A Gallant County

For the descendants of all those who served in the Gloucestershire Regiment or the Royal Gloucestershire Hussars during the First World War.

A Gallant County

The Regiments of Gloucestershire in the Great War

Robin Grist

Pen & Sword
MILITARY

First published in Great Britain in 2018 by
Pen & Sword Military
An imprint of
Pen & Sword Books Ltd
47 Church Street
Barnsley
South Yorkshire
S70 2AS

ISBN 978 1 52673 607 9

Printed and bound in England by TJ International Ltd, Padstow, Cornwall

Pen & Sword Books Limited incorporates the imprints of Atlas, Archaeology, Aviation, Discovery, Family History, Fiction, History, Maritime, Military, Military Classics, Politics, Select, Transport, True Crime, Air World, Frontline Publishing, Leo Cooper, Remember When, Seaforth Publishing, The Praetorian Press, Wharncliffe Local History, Wharncliffe Transport, Wharncliffe True Crime and White Owl.

For a complete list of Pen & Sword titles please contact
PEN & SWORD BOOKS LIMITED
47 Church Street, Barnsley, South Yorkshire, S70 2AS, England
E-mail: enquiries@pen-and-sword.co.uk
Website: www.pen-and-sword.co.uk

Contents

Introduction

Our plumber, Tony Lusty, is partly the inspiration for this book. He remarked one day that one of his ancestors had been killed in the Gloucesters in the First World War but confessed that the family didn't know much about it. I was soon able to tell him that Harold Lusty, from Stroud, had been in 7th Gloucesters, who were fighting to capture Baghdad from the Turks when he died on 15 February 1917, probably from wounds received a few days earlier. This incident made me wonder how many other descendants of those who had fought in the Gloucestershire Regiment might want to find out more about what their life had been like. This, therefore, is the story of the two Regiments of Gloucestershire that fought in the Great War of 1914–1918. I set out to tell the descendants of the men who joined the Gloucestershire Regiment (Gloucesters) or the Royal Gloucestershire Hussars (RGH) during that war where and why their forebears fought.

It was Gordon Corrigan, now a distinguished if controversial military historian but once a fellow officer of mine in the Gloucesters, who in his book, *Mud, Blood and Poppycock*, made me realize that the popular conception of the war was incomplete. It was much more than a troglodyte struggle in the mud of France and Flanders managed by incompetent commanders.

First, the Great War was not only fought just across the Channel. As Harold Lusty's death testifies, it was also contested in Mesopotamia, as well as in Italy, Macedonia, Turkey (Gallipoli), Egypt, Palestine and Syria. Elements of both these Regiments of Gloucestershire served in all these campaigns. My own grandfather was killed in 1918 in Italy in the 1/5th Gloucesters, and for some time I thought he had been fighting the Italians. Only when I looked into it did I realize that in the First World War the Italians were our allies, and he died fighting the Austrians.

Secondly, I learnt that life for those in the Gloucesters and the RGH was much better than often depicted today. It was an adventure; it was often amusing; the food was generally better than at home; the men experienced a comradeship that would never be replicated in the rest of their lives; and they were proud of overcoming the fear that all, with few exceptions, felt. This is not to diminish the terrible loss of life and the tragedy that deaths and life-changing wounds caused, but simply to reflect a wider picture. When a man was killed or died in service there was no more that could be done for him, but for his family it was a different matter; their lives were changed forever. My mother was eight when her father was killed with 1/5th Gloucesters in 1918; 73 years later I was driving her near Ludgershall in Wiltshire when she suddenly pointed to some buildings on the left and said, 'That's where I last saw my father on leave in 1918.' She never forgot him. Lucy Hunt's husband, Owen, was killed in August 1916, leaving her with their eight children; for the rest of her life she kept the back door of 14 Taunton Crescent, Cheltenham unlocked for him to come home.[1] As Sergeant Norman Pegg of 12th Gloucesters (Bristol's Own) said:

> It is the recollection of scenes witnessed which causes me to read, or listen to, with a deep sickening feeling some of the glib descriptive writing or public speaking, official and unofficial, which have from time to time thrust themselves on the people who have stayed at home. To the men who underwent the experience, a battle is not gay, glorious or frivolous, but devilish and murderous.[2]

It would not have been possible to capture the detail of this story without access to the War Diaries of each battalion. These remarkable documents are contemporary accounts of what happened day by day, generally written up by the Adjutant each evening. Many entries are just one sentence, but others record battles with timings and casualties. The latter almost always include without emotion the names of officers, although most will have been close friends and comrades of the writer. More colour is provided by the letters and diaries of participants, many of which are held in the archives of the Soldiers of Gloucestershire Museum in Gloucester Docks. Most of the archives of the RGH are held at the Gloucestershire Archives in Gloucester; the contrast between the momentum of the cavalry engagements in Palestine and the static nature of the war on Western Front is striking. From these sources I hope that I have managed to penetrate a little the 'net curtain' represented by the Second World War, which so often obscures and distorts the events and conditions of the First.

Some may cavil at the title of this book, and it is true that more Victoria Crosses were won by men from other regiments. The Gloucesters, however, had long been influenced by the story that at the Siege of Delhi in 1857 each regiment was asked to nominate two men to receive VCs. Colonel Deacon, who commanded the 61st (South Gloucestershire) Regiment, felt that every man had done his duty and that if an individual were to receive the VC, his comrades would be jealous. So, with the agreement of his men, the Colonel nominated their brave Indian water carriers for the award. No more was heard of the matter. On the other hand, 25 Military Medals were won by men of 1st Gloucesters at Festubert in April 1918, a record for the decoration to a single battalion on one day. Company Sergeant Major William

Biddle MC, DCM & Bar, MM & Bar became one of the most decorated other ranks in the British Army. Clearwell, in the Forest of Dean, is believed to have sent more men to the Great War than any other village in England in proportion to its size, one of whom, Private Francis Miles, did win a VC. Only ten men in the British Army were awarded a DCM and two Bars; one of these was CSM Stanley Phillips of the Gloucesters from Drybrook in the Forest of Dean, who won the DCM with the Gloucesters and the two Bars with the Worcesters in 1918. Finally, over 46,000 men served in the Gloucesters and the RGH during the Great War, yet no single instance has been found of any member of either regiment being charged with either desertion or cowardice. I hope therefore that those who read this account of the Regiments of Gloucestershire in the Great War will agree that Gloucestershire is and was a Gallant County, never forgetting that, until 1974, it included Bristol and South Gloucestershire, which provided many of the soldiers in this story.

Robin Grist

Corton, Wilts

October 2017

Notes

1. J. Devereux and G. Sacker, *Leaving All That Was Dear – Cheltenham and the Great War*
2. Dean Marks, *'Bristol's Own', the 12th Battalion Gloucestershire Regiment 1914–1918*

Acknowledgements

There are thousands of books about the First World War, and I have listed in the bibliography a few that I have found particularly useful. There are also a mass of papers, diaries, photographs, etc. in the Archives of the Soldiers of Gloucestershire Museum, and I am grateful to the Trustees of the Gloucestershire Regimental Museum Trust for allowing me to quote from these. David Read, the former archivist of the Soldiers of Gloucestershire Museum, provided invaluable help in the early stages, and Joe Devereux, who is now a volunteer in the archives, has a remarkable ability to ferret out information about individuals. This story would not have been complete without the help of Colonel Rollo Clifford and his team of historians of the RGH. Major Claud Rebbeck, a former Regimental Secretary of the Gloucestershire Regiment with an exceptional recall and a fine eye, read and commented comprehensively on an early draft. Colonel Christopher Newbould, who has led Battlefield Tours for many years, also read the draft and corrected some major errors, and Colonel Rollo Clifford helped significantly with the RGH input and in ensuring its accuracy. I am grateful to the RGH Trustees for allowing me to use photographs from the Walwin Album that is held for the RGH Trustees at the Gloucestershire Archives, for the help of the staff there while the building was being extended and for the timely assistance of Chris Chatterton, the Museum Director of the Soldiers of Gloucestershire Museum with the photographs. I also wish to acknowledge the assistance and advice of all at Pen & Sword Books, particularly Brigadier Henry Wilson, George Chamier and Matt Jones. Finally, my heartfelt thanks to Louise for her wise advice and superb support over the 46 years of our lives together.

Every effort has been made to contact copyright holders of quotes. The author will be glad to make good in future editions any error or omission brought to his attention.

List of Maps

The maps have generally been adapted to fit the book. The originals can be found at: Maps 1 & 14 – nzhistory.govt.nz/media; Maps 2, 5–7, 13, 26–7 & 33 – The Long, Long Trail; Map 3 – *The Gloucestershire Regiment War Narratives 1914-1915*; Map 4 – *The British Campaign in France & Flanders Volume 1 – 1914*; Map 8 – ww1blog.osborneink.com; Map 9 – Webmatters; Maps 11, 16 & 18 – Wikipedia; Map 10 – National Archives; Map 12 – rslvirtualwarmemorial. org.au/explore/campaigns/3; Maps 15, 23, & 30 – *Palestine* by R Wilson; Map 17 – *The Soldier's Burden*; Map 19 – Families & Friends of the First AIF; Maps 20, 29 & 35 – *The Great War – The Standard History of the World Wide Conflict* by H.W. Wilson; Map 21 – www.vlib.us/wwi/resources/egyptiancampaign; Maps 22 & 31 – *Official History of the Great War Military Operations Egypt and Palestine Volume 1*; Map 24 – kaiserscross.com/media/DIR_534601/e780f5152 0dd886fffff8046fffffff2; Map 25 – Wikimedia Commons; Map 32 – Alchetron.

Part I

THE BRITISH EXPEDITIONARY FORCE (B.E.F.)

Chapter 1

The Regiments of Gloucestershire in the Great War

In 1914, on the outbreak of war, there were just two regiments of the County of Gloucestershire, which in those days included the City of Bristol and what is now South Gloucestershire. The Gloucestershire Regiment and the Royal Gloucestershire Hussars drew their men from the same sources, the cities and towns of the county, the Cotswolds, the Severn Vale and the Forest of Dean. The Gloucestershire Regiment, abbreviated at the time to 'Gloucesters', had a history stretching back to 1694 and more Battle Honours on their Colours than any other infantry regiment. It consisted of two 'regular' battalions, 1st and 2nd Gloucesters, made up of full-time professional soldiers. Until 1881 these had been two separate regiments, the 28th (North Gloucestershire) Regiment and the 61st (South Gloucestershire) Regiment (the numbers simply signified their seniority and related to when they were formed). Thus, although they were officially the 1st and 2nd Battalions, they always referred to themselves as the 28th and the 61st, and continued to do so until 1947, when they amalgamated. One battalion was usually overseas, somewhere in the Empire, while the other was at home, and every ten years or so they would change round. In 1914 the 28th were in Bordon, near Aldershot, while the 61st were in Tientsin in China.

Alone among the major European nations, Britain had no form of conscription and an historic distrust of a large standing army, which apart from being costly was seen as a means for the state to impose its will. The British Army was entirely voluntary, and so, in addition to the 'regular' battalions, there were three 'territorial' battalions in the Gloucestershire Regiment: 4th (City of Bristol), 5th and 6th. These were made up of men who trained one evening a week and at weekends and went to camp once a year, but had other paid employment; in addition, a few regular officers and NCOs ran the administration and training. These three battalions were part of the Territorial Force, which had emerged in 1908 from the Militia and Volunteers, both of whom existed to defend Britain in times of crisis. This tradition was maintained in the Territorial Force, which was for home defence only. Units when 'embodied' could be sent to serve anywhere in the United Kingdom but could not be forced to go overseas, although they could volunteer to do so.

Once the War had started, the Secretary of State for War, Lord Kitchener, quickly realized that the Army was not large enough. He therefore did two things. First, he ordered every Territorial Force battalion to raise a second battalion. As a result, the 4th, 5th and 6th Gloucesters became 1/4th and 2/4th, 1/5th and 2/5th and 1/6th and 2/6th. In due course, each also formed a third battalion, but these were created to train reinforcements for the fighting battalions. Secondly, he recognized that those who had enlisted in the Territorial Force could not be compelled to go overseas. Most did, but he felt the country needed a larger Army. He therefore authorized the formation of 'Service' battalions. Those who joined them agreed to serve world-wide but only for the duration of the War. These were also known as 'Kitchener battalions'. As a result, the Gloucestershire Regiment was enlarged by the addition of 7th, 8th, 9th, 10th, 12th (Bristol's Own), 13th (Forest of Dean) (Pioneers), 14th (West of England) (Bantams) and 18th Service Battalions. In addition, there were the 11th, 15th, and 16th Reserve Battalions and the 17th Territorial Force Battalion, all of whom stayed at home.

In 1914 the Gloucestershire Regiment also had a Regimental Depot at Horfield Barracks in Bristol, where the 3rd (Special Reserve) Battalion was based; as its name implies, it trained recruits for the 1st and 2nd Battalions and ran courses for the Regiment. It was to Horfield that recruits were sent as they joined up.

The other 'Regiment of Gloucestershire' was the Royal Gloucestershire Hussars, abbreviated to 'RGH', a Yeomanry Regiment in the Territorial Force. It had started life as separate Troops of the Gloucestershire Gentlemen and Yeomanry in 1795. In 1834 these troops met at Petty France, near Badminton, resolved to become a regiment and chose as their first commanding officer the Marquess of Worcester, shortly to become the 7th Duke of Beaufort. Since then, succeeding Dukes of Beaufort have been Honorary Colonels of the Regiment. Until 1900 the RGH had not been involved in any fighting, although they had had to deal with affrays 'in support of the civil power', most notably the Bristol Riots of 1831. It acquired the 'Royal' prefix in 1841 from Queen Victoria. During the Boer War the need for mounted infantry was such that the Imperial Yeomanry was formed, in which men of Regiments like the RGH could volunteer to serve. Many did, and members of the RGH formed the 3rd Company of the 1st Battalion Imperial Yeomanry.

The six battalions of the Gloucestershire Regiment that existed in 1914, two Regular, three Territorial Force and one Special Reserve, expanded during the War to twenty-four, sixteen of which saw active service; while the Royal Gloucestershire Hussars increased to three regiments, or 'lines', one of which fought in Gallipoli and the Middle East. This is their story.

Chapter 2

Background to World War One

Although this is an account of the War as it involved just the Regiments of Gloucestershire, their story would be incomplete without some understanding of why it happened. Historians still disagree about the causes of the Great War, largely because there were a variety of factors whose relative importance can never be proved. Furthermore, the outbreak of the War was due to a sequence of events which might have been stopped at any point. As Barbara Tuchman wrote in *The Guns of August*, 'War is the unfolding of miscalculations'; with the benefit of hindsight, surely more would have been done to break the chain, but it wasn't.

The oft quoted cause of the outbreak of war, the assassination of Archduke Franz Ferdinand of Serbia in June 1914, is too simplistic an interpretation. It could be described as the 'trigger', but the conditions for such a catastrophic conflict were more complex and were in place well before 1914. Sibling rivalry, old scores, ethnic and economic tensions, over-large armies, weakened empires and nervous generals are just a few of the factors that led to the War.

Today a major war in Europe is unthinkable, but Yuval Noah Harari writes, 'Between 1871 and 1914, a European war remained a plausible eventuality, and the expectation of war dominated the thinking of armies, politicians and ordinary citizens alike.'[1] Even in 1899, whilst fighting in South Africa, a large proportion of the British Army was retained at home in case the French decided to invade. John Keegan records that in 1899 Tsar Nicholas II of Russia convened a conference at the Hague, warning that 'the accelerating arms race was transforming the armed peace into a crushing burden that weighs on all nations and, if prolonged, will lead to the cataclysm it seeks to avert.' The conference agreed a number of conventions, but none were compulsory and so they were relatively ineffective.[2]

With the exception of France and Switzerland, all the major European nations in 1914 were monarchies, and their rulers were related. King George V, Tsar Nicholas II of Russia and Kaiser Wilhelm II were first cousins. The Kaiser is reputed to have said that if their grandmother, Queen Victoria, had still been alive she would never have allowed them to go to war. This, however, overlooks the dangers of sibling rivalry and nationalistic passion which led to the expansion of armies and navies, the acquisition of more and heavier artillery and the construction of stronger, wider frontier fortifications. The Germans decided in 1890 to build a navy that could defeat the Royal Navy in battle. Britain regarded this as a challenge to its command of the seas, and by 1906 determination to build more and better battleships than Germany was popular public policy. In 1913 France decided to match the military strength of Germany, despite being a nation of 40 million opposed to Germany's 60 million.

Armies have historically made plans. With the introduction of military Staff Colleges in the latter part of the nineteenth century, where officers were trained in staff work, it became normal for them to draw up contingency plans; had they not done, it could be argued, it would have been dereliction of duty. Alfred von Schlieffen was the Chief of the Imperial German Staff from 1891 to 1906. The Schlieffen Plan was designed to secure the position of Germany, sandwiched between France, hostile since their defeat by the Prussians in 1870, and France's long term friend, Russia. His plan was designed to win a short war by first defeating the French in 42 days after mobilization, using about 90 per cent of Germany's strength, before turning to face Russia, who he judged would take much longer to mobilize and move. To achieve this he planned to circumvent the line of fortresses that the French had built along the German border and ignore Belgian and Luxembourger neutrality. His plan relied heavily on the railway network to move troops and logistics to a precise programme. But trains could only take an army to the Belgian border; after that it relied on feet, thousands of them, both human and equine.

There were also a number of alliances or ententes in existence: Serbia with Russia, Russia with France, France with Great Britain and Great Britain with Belgium. One of the snags of alliances is no one knows whether they will be honoured, and if so to what extent. Will it, for example, be a question of token support only? Another important factor was that in Germany, Russia and Austria the sovereign was commander both in name and fact. This was at its most extreme in Germany, where it soon became apparent that the Kaiser did not understand the organization he was supposed to control.

Europe was not at peace in the first decade of the twentieth century. In the Balkan Wars of 1912 and 1913 the Balkan League of Bulgaria, Serbia, Greece and Montenegro had fought to gain much of the territory of the Ottoman Empire in Europe. Austria-Hungary, the weakest of the European great powers, had a dread of ethnic subversion by Serbia so was alarmed when Serbia became larger and began pressing strongly for a union of the South Slav peoples. The murder of Archduke Franz Ferdinand, the heir to the throne of Austria-Hungary, and his wife on 28 June 1914 in Sarajevo by a Serbian nationalist organization was therefore even more serious than it might otherwise have been. For Austria-Hungary a war against Serbia was a necessity, but a general European war was not.

Things now began to go wrong. Instead of reacting swiftly, Austria-Hungary delayed and sought support from its ally, Germany. The Kaiser responded that it could rely on Germany's full support but that it was up to Austria-Hungary to decide what it wanted to do; he then went on holiday. There was disagreement within Austria-Hungary as to whether a note or an ultimatum should be sent to Serbia; the latter would imply war if its demands were not met. Eventually, a note was sent but not until 23 July, 25 days after the assassination. It gave Serbia 48 hours to respond and demanded that Serbia accept an Austro-Hungarian inquiry into the assassination, suppress all anti-Austrian propaganda and take steps to eliminate terrorist organizations within its borders. Churchill, reading it, described it as an 'ultimatum' not a 'note'. Meanwhile, across Europe, the crisis was getting out of control, not helped by many of the key personalities taking their summer holidays. Nevertheless, Serbia was on the verge of agreeing to Austria-Hungary's demands when it heard that the strongly pro-Serbian Tsar, although unwilling to order mobilization, had announced a 'Period Preliminary to War' that morning, 25 July.

Few diplomats understood the inevitability of what was about to happen. Mobilization in one country was bound to trigger war plans in another. The situation was not helped by nervous generals, whose plans were dependent on timely decisions and who were determined not to be caught at a disadvantage. Joffre, the Chief of the French General Staff, warned that every day's delay in ordering general mobilization would lead to the loss of 25km of national territory.

Events now progressed as follows:

26 July. Serbia mobilized its Army, while Russia recalled its youngest reservists.

27 July. The Kaiser was still on his sea cruise, but the German Ambassador to Russia warned of war and said that Germany was anxious to preserve peace, although in reality Germany was trying to delay Russian mobilization.

28 July. Austria-Hungary declared war on Serbia. In Russia all military districts were told that 30 July would be first day of general mobilization.

29 July. An exchange of telegrams between the Kaiser and the Tsar led the latter to order the cancellation of general mobilization.

30 July. Britain was still trying to arrange mediation. France had not implemented any precautionary measures and Germany had not mobilized, but the Tsar was persuaded to change his mind and ordered mobilization.

31 July. Germany issued an ultimatum to Russia which stated that Germany would mobilize unless Russia suspended all war measures against Germany and Austria-Hungary, and demanded a response within 12 hours. Both France and Germany announced that general mobilization would take place on 2 August.

Britain had offered to mediate, but otherwise the Cabinet had not decided what to do. It now agreed that if Belgian neutrality was threatened Britain must act. On 2 August Germany delivered an ultimatum to Belgium demanding to use its territory in operations against France and threatening to treat it as an enemy if it did not comply. Germany also declared war on France. On 3 August Belgium rejected the German demand. Germany crossed the border into Belgium on 4 August. Britain now sent an ultimatum to Germany demanding that military operations against Belgium should cease. Germany did not reply but attacked Liège on 5 August, by which time Britain, France and Russia were at war against Germany and Austria-Hungary.

Many millions of men would die as a result of these decisions and many more millions would be wounded. The world, including Gloucestershire, was about to face the consequences.

Notes

1. Yuval Noah Harari, *Sapiens – A Brief History of Humankind*, Vintage Books (first published by Harvill Secker, 2014)
2. John Keegan, *The First World War*

Chapter 3

1st Gloucesters Join the British Expeditionary Force (B.E.F.)

O
n 1 August 1914, 1st Gloucesters, training near Aldershot, was ordered to return to its barracks at Bordon. It was one of four infantry battalions in 3rd Infantry Brigade in 1st Division. General mobilization was ordered on 4 August. An infantry battalion in 1914 consisted of 30 officers and 977 other ranks, divided into 4 rifle companies. There were 13 riding horses, 43 draught or pack horses to draw 6 ammunition carts, 2 water carts, 3 general service wagons and the medical officer's Maltese Cart, a two-wheel vehicle which carried medical supplies. The battalion headquarters included signallers equipped with 9 bicycles; there were no radios, and communication within the battalion and back to brigade was by telephone wire or runner. 1st Gloucesters required 9 officers and 600 men to bring it up to 'war strength', but reservists were rushing back to the Depot at Horfield Barracks in Bristol, so that just two days later, on 6 August, a draft of 580 men was sent to the Battalion. Seven officers from the Reserves joined on the same day. By 7 August the Battalion was over strength, and by midnight 1st Gloucesters was fully mobilized and ready to move.

It wasn't just a matter of manpower. Peace equipment had to be handed in and war stores issued. Personal kit had to be packed and stored for the duration, at that time expected to be just a few months at the most. The Battalion also needed horses, both riding and draught, which came from the Remount Depot on the 6th but had been used to civilian harnesses and so had to be broken in; this, as can be imagined, led to some entertaining incidents. The Battalion left Bordon on two trains in the early hours of 12 August and shortly after 6.00 am was in Southampton. Here it embarked on SS *Gloucester Castle* and at about 1.00 am on 13 August reached Le Havre. The Gloucesters were one of the first battalions to arrive at Le Havre, where arrangements for disembarkation were minimal. The soldiers assembled in a cargo shed, but it took several hours to unload the horses as each one had to be slung ashore by crane. By 4.00 am, when the last horse was disembarked, all the Gloucesters were asleep; they were allowed to stay put, then moved off at 6.00 am to 100 bell tents allocated to the Battalion in a stubble field, which turned to mud when it rained.

The Battalion was part of the British Expeditionary Force (B.E.F.), which consisted of six infantry divisions and five cavalry brigades arranged into two corps under the command of Field Marshal Sir John French. Each infantry battalion was organized into four companies, each of four platoons. The battalion was commanded by a lieutenant colonel, Alfred Lovett,[1] with a major as second in command, and each company was normally commanded by a captain and each platoon by a subaltern, either a lieutenant or second lieutenant. It was sustained by a quartermaster, invariably a senior other rank who had been commissioned, and his staff. Then, as now, it was the senior other ranks who played a vital part in the effectiveness of the British Army. In each battalion these consisted of the Regimental Sergeant Major (RSM), with a Company Sergeant Major (CSM) in each company; the Quartermaster was supported by the Regimental Quartermaster Sergeant (RQMS), and each company had a Company Quatermaster Sergeant (CQMS).

Despite the small size of the B.E.F. it was exceedingly well trained and equipped, although there were some deficiencies, as this story will reveal. The French had not expected the Germans to ignore Belgian neutrality and had deployed their five armies along the border with Germany. Once aware of the threat, they began to move their Fourth and Fifth Armies to face Belgium, with the B.E.F. on their left and the Belgian Army on the left of the B.E.F.

By 15 August 1st Division was complete in France and 3rd Brigade entrained. There were fifty coaches each bearing the legend 'Hommes 30–40, Chevaux 8',

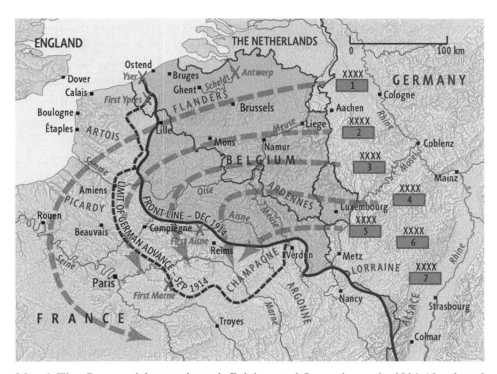

Map 1 The German Advance through Belgium and Luxembourg in 1914 (the dotted arrows show the Schlieffen Plan)

and, as the War Diary records, 'There were no latrines.' Four hours were allocated for entraining, but the Gloucesters did it in an hour. The train travelled via Rouen, where the men could have a wash and get fed before continuing via Amiens and St Quentin to the railhead at Le Nouvion, close to the Belgian border, soon after 6.00 am the next day. It then marched to a concentration area, where for the next few days it trained and planned.

Infantry battalions could only get to the theatre of operations by train and ship. This was standard for 1914/15 and was much more efficient than might be expected. Battalions could entrain in the early hours on the edge of Salisbury Plain and be in Boulogne the same evening. Once in the theatre of operations, a battalion moved either by train or by marching. Trains were used whenever possible, and the whole process of entraining and detraining was soon almost second nature to the men.

Donald Baxter,[2] a Second Lieutenant at the time, recalled in later life:[3]

> Having mobilized from 4 August I found I had about half my Platoon (No.3) made up of Reservists to bring us up to strength. We had to teach them the rifle, as they had never seen this particular one before. They turned out splendid chaps in all situations. When we moved off from Bordon Station on 12 August I was responsible for the baggage together with Charles Wetherall. We all spent a horribly uncomfortable night on the concrete of Le Havre Station and we boarded a train for the Frontier in the morning. At all the Stations going up when the train halted all the girls kissed the soldiers, and the soldiers in return gave their cap badges away. By jove, wasn't the Colonel upset; at one of the halts on the way, he paraded the Battalion and told them they must never do such a disgraceful thing again.

On 19 August the Kaiser issued an Order of the Day:

> It is my Royal and Imperial Command that you concentrate your energies, for the immediate present upon one single purpose, and that is you address all your skill and all the valour of my soldiers first to exterminate the treacherous English; walk over General French's contemptible little Army.

From then on the B.E.F. called themselves the 'Old Contemptibles' with pride, determined to refute the insult.

On 20 August the Germans entered Brussels, already behind the tight timetable of the Schlieffen Plan. They had assumed that the Belgians would not fight or, if they did, that they would be defeated swiftly; both expectations were wrong. On the same day the French ordered the advance into Belgium, and the 3rd Brigade set off with 1st Gloucesters leading. They only marched 8½ miles but it was abnormally hot, the load each soldier was carrying was considerable, the road was dusty cobbles and the reservists were not used to the conditions; ten men had to be evacuated to hospital. The next day, 3rd Brigade continued the advance and on the 22nd reached Maubeuge, where the French Fifth Army was preparing its defences. It halted in a cornfield, but at 3.15 pm marched off to occupy billets just south of the Belgian border. Suddenly, reports of German cavalry 8 miles to the north meant that the battalion turned out to dig trenches north of the village. No sooner had it started this, than it received fresh orders for 3rd Brigade to advance to occupy a line Peissant–Farœulx–Haulchin–Givry. The Gloucesters began to prepare a defensive position at Haulchin using tools that it had to commandeer from the civilian population, who, although enthusiastic, became less so when the men began to take down their doors to help revet the trenches. The 'fog of war' had begun to descend on the B.E.F. and the Allies. The Battalion had covered 35½ miles in two days; it would be the start of many long marches.

Meanwhile, aerial reconnaissance had revealed that the Germans were driving the French back on the line of the River Sambre. It was soon clear that, although the B.E.F. was ready to fight the Germans, it was now 9 miles in front of the French Fifth Army and there were gaps with no troops to fill them. The stage was set for the first battle of the War.

Notes

1. Lieutenant Colonel Alfred Crowdy Lovett (1862–1919) had commanded 1st Gloucesters since 1911. He was commissioned in 1881 and was a prolific artist, mainly of military figures, many in the Indian Army, and had exhibited at the Royal Academy. He commanded 1st Gloucesters at Mons, in the Retreat from Mons, at Aisne, and during the First Battle of Ypres until the latter stages of the Battle of Gheluvelt, when the two divisional commanders were wounded by a shell and he took over command of 3rd Brigade. He was made a Companion of the Order of the Bath (CB) for his conduct in 1914. He subsequently commanded East Lancs Reserve Div (TF) 1916–1919, I/C Yorkshire Coastal Defences. His two sons served in the Gloucesters.

2. Donald Baxter MC, TD (1892–1969), always known as 'Bob', was commissioned into the Gloucesters in 1913. He was awarded the MC for his gallantry at Langemarck in 1914, where he was severely wounded in the groin and evacuated. He rejoined after a year and commanded A Company. After the Somme he commanded 1st Divisional Training School. He retired in 1920 to be the managing director of the family brewery business at Sherborne until 1951. He joined 4th Dorsets (TF) in 1922, later commanding the Battalion, and was Honorary Colonel 4/5th Dorsets after the Second World War.

3. Colonel Donald Baxter MC, 1st Gloucesters, 'Reminiscences of August 1914'.

Chapter 4

Mons and the Retreat
from Mons with 1st Gloucesters

The Battle of Mons was a subsidiary part of the Battle of the Frontiers being fought along the French border. The B.E.F. took up defensive positions along the Mons–Condé Canal against the advancing German First Army. Both sides were surprised, the British by the weight of the German artillery fire, the Germans by the accuracy and rate of the rifle fire of the British infantry. Captain Walter Bloem of the German 12th Grenadier Regiment wrote:[1] 'Here we were as if advancing on a parade ground . . . away in front a sharp hammering sound, then a pause, then a more rapid hammering – machine guns!' This highlighted the difference between the German and British Armies at the start of the war. The Germans were a Continental army who had learnt the value

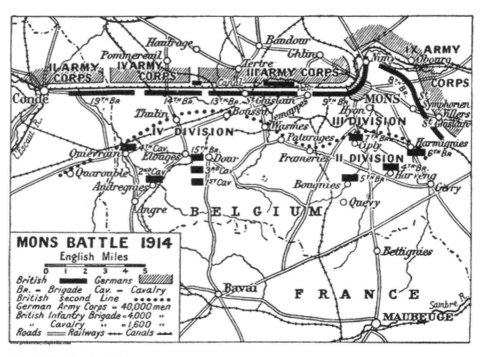

Map 2 The Battle of Mons

of artillery, which they had expanded, making heavier guns with longer ranges and stockpiling large amounts of ammunition. The British Army's experience was based on garrisoning the Empire, and the tribesmen of the North-West Frontier in India and the Boers in South Africa had been shown to be superior marksmen. So what was described, rather quaintly, as 'musketry training' became a priority (muskets had been replaced by rifles in about 1870). One of the consequences of this was that the British Army had no steel helmets. These first began to be issued in 1915 and then they were only available to those in the front line; only in 1916 were there enough for everyone. Without a steel helmet, the only protection from artillery fire is to get below ground level in a ditch or a trench. (In some other respects the British Army was better equipped. The French were still wearing blue coats and red trousers at the start of the War).

The B.E.F. position formed a dog-leg: II Corps faced north astride the canal, whilst I Corps faced east to join up with the French Fifth Army and prevent the Germans outflanking II Corps. As a result, neither 3rd Brigade nor 1st Gloucesters was involved in any significant fighting. The Battalion War Diary describes the confusion:

24 August – HAUCHLIN – After midnight there was a good deal of rifle fire to our left. 3am. Orders received to hold our position at all costs so we made all preparations to have ammunition, water and food in the trenches. 5am. Received an order to be prepared to retire at short notice as a general retirement of the British force had been ordered. Got away at 7.15am with C Company as rearguard. B Company got detached and retired parallel to the BINCHE–BAVAI road but rejoined the Battalion when it had got to BETTIGNY. The Battalion had been ordered to retire across country parallel to the BINCHE–BAVAI road but as the transport had not been sent ahead it was decided to march via CROIX LEZ ROUVEROY, where the Queens had taken up and entrenched a defensive position. As soon as the rear party had got through the Queens' lines a German cavalry patrol of 6 men came up within 500 yards of the rear party. The Queens opened fire and 5 of the patrol were knocked over, one escaping . . . The 3rd Inf Bde was assembled at BETTIGNY and resumed its march at 5.40pm via GOGNIES—CHAUSÉE–PEIGNES to NEUF MESNIL where we billeted.

(Those writing War Diaries were required to use capital letters for all place names to improve legibility; occasionally the spelling is imaginative).

Although initially planned as a simple tactical withdrawal, the British retreat from Mons lasted for two weeks and took the B.E.F. to the outskirts of Paris before

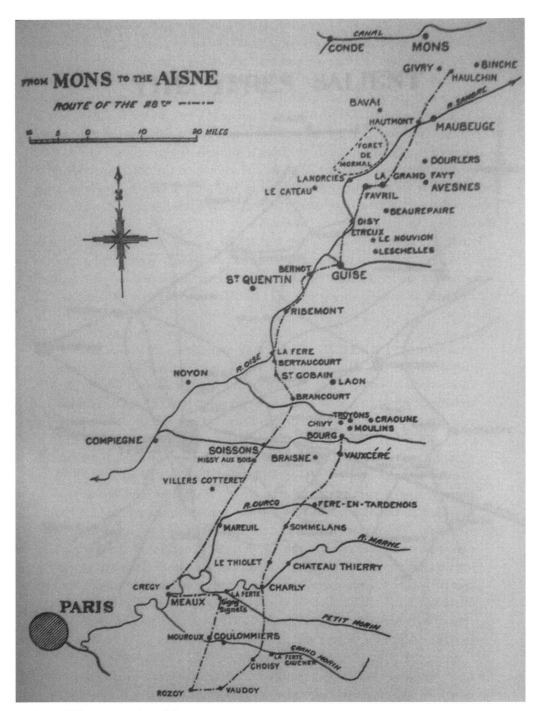

Map 3 The Retreat from Mons

it was able to counter-attack, together with the French, at the Battle of the Marne. I[st] Gloucesters marched 200 miles in thirteen days from Hauchlin to Rozoy, which they reached on 5 September. En route, it had its first engagement with the Germans at Landrecies, on 26 August. The Battalion occupied a position to the south of the village to cover the withdrawal of the rest of the Division. Shallow trenches were dug, and at about noon enemy columns were seen moving across the Battalion's front some 1,000yds away. Two guns sited in the Gloucesters' front opened fire and the enemy dispersed. Then a German aeroplane flew low overhead, located the trenches and directed artillery fire on to them, while German infantry started to attack the position. By this time the object of delaying the enemy had been achieved, and the Battalion fell back and continued to retire with the rest of the B.E.F. In this, the first encounter with the enemy, the Battalion lost five men killed.

Second Lieutenant Baxter recalled[2]:

> Eventually we marched into the Landrecies Area (Belgium) when I had a sudden order from Captain Rising to line the hedge on the right. I found myself alongside a platoon of C Company commanded by Charles Wetherall, who then gave a perfect Fire Order; the first Fire Order I had heard in war. The result of our Fire Orders was however two bursts of enemy shrapnel over our heads. Our first officer casualty was Captain Guy Shipway who was mortally wounded by a sniper; a great waste of a valuable officer who had just been through the Staff College. We could see in the distance the enemy moving across our front. In this little battle Captain Rising was ordered to put out a Detached Post on some cross roads . . . when a runner was sent to call it in, it could not be found. The whole post was captured: it was so detached with no communications. Never did I hear of a Detached Post being put out again. I may say this was very close country. We were all told to collect on the road: we had started our retreat. I was rear Platoon of the Battalion. We camped our first night in a stubble field. A piercing wind was blowing and it was decided by the Company Officers that we should get on top of a hay rick and there spend the night. It was one of the coldest nights I have ever spent. Why we went on the top of the rick instead of the sheltered side nobody knows. We marched back for about thirteen days; every night we pulled down the corn stooks and every soldier had as good a bed as possible, but very little food. Later on the A.S.C.[3] used to dump tins of bully beef and biscuits at the end of each day on the roadside.

The remainder of the retreat was accomplished without major incident, but Second Lieutenant Baxter gives more detail:

When we mobilized the Colonel distributed the drummers as orderlies to the Platoon Commanders. My drummer was Drummer Fluck. He was a splendid fellow, never too tired to blow his pipes (Irish pipes). This kept the Platoon together in a wonderful way: we owed a lot to him . . . No doubt, later on all drummers were withdrawn and reformed the Fifes and Drums again. The march discipline of the 1st Gloucestershire Regiment on this retreat was the best in the 3rd Infantry Brigade . . . Morale was high. Meanwhile as the days went by steadily marching along the straight roads of France under the pitiless sun we got very thirsty, so every evening we used to go to a cottage well and fill our water bottles: what wells, what water! I lived on the biscuits served out to us and chocolate. We were told the biscuits were left from the South African War. Very hard, and they robbed me of thirteen bits of stopping from my teeth! The chocolate was bought from one of our good Interpreters who scoured the surrounding districts for it. At this stage bully beef could not be managed. One Interpreter, a lusty fellow, used to play rugger for France. The last two or three days of the march my legs got so thin that my puttees would not stay on my legs.

The German plan was to capture Paris in 42 days. On 4 September a delighted Kaiser reported: 'It is the thirty-fifth day, we are besieging Rheims, we are thirty-five miles from Paris.' The German plan specified that there would be a decisive battle by the fortieth day to decide the outcome of the war on the Western Front. The Germans estimated that by the fortieth day the Russian Army would have deployed sufficient strength to launch an offensive in the east and troops would need to be moved from France to counter this. So far, although the Allies had been driven back they had avoided being enveloped on their left, as the Germans intended. On 5 September German orders were issued for what should be this decisive action, the Battle of the Marne. The Germans had, however, deviated significantly from Schlieffen's plan and presented the Allies with a fleeting opportunity to change the course of the War; they took it.

Notes

1. Captain Walter Bloem, *The Advance from Mons 1914: the Experience of a German Infantry Officer*, Helion, 1963.
2. Colonel Donald Baxter MC, 1st Gloucesters, 'Reminiscences of August 1914'.
3. Army Service Corps. It was granted the 'Royal' prefix in 1918.

Chapter 5

To the Aisne with the 1ˢᵗ Gloucesters

The Germans had not stuck to the Schlieffen Plan. Their First Army was meant to go to the west of Paris but had, for various reasons, drifted east and exposed its flank to the Allies. The Allied Advance to the Aisne, which lasted from 6 September to 1 October and included their victory at the Battle of the Marne (6–10 September 1914), ended the month-long German offensive. The counter-attack by six French field armies and the B.E.F. along the Marne River forced the German Imperial Army to abandon its push on Paris and retreat north-east.

On 6 September 1ˢᵗ Gloucesters was at Rozoy, when it received orders cancelling further withdrawal; the Allies were about to advance. The Battalion moved to Vandoy and the next day 3ʳᵈ Brigade formed the right flank of the B.E.F. as it advanced. The Gloucesters crossed the River Marne on 9 September and at about midnight, at Ferme de Lille, one German officer and nine men, who had been cut off, surrendered after a few shots had been fired. This apart, the Battle of the Marne was without incident for the Battalion.

The advance to the Aisne continued on 10 September, but 1ˢᵗ Gloucesters remained until the next day, when it moved to Villeneuve-sur-Fère. On the way it was warned that the Germans were near Perles but found no trace of them. The War Diary of 3ʳᵈ Brigade on 10 September comments:

> The general impression gained by all those who have actually been in touch with the Germans is that we have nothing to fear or learn from their infantry or cavalry, who are both said to shoot very badly, but that their machine guns and artillery are very good and very well handled.

On 14 September 1ˢᵗ Gloucesters caught up with the Germans. The River Aisne is a deep, wide river that can only be crossed via bridges. The Germans had selected the crest along the high ground behind the Aisne to create a strong position from where they could halt the Allied advance. The Gloucesters, unaware of the Germans' intentions, set out with the rest of 1ˢᵗ Division from Bourg-et-Comin on the Aisne, heading for Athies-sous-Laon, about 15 miles away. The Germans were shelling the river crossings, and progress was slow as the men climbed up from the valley through folds in the ground towards the Chemin Des Dames ridge; 1ˢᵗ Gloucesters was the Brigade reserve. The leading battalions were soon engaged by the enemy,

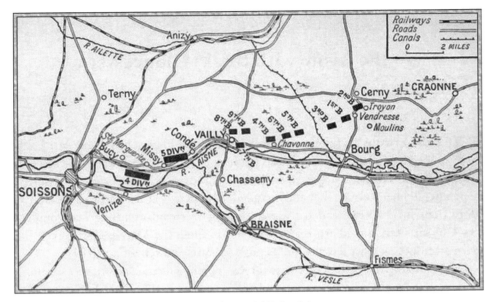

Map 4 British Advance at the Aisne ('3rd B' is 3rd Brigade)

and when the Germans launched a counter-attack, two Gloucester companies were sent with a company of the 2nd Battalion, The Welch Regiment, which was also in 3rd Brigade, to repulse it; but in the event, this was done by the artillery. Support was now needed by 1st Guards Brigade, so B and C Companies were detached from the Gloucesters to reinforce it. They moved into a quarry, and some platoons were pushed forward, where they were shelled, but once it was realized that there were no enemy infantry to their front they were withdrawn, having suffered some casualties. D Company was then sent to 1st Guards Brigade as brigade reserve, but by 6.00 pm the situation had improved and A and B Companies rejoined the Battalion, while D Company moved to Vandresse as Divisional Reserve. At dusk, 3rd Brigade was ordered to move forward to the ridge line, and B and C Companies, led by the Brigade Commander, advanced through Chivy but then came under fire. After a period the firefight died down, but the Brigade Commander was missing, although he eventually reappeared. The remainder of the night was quiet, but the next morning a German advance was stopped, partly by four Gloucester marksmen. During the day the Gloucesters suffered more casualties from German artillery but were better off than some battalions, particularly in 1st Guards Brigade. This was the Battalion's first serious action of the War, as the War Diary makes clear: '2 Lt R. K. Swanwick – killed, Lt D. Duncan slightly wounded in the left upper arm by the splinter of a shell, 2 Lt Hon. N. F. Somerset grazed on the head by the splinter of a shell, 10 killed, 70 wounded, 3 missing.'[1]

The fighting was by no means over, and 1st Gloucesters remained in action for the next twelve days. What had changed was the nature of the battle. Neither side was able to advance successfully, and the trench warfare that would dominate the Western Front for the next four years had begun. One other thing had changed, which would become a feature of much of the rest of the war in France and Flanders: it began raining, so the ground became soft and muddy. Another factor was the strength of the German artillery. By contrast, the British had fewer guns, with shorter ranges and less reliable ammunition, and lacked the capacity to manufacture the quantities needed for what was to prove a vital necessity on the Western Front. The Battalion War Diary for 16 September records: 'At 6am the Germans began shelling again. They appear to have a battery at COURTECON with an unlimited amount of ammunition; it fired all day distributing its fire in all directions.'

On 17 September the Germans attacked 2nd Brigade, and although this was repulsed, both sides suffered heavy casualties and the Gloucesters were sent to reinforce it. The Battalion took up a position along the Chemin Des Dames, which they held until 2nd Brigade was relieved during the night of the 19/20th. During this time one of the companies was detailed to fill in some German trenches, which they did, burying German dead along with three abandoned machine guns, although they brought back one gun and a German drum.

On 20 September, a draft of one officer and ninety-six men arrived as reinforcements, and on 27 September this signal was received:

> I am intensely proud of the courageous spirit and stubborn endurance with which all bns of the 3rd Bde have the severe trials of the past 14 days. The already famous Bns [1st Queens, 1st South Wales Borderers, 1st Gloucesters, 2nd Welch] composing the Bde nobly added to their proud history by their recent deeds and this knowledge should brace them to face a continuance if necessary, and to renewed efforts towards final defeat of the enemy. I am sure everyone knows how greatly I have felt for them in the hardships endured & how deeply I deplore the loss of so many gallant comrades of all ranks. Signed H.J.S. Landon Brig Gen.

During the night of 27/28 September 3rd Brigade was relieved, and 1st Gloucesters moved back to Bourg-et-Comin, where they were reunited with their baggage, before moving on to Pagan. The respite was short-lived; on 1 October the Battalion became Divisional Reserve at Moulins. Here it remained, principally improving the defences, until the whole Division was relieved by the French on 16 October. The Gloucesters had suffered less than some of the battalions in 1st Division in the Battle of the Aisne, but more severe tests were to come.

Note

1. The Hon Nigel Fitzroy Somerset CBE DSO MC (1894–1990) was descended from the Duke of Beaufort through Lord Raglan who led the charge of The Light Brigade in the Crimean War. Nigel Somerset was wounded again during the First Battle of Ypres and, when he was discharged from hospital, went to Mesopotamia to command a Light Armoured Battery equipped with Rolls-Royces for the rest of the War. In 1938 he took over command of 2nd Gloucesters, went with them to France where in May 1940 he was promoted brigadier to command Somer Force, which included 2nd and 5th Gloucesters, and held Cassel and Ledringham in the Dunkirk perimeter for four days, thus buying time for the evacuation from the beaches. Nigel Somerset was captured, along with most of 2nd Gloucesters and spent the rest of the Second World War in captivity. He died in 1990 aged ninety-six.

Chapter 6

1ˢᵗ Gloucesters at Ypres in 1914

By mid-October 1914 the options for both sides were limited. The British had to secure their supply lines through the Channel Ports; the French needed to prevent the Germans outflanking the Allies to the north; while the Germans, who were now also fighting the Russians on their Eastern Front, knew that if they could get to the coast they could cut off the British and France might then be defeated. The focus of the struggle was the Belgian city of Ypres. It was eventually a victory for the Allies, since Ypres remained in Allied hands, but the cost to all regiments of the B.E.F. was tragic. When 1ˢᵗ Gloucesters marched through Poperinghe on 20 October there were 26 officers and more than 1,000 men in the Battalion. Four weeks later, 2 officers and fewer than 200 men marched back. Two DSOs, 2 MCs, and 6 DCMs were awarded to members of the Battalion. Ten officers and 189 other ranks had died, 11 officers and 413 other ranks had been wounded,[1] 3 officers and 62 other ranks had been taken prisoner, and 285 were sick.

The Gloucesters moved by train to Cassel and on 20 October, along with the rest of 3ʳᵈ Brigade, marched to Poperinghe, advancing the next day to Langemarck to attack Poelcappelle Station and village. The Gloucesters' task was to take and hold the hamlet of Koekuit to the north of Langemarck. C Company, under Lieutenant Wetherall, captured the hamlet and defended it against repeated attacks with rifle fire of a quality which astonished the enemy. After four hours the situation had become desperate, and a sudden assault by 200 enemy was only stopped with difficulty. The small force was dwindling rapidly, although sixteen men of the Scots Guards had reinforced it. Thirty more men were spared from another company, and the position, which was the key to the defence, was held. However, it was now a sharp salient, so at midnight they withdrew without further losses. Lieutenant Wetherall was awarded one of the first Military Crosses of the War.[2]

On 22 October things were relatively quiet, but at 2.30 am the next morning Captain Rising and two platoons of A Company were sent to fill a gap on the outskirts of Langemarck. When the situation became critical, they were joined by another platoon from D Company. Brigadier General Landon, the commander of 3ʳᵈ Brigade, wrote in a letter:

> We had a great fight yesterday and were attacked all day: the Brigade did splendidly and inflicted great loss on the enemy . . . the Gloucesters

(100 strong) fired over 500 rounds per man, lost all their officers and many N.C.O.s, had the Germans within 50 yards, and not a man retired. Some of their bayonets were shot off their rifles and they had over sixty casualties. A grand performance.

An official account of the battle stated:

> Many fine deeds of valour were done. In one of these Captain R. E. Rising of the Gloucestershire Regiment, with ninety men, defended a point with such heroic tenacity that when some days afterwards the Brigadier attempted to get the names of the survivors for commendation not one could be found.

Bobby Rising, who was forty-three and whose home was in Norfolk, was awarded a DSO (he was to be mortally wounded on 7 November 1914 in the fighting near Zillebeke). Sergeants T. Eddy and T. Knight together with Private W. Crossman of A Company were all awarded the DCM; the official citation is unique in that it mentions the work of each member of the two platoons of A Company. Sergeant J. Wilson of D Company was also awarded the DCM.

On 24 October 1st Gloucesters was relieved and marched to a position 2km east of Ypres on the road to Gheluvelt. On 28 October 1st Division placed 1st

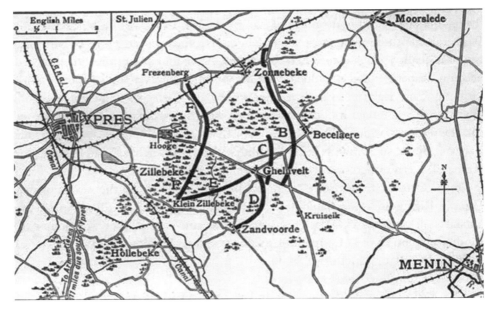

Map 5 The British Positions Prior to the First Battle of Ypres

Gloucesters 'in reserve' to 1st Brigade who, the next day, ordered the Battalion to advance in thick mist to check a German attack which had overwhelmed two of the forward battalions. The Gloucester companies moved independently. Soon, all the officers in C Company were killed or wounded, and it ceased to exist as a coherent force. The few men who had not been hit attached themselves to other companies, or even other regiments, so great was the confusion. D Company pushed along the Menin road, where it helped to rally the remnants of 1st Brigade. It was attacked repeatedly as Germans poured through a gap passing some 400 to 500yds to their north; no other British troops were in sight as they strove to stem the enemy flow. A Company had advanced behind C Company to the assistance of the Black Watch and Scots Guards. On arrival, it was attacked suddenly from the flank and rear. After an almost hopeless resistance, all were killed, wounded or taken prisoner. B Company, advancing behind D Company, crossed the Ypres–Menin road and pushed on towards Kruiseck. Fighting most of the way, it reached the rising ground to the south of the road, about 800yds beyond Gheluvelt. Here it was stopped and slowly driven back. D Company was also forced to withdraw. Soon after noon, the remainder of the 3rd Brigade was sent to assist 1st Brigade. This relieved the strain on the Gloucesters, and the remnants of the Battalion withdrew to the line from which they had advanced twelve hours previously.

The night of 29/30 October was quiet. Early next day, a bombardment followed by a German assault reduced Gheluvelt to ruins. It was touch and go as to whether the British line could bend any more without breaking, and 1st Gloucesters was ordered to collect the men streaming back along the Menin Road from the confusion in front and send them forward again. Counter-attacks were organized, and companies, acting on their own, were able, after desperate fighting, to hold the Germans. At about midday D Company, now only eighty strong, was ordered to recapture a trench to the north of the Menin Road. It advanced under heavy shellfire, then saw that the trenches were still held and the break was further south. Accordingly, it moved across open ground to a sunken road, where the remaining thirty men rallied. From here they attacked, but within a few yards the company commander and fifteen men fell and the remainder were overwhelmed and taken prisoner. By early afternoon the situation was so bleak that it looked as if the Germans would break through. At this point 2nd Worcesters, in a famous counter-attack, drove the Germans back. The remnants of 1st Gloucesters continued to hold their position on the Menin Road, and by 9.00 pm the British line had been stabilized and the Germans were too exhausted and disorganized to mount further attacks. Private Shipway, a signaller attached to Brigade Headquarters, was awarded a DCM.[3] He had been given a message to take up to 1st Gloucesters:

An orderly from the South Wales Borderers was also given a note to take to his battalion. They set out together, but after going a short distance up the Menin road the South Wales Borderer orderly was knocked off his bicycle by a piece of shrapnel and killed. Shipway took on both messages, delivered one to the Gloucesters and obtained leave to take the other to the South Wales Borderers, who were up in the front trenches. He had to advance under very heavy shellfire, and along the rear of the trenches for 3–400 yards, with little or no cover from fire or view. He delivered his message and obtained a receipt. He was then wounded in the hand and wrist but immediately volunteered to take back an answer to Brigade.

There was now a pause. The Official Historian wrote:

> To give a true picture of the long hours of patient & stubborn resistance there should be some mention on almost every page of bursting shells, blown-in trenches, hunger, fatigue and death and wounds . . . it must be remembered that the fighting was almost continuous, hardly interrupted at night and that the troops had no rest . . . they must be imagined as fighting in small groups scattered along the front in shallow trenches, often separated by gaps amounting to two, three or even four hundred yards . . . it was only at night that supplies could be got up to the troops and the wounded removed.

The Gloucesters, who were only about 300 strong, spent 1–5 November in Heronthage Wood. There is no Battalion War Diary for this period, just four pages of notes which include: 'About 200 men arrived under Captain Pritchett but no record was kept as the drafts went straight into action on arrival.' The Battalion was ordered to clear the Germans out of the wood just east of Zillebeke on the 6th. Held up by wire and machine gun fire, the Gloucesters spent the day in the open, only able to withdraw after dark. A fresh assault the next day failed in the same way, and the notes record: 'Roll Call that night 213. Casualties roughly 300 mostly killed and missing'. Lance Corporal G. Royal, a bandsman before the War, who had become one of the many gallant stretcher-bearers, was awarded a DCM for his conduct in rescuing and looking after the wounded.

The Germans now mounted their final attack with twelve fresh battalions of Prussian Guards at Nonne Bosschen on 11 November, where they were stopped and thrown back by the 2nd Oxford and Buckinghamshire Light Infantry in a famous charge. Everard Wyrall wrote:[4]

> None of the survivors who were present at Ypres on 11 November 1914 will ever forget the final and violent effort of the Germans on that day to

break through the British line . . . Four of the most renowned regiments of the German Army, each consisting of three battalions of fresh troops, advanced against a thin line of British troops who for three weeks had been engaged in incessant fighting and were almost worn out from fatigue.

The role of 1st Gloucesters was relatively modest. It was in the Corps Reserve and at 10 o'clock advanced to the south-east of Hooge Chateau. An hour later it advanced again to the crossroads 600yds south of Westhoek. A small part of the Battalion then combined with troops of 2nd Division to counter-attack and clear Nonne Bosschen Wood. Later, the whole battalion took up a new position, which it held for the next four days. Shortly after midnight on 15 November, the First Battle of Ypres was over, and 1st Gloucesters marched to Outtersteen, where they were able to undertake a complete reorganization with 320 badly needed reinforcements. After the War it was decided that there should be four battle honours: 'Ypres 1914', 'Langemarck 1914', 'Gheluvelt' and 'Nonne Bosschen'. All four were awarded to 1st Gloucesters.

Notes

1. The term 'wounded' can be misleading. It included everyone treated at the Regimental Aid Post, from those with life-changing injuries to those needing a shell splinter removed and who might be back in action the same day. These figures therefore include some individuals wounded twice or even three times.
2. Lieutenant General Sir Harry Edward de Robillard Wetherall KBE, CB, DSO, MC (1889–1979), always known as 'Charles', was commissioned into the Gloucesters in 1909. He commanded 4th Oxs and Bucks LI in 1917 and in 1918 was seriously wounded. He commanded 1st Yorks and Lancs in 1936 and then 19 Brigade in 1938. He was GOC 11th African Division in Abyssinia in 1941, then GOC East Africa Force before becoming Commander-in-Chief Ceylon in 1943 until he retired in 1946. He was the Colonel of the Gloucestershire Regiment from 1947 until 1952.
3. John Shipway DCM was born in Chippenham and enlisted in the Gloucesters in 1903. He was wounded again on 27 November 1914 and transferred to 2nd Gloucesters in August 1915. After the War he was employed by Westinghouse in Chippenham. His twin sons, Douglas and Ronald, were both wounded with 1st Gloucesters in Burma in the Second War. John Shipway's younger brother W. G. Shipway was commissioned into 1/4th Gloucesters.
4. Everard Wyrall, 'The Gloucestershire Regiment in the War 1914–1918'.

Chapter 7

1st Gloucesters Defend Givenchy and Endure the Winter of 1914/15

The nature of the War on the Western Front now changed. The initial German invasion of France had been checked. What followed was a series of attempts by each side to outflank the other, but these also failed, so static warfare ensued, and a line of defensive trenches 450 miles long from the Belgian coast to the Swiss border was established.

On 1 December Field Marshal Sir John French, Commander in Chief of the B.E.F., inspected 1st Gloucesters and congratulated them on their gallant conduct. Two days later, HM The King inspected the whole of 3rd Brigade. Few of those on parade had ever seen King George V except in photographs, so this must have been an impressive event. Generally, the Battalion was able to rest and train, but on 20 December this came to an abrupt end. At daybreak the Germans began a heavy artillery barrage on the Indian Corps from Cuinchy to Neuve Chapelle. At 9.00 am ten mines were exploded under the British trenches in front of Givenchy, followed by a German attack; a critical situation soon developed there, as it did in front of Festubert, where the enemy had secured a 300yd breach in the line. At 6.30 pm 3rd Brigade, including 1st Gloucesters, marched to Merville. At 4.00 am the next day they continued to Béthune, where they arrived, with the Gloucesters leading, at 8.00 am and halted for breakfast. At 12.30 pm 1st Division launched an attack to retake the trenches lost by the Indian Corps, with 1st Brigade on the right of the Gloucesters and 1st Battalion, South Wales Borderers (SWB) on the left. In fierce fighting they gained about 500yds by nightfall. An order to continue the attack the next day was subsequently cancelled, and the Division dug in where they were. Amongst much other gallantry, Thomas Harding was the only surviving NCO in his platoon, having remained for two days under heavy fire 50yds from the German trenches. He was awarded the DCM.[1] Lieutenant Colonel Lovett wrote:

> In the advance to the attack there was a gap on left and touch could not be secured with SWB. This was eventually filled by A Company, Welch Regiment. C Company under Captain Pritchett eventually diverted to right to fill gap between 3rd and 1st Brigades. This officer reached the enemy's trenches with a few men only, not sufficient to make an entry. The attack was carried out over such muddy ground, and intersected

with dykes, that rifles became clogged with mud & useless – bayonets could not be fixed. No reply could be made to the hostile fire and the line could not be pushed within 300 yards of the enemy's position as they were using a very heavy machine gun and rifle fire and losses became very heavy. Here the battalion entrenched on a front of about 300 yards . . . No 5957 Lance Corporal F Bailey and 9796 H Mann remained with Captain Pritchett when that officer was wounded within 25 yards of the enemy's trenches from the night of 21st until early morning 23rd when Captain Pritchett was brought back. They placed their officer under close fire of the enemy in a place of comparative safety.

Walter Pritchett died of his wounds five days later. He was thirty-five. Lance Corporal Mann died in April 1916.

On 21 December 1914 Lieutenant Claude Templer was taken prisoner while reconnoitring an enemy position near Givenchy. He subsequently made thirteen attempts to escape, was eventually successful in 1917 and was granted a private audience with King George V. His heroism so impressed Field Marshal Sir Henry Wilson that he ordered the publication of a pamphlet, 'Behind the German Lines'. After his escape, he rejoined 1st Gloucesters and was killed on 4 June 1918 by a chance shell while returning from a successful raid on enemy trenches.[2] The following message was subsequently circulated:

> Sir Douglas Haig wishes to express to the troops his appreciation of the excellent work done by the 1st Div on 21st and 22nd Dec in exceptionally difficult circumstances. The GOC 1st Division has reported that in this action the following battalions rendered conspicuously gallant service:
>
> 2nd Bn Royal Munster Fusiliers, 2nd Bn Welch Regt, 1st Gloucestershire Regt, 1st Coldstream Guards
>
> Sir Douglas Haig has read these reports with great pleasure.

The British line had been secured but the price was high. The Gloucesters had two companies forward in the front line and two in reserve and kept changing these around for the rest of December. There appear to have been no other battalions available to achieve a relief, and it must have been a miserable time, as the front line trenches were full of water. So ended 1914 for 1st Gloucesters, who had seen a lot of action and could boast of being one of the few battalions that had never lost its trenches. Their gallantry had been recognized by the award of 1 CB, 2 DSOs, 3 MCs, 8 DCMs; 7 officers and other ranks had been Mentioned in Despatches.[3] As R. M. Grazebrook wrote,[4] 'Assuredly a gallant record of a gallant Regiment from a gallant County'.

1st Gloucesters had arrived in France in August with 30 officers and about 1,000 other ranks, and had subsequently received reinforcements. By 31 December 17 officers and 276 other ranks had died, 17 officers and 719 other ranks had been wounded and 4 officers and 78 other ranks had been captured. In addition, 5 officers and about 464 other ranks had been taken sick. These stark figures hide the confusion and despair that existed at the time. Miss Gertrude Bell, better known for her work as a political officer, administrator, spy and archaeologist in the Middle East, went to Boulogne on 21 November and was soon running the Red Cross Wounded and Missing Enquiry Department. This tried to help the many people attempting to find out whether their husbands, sons, or fiancés were dead, lying wounded in one of the many hospitals or prisoners of war. In many cases it would be weeks before they knew. There were just three Campaign Medals issued for the Great War, but two were very similar. The 1914 Star was only given to those who served in France and Belgium between 5 August and midnight on 22 November 1914. It had a narrow bronze strip sewn on to the ribbon inscribed '5 Aug–22 Nov 1914'.

The Gloucesters remained near Givenchy until relieved by an Indian Brigade on 7 January, when it withdrew to Béthune. Here the men could at last get a wash and shave. Two officers and three NCOs were granted four days leave to England, and 25 per cent of the Battalion were allowed out into the town at a time. The break only lasted five days as 3rd Brigade began relieving 1st Brigade on 12 January and the Gloucesters spent the rest of January in the trenches at Givenchy. The companies were rotated every two days so that the men were only in the front line for 48 hours. Up to three men were wounded virtually every day, and the weather was dreadful. The War Diary of 20 January summarizes the situation: 'Weather conditions still extremely bad for trenches. Men undergoing great hardships during their 48 hours on duty owing to wet and sharp frost at night. In spite of this all ranks are most cheerful. 1 man wounded.' The next day the diary records: 'No change in situation. Great difficulty experienced in keeping trench fit to occupy on account of continual collapse of parapet owing to water.'

There was a diversion on 24 January, when the Germans shelled a lock, doing little damage and causing no casualties to the men but killing a lot of fish, which 'the men caught with nets during intervals in the shelling'. This was the prelude to a more serious situation, as the next day, after a 45-minute artillery bombardment, the Germans attacked Givenchy. The Gloucesters managed to halt the attack with small arms fire, although some attackers got to within 40–50yds of the forward trenches. However, the Germans broke through the battalion on the immediate left of the Gloucesters and into Givenchy itself. There was a risk of their getting into the Battalion's trenches, until a half company of the Black Watch 'carried out a brilliant counter-attack', which completely restored the situation. Three officers and 9 other ranks were killed, and 1 officer and 27 other ranks were wounded. Private Joseph Harper[5] was awarded the DCM: 'When the bombardment by the enemy was very fierce he volunteered to convey a message under very dangerous circumstances to the front trench. This act of gallantry entailed the crossing of 800 yards of fire-swept ground on two occasions.'

The overall strength of 1st Gloucesters was, nevertheless, gradually increasing. In January three drafts arrived, totalling 2 officers and 280 other ranks. The Battalion received a message on 26 January: 'With reference to recapture of Givenchy, Sir John French sends his congratulations to all concerned.' The Battalion was relieved on 3 February when 3rd Brigade became the Corps Reserve some 14 miles to the rear, well out of artillery range. Here it remained for most of the month, receiving more drafts, which included some individuals who had been wounded on the Aisne. Now recovered, they brought much needed experience. Once the wounded evacuated to England had been found fit to return to duty they joined 3rd Gloucesters, where they could help to train new drafts and get physically fit before rejoining their battalion. A draft of 202 men arrived on 7 February, and the War Diary records: 'Reconstruction of companies and platoons with newly arrived reinforcements'. Besides training, there was a 'regimental concert' on the 18th and news of the award of gallantry medals.

On 25 February 1st Gloucesters went back into the line at Festubert, but it was noted: 'A great change has now taken place in the situation at this spot. Trenches have been replaced by strong breastworks and consequently great difficulty in coping with waterlogged trenches has ceased to exist. The enemy shows much less activity.' The Battalion was relieved on 7 March and spent several days standing by to support an Indian Corps attack, but were not needed. Having organized a Battalion boxing competition, they took over the line at Neuve Chapelle on the 23rd. There, an American war correspondent, Frederick Palmer, spent a night in the trenches with them. He had started his career in 1897 and by 1914 had covered six different wars, gaining wide experience of reporting war and judging morale. He would have found a battalion coping with both the weather and the Germans, cheerful and confident.

Notes

1. Sergeant Thomas Harding DCM had first enlisted in 1902 and had served in South Africa but was discharged in 1905. Like many others, he re-enlisted in 1914 and survived the War, being discharged in October 1919, aged thirty-six; his medals are in the Soldiers of Gloucestershire Museum.

2. There is a memorial to Claude Templer in the Chapel at the Royal Academy, Sandhurst. A collection of his work, written while a prisoner, *Poems and Imaginings*, was published in 1923.
3. Those Mentioned in Despatches received no visible sign of the award prior to May 1919, when a Certificate was issued. In January 1920 they were entitled to wear a bronze oak leaf on the ribbon of their Victory Medal.
4. Captain R. M. Grazebrook OBE, MC, 'The Gloucestershire Regiment War Narratives 1914–15'.
5. Joseph Harper came from Bristol and enlisted in the Gloucesters in September 1914. The Lord Mayor of Bristol presented him with his DCM. Nine months later he was wounded at Aubers Ridge and lost the use of his right arm. He was aged thirty-six, and was discharged on 20 July 1915.

Chapter 8

2nd Gloucesters arrive from China

The other regular battalion of the Regiment, 2nd Gloucesters, had left Portsmouth in 1909 and was in Northern China when the War broke out. The Chinese had granted concessions to a number of European countries, and the British Concession in Tientsin consisted of about 200 acres leased in perpetuity to the British Government, who subleased plots for businesses to establish themselves. The Gloucesters were part of the British garrison.

Initially, there was some confusion about the task of the Battalion. The Germans had been granted a concession at Tsingtao and they had turned it into a port and naval base garrisoned by about 4,000 troops, which the Japanese, Britain's allies, had decided to blockade. The British Government, apprehensive of Japanese intentions, sent 1,500 troops to assist its allies, and 2nd Gloucesters expected to be part of this force. However, probably due to the situation in France, at 24 hours' notice 2nd Gloucesters was ordered to sail with families for England on the P&O *Arcadia*. The journey took eight weeks, before they eventually arrived at Southampton on 8 November 1914. One horse accompanied the Battalion, 'The Sikh', owned by the Adjutant, Lieutenant Alec Vicary.[1] The story of 'The Sikh' is a remarkable one as he accompanied 2nd Gloucesters throughout the war to France and Salonika, and afterwards to South Russia.

On arrival, 2nd Gloucesters travelled to Winchester. The men cannot have been fit after so long on board, but casualties in Flanders made it imperative that any fresh regular battalions joined the B.E.F. as soon as possible; the First Battle of Ypres had not ended and there was no indication as to when it would. The Battalion joined 81st Brigade of 27th Division and immediately began to draw kit to mobilize. The Commanding Officer was Lieutenant Colonel George Tulloh, who although a Scot (he came from Roxburghshire) had been commissioned into the Gloucesters in 1887 and had fought in the Boer War. He had taken over command in China just days before the outbreak of war.

Having been away for so long it was thought essential to let the men have leave, and on 14 November half the Battalion were allowed away, only to be recalled the next day. Giving leave to half was clearly felt to be excessive, so the practice began of sending 20 per cent at a time away for 5 days. A note in the battalion War Diary records, 'Boots are of inferior quality.' Two officers and 33 men were detached to form part of the Divisional Cyclist Company, part of the Army Cycling

Corps, which had its own cap badge. Their role was to provide reconnaissance and communications.

A month after arriving at Southampton, the Battalion was up to full strength. Besides 'The Sikh', another animal joined the ranks at Winchester. 'Buller', as he was swiftly christened by the men, was a huge bull terrier, who appeared suddenly and who was to guard the transport lines throughout the War. He was never defeated by another dog. By 17 December 2nd Gloucesters had completed mobilization in less than six weeks. The Battalion marched the 13 miles to Southampton the next day and embarked for Le Havre. Lieutenant George Power[2] wrote home:

> We are all tucked away in a large shed at a certain place in the pleasant land of France and expect to move up by rail soon. We got dry by degrees on board and were quite comfortable although rough and rather cold for an hour or so. To-day is lovely.

On 19 December the Battalion entrained and set off for Aire, about 50km west of Ypres, where it was accommodated in French barracks. On 22 December, George Power wrote:

> D. Burges [Dan Burges, who was to win a VC in 1918] and I are, this night, at a railway goods station rather cold and dinnerless and the prospect of being up all night for no reason at all. We had a very tedious journey in the train, also rather cold, but by filling the carriage up with hay we managed to make it very comfortable in the end . . . Now we are in billets in another town. The men are in barracks but the officers are in the town. I am billeted on a maker of paints; my arrival was rather comic. Knowing how much French I can speak, you can imagine the scene, I expect. The landlady is very small and rather plain, wife of maker of paints. We had a long discussion as to whether she could give me space to cook or not. It was eventually decided she could not, so we proceeded upstairs to view the chamber. Quite a nice looking room in which a charming looking maiden, in an extraordinary dress, was making the bed. The room was evidently hers and she was very fed up at having to turn out, and when I could not understand a remark of the landlady, she repeated it at the top of her voice. I expect she will trot back again tonight as I am on this outpost job. Funny world.

He wrote again on Christmas Day:

> We are still quite comfortable and dry . . . We got a present from Princess Mary this morning. I am sending you the card. All the men got

a card from the King and Queen, but the officers did not. I am rather disappointed. Last night it froze a bit and has dried the ground a bit. The C Company Mess is a very happy affair indeed. The Christmas Dinner consisted of beef and rum; very good! So far, no mails and baccy was getting a bit short. Luckily Princess Mary's baccy turned up . . . It is getting rather late and I must go the house of the maker of paints. Had a bath today – wonderful the amount of dirt that came off – the first since leaving England. Mrs land-lady lodgings does not understand baths. It is as much as she can do to empty the slops.

2nd Gloucesters remained in Aire for the rest of December, 'generally squaring up' as the War Diary describes it. Every man was issued with extra-large boots that could be worn over two pairs of socks and was given a third pair. Looking after feet was vitally important, given the marching that was required. The men also carried out musketry training, learnt to load the wagons by day and night and dug trenches, although they quickly discovered that the ground was impossible and so built parapets. Several officers were sent to 1st Gloucesters to learn more about the intricacies of trench warfare. The weather was by now cold and wet, and the men were provided with fur waistcoats. Sixteen braziers were issued and must have been in great demand.

By January 1915 the situation on the Western Front had become the deadlock that would persist for the next three years. The German plan had failed. They had not captured Paris, and the Russians had mobilized far more rapidly than expected and by September were threatening East Prussia. This was partly the reason for the German retreat and the order given by Field Marshal Helmuth von Moltke, the German Chief of Staff, on 11 September to move to positions behind the line of the River Aisne and its tributaries. He directed: 'The lines so reached will be fortified and defended.' The Kaiser replaced Moltke two days later. Nevertheless, by taking up positions behind the river, the Germans had seized the advantage. The order initiated trench warfare, for which the Germans were better equipped than any other army at the time. Critically, the line chosen on the high ground above the river enabled the Germans to look down on the Allies, observe movement and direct artillery fire. It also meant that the Allies' trench line would be, in many cases, on the flood plain.

On 7 January 1915 the Battalion, along with the rest of 81st Brigade, marched to Dickebusch, south of Ypres, in preparation for their first spell in the trenches. It was also their first experience of taking over the line at night, something all battalions would become well accustomed to; but initially it must have seemed alarming to be squelching along communication trenches with the occasional artillery shell exploding nearby and any exposed light immediately drawing fire from a sniper.

Map 6 The Western Front 1915–1918

The Battalion took over the line near St Eloi from 2nd King's Shropshire Light Infantry (KSLI). The War Diary for 11 January records the first impressions:

> Artillery fire carried on all day, particularly heavy between the hours of 2pm and 4pm. Artillery fire ceased at nightfall. At 6.30pm there was very heavy rifle fire, which lasted about 20 mins after that there was continued sniping all night. Snipers between our fire trenches and Battalion Headquarters were very annoying. Great difficulty about water & rations, which had to be fetched from KRUISTAAHOCK a mile in rear of Headquarters. Rations were eventually man-handled to Headquarters and issued there, this took from 9pm to 3am. Platoons sent men direct to KRUISTAAHOCK for water.

The Gloucesters were relieved at 9.00 pm on 12 January by 2nd Duke of Cornwall's Light Infantry (DCLI) and marched back to the same billets in Dickebusch. The casualties from these first 48 hours in the trenches were 12 wounded, 5 missing and 2 'unfit to march'. Only one of the missing, Albert Roberts, who was twenty-six and whose parents lived at 36 Swindon Place, Cheltenham, had been killed. The others were either lost or prisoners, probably the former. The Adjutant, Captain Alec Vicary, noted in the margin of the War Diary:

> Braziers in trenches useless as they sink into the mud. Long stands to put them on would remedy this. Going into trenches men must take 2 days rations. If men are in fire trenches more than 24 hours, efficiency will suffer greatly. 24 hours is as much as a man can endure up to his knees in water.

This was a lesson learnt throughout the British Army. It led to the system, whenever possible, of battalions spending four days in the line, with two companies in the front line and two in the support line. This was followed by four days in the reserve trenches and four in billets out of the line completely. The staff work required to organize these regular reliefs was significant and is one of the little recognized achievements of the War, vital as it was for maintaining morale.

On 13 January 2nd Gloucesters marched the 6 miles from Dickebusch to Mount Kokerelle, but their first short spell in the trenches had taken its toll. Fifty-four men had to be carried on carts and there were many stragglers. The War Diary records, 'A large number of men were very done up and we had great difficulty in getting them along.' The Gloucesters were back in the same trenches near St Eloi on 16 January, and this routine continued until the 23rd, when they marched the 6 miles to Westoutre to be Divisional Reserve. Here there were good billets and an opportunity for every man to have a bath, clean underclothes and six days' rest. In his letter of 27 January, George Power wrote:

Kaiser's Birthday today. Deuce of a scrap somewhere last night, by the row. Thank goodness they did not turn us out for it. I think this is No. 13, but I am not sure. I forgot to number the last two, I think. Still very cold, but no rain, which is a great thing. There was a little snow last night and the fields were slightly white this morning. This morning the entire Army is being washed. They walk over to the brewery, about 2 miles, and have a much needed hot bath and clean things given to them.'

Throughout February and until 23 March the routine continued. Every two days the Gloucesters and 1st Argyll and Sutherland Highlanders (1 A&SH) relieved one another, and there were occasional breaks as Divisional Reserve for rest and baths. On 14 March the enemy attacked 82nd Brigade and captured some trenches but were driven back with a counter-attack that involved a platoon from C Company. The German artillery and snipers, however, meant that on almost every day in the line there were casualties: during the period from 7 January to 23 March the Battalion suffered 168 casualties from enemy action of whom 34 died. Sickness had a much greater impact on the Battalion: in January 1915 222 were taken sick, in February, 144, and in March, 84. The first mention of issuing gumboots before the men went into the trenches was on 5 March. On Easter Sunday, 4 April, the Battalion marched to Ypres itself. April 1915 would provide a severe test of 2nd Gloucesters and many others.

Notes

1. Alexander Craven Vicary CB, DSO & Bar, MC (1888–1975) was born in Devon and commissioned into the Regiment in 1908. He rose through the ranks of 2nd Gloucesters, winning an MC in June 1915, to become CO of 2nd Gloucesters in November 1917. He was awarded the DSO in June 1918 and a Bar in September 1918. When he married Kathleen Hilton Green from Alderley, Gloucestershire in 1919, their wedding presents include a silver salver inscribed with the 590 names of the NCOs and men of 2nd Gloucesters, a unique tribute. He retired to Chagford in Devon in 1930 but rejoined the Army in the Second World War and was made a CB. He was Mentioned in Despatches six times. His younger brother, John, was also in the 2nd Gloucesters.
2. Edward George Hugh Power (1887–1981) was commissioned into the Gloucestershire Regiment in 1908. He went with 2nd Gloucesters to Macedonia, where he became Commandant of the Machine Gun School. His letters and other artefacts are in the archives at The Soldiers of Gloucestershire Museum in Gloucester Docks. His letters provide an excellent contemporary insight into life in the Battalion at the time.

Chapter 9

2nd Gloucesters at Ypres in 1915

The Second Battle of Ypres, fought in April/May 1915, was the result of the only major attack launched by the Germans on the Western Front in 1915. Although the Allies were driven back from the outer rim of the Ypres Salient, the Germans failed again to take Ypres itself.

Late on the afternoon of the 22 April, the Germans released chlorine gas over a 4-mile front. The Allies were completely unprepared and the impact was terrifying. The French Territorial and Colonial Moroccan and Algerian troops that held the Allied line at this point suffered about 6,000 casualties, many of whom died within ten minutes whilst others were blinded. The Germans had not expected the gas to be so effective and were unable to exploit the gap in the Allied Line that it created. The forces they had available were limited, and they too had suffered casualties in releasing the gas. As a result, those Germans who did advance did so with great caution, not knowing what the after-effects might be. Canadian troops on the flanks of the breakthrough counter-attacked successfully, although some battalions experienced significant losses.

Like all the major battles in the First World War, the Second Battle of Ypres was broken down subsequently into a series of separate actions: Gravenstafel Ridge (22–23 April), St Julien (24 April–5 May), Frezenberg (8–13 May) and Bellewaarde (24–25 May). For 2nd Gloucesters, like others, the action was continuous, but until 8 May it principally consisted of being shelled daily and suffering casualties as a result. In April 1915 the Battalion was still rotating in the trenches with 1st A&SH, four days in the line, followed by four out. It was relieved at 1.00 am on 21 April and marched back to Sanctuary Wood, which, sadly, was no sanctuary. The chlorine gas did not reach the British positions but there was heavy fighting around Hill 60. As a result, the 1st Royal Scots had not been relieved, and 2nd Gloucesters were ordered at about 2.45 am on 23 April, to replace them. The Germans' shelling and heavy machine gun fire meant the Battalion was delayed and did not reach the Royal Scots until it was getting light; the Commanding Officer of the Royal Scots refused to be relieved, and 2nd Gloucesters therefore returned to Sanctuary Wood, having lost eight other ranks.

The village of St Julien had been well to the rear of the 1st Canadian Division until the poison gas attack of 22 April, whereupon it became the front line. Two days later, the Germans released another cloud of chlorine gas, this time directly

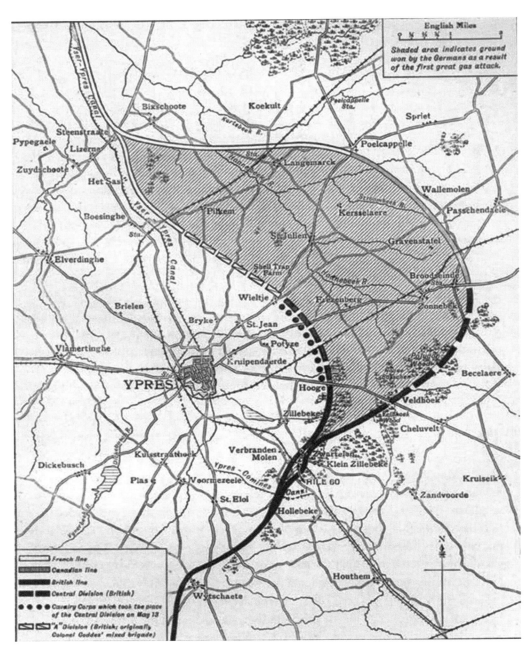

Map 7 Second Battle of Ypres

towards the re-formed Canadian lines just west of the village. On seeing the approach of the greenish-grey gas cloud, the Canadian troops urinated on their handkerchiefs and placed these over their noses and mouths. This countermeasure was ineffective, however, and the Canadian lines broke, allowing German troops to take the village. The Gloucesters were ordered to march as fast as possible over open country towards Potije, but in the event they were not needed and returned to the shelters in Sanctuary Wood.

Until now there had been no preparation for gas warfare. Men were ordered to tie socks soaked in urine over their mouths whenever they saw the yellow clouds of chlorine gas. These were not efficient, but soon more effective cotton waste and gauze respirators were issued, which remained in use until a flannel smoke-helmet with a mica eyepiece was issued at the end of May. George Power wrote on 24 April:

> These are strenuous days. Fritz fairly on the bounce and lots of really big stuff flying about. Fritz is using sulphuric acid in his shells, which has the most discomforting effect. It makes your eyes awfully sore and if you get enough of it, it chokes you. So you see we are fighting perfect gentlemen in every way . . . The noise during the last three days has been perfectly ghastly and the fumes from the German shells very unpleasant. But the worst things have an end sometime. [Two days later] An extraordinarily noisy day . . . Alas my poor good billet has fallen down; a victim of a very large shell sent over by Fritz.

The Gloucesters moved into the front line on 28 April and began the rotation of companies in and out of the line until the Battle of Frezenberg. George Power was as confused as everyone else when he wrote on 5 May:

> This last fortnight has been distinctly trying. Continual shelling all day and night and anxiety as to what the situation really is. Nobody seems to know, or if they do, they do not tell us…The weather is perfectly heavenly, which is a great blessing, as at present I have no kit beyond what I stand up in and badly need a bath. Such is war – Vive la France . . . Please send me a piece of soap! Some day soon there is going to be a mighty washing of the person and raiment. The inconsiderate and uncleanly Hun has destroyed my laundry with a 17 inch shell. Luckily none of my clothes was there, but all the apparatus of cleansing garments has vanished in a cloud of smoke.

The conduct of 2nd Gloucesters during the Battle of Frezenburg Ridge would have made their famous predecessors, the 61st (South Gloucestershire) Regiment,

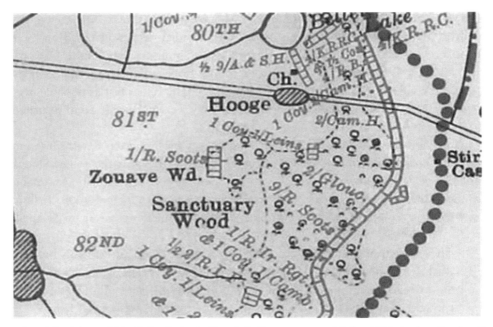

Map 8 Position of 81ˢᵗ Brigade including 2ⁿᵈ Gloucester on 8 May 1915 during Battle of Frezenberg Ridge.

proud. On 8 May the Germans began an attack on 27ᵗʰ Division and the following day assaulted 2ⁿᵈ Gloucesters from Stirling Castle, after a 10-minute heavy bombardment followed by intense small arms fire, then another bombardment, again followed by machine gun and rifle fire. The Battalion was deployed with two companies forward (D Company on the right, B on the left), with A Company in close support behind and C Company as battalion reserve with Battalion HQ. The Germans concentrated their efforts on B Company. There were few British guns, and in any case these had little ammunition, but a Belgian battery did what it could to help. Platoons of the forward left company were cut off, and the company commander ordered all but ten men per platoon to try to withdraw, but the intensity of the German fire made movement almost impossible. One wounded platoon commander, Lieutenant E. D'O Aplin,[1] got back with just three men, the sole survivors of his platoon.

When the Germans assaulted, they did so in strength and, despite suffering heavy casualties, were soon able to get into some of the left forward trenches and, more seriously, into the communication trenches behind. The close support company rushed forward to support what was left of the forward company but was unable to dislodge the Germans, losing men in hand-to-hand fighting. The Battalion reserve company, along with Battalion HQ, occupied the reserve trenches about 250yds behind the main line. Two companies of Leinsters were ordered forward to help. There was no communication between groups except by runner, and the ground was not only a morass of mud and shell holes but covered in a tangle of fallen trees, a hazard for both sides. When Battalion HQ learnt that the Germans were still holding the forward trench, the battalion reserve bombing parties advanced to turn the enemy out. (Throughout the Great War hand grenades, as they are now known, were referred to as 'bombs', and bombing parties or sections of specially trained men were often used to clear enemy trenches). Two parties got within 20yds of the Germans, but the attempt failed. As Everard Wyrall wrote,[2] 'Many brave actions were performed during that heavy fighting.'

A counter-attack organized by Brigade Headquarters for mid-afternoon also failed, but not until great acts of gallantry had got some of the Gloucesters to within 15 to 20yds of the enemy; at this point the Commanding Officer, Lieutenant Colonel George Tulloh, was killed, and there appeared to be only Captain A.C. Vicary and five subalterns left. At about 5.30 pm Captain Vicary crawled forward and found Major Nisbet and three other officers and a few men still holding out and led them back. Major Nisbet[3] took over command. The Brigade Commander ordered no further attacks; the Battalion was to consolidate on the old Main Line. During the night the line was handed over, and the Gloucesters, with their wounded, marched back to the GHQ Line of reserve trenches. But it was not over.

On the evening of 11 May, less than two days later, the Battalion was sent forward as the enemy had seized part of the front line from the Camerons. It included a small hill, which the Brigade Commander felt must be retaken at all costs. Captain A. C. Vicary volunteered to recce the situation and found the Germans digging in on the hill. He reported back, and an attack by the Leinsters failed, so B Company under Captain Julian Fane were ordered to retake the hill, which they did with fixed bayonets. At 4.45 pm, having been subjected to heavy artillery and machine gun fire, the Company was forced to withdraw and the Germans retook the hill. B Company regrouped and an hour later drove the Germans off again and held the hill until the next day. Captain Fane reported, 'I can go on taking the damned hill as often as you want, but I cannot hold it.' In the period 8–13 May, 2nd Gloucesters casualties totalled 262 all ranks, of whom 86 died in action, but as Everard Wyrall comments,[4] 'But for the continuous gallantry of Lieutenant Sherlock [the Medical Officer] and his band of stretcher-bearers, the number of men lost would have been far greater.'

George Power, who was by now the Brigade Machine Gun Officer, wrote on 15 May:

A much quieter day. Let us hope things are settling down here after a thorough shake up. My poor Regiment; it has done splendidly.

The Brigade has had telegrams from Joffre and sundry big-wigs, but what we want more than millions of telegrams, is a rest. Get somewhere where we cannot hear a gun and a bath is not completely non-existent . . . The *Lusitania* incident is pretty bad. How this war has brought out the utter impotence of America in European politics . . . The truth is they are quite powerless and Germany knows it.

Sir John French inspected the Brigade on 20 May and said:

Your Colours have many famous names emblazoned on them, but none will be more famous than that of the Second Battle of Ypres. I want you one and all to understand how thoroughly I realise and appreciate what you have done.

The Gloucesters were spared further fighting, although early on 25 May 28th Division suffered a major gas attack and 2nd Gloucesters moved at short notice to Vlamertinghe near Ypres but remained in reserve until relieved on 28 May. The Second Battle of Ypres was over, and the Germans had not taken the town. The Battalion had suffered 587 casualties, over half its strength, of whom 134 had died. After the War 2nd Gloucesters were awarded all five Battle Honours: 'Ypres 1915', 'Gravenstafel', 'St Julien', 'Frezenberg', and 'Bellewaarde'. The Battalion now marched south with the Division to the more peaceful and comfortable sector east of Armentières, where the summer months of 1915 would be spent.

Notes
1. Elphinstone D'Oyly Aplin, who came from Budleigh Salterton in Devon, died of his wounds four days later.
2. Everard Wyrall, *The Gloucestershire Regiment in the War 1914–1918.*
3. Francis Courtney Nisbet DSO (1870–1953) joined the Regiment in 1890. He was taken prisoner outside Ladysmith in the South African War. From 1916 to 1918 in Macedonia he commanded the 8th DCLI and a brigade, gaining the DSO, the Serbian Star of Karageorge and was Mentioned in Despatches five times. He commanded 1st Gloucesters after the War in Ireland. Retired as Hon. Brigadier-General in 1921. He was a fine sportsman and athlete in his day.
4. Wyrall, op. cit.

Chapter 10

1ˢᵗ Gloucesters at the Aubers Ridge

At the beginning of 1915 the question of how to break the stalemate on the Western Front occupied the best military brains on both sides. It wasn't enough to break the opposing trench line; the breakthrough had then to be exploited to force a large scale withdrawal. The first major attack of the war by the British Army was at Neuve Chapelle in March 1915; no Gloucester battalion was involved. It was not a success, but there was a feeling that with a heavier artillery bombardment and more reserves to follow up it might have been. The Germans had broken the Allied line when they used gas for the first time in the Second Battle of Ypres but had failed to use the opportunity presented.

Meanwhile, politicians at home pressed for action and success. What had also become increasingly apparent was that the ground the German held south of Ypres gave them a significant geographical advantage: the ridges of Aubers and Messines allowed them to overlook the Allies and direct artillery fire effectively. Allied planning began to focus on which railway lines supported the Germans, on the basis that if these could be cut then the enemy would be forced to withdraw. Two railway systems supplied the Germans holding the salient between Flanders and Verdun, and it was decided to mount offensives on the shoulders of the salient in the north, at Aubers and Vimy, while in the south attacks would be launched against the Champagne Heights.

This was the background to the Battle of Aubers on 9 May 1915, in which 1ˢᵗ Gloucesters took part. The Battalion had remained in the Neuve Chapelle area since the visit by the American war correspondent in March, going in and out of the trenches. There was constant shelling and sniping, and in this period twenty-two other ranks died and some were taken prisoner. Generally, in the early stages of the war, prisoners were treated well. It was only later, when the whole German population was short of food, that Allied prisoners also suffered from hunger.

The ground over which the British attacked at Aubers was difficult. It was flat and intersected with drainage ditches, some of which were 10–15ft wide; too far to jump. There was also little cover, and the German positions, which were 100 to 500yds from the British, were difficult to identify. The Bois de Biez, a thick wood, lay behind the German front line, and the ground rose gradually to the

Aubers Ridge, from which the Germans could observe the British lines. The British plan was to launch a pincer movement: 8th and 7th Divisions would attack from the north, while 1st Division and the Meerut Division would do so from the south.

Although 3rd Brigade was one of the assaulting brigades in 1st Division, 1st Gloucesters was in reserve with orders to attack the German positions in the direction of the Ferme du Bois Distillerie, once the leading battalions had advanced. Initially, C Company (Captain A. W. Pagan) was on the right and B Company (Captain A. St J. Blunt) on the left, with D Company (Captain F. C. Finch) in the second line. The leading battalions went 'over the top' at 5.30 am and were quickly cut down by heavy machine gun fire; unbeknown to the British, the Germans had considerably strengthened their positions since Neuve Chapelle. By 6.00 am the advance had halted, with many men pinned down in no-man's-land. Some of the Munsters from 3rd Brigade had reached the German trenches but all were killed or captured. Meanwhile, the Gloucesters had reached the Allied forward trenches without many casualties but found the trenches crowded with men from the leading battalions who had managed to get back. After a further intense bombardment the Gloucesters' assault began at 7.00 am. After about 40yds they were held up by heavy machine gun fire. No further advance was possible, and they were ordered to retire. C Company had lost 62 all ranks.

By 8.00 am Haig was aware that the attack had failed, but the reports underestimated the losses and the problems encountered. He was also told that the French had been more successful at Vimy in the south and so decided to launch a further attack at noon, although this was put back to 4.00 pm when it was realized how long it would take to get fresh troops into position. The Germans, meanwhile, continued to bombard the British positions and had moved reinforcements into the area opposite 1st and Meerut Divisions. The Gloucesters then received orders to repeat its assault at 4.00 pm. This time, D Company was on the right with C Company behind, A Company (Captain R. D. Scott) on the left with B Company behind them. Directly the bombardment ceased, hostile machine guns fired heavily. D Company suffered severely while crossing the parapet; A Company less so. Captain F. J. Brodigan led D Company (Captain Finch had been wounded earlier in the battle) with great gallantry for about 120yds under heavy machine gun fire, until they were held up and he was killed. His father, Colonel Francis Brodigan, had served with distinction in the 28th (North Gloucestershire) Regiment in the Crimean War, and he himself had joined the Gloucesters in 1902. A Company did not get as far before being stopped, and 1st Division ordered the Battalion to retire when it was seen that advance was impossible. It had suffered 264 casualties, of whom 74 died. Among

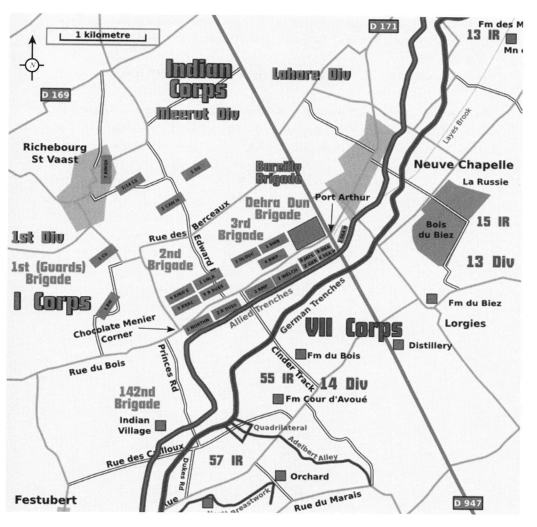

Map 9 Aubers Ridge (Southern Sector), 9 May 1915

those killed was Second Lieutenant Frank Lawrence, brother of T. E. Lawrence, better known as 'Lawrence of Arabia'.

To end what had been a disastrous day for the British Army and the Gloucesters, the War Diary records:

> Battalion was relieved from the trenches by Royal Berkshire Regt and had assembled at Windy Corner by midnight . . . Battalion was ordered to proceed to Le Touret to meet Staff Officer who would direct it to billets. Arrived at 3.15am. Staff Officer was not forthcoming and

battalion remained on roadside till 5.15am while Adjutant searched for billets eventually found to be at Cornet Malo. Marched in at 6.15am and rested.

Tuesday May 11th. Rested. Draft of 50 joined from 3rd Battn.

The lessons – poor intelligence, lack of surprise, ineffective artillery support and a failure to match the German ability to move reserves rapidly – would not be learnt until many more attacks had failed and men had been killed or wounded as a result.

Part II

ENLARGING THE ARMY

Chapter 11

Expanding the Territorial Force

Back in England, life had changed dramatically for members of the RGH and the 4th, 5th and 6th Gloucesters. All were volunteers with jobs outside the Army which they had to give up; some had been Territorials for many years; almost without exception, they had deep roots in Gloucestershire, including the city of Bristol.

Yeomanry Regiments at full strength consisted of 26 officers and 523 other ranks, so the RGH needed to expand. The commanding officer was a lieutenant colonel, and there were three squadrons each with four troops. At full strength, a Yeomanry Regiment had 528 riding horses, 74 draught horses, 6 pack horses, 18 carts or horse-drawn wagons and 15 bicycles. One of the differences between the regular cavalry and the yeomanry was the latter's relationship with horses; most yeomen had lived with horses since they were children. In the nineteenth century a basic requirement for the yeomanry was that both officers and men should be able to provide a suitable horse and saddle; and although this had long ceased, a familiarity with horses and their well-being was instinctive. The RGH were part of the 1st South Midland Mounted Brigade. On 12 August, just eight days after mobilization, the brigade moved to Bury St Edmunds, where it trained but was also kept ready to deal with enemy landings, in case these materialized. At the end of August, the brigade moved to Newbury racecourse, where it became part of 2nd Mounted Division, and went back to defend the North Norfolk coast.

The 4th (City of Bristol) Battalion, The Gloucestershire Regiment, had its headquarters at Queen's Road, Clifton, and the Lord Mayor of Bristol was the Honorary Colonel of the Battalion. 6th Gloucesters was also a mainly Bristol battalion, recruiting from the city and the south of the county, whereas 5th Gloucesters recruited in the centre and north of Gloucestershire and in 1914, its headquarters were at The Barracks, near Gloucester Prison, in the city.

The RGH and the three Gloucester Territorial Force (TF) battalions were all ordered to mobilize on 4 August. There was a legal problem to be overcome, since the men were only committed to serve within the United Kingdom and could not be sent overseas unless they volunteered to go. In 1910, those serving in the TF were asked to 'nominate' for Imperial Service overseas in the event of mobilization; only 10 per cent elected to do so. There was therefore some uncertainty as to what would happen in 1914. In the event, the mood of the country was such that virtually everyone volunteered to go overseas. Norman Edwards, a draughtsman at the Bristol Wagon Works, wrote in his diary:[1]

> Gradually the conviction was growing within me that this was almost a holy war. Germany in her brutal violation of Belgium, her contempt for treaties and her ruthless militarism, appeared to me to be the greatest menace to righteousness and freedom that the world had ever known . . . It came home to me that, as a believer in God and Christ, I must give my service to stay this menace to civilization . . . No thought of killing my fellow men entered my mind, but I felt I must offer my services to the country in the hour of her need . . . so on a glorious morning on the 2nd September, 1914, I left my digs and instead of going to the works, I walked up the Cotham Road to the Headquarters of the 6th Bn of the Gloucestershire Regiment and after waiting in queue for three hours I enlisted and became No 2912 Private H.N.Edwards.

Although the TF units needed more training and to be brought up to full strength before they could be sent into battle, they had a structure and experience. When Lord Kitchener instructed each infantry regiment to double the number of its TF battalions, the Gloucesters did this by dividing their existing battalions into two, thus creating 1/4th and 2/4th, 1/5th and 2/5th and 1/6th and 2/6th Gloucesters. This meant promotion, and although the first battalions kept more of the privates and the second battalions more of the new recruits, there was sufficient experience in both to enable rapid progress to be made. Likewise Kitchener decided, in early September 1914, to increase the number of yeomanry regiments but in a slightly different way. The RGH formed 1/1st RGH, a first Line regiment liable for overseas service, and 2/1st RGH, a second Line regiment for home service only.

1/4th, 1/5th and 1/6th Gloucesters were in the 48th (South Midland) Division. Recruiting needed to be rapid, and at a meeting at Shire Hall, Gloucester, Major John Collett, who would shortly be promoted to command 1/5th Gloucesters, called for 25 men to enlist in the Battalion. Among the audience were men from the Gloucester Rugby Club, and as a result nine members of the 1913/14 team joined 1/5th Gloucesters. Each battalion also required a medical officers and padre. On 16 August 1914 the War Diary recorded: 'Rev G. F. Helm joined the Battalion as Padre, complete with straw hat. Jolly good chap.' This brief entry was to prove accurate. George Francis Helm was the Padre of 1/5th Gloucesters and editor of the *Fifth Gloster Gazette* for most of the War and remained a TA Chaplain until 1942. He was at various times vicar of All Saints, Gloucester, vicar and rector of Stroud and rural dean of Dursley.

In August 48th Division moved to Essex; 1/4th and 1/6th Gloucesters were in 144 (Gloucester and Worcester) Brigade and 1/5th Gloucesters was in 145 (South Midland) Brigade. Private Thomas Nash, of 1/4th Gloucesters, recalled his arrival at Danbury, near Chelmsford:[2]

> Long lines of tents loomed ghostlike in the darkness, showing us our future quarters, and the clanking of tools as a Company came in, wet and exhausted after digging trenches, warned us of our future work. We were issued with blankets, those Army blankets, which serve so many purposes, and so many men, before fulfilling their last use as a shroud to the dead. Then tents were allotted to us, one tent to twelve men, twelve tired, hungry, bad-tempered men. We had not fed since 6 a.m. that morning and we had no food that night. We soon realized that hunger was to form one of the main features of our new life. We bought a candle from one of the Corporals for a shilling and spent the evening in settling down and giving away our idiotic possessions to the trained soldiers of the Battalion, who came to pull our legs and to cadge all they could . . . We discovered later that one candle had been issued to each tent, but had subsequently been collected before our arrival by the N.C.O.s in order that they might later be peddled at a profit.

In his diary, nineteen-year-old Private Albert Edwards from Portishead, who had joined 1/6th Gloucesters, recalled the journey from Bristol to Essex:[3]

> On 1 December, my parents came to Portishead Station to see me off on the 6.55 A.M. train. I took a 'return' workman's ticket to Clifton Bridge at a cost of 3d and, in due course, marched from Headquarters to Temple Meads and there joined the train for London. The journey was of special interest to me as I had never been to London in my life. I am afraid we saw nothing of London, as we quickly went 'underground' at Paddington and emerged at Liverpool Street Station . . . It was almost dark when we de-trained at Chelmsford and began our march towards Danbury. By the time we had passed through the village we saw a sign post marked 'Little Baddow', and through the lanes we marched for about three or more miles and, as we marched on, small groups were detached and stayed behind. Finally, our turn came, and four of us were told to 'go to that cottage and report to Corporal Smith' . . . We four 'newcomers' were each placed in one of the rooms of this red-brick, semi-detached cottage. A meal was sent over to us from the cook-house, a short distance down the road, and we

were soon 'to bed'. Bed consisting of three blankets, overcoat or tunic for a pillow, and bare boards.

Some were made more welcome than others. When Wilfred Gough of 2/5th Gloucesters died a few years after the war, his landlady from Chelmsford travelled to attend his funeral in Gloucester.[4]

Second Lieutenant Cyril Winterbotham[5] of 5th Gloucesters wrote in a letter on 8 October:[6]

> I am rather depressed at my complete ignorance of drill and I fear I made a poor figure in command of my company (they split the recruits into small companies and gave us subalterns one each) . . . They are a splendid lot of men our recruits, mostly intelligent well set up young men – many of them undergrads ranging down to good country lads with names like 'Stinchcomb'. They obeyed well and treated me well when I made a fool of myself which was not infrequently.

Later in the same letter describing shooting practice on the range, he wrote:

> Kitchener men were all around us as we shot – they didn't look at all so bad at a distance, but the correct Territorial attitude is one of patronising approval.

48th Division remained in the Chelmsford area until the end of March 1915, when they set off for France and Flanders. Albert Edwards, the nineteen-year-old with 1/6th Gloucesters, wrote:[7]

> March 31st 1915. We have only left England an hour ago, and the eyes of all are turned to the south to catch a glimpse of France – the land of our Great Adventure. It is a novel experience for the majority of us – few of our fellows have left their native land before. Most of us were civilians six months ago, while it is only four month ago since I left home. Now, we are fully trained . . . Britain has called for us! Thank God she has not called in vain.

After further inspections and training the Battalion moved into the front line in early May at Ploegsteert Wood in the Ypres Salient.

Meanwhile, in early September 1914, 2/4th, 2/5th and 2/6th Gloucesters had been formed and allocated to 61st Division. Initially, no uniforms were available, so the men wore civilian clothes with a square of white silk on the lapel inscribed with each man's battalion. The battalions were composed of men from many trades and professions; 2/5th Gloucesters included Members of Parliament, poets, lawyers, bakers, accountants, drapers, musicians, conjurors, butchers, sugar magnates, farm labourers and artisans of every sort. The 2/5th Gloucesters Officers Mess was at the Gloucester Club, and the men were billeted in the city. In February 1915, 61st Division began assembling at Northampton and moved in April to Chelmsford, to train for the War.[8]

Notes

1. James Bonsor, 'I did my Duty – First World War experiences of H. N. Edwards as seen through his accounts and recent interviews'.
2. Thomas Nash, *The Diary of an Unprofessional Soldier*.
3. Diary and letters 1915–1918 of Sergeant A. G. Edwards.
4. Robert Brunsdon, *The King's Men Fallen in the Great War. The King's School, Gloucester*.
5. Cyril William Winterbotham was the youngest son of Alderman James Winterbotham JP and his wife, Eliza. Cyril was a Cheltenham barrister before the War and the Liberal candidate for the Cirencester Division. His brother, Percy, was Adjutant of 1/5th Gloucesters, and his sister, Clara, later became Mayoress and Alderman of Cheltenham for many years. Cyril's letters have been transcribed and are in the Archives of the Soldiers of Gloucestershire Museum.
6. Winterbotham letters, transcribed by Miss Iona Radice.
7. Edwards, op. cit.
8. The War Diary of 2/5th Gloucesters is the only one to record the day-by-day training at Chelmsford.

Chapter 12

Raising the Service Battalions of the Gloucesters

T he raising of the Service Battalions is one of many remarkable stories of the Great War. On 6 August 1914 Parliament authorized an increase of half a million men in the Army. The poster 'Your King and Country Need You', which explained the terms of service, was published on 11 August and called for the first 100,000 to enlist. This target was reached within two weeks. The situation was completely different to the expansion of the Territorial Force; the Service Battalions had no history, no base and no structure, but consisted simply of an enormous number of enthusiastic young, and not so young, men without any military experience flocking to recruiting offices all over the country. As a result, their first Commanding Officers, supported by NCOs from the Regiment, were particularly important, for they determined the sort of battalion each one became. This, combined with where they came from, city, town or village, gave each an individual character of its own.

Those wanting to join the Gloucesters were examined medically, enlisted and sent to the Regimental Depot at Horfield Barracks in Bristol, where they were allocated to a battalion. Although each battalion was largely raised from a particular area, such was the keenness of young men to join up that if their own local battalion was full they would travel to where there were still vacancies. As a result, all the Gloucester Service battalions included some men from outside Gloucestershire.

7th Gloucesters was raised in Bristol in August 1914 with recruits from the city and South-West England. It was in 39th Brigade in 13th Division and based initially at Tidworth. The Battalion never served in France and Flanders but fought at Gallipoli and then in Mesopotamia and Persia (Iraq and Iran today). Lieutenant Colonel Richard Price Jordan raised the Battalion and commanded it throughout the war, except when he was recovering from wounds. He had joined the Gloucesters from the Militia in 1889 and won a DSO with 2nd Gloucesters in the South African War. Much loved by his men, he was created CMG in 1918 and after the War commanded 2nd Gloucesters, before retiring in 1922.

8th Gloucesters was a Gloucester-based battalion in 57th Brigade in 19th Division. The Battalion went to the Western Front in July 1915, where it remained throughout the War. It was raised and commanded until December 1915 by Lieutenant Colonel Joseph Scovell Hobbs, who was commissioned into the Gloucesters in 1881 and served in St Helena with 4th Gloucesters during the South African War.

9th Gloucesters was raised in September 1914 with new recruits from Bristol once 7th Gloucesters was full. It joined 78th Brigade in 26th Division and deployed to France in September 1915 but was only there for two months, because in November it went to Marseilles and embarked for Salonika. The Battalion was raised by Lieutenant Colonel Charles Vines. He was fifty-six and had been commissioned into the Gloucesters in 1878. During the South African War he commanded both 1st and 2nd Gloucesters and was extremely popular. He retired in 1907 and rejoined in 1914 to raise 9th Gloucesters, but because of his age was not allowed to go overseas with them.

10th Gloucesters was recruited primarily from Cheltenham, although soldiers from other parts of Gloucestershire, particularly the Forest of Dean, and the surrounding counties were to be found in its ranks. In his book, *In the Shadow of the Lone Tree*, Nick Christian explains how they were forged into a battalion that would display outstanding courage at Loos in September 1915. Its Commanding Officer was Lieutenant Colonel Henry Edward Pritchard, who had been in the Indian Army and was brought out of retirement to raise the battalion.

There were many challenges to be overcome in the early days. During October 1914, 8th, 9th and 10th Gloucesters were sent to Codford in Wiltshire for initial training. Sergeant Ernest Chadband later recalled:[1]

> Codford was a terrible place to pitch a camp. Well, we all rioted and went on strike as we could not sleep. Wet ran down the hill and through the tents so we protested to go to bed. The 8th, 9th and 10th Gloucesters guards turned out with pick handles but with no avail. We let the tents down on those who would not come out and in almost three days the 9th and 10th were billeted in Cheltenham and the 8th in Weston-super-Mare.

10th Gloucesters went to Lansdown Crescent in Cheltenham. Here it thrived, drilling on the grass in the front of the Crescent, marching to Gloucester and back and learning tactics and drill on Cleeve Hill. By May 1915 the Battalion was ready for Divisional training on Salisbury Plain. Here the men were at last issued with rifles but only got half a dozen rounds each to practise with.

The raising of 12th Gloucesters is splendidly described by Dean Marks in *Bristol's Own, the 12th Battalion Gloucestershire Regiment 1914–1918*. A meeting of the Bristol Chamber of Commerce on 12 August 1914 felt that Bristol's response to Lord Kitchener's appeal had been inadequate. The Bristol Citizens Recruiting Committee was therefore formed and the Colston Hall opened as a special recruiting centre on 14 August; by 2 September 2,274 men had enlisted. It was soon clear that many of these recruits wanted to join a special Bristol Battalion, which led to the creation of 12th Gloucesters (Bristol's Own). Its commanding officer was Colonel William Burges.[2] When the battalion was ready to move to France, he was ordered to hand over command, a bitter disappointment; he was fifty-nine. Initially, there was no uniform or equipment for the Battalion, and those who enlisted stayed at home but had to attend parades on the Artillery Grounds, Whiteladies Road, each day. In mid-June the Battalion moved to a camp at Wensleydale in Yorkshire and then to Whitburn for firing practice, before moving to Codford on the edge of Salisbury Plain. In his *History of Armed Forces on Salisbury Plain* N. D. G. James recounts:[3]

> Each day the different regiments would march off headed by their band and complete with field kitchens drawn by mules. The kitchens were mounted on wheels and were fitted with a fire grate and chimney so that the food was cooked as the column marched along.

Eventually, on 21 November 1915, after over twelve months' preparation and training, 12th Gloucesters (Bristol's Own) crossed to Boulogne as part of 95th Brigade in 5th Division. There were 31 officers and 990 other ranks, commanded now by Lieutenant Colonel Martin Archer-Shee DSO, MP.[4]

It was soon evident that there was a requirement for additional men to dig trenches and protect them with wire, etc., so relieving line battalions, who otherwise were sacrificing rest in order to improve defences. As a result, an Army Order in December 1914 allocated a Pioneer Battalion to each of the B.E.F. Divisions. On Christmas Day 1914 the *Dean Forest Mercury* reported that the local MP, Sir Harry Webb Bt, was to raise a new Pioneer Battalion from the Forest of Dean. He was Liberal MP for the Forest of Dean from 1911 to 1918 and a director of several South Wales collieries. This was 13th Gloucesters, recruited initially from Forest of Dean miners but not for the first time; 500 years earlier, in 1415, when Henry V embarked for the Agincourt campaign in France, his army included a company of 120 miners from the Forest. 13th Gloucesters also included men from South Wales and North-East England. During 1915 the Battalion trained at Malvern and in Yorkshire before joining 39th Division as Divisional Pioneer Battalion. Private Woodrough recalled:

> I joined up at Sunderland in 1915 & when I got down to Cinderford in the Forest of Dean I settled down straight away. I liked the training. We had no uniforms at first, you know, like Dad's Army. We went for a Route March to a place called Lydney. The people turned out in droves & we had to march into the Church Hall for tea & a Concert. The Chairman gave it out that the Local People would like some of the Soldiers to Perform so it was not long Before the North Country Lads had me up, as they knew I was a Whistler. Besides performing at Theatres on Tyneside, & Picture Halls, I did a lot of Charity work at Workhouses & Children's Homes & Blind Schools . . . On Route Marches through the Forest of Dean, whoever was in charge, anyone who could play the Mouth Organ, I was put beside him & had to Whistle to Our Lads Marching.

Many fit young men were being rejected because the minimum height for a recruit was 5ft 3ins, so in November 1914 it was decided to form 'Bantam Battalions' consisting of men 4ft 10ins to 5ft 3ins in height; 14th Gloucesters (West of England), raised in May 1915, was one. It was commanded by Lieutenant Colonel Gerard Roberts. He came from Co Durham, where his family ran a carpet business, and had served in 4th Bn Durham Light Infantry (DLI) from 1897 to 1903. On the outbreak of war he volunteered for active service in the DLI but in August 1915 he was transferred to command the newly formed 14th Gloucesters. The men were recruited mostly from Bristol and Birmingham, and in August 1915 the Battalion joined 105th Brigade, 35th (Bantam) Division. At one stage they were warned for Egypt, but this was soon changed, and on 31 January 1916 14th Gloucesters arrived in Le Havre from Southampton.

The last Gloucester battalion to see active service in the War was 18th Gloucesters, which only came into existence on 20 June 1918, at Clacton-on-Sea, five months before the end of the War. It was raised by Lieutenant Colonel Noel Frederick Barlow MC, who had commanded 5th Ox and Bucks LI until it was disbanded. The Battalion joined 49th Brigade in 16th (Irish) Division and landed in France on 1 August 1918, with 41 officers and 709 other ranks. The 16th Division had originally gone to the Western Front but, having suffered heavy casualties, was sent back to the UK to be reconstituted with fresh battalions. One of these was 18th Gloucesters.

There were more Service Battalions of the Regiment that never saw active service. 11th Gloucesters was a Reserve Battalion from 1914 to 1915; 15th Gloucesters existed from 1915 to 1917 as local reserve battalion for 12th Gloucesters (Bristol's Own) and became 93rd Training Reserve Battalion; 16th Gloucesters was a local reserve battalion for 13th Gloucesters and became 94th Training Reserve Battalion.

Notes

1. Nick Christian, *In the Shadow of Lone Tree. The Forging of the 10th Gloucesters and the Ordeal of the First Division at the Battle of Loos, 1915.*
2. William Edward Peter Burges OBE, DL, JP (1856–1938), a Bristolian educated at Clifton, was commissioned into Royal South Gloucestershire Militia in 1880. It became the 3rd Militia Battalion, The Gloucestershire Regiment in 1881, and he commanded it from 1905. On the outbreak of hostilities in 1914, although he had retired, he immediately offered his services and was given permission to raise 12th Gloucesters. Keen on musketry, he was always proud of the fact that the highest individual score in shooting amongst the new armies was made by a member of his Battalion. In 1920 he was appointed Honorary Colonel of 3rd Gloucesters, an appointment he held until his death in 1938, when his name was the only one appearing under the heading of the 3rd Battalion in the Army List.
3. N. D. G. James, *Plain Soldiering: History of Armed Forces on Salisbury Plain.*
4. Martin Archer-Shee had joined the Royal Navy in 1886, aged thirteen. He resigned in 1890 to join the Army and was commissioned into the 19th Hussars. He fought in the South African War, where he was awarded the DSO and taken prisoner. He resigned from the Army in 1905 and in 1910 was elected MP for Finsbury Central. He remained an MP whilst commanding 12th Gloucesters.

Part III

GALLIPOLI

Chapter 13

The Gallantry of 7th Gloucesters on Chunuk Bair

O n 25 April 1915 the British 29th Division landed in three places at Cape Helles on the tip of the Gallipoli Peninsula in Turkey. Simultaneously, the Australian and New Zealander Corps (ANZAC) went ashore half way up the peninsula at a place known ever afterwards as Anzac Cove.

The reasons for mounting the ill-fated Gallipoli campaign, in which both 7th Gloucesters and 1/1st RGH fought, were many. The Ottoman Empire had sided with the Central Powers and declared war on the Allies. Founded when the Turks captured Constantinople in 1453, the empire had grown in power and influence during the sixteenth and seventeenth centuries. Although in decline by 1914, it still controlled much of the Middle East. Most significantly, it endangered Russia's southern flank, ruled what is now Iraq and its oil fields and threatened the Suez Canal and the British link to India. Russia wanted to seize Constantinople and recover the seat of Orthodox Christianity from Islam. It also wished to gain control of the Bosphorus and the Dardanelles. Thus any offensive against the Ottoman Empire was enthusiastically encouraged by the Russians.

The deadlock on the Western Front and the prospect of indefinite trench warfare was considered by impatient politicians as a crisis requiring a completely different approach. One option was to open a new front and bring relief to Russia, which had been attacked by the Ottomans in the Caucasus. In January 1915 the Russian Commander-in-Chief, the Grand Duke Nicholas, sent a telegram to Britain appealing for help. Kitchener, as Secretary of State for War, made it clear that no troops could be spared but thought that a demonstration in the Dardanelles might have some effect. The Dardanelles strait, part of the link between the Mediterranean and the Black Sea, is 30 miles long and at its narrowest point less than a mile wide. Churchill, who was then First Lord of the Admiralty, seized on the idea, which had been lurking in his mind ever since he had sent the British Aegean Squadron to bombard the forts at the mouth of the Dardanelles. It succeeded in hitting an Ottoman magazine and thus disabling several heavy guns. While this encouraged Churchill to see the Dardanelles as an opportunity, it alerted Constantinople to the threat, and the Turks began, with German help, to strengthen their defences.

It wasn't until 18 March 1915 that a British and French force that included sixteen battleships and a host of minesweepers, cruisers and destroyers, steamed into the mouth of the Dardanelles and for the first few hours made good progress. Then an undetected line of mines began to cause havoc, so that by the end of the day the fleet was withdrawn after 3 battleships had been sunk, 2 more were put out of action and 3 others had suffered damage.

Meanwhile, despite Kitchener's reluctance, a base on the Greek island of Lemnos had been established from which to launch a landing force should the naval assault fail. This force would land on the west coast and take the guns guarding the Dardanelles from the rear. The Mediterranean Fleet could then steam through the Dardanelles and bombard Constantinople. The Force consisted of 29th Division, the Royal Naval Division, the Australian and New Zealand Army Corps (ANZAC) of three divisions and a French contingent of divisional size. On 25 April 1915 these troops landed. Neither 7th Gloucesters nor 1/1st RGH were involved, so it is not necessary to go into the detail of what happened here. Suffice it to say that the plan was improvised, the intelligence faulty and the force simply not large enough for the task unless the Turks failed to respond effectively to the landings. They did not fail. At Cape Helles 12 Victoria Crosses were won on the 25th, 6 by the Lancashire Fusiliers and the other 6 by the sailors landing the troops.

The Turkish commander defending the area of the ANZAC landing was Mustafa Kemal, who would become President of Turkey and is better known today as Atatürk. He later claimed that his orders to the 57th Regiment were: 'I don't order you to attack. I order you to die. By the time we are dead, other units and commanders will have come to take up our place.' By 4 May the Turks had lost 14,000 men, the ANZACS nearly 10,000, but Kemal, recognizing that he couldn't drive the enemy into the sea, ordered his men to dig in, thus enclosing an area 1,000yds deep and a mile and a half around the perimeter, most of which was on a 45° slope, but in places was perpendicular. In the south, 29th Division had managed to advance about 3 miles from Cape Helles but could go no further. Another stalemate had been achieved; the only options for the Allies were to add more troops or withdraw. It would be many more months before the latter course was adopted.

Seven more divisions now joined the campaign. The first two, in June, reinforced 29th Division in the south. Then, in July, 13th (Western) Division, which included 7th Gloucesters, arrived, and by August the Mediterranean Expeditionary Force had swollen to 15 divisions, 10 British, including the Royal Naval Division, 3 ANZAC and 2 French.

On 19 June 1915 7th Gloucesters sailed from Avonmouth for Alexandria and then on to Mudros on the Greek island of Lemnos, the Allied base for the Gallipoli campaign. It landed, together with the rest of the Division, at Cape Helles, to relieve the 29th Division on 11 July and began to take casualties from snipers the next day; by the time the Battalion was withdrawn to Mudros at the end of July,

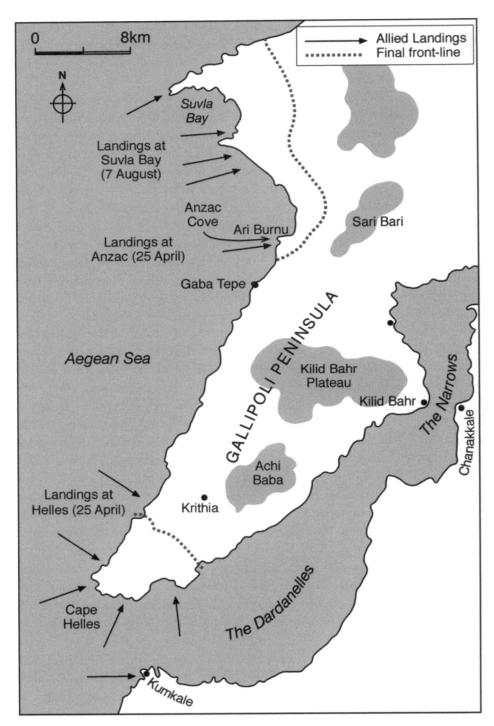

Map 10 Gallipoli

24 men had been hit but none had been killed or died of wounds. After a few days preparation the Battalion embarked and sailed to Anzac Cove, which it reached on 3 August, to reinforce the ANZACs.

Once the ANZACs had been joined by 13th Division and 29th Indian Infantry Brigade they numbered about 20,000 front line infantry to launch an offensive against the Sari Bair range of hills. The plan was for the New Zealand and Australian Division, with most of 13th Division, to advance north of the ANZAC perimeter. There were two assaulting columns; the one on the right was to advance up Rhododendron Spur to Chunuk Bair, and it is this advance that concerns the story of 7th Gloucesters. The attacking columns were to set off at 10.30 pm and reach the ridge an hour before dawn. The intention was to take further objectives once Chunuk Bair had been secured.

The advance began as planned at 10.30 pm on 7 August. Rhododendron Spur ran from the beach to the peak of Chunuk Bair. There were four enemy outposts that had to be cleared before the main assault could start up the ridge. This was done by the New Zealand Mounted Rifles Brigade, and although it was successful, the operation was now running about two hours late, making reaching the summit by first light difficult. The main part of this assaulting force was the New Zealand Infantry Brigade commanded by Brigadier General Francis Johnston. The Brigade made good progress on the north side of the spur and by 4.30 am, shortly before dawn, had reached 'The Apex', which was only about 500yds from the summit, where there were only a few enemy at the time. However, the Canterbury Battalion on the south side of the spur had been held up, and Johnston made what was, with hindsight, the fatal decision to wait for them to arrive before launching a final assault. By 8.00 am the enemy had reorganized and strengthened their defence of Chunuk Bair, and the opportunity for a swift victory had been lost. Nevertheless, the Divisional Commander ordered the assault to continue, and the New Zealand Auckland Battalion advanced another 200yds to 'The Pinnacle', where the 300 men who had made it tried to dig in on the stony ground, from which it was a straight climb to the summit. The New Zealand Wellington Battalion was now ordered to continue the attack, but their commanding officer refused, stating it was hopeless and that he would take Chunuk Bair at night. Meanwhile, 7th Gloucesters, who had been in reserve and were about 1,000 strong, were ordered to reinforce the Wellington Battalion and began planning a night attack.

The Battalion War Diary for 8 August records the confused events:

> Battalion received orders to stand to arms at 3am to form the left of an attacking first line, the Wellington Battalion being on the right. Other battalions formed lines in rear. The Wellingtons started forming up at 3:30am with two 7th Gloucester Companies, B & D (B on right) in

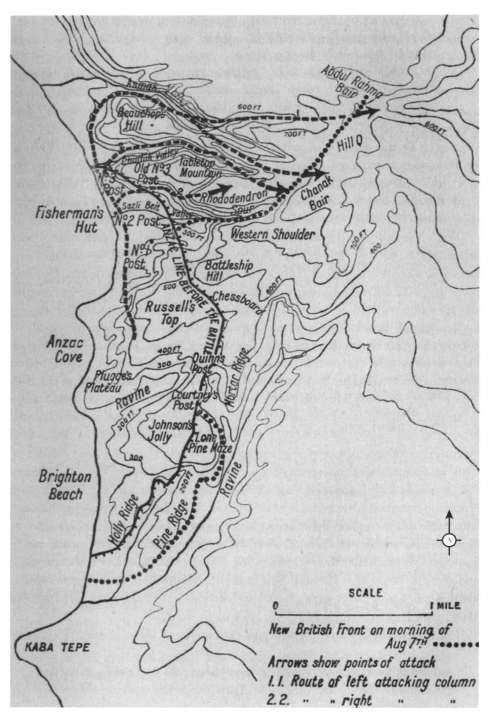

Map 11 Battle of Sari Bair

the first line and A & C Companies in the second line. The advance started at 4:15am before D Company was quite in position and C Company (less 2 platoons on detachment) was still filing up the mule track. Longer time would doubtless have been given for the preliminary formations had it been realized how difficult filing along a mule track in the dark, with dug outs on either side, was. The advance started. A short while after starting the two left platoons of the first line came under enfilade m fire from the left and were practically wiped out, the few remaining men of these platoons remaining in this place. The advance was continued for some distance when the ground began to fall away steeply which in conjunction with the fact that the Companies were under enfilade fire caused the Company Commanders to wheel into line. About this time a staff officer of the New Zealand Brigade came up and ordered the companies to move to the right and gave his information that the Wellington Battalion had taken the hill Chunuk Bair. This movement brought the line of Glosters advancing towards the Sazli Beit Dere, which they crossed with the right rather advanced. Beyond the Southern slope of this Dere the line entrenched with the left about 60 yards beyond the Dere and the right about 200 yards. Owing to change of direction there was a considerable intermixing of companies and units. The right of this line had afterwards to retire and dig in further back to escape enfilade fire (shell) from the right. The Turks were continuously attacking the line which in many cases had no time to entrench more than 6 inches. In spite of these attacks and heavy losses, especially in officers and senior N.C.Os, the line was held until relieved. Every officer and every C.S.M & C.Q.M Sgt were either killed or wounded and the Battalion consisted of groups of men being commanded by junior N.C.Os or privates. When the relieving troops arrived at dusk, most of these groups either went back or were sent back by officers of other Corps and continued for three days to re-join Battalion Headquarters in Overtons Gully.

The Commanding Officer, Lieutenant Colonel Jordan, was severely wounded but was propped up and fought on as a sniper. Both the Battalion Second in Command and the only other Major were killed, as well as seven other officers. Three of the five Company Sergeant Majors had been killed, along with 200 Other Ranks. Fighting continued until 10 August and then petered out. The War Diary does not record the number of wounded, but on 1 September the effective strength was recorded as 8 officers and 263 other ranks, about a quarter of what it had been a month earlier.

General Sir Ian Hamilton wrote of the 7th Gloucesters in his Dardanelles Despatch:

> On they went, until, with a last determined rush, they fixed themselves firmly on the south-western slopes and crest of the main knoll known as the height of Chunuk Bair . . . The 7th Gloucesters suffered terrible losses here. The fire was so hot that they never got a chance to dig their trenches deeper than some six inches, and there they had to withstand attack after attack. In the course of these fights every single officer, company sergeant-major, or company quartermaster-sergeant was either killed or wounded, and the battalion by midday consisted of small groups of men commanded by junior non-commissioned officers or privates . . . Chapter and verse may be quoted for the view that the rank-and-file of an army cannot long endure the strain of close hand-to-hand fighting unless they are given confidence by the example of good officers. Yet here is at least one instance where a battalion of the New Army fought right on, from midday to sunset, without any officers.

Chapter 14

1/1ˢᵗ RGH Join the Gallipoli Campaign Dismounted

I t is now time to catch up with 1/1ˢᵗ RGH, who had been defending the Norfolk coast, until warned for overseas service in March 1915. Although the threat to Egypt was partly reduced by the movement of Indian, Australian and New Zealand troops through the Suez Canal on their way to the Western Front, the British Government decided to reinforce the garrison there with the 2ⁿᵈ Mounted Division. 1/1ˢᵗ RGH embarked initially for Malta on 11 April 1915 but sailed straight on to Alexandria, where it arrived on 24 April. The Regiment consisted of 27 officers, 512 other ranks, 485 horses, 70 mules, and 17 vehicles, divided into a headquarters and three squadrons. Prior to its departure, mules replaced all the transport and Maxim gun limber horses, which as the Anonymous RGH Trooper[1] writing as the *Gloucester Journal* 'Journalist at the Front' commented,[2] 'gave their riders a few exciting afternoons. They were terrors to groom, as they have what seem to be double-jointed reciprocating-action legs, which kick impartially in all directions with lightning rapidity.'

The RGH spent three months experiencing the delights and difficulties of Egypt in the searing heat of the summer months, before being ordered, on 11 August, to be prepared to embark for the Dardanelles, dismounted as infantrymen, and reorganized into two squadrons and a Regimental HQ. Four days after the fighting on Sari Bair petered out, the British 2ⁿᵈ Mounted Division, with 1/1ˢᵗ RGH in the 1ˢᵗ South Midland Mounted Brigade, sailed from Alexandria. The RGH was organized into two squadrons, numbering 15 officers and 346 other ranks, under the command of Lieutenant Colonel Bill Playne, whose family owned Longfords Mill and lived next door at Longfords House, Minchinhampton. He had commanded 3ʳᵈ Company, 1ˢᵗ Imperial Yeomanry during the South African War. The RGH took 36 mules and 9 vehicles and arrived at Mudros early on 17 August. Here, a 'first reserve' of officers was left, while the remainder transferred to a paddle steamer, *Queen Victoria*, which had previously worked the Isle of Man run, for the trip to Suvla Bay on the Gallipoli Peninsula, which they reached at midnight on the same day.

The first landing on Suvla Bay, on 6/7 August, was designed to break the stalemate that had arisen on the other two Gallipoli beachheads at Cape Helles and

Anzac. It took the Turks completely by surprise and was unopposed, but failure to support this opportunity and press forward to Scimitar Hill, which was the immediate objective of the landing since its capture would make the landing at Suvla more secure, allowed the Turks time to respond. The Corps Commander was unwilling to advance without artillery support, and as a result the landing force did not move far from the beach until 8 August, by which time the Turks had moved forces to oppose them. It was not until 9 August that the British began a concerted advance towards the high ground, and fierce fighting followed before the British were driven off the ground they had taken. Another effort the following day by 53rd (Welsh) Division was another failure, and 54th (East Anglian) Division fared no better the next day. On 15 August the Corps Commander was sacked, and his successor decided that he must secure the ground the Corps held and link up with the ANZACs to the south. This involved the capture of Scimitar Hill, the W Hills and Hill 60. The troops involved included the unmounted 2nd Mounted Division and 1/1st RGH.

The Battle of Scimitar Hill, on 21 August, was the largest single-day attack by the Allies during the Gallipoli Campaign and also their last offensive. It was a failure, although the Turks had to use all their reserves to stave off defeat. 2nd Mounted Division's task was to support the infantry in the attack on the Gallipoli hills. On 21 August the Division advanced across the Salt Lake to Chocolate Hill in support of two Brigades, 87th and 86th, of 29th Infantry Division, who were to capture Scimitar Hill and Hill 112. Hill 112 was the objective of 86th Brigade supported by 5th Mounted Brigade, comprising the RGH, the Queen's Own Worcestershire Hussars and the Warwickshire Yeomanry.

After a short pause, they moved over Chocolate Hill to the adjacent Green Hill, coming under heavy fire as they crossed the intervening saddle. This advance resulted in 1 officer and 9 other ranks of 1/1st RGH being killed and 4 officers, including the Commanding Officer, Bill Playne, and 44 other ranks being wounded. Major Henry Elwes[3] took over command of 1/1st RGH. 87th Brigade on the left, supported by 2nd Mounted Brigade, was heavily enfiladed and had to retire. This left 5th Mounted Brigade unsupported on the left and right and it retired to Chocolate Hill. Major Palmer, with A Squadron, was the last to withdraw.

General Sir Ian Hamilton wrote of the Mounted Division in his Dardanelles Despatch:

> The advance of these English yeomen was a sight calculated to send a thrill of pride through anyone with a drop of English blood running in their veins. Such superb martial spectacles are rare in modern warfare. Ordinarily it should always be possible to bring up reserves

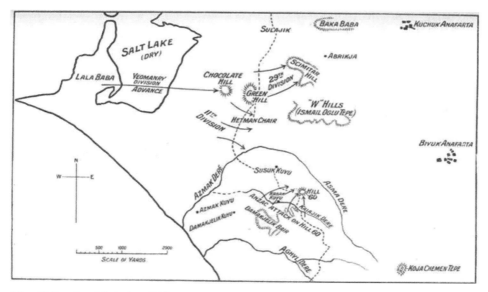

Map 12 Battle of Scimitar Hill

under some sort of cover from shrapnel fire. Here, for a mile and a half, there was nothing to conceal a mouse, much less some of the most stalwart soldiers England has ever sent from her shores. Despite the critical events in other parts of the field I could hardly take my glasses from the yeomen; they moved like men marching on parade. Here and there a shell would take toll of a cluster; there they lay. There was no straggling; the others moved steadily on; not a man was there who hung back or hurried.

The personal diary of Captain Tim Cripps[4] of the RGH describes events. The following are extracts:[5]

August 19 – Suvla Bay. The boat we landed in was a Bristol pleasure steamer – a good omen. Country here very broken with low, thorny scrub, rocks and stones on clay soil. Shelling. Dug ourselves into temporary graves – just long enough to hold me – 2ft deep and built up all round with earth, a stone at my head, two pieces of wood (that I had found floating in the sea) in the middle, and my mackintosh sheet as a sun shelter. The firing line about three miles off. Worst job fetching water, all of which comes from Alexandria by ship. The men are wonderful; they make jokes all the time. I bathed in the afternoon. Smith[6] had a shell in the water when he was bathing. Warships reply to the Turks now and again. It is a dry country and you don't want a lot of washing. Drinking water very scarce.

August 20 – A five inch centipede wished to share my valise with me. Weather good; warm in the day, cold at night. This morning we had a lesson in bomb throwing. I am dying to have a go. One of us has to be left behind with each squadron, and I tossed up with Gething and lost! So I shan't see the beginning of it I suppose. I am so sorry I shall be parted from Smith: all servants go in the firing line.

August 21- Regiment have gone to Lala Bay in reserve. The flies are beginning. We live entirely on bully and biscuit and lime juice.

August 22 – At three o'clock the show began yesterday. Micky (Lord Quenington) and I went up the hill a bit to see the most wonderful panorama of low ground to the sea, with high hills in the distance all round. The ball began with artillery fire and warships shelling the ground we were to advance over, and then you could distinguish bodies of infantry all over the place. We could see the whole thing: the distance up to six miles and the battery close below us being shelled whenever they spotted it. I shall never forget the sight. Micky and I both said we wished our wives were there, to be quite close and practically safe and see a big battle from a unique position!

August 23 – I am up here, commanding the Squadron, on Chocolate Hill – as all the officers and sergeants except my young sergeant, Philp, were hit or killed – in the support trenches; in a dug-out with Micky, very deep and narrow, and the wind blows a shower of dust on us every few minutes. The Regulars, 29th Division, say the sight the day before yesterday of our men marching in spite of very heavy shelling was wonderful.

In 1922 an RGH officer went back to Gallipoli. In a letter describing what he had found he wrote:[7]

It was most interesting reconstructing some of the operations again, and taking my seat in a comfortable stall in the Turkish Lines on Chunuk Bair. The Suvla theatre of operations lay in a piece of country like a saucer, with a bit broken out where the sea would be, commanded from everywhere as regards observation and fire. I doubt whether the capture of Scimitar Hill and Ismail Oglu Tepe and Anafarta would have helped us or even had we got Kavak Tepe whether we should again have been faced with ranges of hills and subsidiary spurs, all of which were densely bushed.

Anzac is incredible; the impossible somehow made possible – a network of hills, precipices, ravines, and gullies all choked with bush and all directly under Turkish observation and fire – and yet they stayed there and gained ground . . .

The more I studied it the more impossible it appeared, and as a tactical problem would, I think be turned down. Once the surprise of landing and capture had failed there would be no hope of success, unless carried out on a colossal scale, and I doubt whether Gallipoli would lend itself to anything colossal. All that seems to have been achieved is a remarkably fine example that if people will defy all the principles of warfare they must expect failure. It is rather sad, though, to think of all the good lives thrown away for nothing.

Notes

1. The 'journalist' was almost certainly Cpl William (Dickie) George Richards, who had been a reporter with the *Gloucester Journal* and transferred from the RGH to the RE in late 1917. His reports have been edited by Lawrence Birkin and published as *A Trooper's Diary*.
2. Lawrence Birkin (ed.),   *A Trooper's Diary – The Royal Gloucestershire Hussars on Service 1914–1918.*
3. Henry Elwes had been commissioned into the Scots Guards and had won a DSO in command of 8ᵗʰ/9ᵗʰ Royal Irish Rifles. He was the grandfather of Sir Henry Elwes KCVO of Colesbourne Park, who was Lord Lieutenant of Gloucestershire from 1992 to 2010.
4. Edgerton Tymewell Cripps MC (1874–1957). Always known as 'Tim', he was the son of Edward and Ada Cripps of Ampney Park, near Cirencester. He became ADC to General Chetwode, the Commander of the Desert Column, for the last phase of the campaign in Palestine, was discharged in 1922 and was a director of Cirencester Brewery, which was a Cripps family firm. He and his wife lived at South Cerney Manor. His diary, with copies of his letters to his wife, is in the Gloucestershire Record Office (D4920/2/2/3/4).
5. Frank Fox, *The Royal Gloucestershire Hussars Yeomanry 1898–1922.*
6. Benjamin Smith, who was Tim Smith's batman/servant, was born in Coates, near Cirencester and employed as a private groom and chauffeur. Towards the end of the war, when Archibald Wavell (later Lord Wavell) joined the Egyptian Expeditionary Force, Benjamin became his batman. After the War he returned to live in South Cerney.
7. Fox, op. cit.

Chapter 15

7th Gloucesters and 1/1st RGH Withdraw from a Failed Campaign

1/1st RGH remained on Chocolate Hill, while the fighting around Suvla Bay continued until December. The 7th Gloucesters, survivors of the Battle of Sari Bair, were withdrawn at the end of August and the Battalion was brought back up to strength. It was then deployed in and out of the trenches at Suvla Bay, where it was continually subjected to sniper and shellfire, resulting in a steady trickle of casualties. Edward Bazeley, who had been born in Matson, Gloucester recalled:[1]

> I remember one wall of our shelter had been lined with tins of the much hated gooseberry jam. Breakfast consisted of sweet black tea, weevilly army biscuits (reputed to be surplus from the Boer War) and jam, to eat which one had to compete with myriads of large black flies . . . In the ensuing months, the enemy made violent attacks on our right flank, hoping to drive us and the Anzacs into the sea. These were accompanied by deafening artillery duels in which the Navy took a prominent part. I think we suffered as many casualties from dysentery as from wounds. But now the Bulgarians, who had come in on the side of the Turks, began to send them large consignments of more modern artillery and shells, with which they constantly bombarded us from the slopes of Sari Bair. Our trenches were badly enfiladed by accurate fire from Turkish snipers one of whose bullets pierced the peak of my cap. (Steel helmets were not issued to us owing to the extreme heat and our topis protected us only from the sun). In addition to being lucky I must have been tough, for – as fellow officers went sick – I had to take charge of our bombers, trench-mortars and four Vickers machine guns.

Due to the losses during the Battle of Scimitar Hill, 2nd Mounted Division had to be reorganized and the remnants of 1/1st RGH, together those of the Warwickshire Yeomanry and the Queen's Own Worcestershire Hussars, formed the 1st South Midland Regiment (Warwickshire, Gloucestershire and Worcestershire Yeomanry). Tim Cripps gives a vivid impression of what life was like:[2]

August 25 – Support trenches Chocolate Hill. Haven't had my boots off for four days. We eat out of our mess tins. Flies very bad.

August 26 – Front line trenches. Digging ammunition trench in moonlight, sniped all the time. Trench very smelly. Four dead Turks found buried in corner. You can't imagine how interesting and beastly it all is. Sniping constantly and bursting of shells. One man dropped his sham teeth in the battle the other day and had to go to hospital as he cannot bite the biscuit; it is just like dog biscuit.

August 27 – Chocolate Hill. Heavy shelling. We lost several men. Doctors and stretcher-bearers earn V.C.s every day. Flies are awful. An enamel cup to wash in. Taking up rations with mules. Sniped all the way. Boxes constantly coming off the mules. Ground garnished with dried thistles and dead men. Trenches most complicated and face different ways. One has to be careful with cuts; they fester. Teaching the men to throw bombs.

September 3 – Chocolate Hill. Poisoning from swarm of flies. Living on malted milk which is supplied to men who are ill.

September 7 – Cator House trenches. Clay soil, very damp. Heaps of water. Fairly safe place, but flies very bad. Lots of hedges and trees and scrub, fig trees, elms and poplars. We crave for sweet things.

September 16 – Cator House trenches. Cold and wet. Men very cheerful. Communion service held in trenches. We are getting very weak – started 320 and now muster 180. Mostly dysentery attacks. We get a wash most days if we are not too busy.

September 21 – Lots of blackberries close by. I crawled out and picked my cap full. I am going to give them to the cook to mix with rice. The weather just now is perfect, hot in the day, but cool at night. Clouds of flies.

September 26 – Reserve trenches. We, the officers, have a row of dug outs 7ft long by 4ft wide and 4ft deep, with a communication trench at the side. They are like cupboards. No head cover. Quite restful here, as we can only hear the snipers in the distance. A depressing thing is seeing your best men going down with dysentery. Horlicks's malted milk is the proper diet[3] . . . I have taken my trousers off the last two nights and got inside my flea bag with only a shirt on. Very comfortable after sleeping with all one's clothes and boots on for the last three weeks. The brigade is now only 250 men, started with 960 men.

Whilst casualties from wounds due principally to shelling were frequent, far more men succumbed to disease, mainly dysentery. Those who needed to be evacuated faced long journeys to base hospitals. Field Ambulances and Casualty Clearing Stations had been established on the Gallipoli Peninsula but were not immune from shellfire. Even the nearby island of Lemnos, from which the landings were launched, was four hours sailing away and the base for the campaign was Alexandria, 650 miles away. In early October Tim Cripps fell ill with dysentery:

> October 2 – I wish I could let you know (but I can't) that Tom Strickland and I are going on sick leave on a hospital ship this afternoon. It will be rather nice to get away from the sound of guns day and night for a bit . . .
>
> October 3 – Hospital ship *Gameka*. Here I am, with Tom and a ship full of wounded and sick, getting into Mudros, where we shall know our fate. We hope to be sent to Malta, as the sea trip would do us good. Also Mudros is a poisonous place and the hospital very full and not too well run. I have had dysentery for a fortnight and am got rather weak . . . I know I am no use as I am, so it is no use fighting against it.
>
> October 12 – I am to go to Alexandria, into hospital there. I suppose I shall get three weeks' rest, but I shall get back as soon as I can. We have enjoyed a dead calm, nice and cool, and we have just eaten and slept and washed, the three things you appreciate most. We shall be at Alexandria this evening.

Tim Cripps was clearly more unwell then he thought. After five months in various hospitals, most of the time in Bristol Infirmary with dysentery and then in London, at 17 Park Lane, for an operation, he sailed for Alexandria in July 1916.

Gradually the strength of 1/1st RGH declined until, at last, on 18 October, it consisted of just 95 men, of whom 4 were 'no duty' and 23 were 'light duty'. Eight other ranks had died of wounds or disease. It was withdrawn to reserve trenches and finally left Suvla for Mudros on 31 October 1915, leaving one officer and ten men of the machine gun section attached to the Scottish Brigade. The Brigade left Mudros on 22 November, by which time the strength of the RGH had increased, due to reinforcements arriving and the sick being fit for duty again, to 183. On reaching Alexandria, each regiment was re-formed and remounted.

7th Gloucesters remained on Gallipoli. One might expect the conditions in the Mediterranean to have been significantly better than on the Western Front; they weren't. On 1 September the effective strength of 7th Gloucesters was 8 officers and 263 other ranks. As a result of a series of reinforcements, by 28 October this had increased to 25 officers and 676 other ranks, but by 1 December enemy actions and sickness had reduced this to 10 officers and 250 other ranks. Conditions deteriorated as winter approached; several men died of exposure, and cases of frostbite were common. Percy Morgan remembered the terrible conditions:[4]

> The Front Line was rough, with rain and cold and we fought up to our knees in freezing water. As a respite, we were sent to the reserves and climbed in to any hole we could find, lying cramped up all night. In the morning our boots were so frozen that we had to wait for them to thaw out before we could put them on again . . . When we returned to the firing line, most of us were so frost bitten that we could hardly walk about.

(Percy was eventually evacuated to Malta on 6 December with severe frost bite to hands and feet.) A heavy rain storm on 26 November flooded the trenches and some men drowned. Edward Bazeley recalled:[5]

> At the end of November a spectacular thunderstorm raged throughout the Gallipoli peninsula, bringing an icy deluge of rain and hail, followed by a north-easterly gale, more violent than we or the men in the ships off the shore, had ever experienced before. Quickly the gullies and trenches became raging torrents. Enemy casualties, washed down in the flood-water, mingled with the bodies of British soldiers, many of whom were swept away, or drowned in their dugouts before warnings or rescuers could reach them. The only chance of survival along a four mile front was to leap out of trenches filled to the brim, and attempt to scratch what shelter one could in the mud behind the parados. Overcoats, equipment, precious water-bottles and stores – all were swept away in a few minutes. Drenched and shivering in the bitter wind, surrounded by scenes of indescribable horror, no less than 15,000 soldiers went down with frost-bite. Field ambulances and hospital ships were quickly choked with casualties.

7th Gloucesters left Suvla for Mudros on 17 December 1915, but it was not the end. After a week's rest, the Battalion sailed back to Cape Helles to cover the final withdrawal from there. Here it was attacked on 7 January 1916 and suffered 6 men wounded, 2 of whom subsequently died. Eventually on 8 January, 7th Gloucesters embarked on SS *Ermine* but did not leave the Dardanelles until 21 January. The whole campaign, except the withdrawal, had been a disaster for the Allies. Suvla, Anzac and Cape Helles were withdrawn in sequence under the noses of the Turks without a single casualty – an astonishing feat. Both 7th Gloucesters and 1/1st RGH had reminded everyone that Gloucestershire was a gallant county. General

William Birdwood, who had been educated Clifton College in Bristol, had gone to Gallipoli in command of Australian and New Zealand Corps. In October 1915 he became the Commander of the Dardanelles Army and led the successful evacuation of the Allies. He considered the 13th Division, which included 7th Gloucesters, commanded by General Maude, the best division in the Army.

Notes

1. Memoir of Edward Bazeley,7th Gloucesters and Machine Gun Corps.
2. Captain Edgerton Tymewell Cripps, RGH, diary.
3. Gerald Horlick, whose father and uncle had invented 'Horlicks', was in 1/1st RGH.
4. Memoir of Percy Morgan 7th Gloucesters.
5. Bazeley, op. cit.

Part IV

July 1915-June 1916 on the Western Front

Chapter 16

The Service Battalions of the
Gloucesters Reach the Western Front

B y the latter half of 1915 the Service Battalions of the Gloucesters were ready to join the fighting on the Western Front; 7th Gloucesters had already embarked for Gallipoli. The first to arrive in France was 8th Gloucesters on 18 July 1915, under the command of Lieutenant Colonel Joseph Hobbs, who had raised and trained a first class battalion. It was part of 57th Brigade in 19th (Western) Division and would remain in France and Flanders throughout the War, winning more Battle Honours than any other Service or Territorial battalion of the Gloucestershire Regiment. A total of 42 officers and 931 other ranks would die; 2 members of the Battalion would win Victoria Crosses; and A Company of the Battalion would be awarded the 19th Division Butterfly Badge of Honour. These events were all in the future as they began going into the trenches in the Laventie area on 9 August. On most days there was some shelling, and snipers were active on both sides.

A month later, on 9 August, 10th Gloucesters landed at Le Havre under the command of the ex-Indian Army officer, brought out of retirement, Lieutenant Colonel Henry Pritchard. On arrival the Battalion was inspected; the written report stated:

> Personnel (strength) 30 Officers 985 Other Ranks. Establishment 30 Officers 995 Other Ranks. Health of Personnel: V Good, Cases of Venereal NIL. Numbers inoculated 1015 (once) 1015 (twice). [It goes on to list all the weapons and equipment, including] 'Vehicles – Establishment Complete, inclusive of 4 G.S. waggons, 11 Limbered waggons, 4 Travelling kitchens, 2 Water carts, 1 Maltese cart [a lightweight two wheel cart hauled by a pony, ass, mule or two men; the Maltese cart was often used by Medical Officer to carry surgical panniers], 1 Officers Mess cart, 9 Cycles . . . Horses (numbers and types) 12 Riding, 17 Light draught, 7 Heavy draught, 36 Mules.

10th Gloucesters had been selected to replace 1st Battalion Scots Guards in 1st Brigade, in 1st Division, which had joined the B.E.F. in August 1914. Those who had experienced the fighting in France and Flanders for a year had lost some of their enthusiasm, and it was felt that inserting some of the New Army battalions would make the Division more effective. The Battle of Loos would test this assumption.

9th Gloucesters, another Service Battalion raised in Gloucestershire, was in 78th Brigade in 26th Division. It landed at Boulogne on 22 September, under the command of Lieutenant Colonel Julian Fane,[1] who had only taken over command four days before the Battalion sailed. 9th Gloucesters did not spend long on the Western Front because on 9 November 1915 it left via Marseilles for Salonika. It spent one short period in the trenches, from 29 September to 6 October; the Battalion would return to the Western Front in July 1918.

12th Gloucesters (Bristol's Own) landed at Boulogne on 21 November 1915. From there the Battalion moved to the Somme in December, joining 95th Brigade in 5th Division. The Battalion had arrived as winter set in and moved initially to Buisny L'Abbe – a small village not far from Abbeville, described by their commanding officer Colonel Archer-Shee M.P. as 'As miserable a village as any we were billeted in', although the Battalion War Diary records, 'Billeted in comfortable billets'.

The last Service Battalion of the Regiment to arrive during the twelve months from July 1915 to June 1916 was 13th Gloucesters (Forest of Dean) (Pioneers), under the command of Lieutenant Colonel Aubrey Boulton, who had initially been the Adjutant. It landed at Le Havre on 4 March 1916 as the Pioneer Battalion of 39th Division. After a cold, rough crossing the band was ordered to play the men ashore – 'Their instruments were cold, and it sounded terrible but the drums beat alright'.

One of the benefits of the arrival of the Service Battalions was that each man had to spend less time in the front line. Although some camps had been built, most of the men were billeted in villages and towns behind the front line. Tired, hungry and wet men arriving from the trenches or battle needed to be accommodated swiftly and efficiently, so each battalion had a billeting party. The 10th Gloucesters War Diary in August 1915 records: 'Billeting party consists of Quartermaster, Interpreter, 4 Company Quartermaster Sergeants, 4 Company Billeting Orderly Guides, Sanitary Sergeant and 4 sanitary men.'

There are many photographs and images of the destruction wrought in France and Flanders, but what is often overlooked is that this only took place along a narrow strip perhaps 4 miles wide but 400 miles long, from the North Sea to Switzerland. As the war progressed this became more fixed, as each side constructed ever more impregnable defences. Therefore beyond the range of the artillery on either side, about 10,000yds, the countryside was untouched and billets were safe. This, of course gave an opportunity to local entrepreneurs, and shops, cafés and restaurants flourished.

The number of men who needed to be treated by the Medical Services for disease far exceeded the number wounded in the fighting. On the Western Front from 1914 to 1918 the number of British wounded by enemy action was 1,988,969 (36 per cent) while the number of sick or injured (non-battle casualties) was 3,528,486 (64 per cent). Vaccinations for many infectious diseases did not exist at the time, and so men caught mumps, measles, chicken pox, etc., and it was not unusual for complete companies to be put into 'isolation' to prevent these spreading. Trench foot, from standing in waterlogged trenches, was a regular problem and, during the winter, so was frostbite. The greatest cause of sickness, however, was venereal disease. It was not a crime to contract the disease, but concealing it was. In most villages and towns behind the lines were brothels that were licensed by the French. Each case of VD required a month of intensive hospital care before the man was able to return to his unit, and moral pressure from home prevented the use of the most obvious way to reduce the number infected, the issue of prophylactics. Fortunately, there are no records of how many Gloucesters or troopers of the RGH contracted VD.

Notes

1. Julian Fane DSO (c.1877–1953) was commissioned into the Regiment from the Militia in 1898. He was descended from an ancient regimental family, Fanes having served in the 61st (South Gloucestershire) regiment since 1775. Julian Fane had commanded a company of 2nd Gloucesters at the Second Battle of Ypres before taking over command of 9th Gloucesters on 18 September 1915. He later commanded 4th KSLI and 8th Gloucesters. After the War he commanded 1st Gloucesters from 1925 until he retired in 1929. His nephew, also Julian Fane, was with the 2nd Battalion in the retreat to Dunkirk in 1940 and later won an MC in Normandy.

Chapter 17

Life During Summer and Autumn of 1915

To suggest that those arriving in 1915 in France and Flanders might have enjoyed themselves may seem unexpected, but it is true. Apart from the Battle of Loos in September/October, at which both 1st and 10th Gloucesters demonstrated great gallantry, there were no major attacks by either side on the Western Front from May 1915 to the start of the Somme Offensive in July 1916.

Life was not without excitement, however; the trenches, which were regularly shelled, had to be manned, and there was always the risk of snipers. Private Norman Edwards, the Maxim gunner in 1/6th Gloucesters, did his first spell in the trenches in April 1915 at Ploegsteert Wood in the Ypres Salient. He described the experience:[1]

> Birds sang, flowers were blooming and the exquisite green of the trees, which were little marred except in the eastern edge of the wood, made it difficult to realize that here in the previous October a bitter and bloody struggle had ended in the Germans being pushed back two or three hundred yards where they were now firmly entrenched. [When they were replaced, he wrote:] We were relieved towards evening, and as we got clear of the wood and came trailing across the fields loaded with equipment, tired and filthy the sun shone with a watery brightness. Every tree and house stood out vividly and I experienced one of these moments, which came rarely enough in life time. One had prepared for it I suppose in the months of training, but suddenly a flood of happiness welled up that almost brought tears to my eyes, so keen was the sense of it. For a brief spell I had been truly serving, enduring the discomfort, and facing death, an actual unit in the fore-front of the battle line that was defending not only my country but freedom, democracy and civilization.
>
> [For him the sinking of the *Lusitania* had been significant.[2]] More than ever I vehemently argued that we should not degrade ourselves by using this foul weapon [gas]. But when the details of the *Lusitania* tragedy became known I could argue no more. That outrage of humanity caused a reorientation of my ethical thinking . . . and I was later to learn that my reaction was typical of all decent people throughout the civilized world.

The German press might rejoice, but the firing of that torpedo settled the fate of the German empire.

The 1/4th Gloucesters War Diary gives a flavour of their early experiences:

26 May 1915. Battalion in Trenches – Night very bright and men working on new trenches constantly fired on if they showed themselves in the open. Officers' patrols out along the whole front from 12 to 2.A.M . . . A Band in German trenches played the Austrian National Anthem followed by much cheering.

Soon after his arrival in France Second Lieutenant Cyril Winterbotham wrote to his mother:

Here I am to all outward appearances a military man . . . Sometimes the boys are annoying but I am rather fond of them good or bad. They haven't done much except eat their heads off and do some marching. The roads are fearful after those in England – they fancy these appalling sets in these parts and the side roads are terribly rutty . . . The men are awfully shocked at French sanitation and the innumerable stinks. Quite a crowd who refused to be inoculated before they left England came and asked to be 'done' yesterday. One man whose letters I censored said he wished he'd been inoculated all over instead of only his left arm. The censoring is a bit of a sweat but I know how much all of you will be wanting letters from me so I and the other Company officers stick to it.

There were also, inevitably, training accidents. One of the first in 1/5th Gloucesters on 6 May 1915, was when Second Lieutenant Henry Guise, the son of Sir William Guise Bt of Elmore Court, Gloucester, was training his platoon grenadiers in the use of 'jam tin grenades'. One went off, accidentally killing him and one of his soldiers, and wounding six others. One of those wounded was nineteen-year-old Private George Fear from Cheltenham; one of Henry Guise's fingers was embedded in his arm, and he was sent to a Red Cross Hospital in Stourport to recover. He was later killed at the Battle of Bazentin during the Somme Offensive.

Baths became a highlight of most infantrymen's lives; they were important for morale. Norman Edwards wrote:[2]

Who can forget the Baths at Pont Nieppe. The site was an old brewery adjoining the River Lys, and after divesting of our outer garments, our tunics and trousers, tied together with our identity disc cord, were put through a delousing machine. We were then marshalled in shirt and pants, and a motley crew we looked. From this part of the building we proceeded to the wash house and en route were in full view of the main road, whereon the village maidens foregathered. The wash house contained several huge vats and here after peeling off our remaining clothing we were split into dozens, each group being allotted a vat. There was a rush, a scramble and twelve naked bodies were immersed up to the neck. For five glorious minutes we enjoyed the benison of hot water, and were then ordered out and at five minutes fifteen seconds a cold hose was turned on the laggards. A clean shirt and a pair of pants and socks were handed out, and with these you returned to the first building for your 'deloused' tunic and trousers. Of course some unlucky wight would be unable to find his trousers and would wander about like a lost sheep with his shirt tail flowing behind him and probably be given a pair yards too big, which he wore until he could scrounge another pair, or arrange 'accidentally' to rip beyond repair on the next wiring party.

Cyril Winterbotham wrote about a convent, where he was able to go for a bath, run by Sister Matilde. He described how, when the Germans shelled it, she 'was chiefly concerned for the soldiers billeted there. Said she, "I got up to help them dress. They told me I ought to be in the cellar. But I think it's much better to be killed doing your duty than shivering in the corner of a dark cellar."'

Many men were regular churchgoers at home, much more so than their descendants a century later, and 'divine service' was held by Battalion padres whenever possible. Norman Edwards described one in Ploegsteert Wood:

At the back of the house in a leafy glade the simple altar was set up and the sacred elements placed on a snow white cloth. A handful of slightly self-conscious men gathered and reverently obeyed the old Padre who bade us, 'Draw near ye that do earnestly repent.' Here in God's pure air with the sunshine beating down on our heads the words were pregnant with meaning. [In September 1915 it had been a year since he had joined up and he reflected:] I did not regret having done so. I had seen much and learned many things, to respect courage and true worth in illiterate and ill-bred fellows that I would have considered outside the pale a year ago . . . The fellow with the yellow streak, no matter how exalted his rank, automatically ceased to count. One saw men as God sees them, and realized that intonations of speech, manners, knowledge and ignorance, wealth and poverty and the minor refinements are so much veneer, and a good bombardment stripped it off and revealed the quality of the stuff underneath.

When not in the trenches men could use time off to get away, as Norman Edwards recorded:

> Dennis and I wandered off to find the Gloucester artillery who were stationed somewhere below Neuve-Église . . . On the return journey we stopped at an estaminet and I was struck by the unusual beauty of two Flemish girls who served us . . . The following day three of us set off for the engineer's billets along the Romarin Road and had a swim in the big pond, followed by a banquet of omelette, pomme de frite, and bread and butter, the whole washed down with delicious coffee.

All battalions held 'sports days', which were designed to be fun and keep everyone fit. Norman Edwards describes one:

> The sports were held on the village green. A scratch band regaled us with lively tunes. Micklem [the CO] turned up in a priceless pair of pale brown leather breeches with bright yellow flashings, and the general graced us with his company but he was quite overshadowed by Patsy McGrath and Ted Thompson. Both were battalion characters. Patsy, a typical Irishman generously endowed with native wit, and Thompson a snub nosed comedian of the doleful variety. Thompson appeared in the costume reminiscent of the dame at a pantomime and Patsy as a dude with top hat and frock coat. Their garb, like a magic coat, freed them from the trammels of discipline, and they fooled to their hearts content, N.C.Os and officers in particular being singled out as objects of their wit.

Cyril Winterbotham was a keen fisherman and eventually acquired a rod but only managed one day's fishing 'in a beautiful little stream that runs all down the valley . . . I only rose one fish and that I missed.'

When men started being allowed to go on leave to England, they began to bring back spools of film. Cameras were forbidden, so Norman Edwards explained how they managed:

> To avoid any risks we cut a slot in the bottom of a water bottle just large enough to take a spool. The spools were then pushed up into the body of the bottle and khaki felt sewn back over, completely covering the hole. This was most successful, and each time a man went on leave he left his own bottle and took the photographic one.

There were other activities to maintain interest. The *Fifth Gloster Gazette* was first produced as a brief newsletter in April 1915 on the initiative of the Commanding Officer, Lieutenant Colonel John Collett, and, as such, is thought to have been the first British trench journal. By the winter of 1915/16 it had developed into a printed publication with a circulation of 1,500 copies and had become an outlet for varied artistic talents, particularly those of poets and cartoonists. It was designed to maintain morale and its strap-line declared it was to be 'a chronicle, serious and humorous, of the Battalion while serving with the British Expeditionary Force'.[3] There were 25 issues in all, the final one appearing in January 1919, and its initial success was largely due to the Battalion's Padre, the Reverend G. F. Helm MC. Both John and Gilbert Collett, who worked for the family chemical works, J. F. Collett of Gloucester, had joined 5th Gloucesters before the war.

Meanwhile, back in England, 2/1st RGH, commanded by Lieutenant Colonel R.P. Sandeman, had joined the 2/1st South Midland Mounted Brigade and in March 1915, when 2nd Mounted Division was warned for overseas service, took over coastal defence in north Norfolk as part of 2/2nd Mounted Division. Nearly two years later the demand for horses on the Western Front meant that like many other Second Line Yeomanry Regiments, it converted to a cyclist unit. 2/1st RGH remained in East Anglia until April 1918, when the Regiment moved to Ireland and was stationed in Dublin, still equipped with cycles. The expansion of the RGH continued when 3/1st RGH was formed in 1915, principally to train reinforcements.

In addition to 3/4th, 3/5th and 3/6th Gloucesters, which all trained reinforcements, there was one more Territorial Force Battalion in the Regiment about which little is known: 17th Gloucesters existed from 1917 to 1919 and served at home.

Notes

1. James Bonsor, 'I did my Duty – First World War experiences of H. N. Edwards as seen through his accounts and recent interviews'
2. Ibid.
3. Christine Beresford and Christopher Newbould (eds.), *The Fifth Gloster Gazette 1915–1919: A Trench Magazine of the First World War*

Chapter 18

Overview of the Battle of Loos

The Battle of Loos in September/October 1915 was a major Allied offensive by 25 divisions (19 French and 6 British). They were supported by two British cavalry corps, whose role was to exploit the planned breakthrough. The Germans had thinned out on the Western Front to strengthen their forces in the East against Russia, and the Allies intended to take advantage of this. Whilst sound in theory, the offensive's execution proved a disaster for the British Army. The artillery did not have enough ammunition to neutralize the German machine guns or cut the wire, and much of it was faulty. The bombs the men carried would not function. The wind was insufficient to take the chlorine gas, supposed to make up for the lack of artillery, across to the German trenches; instead, it poisoned some of our own men waiting to assault. Despite all these difficulties, in some remarkable examples of determination and courage the British did break through the German lines in several places, but failed to exploit this initial success before the Germans reacted effectively.

The first day of the Somme offensive in 1916 is notorious for the massive slaughter of many of the 'New Army' battalions. It was, however, ten months earlier at Loos that these enthusiastic volunteers were first tested in battle and 10th Gloucesters and 8th R Berks, who had both replaced Guards battalions in 1st Brigade the previous month, demonstrated courage and determination, despite horrendous casualties, to break through the German lines. The initial assault was by six divisions: the two in the centre were 1st Division, which included 1st and 10th Gloucesters, and 7th Division.

Most of the battalions in the leading divisions spent the six days prior to the battle carrying cylinders of chlorine gas up to the front. On 21 September the British artillery barrage on German positions began and was continuous until the attack was launched on 25 September. On 23 September a violent thunderstorm flooded the communication trenches, so the assault brigades moved up through standing water; all reported in position by 2.30 am. In some cases the most advanced troops were only about 200yds from the enemy. Meanwhile, two reserve divisions of XI Corps begin their final 7-mile march to the battle area at 7.00 pm, but were constantly delayed by road traffic and halts at level crossings. A military policeman stopped some units moving through Béthune because they were without passes! The Guards, 21st and 24th Divisions of XI Corps moved up through the night, eventually halting on average 6½ miles from the front.

The initial assault was launched at 6.30 am on 25 September, 40 minutes after the gas had been released; in places, due to insufficient wind speed, the gas lingered around the assaulting battalions, causing casualties before they started. By noon, however, there was some cause for optimism. The German line had been broken in several places, particularly on the right, although on the left the two divisions had failed to make any progress. Casualties across the front had been extremely heavy, and in many places too few officers remained to maintain direction or cohesion. Nevertheless, what happened next would decide the success or otherwise of the British plan. Had the reserves been far enough forward and well organized to exploit the initial success, the breakthrough might have been achieved; but Sir John French, the Commander in Chief of the B.E.F., had kept the bulk of them too far back and under his command for too long, despite protests from General Douglas Haig, the Commander of 1st Army. As a result, the reserves joined the battle piecemeal, too late, exhausted and in many cases hungry. Meanwhile, the Germans had reacted with remarkable speed, reorganizing and reinforcing. By nightfall the opportunities for the British that had existed in the early afternoon had been lost, and many of the reserves were being used simply to strengthen the defence of ground captured in the morning.

On 26 September the Germans counter-attacked in several places during the night, and it rained heavily. By dawn the Germans had not only recovered but had improved their defences, particularly with wire. Attempts to continue the advance with the reserves failed; twelve attacking battalions suffered 8,000 casualties out of 10,000 men in four hours. By nightfall at least three of the reserve divisions had been shattered and needed to be relieved. Loos and Hulluch were held, although the Germans remained in possession of Hill 70 and the Quarries. At 11.30 pm First Army ordered consolidation of the line and the creation of a new general reserve of two divisions.

Another day of fierce fighting on 27 September saw both sides attacking and counter-attacking. A British attempt to capture Hill 70 at dawn failed, and a further attempt later in the day was abandoned at the last minute. The Germans attacked in Stone Alley adjacent to the Vermelles–Hulluch road but were beaten off, although those holding Fosse and Slag Alleys were now totally exhausted, having had no sleep, food or water for 48 hours, and were eventually forced to withdraw. Chalk Pit and Chalk Pit Copse were captured and held by the British. By nightfall, the British positions across the front were thinly held. The vital positions at Fosse 8, the Quarries and Hill 70 had all been lost or not captured, and the Germans had been able to increase their strength by moving reserves from the French front. In places, the British had retreated to their starting positions, having suffered over 20,000 casualties, including 3 major generals. It was time for the Allies to rethink their intentions. New plans were therefore agreed, which included a renewed offensive towards the Haute Deule Canal on 4 October, although subsequent events delayed this until 13 October, by which time it made no sense at all.

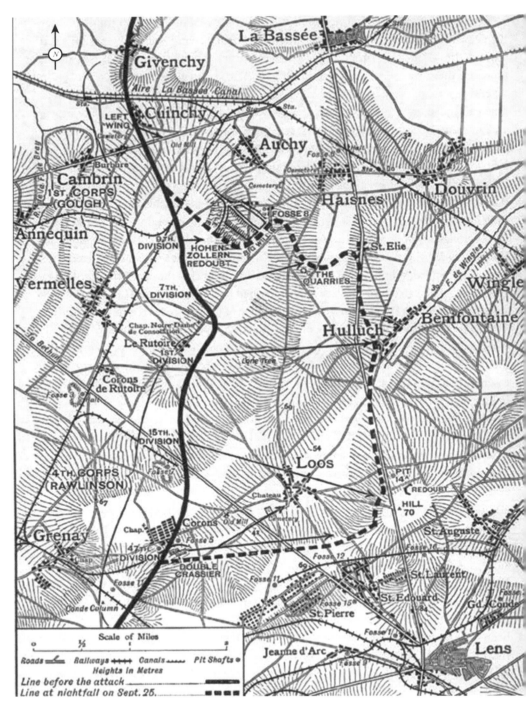

Map 13 The Battle of Loos, 1915

Over the next ten days the fighting continued. It was generally localized, but this did not diminish its intensity for those involved. Three Victoria Crosses were won. Much of the fighting was in the area of the Dump, Fosse 8 and the Hohenzollern Redoubt, but neither of the Gloucester battalions was involved. The French offensive further south was halted on 1 October, allowing some French units to relieve British ones, albeit two days later than planned due to the weather and the volume of traffic on the roads.

On 8 October the Germans launched a major counter-attack by five regiments, each of three battalions, to recapture much of the remaining lost ground. Foggy weather meant that observation was difficult, so their artillery preparation was inadequate and the Allies were in well constructed positions behind intact wire. The Germans were repulsed with 3,000 casualties but managed to disrupt the British preparations for a fresh attack.

After four more days of local attacks and counter-attacks the British renewed the offensive on 13 October and achieved virtually nothing, except a large number of further casualties. The Battle of Loos was over. The British casualties were more than 61,000. About a quarter of 10th Gloucesters had died, and the Battalion would never be the same. However, they had shown a courage and determination that could, had the reserves been better placed, have led to a much more successful outcome. Much of the debate afterwards concentrated on this single issue, leading eventually to the resignation of Sir John French and his replacement as Commander-in-Chief by Douglas Haig. The other lessons that might have been learnt, such as the failure of artillery to breach barbed wire or penetrate German dugouts, were overlooked, largely because the artillery ammunition had been so unreliable and some wire had actually been breached. These lessons would be repeated on the Somme nine months later.

Chapter 19

10th Gloucesters Lead the Assault at Loos[1]

Before the battle, Lieutenant Clement Symons of Lydney wrote to a friend in Bath:[2]

> A very few lines before the fun starts. I have been up in the trenches since the 14th bringing up all sorts of things to the firing line. We were a fatigue party and have had about twelve hours sleep in the last three days. We moved back last night to join up with the rest of the battalion. We are now on the march for either death or victory . . . We feel so happy and everything points to a great success. The Huns are being strafed terribly and will be for a day or two longer . . . I shall be able to tell you full details in a few days, I hope. Look out for good news in four or five days from now.

Clement Symons was killed on the opening day of the battle.

10th Gloucesters and 8th R Berks led the assault by 1st Brigade on the left of 1st Division, with 2nd Brigade on their right, at 6.30 am. Several officers and 95 men from No 1 Company were left at Gosnay in isolation because of an outbreak of mumps. The Germans' wire entanglement, into which gaps had been torn by bombardment, proved a considerable obstacle, and the wind was more favourable to the enemy than the British. Private William Jennings wrote:[3]

> The gas caused a lot of trouble and men were lying in the trench bottom foaming at the mouth. On the whistle we climbed out of the trench up stepladders. Our own barbed wire was supposed to have been cut during the night by sappers, but the only gap I could see was on my right. Private Bertram Taylor was next to me and as he tried to pass through the gap he was shot dead. I crouched to see how I could get through, but a bullet shattered my rifle and took away my left thumb and forefinger. Another bullet grazed my chin and tore a hole in my gas helmet. Someone crouching on my left was also hit and fell. I bent down to help him, but an NCO ordered me back into the trench. I tore off my gas mask and splashed some water on my face from the trench bottom on to my bleeding chin, not realising I was breathing in gas lying in the trench.

William Jennings survived and was evacuated back to a hospital in Weymouth, but because he had lost his trigger finger he never went back to the front. Bertram Taylor came from Kirkham in Lancashire.

Despite these setbacks, by 7.15 am the two battalions had taken the German front line trenches and were continuing to advance. By 8.00 am they were in Gun Trench, an intermediate line running south of the Hulluch quarries and about 1,200yds from their start line. They met strong resistance at the German support and reserve trenches and by now were suffering heavy casualties; so the Brigade support battalion and reserve battalions, 1st Camerons and 1st Black Watch, joined in the battle and pressed the advance on towards Hulluch. There were problems with the bombs (grenades), as the Battalion War Diary explains: 'Our bombers suffered severely, their bombs in the main refusing to explode as the Brock firelighters had got wet with the rain, which fell in the early morning.'

Meanwhile, on their right, 2nd Brigade was unable to advance due to German resistance in the area of Lone Tree, where four VCs were to be won in the fighting. As the battle continued, officer casualties, together with smoke and fog, led to considerable confusion. By 10.55 am the advance had effectively been halted by German resistance at the third line. Despite German counter-attacks in the afternoon, the remnants of 1st Brigade held on to the ground captured. By 6.30 pm the remnants of the four battalions were dug in behind the Lens–La Bassée Road in front of Hulluch. At 11.30 pm the Germans launched a further counter-attack but were beaten back. 10th Gloucesters were reduced to 60 all ranks in this position; 163 all ranks had either been killed in action or died of wounds, and the rest were casualties or lost. The Battalion continued to hold the position taken throughout 26 September until relieved during the night, by which time its strength in the forward position had risen to 130 as stragglers came in. The next day, the Battalion was withdrawn completely and marched to billets in Les Brebis. Here Lieutenant Colonel Pritchard, the Commanding Officer, was evacuated on the orders of the Brigade Commander[4] – 'his health had given way, and the Medical Officer reported that in his opinion he was no longer able to carry on.' In fact, he was broken-hearted at the destruction of the Battalion he had raised and loved. Twelve years after the war, he wrote to an old sergeant of the 10th:

> When those of us who remained alive were ordered back to Les Brebis [sic] to re-organize, and to evacuate our lines, I well remember crossing over the battlefield, seeing our men in rows, dead, with their faces turned towards the enemy, their faces lighted up by the pale and tender gleams of moonlight struggling thro' the storm clouds. Through those unforgettable scenes we passed, as we traced our way thro' the lines of our heroic men. It was my fate I should never again lead such men. I was stricken with grief, stricken with the strain of those few days of such intense effort.

As the Battalion second-in-command and all the company commanders were dead or wounded, Major H. Sutherland of the Black Watch took over the Battalion and remained in command for the rest of the War.

By 30 September the return of further stragglers and those with minor wounds raised the total to a 'ration strength' of 11 officers and 373 other ranks and a 'fighting strength' of 9 officers and 276 other ranks, with a further 96 men still in isolation at Gosnay. Private Bill Williams wrote on 3 October to John Emery, his old headmaster in Monmouth:[5]

> Just a few lines from the front, or what people call somewhere in France, we call it a place unknown. We have been out of the trenches about three days after being in them for eleven days, and very thankful I am to have a few days' rest. I daresay you have been reading in the papers of the success of the Allies. Well, we were in a bayonet charge at Hulluch. We battered and bayoneted the Germans for about two hours without stop and took four lines of trenches at tremendous cost. We took about 1,700 prisoners with the help of the Scottish. There is one honour to the 10th, we led the charge and had a very fine name. We were told by the General we had done what no other Regiment had done for the last 10 months and that was to rout the Germans from their snug abode, because they can dig trenches like moles and make them like a palace. I have got a few souvenirs, and if I live long enough to see the old homestead again I will let you have some. It was on September the 25th we started the advance and we stuck to our posts and not a man lacked courage. The smoke was very thick like a fog; you could not see far especially with gas helmets on, but we kept rushing on and on, all eager to get at the foe not thinking of our own lives. Many a time did I lift up a prayer and ask Him above to save me from those death hunters. No one can tell what the feeling is; only those that have been through it . . . Hoping this will find you and your family in the best of health as I am fairly well at present
>   I beg to remember yours most sincerely,
>   William J. Williams

Bill Williams was killed in the attack on 13 October and has no known grave. He was twenty-two.

On 9 October 10th Gloucesters received 90 men as reinforcements, and by this time the men who had been in isolation had also rejoined. On 11 October the Battalion moved into battle positions for the new offensive, and at midnight on 12 October took up positions in the firing line in preparation for the planned assault at 2.00 pm the next day, west of the Lens–La Bassée road. After a puny preliminary artillery bombardment and gas attack the two leading companies failed to reach the objective owing to heavy rifle and machine gun fire from the enemy trenches; at nightfall they were compelled to fall back on to the original line. Private William Daffurn wrote:[6] 'It was far worse than on the 25th. The Germans were waiting for us. They held their fire until we were almost on their wire then cut us down.' Sixty all ranks died either killed in action or of wounds received. The Battle of Loos was over.

Lieutenant General Sir Henry Rawlinson addressed 1st Brigade after the battle:[7]

As Commander of the 4th Corps I have come here today to inspect you, and to thank you for the magnificent work you did on September 25th last, especially the two battalions that led the assault – the 8th Royal Berkshires and 10th Gloucesters – supported by the 1st Camerons. I have been over the ground since, and, standing the other day on the old first line of German trenches, and taking into consideration the nature of the ground and the strongly fortified condition of those trenches, I must say it seemed to me a marvel how you managed to take the position. I can assure that no more brilliant feat of arms has ever been performed by a body of men during this present war, and I am proud to have such regiments under my command . . . Of the courage and fearlessness of the two leading battalions who were ordered to take the first-line German trench, I cannot speak too highly, for on their efforts depended much of the success of those following them. Having taken the first-line trenches, you wisely pushed forward and took the third and the fourth, and some of your gallant comrades, I feel safe in saying, actually got into and took possession of some houses in Hulluch. The 2nd Brigade on your right was not at first successful, and the fine courage you displayed in pressing on, with your flank exposed, is worthy of all admiration, and the great lesson to be learnt from it is that, in battle, it behoves a battalion to push on irrespective of anything that is happening on their flanks. It has pleased me greatly to ride through your ranks today, and to notice the fine spirit displayed by all, also to see the improvement in your condition since coming to rest . . . I wish to thank you again for your work on September 25th last, especially the battalions who led the assault.

Notes

1. Most of the quotes in this chapter are taken from *In the Shadow of the Lone Tree* by Nick Christian, which includes more contemporary material and a fuller account of the battle.
2. Nick Christian, *In the Shadow of Lone Tree. The Forging of the 10th Gloucesters and the Ordeal of the First Division at the Battle of Loos, 1915.*
3. Ibid.
4. Ibid.
5. Ibid.
6. Ibid.
7. Ibid.

Chapter 20

1st Gloucesters Defeat a German Counter Attack

One of the extraordinary things about a battle is how two battalions fighting in the same area on the same day can have such different experiences. 1st Gloucesters had been fighting in France and Flanders for over a year, and the men were both battle-hardened and realistic about war. At the start of the battle, being in 3rd Brigade, the reserve brigade of 1st Division, the Battalion was not part of the initial assault. It arrived in position at 4.00 am and began to move forward at about 11.30 am; then, at 2.15 pm, the Battalion was placed at the disposal of Commander 2nd Brigade, which was still held up. He ordered 1st Gloucesters to get behind the Germans still holding the area of Lone Tree. As they did this, the Germans surrendered. At 4.00 pm the Battalion was ordered to cease the flanking movement and advance direct to Bois Hugo and make good the wood. It achieved this without difficulty and dug in all night in heavy chalk. No one had been killed. An officer described their advance on 25 September:[1]

> For some time there was no sign of war, a lull having set in over the neighbouring battlefield. It was rather exciting to advance over coarse autumn grass of fields that had been neither cultivated or grazed since the war began and had for so long been in German territory.

The next morning, 26 September, 1st Gloucesters was relieved by 8th Lincolns at 5.00 am, but this move was hampered by heavy enfilade and rifle fire that caused casualties, including 14 dead. The Battalion rejoined 3rd Brigade and was ordered to move into the German first line trench south of Bois-Carre. An officer described the scene: 'It was a fine, fresh morning, and moving by way of the Lone Tree, one watched with interest the various activities which were going on in connection with the clearing of the flotsam of the battlefield.' The Battalion continued to hold this trench until they relieved 8th R Berks in the position they and 10th Gloucesters had reached on the first day, during the night of 27/28 September.

Lance Corporal H. E. Herbert wrote home describing the experiences of 1st Gloucesters on 25/26 September:[2]

> I have got through once again, we have had some stirring times lately and there is better news than on 9 May [Aubers Ridge]. We were in the reserve

when the attack was made. Some of our side soon broke through and we went into the front line, but there was a keep with about fourteen machine guns in it that held us up for a long time. At last our men outflanked them and about 200 Germans surrendered to the Gloucesters. Then we crossed their trenches and made an advance. We must have advanced three miles. There were scouts out in front of us to see if there were any Germans about. We went through a wood and came to a railway and then had orders to dig ourselves in. It did not take us long to get some head cover, for the Germans were just in front of us and opened fire. We held the position until morning and were then relieved, for which we were not sorry as it had been raining and we were all wet through. We came back to what had been the German's front line . . . The Germans were comfortable, for in the dug-out we occupied they had a bed, a stove, a table and chairs, and oil cloth for the floor. They even had a bookshelf there, so it came in just right for us, and we were glad at the time they had such places. Through the day we could hear our fellows making an attack in different places, of the Germans counter-attacking, but the Germans were repulsed everywhere. If our men had to retire from a position they soon retook it, and they were still pushing on. We were relieved from the trenches but I don't know for how long.

During the night of 29 September 1st Gloucesters was relieved and went into billets at Noeux les Mines. The Battalion casualties from 25 September until relieved were 102, of whom 20 died, including the Regimental Medical Officer, Captain Robert Montgomery.[3] He was killed as he rose from treating a wounded soldier. The majority of casualties occurred in the relief by 8th Lincolns on the 26th. The Battalion remained in billets at Noeux les Mines from 30 September until 5 October. On the 2nd there were bathing parades at the mine baths and on the 3rd a Church Parade.

At 5.30 pm on 5 October the Battalion marched to Loos to relieve 5th R Berks and one company 9th Essex in the Chalk Pit sector. The relief was completed by midnight. For the next two days the Battalion was shelled continuously along the line of Chalk Pit Wood. The Chalk Pit Sector was one of the objectives of the German counter-attack on 8 October. After the war Lieutenant-Colonel 'Patsy' Pagan[4] recalled events:[5]

The morning of the 8 October opened fairly, though the air was cold; hostile shelling had abated, and life in the line seemed pleasanter than it had done on previous days. At 11 a.m. shelling began; by 11.30 a.m. it had become a definite bombardment; it continued with increasing intensity until 4.15 p.m. In enfilade and from the front, the Chalk Pit and the trenches on either side of its salient were overwhelmed with a hail of 8-inch and 5.9-inch shells; the fire was the severest to which the regiment was ever subjected during the war. Traverse after traverse was knocked in and flattened out; casualties increased steadily.

There was nothing to be done but to sit still and to await the infantry attack which obviously would succeed the bombardment. The passive watchers in the trenches actually saw shells arriving in showers of tiny specks; each cluster of specks, a fraction of a second after its appearance, resulted in a series of rending crashes. A remarkable experience, but after the first hour or two, one which shook one's moral fibre considerably, despite all efforts to feel, and to appear, light-hearted. The men bore the strain – nearly 5 hours of it – with admirable calmness though they failed to grasp the fact that the enemy would not attack with infantry till their guns stopped; it was continually necessary to prevent them from clambering on to the fire step to see how things were going. All communications had been cut early in the proceedings and the smoke and dust of the bombardment blotted out the line completely to observers from behind. An appreciable period had elapsed after the show was over, before the higher commanders were aware whether we still held the line or whether the enemy had got it.

The bombardment stopped at 4.15 p.m. with noticeable suddenness. Immediately the German infantry, issuing in dense masses from the portion of the Bois Hugo opposite the Chalk Pit and from their trenches running northward from the wood, advanced against our line. Thin skirmishing lines only moved against the Munsters on the right . . . its main weight was flung against the Chalk Pit and the trenches on each side of it. As the shelling stopped every man was instantly on the fire step, pumping well aimed lead into the on-coming hordes. The machine guns, well sited at the salient of the line, did great execution, while at the very moment that the German gun fire ceased our supporting artillery, that of the 15th Division, opened with every gun on the attackers . . . their opening was timed to the second and their fire was accurate and effective. Combined with that of the infantry, it rapidly dealt with the situation; the advancing troops of the enemy, suffering very heavily, first wavered, then checked and finally stopped altogether. None, save one unarmed German, a sailor who said that he disliked land fighting, got within 40 yards of our line. Desultory shooting on our part went on till dusk, but within 10 minutes of its start the attack had been broken, and the attackers were trying, at great cost to themselves, to get back to the cover of the woods.

It is estimated that 6 battalions were employed by the enemy in the attack at the Chalk Pit; their casualties must have been heavy. There is little doubt that they expected that their intense bombardment would have subdued all resistance and that they would have overrun our position easily; on this occasion they counted without their host. The regiment lost about 130 men during the day, but had a good fight; all ranks were overjoyed thus to get their own back, not only for the shelling they had endured earlier in the day, but also for the never forgotten ninth of May [Battle of Aubers]. In many cases, when the shooting began, wounded men, stripped of their shirts for the dressing of their wounds, were on the firing step taking their part in the battle; it was instructive to hear eager marksmen counting aloud the number of their hits as they obtained them.

1st Gloucesters lost 22 killed and 101 wounded and, having been relieved at 11.00 pm by 1st South Wales Borderers (SWB), moved into support trenches east of the Loos–La Bassée road. The Battalion remained in this position until 12 October, where they were shelled regularly. On 12 October 1st Gloucesters relieved 1st SWB in the front line in preparation for the assault the next day. At 2.00 pm on 13 October the Battalion launched its final assault of the Battle of Loos without any success, suffering 55 casualties, of whom 7 died. The Battalion was relieved by 1st SWB at about 10.00 pm and moved into the support trench. The next day the Battalion was relieved again and within hours had entrained for Lillers, well to the rear.

    The Battle of Loos was over, but there was a postscript, which Lance Corporal Freeman[6] from Churchdown, Gloucestershire described. He was one of 208 men of 10th Gloucesters picked to form up alongside others of 1st Division to be reviewed by King George V on 28 October:[7]

We had to march about 15 to 20 miles for the King's inspection, it was a miserable day. We arrived at this place, Louvener, and were placed in a position in this ploughed field with mud over our boot tops. At last the King came along with his staff on horseback; all the men were at attention presenting arms. However, after passing our Division, something happened, for the King fell off his horse and was hastily taken away by car. I don't think he was seriously hurt.

Notes

1. Nick Christian, *In the Shadow of Lone Tree. The Forging of the 10th Gloucesters and the Ordeal of the First Division at the Battle of Loos, 1915.*
2. Ibid.
3. Captain Robert Montgomery RAMC (1888–1915) was the son of Robert and Margaret Montgomery of Liberton Brae, Midlothian, and had joined the RAMC in 1913 on graduation from Edinburgh University. He was Mentioned in Despatches.
4. Alexander William Pagan (1878–1949), known affectionately as 'Patsy', served the Gloucestershire Regiment faithfully all his life. As a subaltern he fought in the South African War. He captained the 2nd Battalion team that won the Army Rugby Cup in 1910. After taking over the 1st Battalion on 28 July he remained in command for much of the rest of the war, being wounded three times; his bravery was legendary. He was the Colonel of the Regiment from 1931 to 1947.
5. A. W. Pagan, *Infantry*.
6. Leonard Freeman was the youngest of three brothers who enlisted in 1914. Their mother lived in Pirton Lane, Churchdown, Glos. His brother Arthur was killed on 25 September. Leonard survived Loos but was seriously wounded in May 1916 and never fully recovered, dying in 1935 aged thirty-nine.
7. Christian, op. cit.

Chapter 21

Life between the Battles –
Winter and Spring 1915/16

By 1 December 1915 2nd and 9th Gloucesters had departed for Salonika, leaving 1st, 1/4th, 1/5th, 1/6th, 8th, 10th and 12th Gloucesters on the Western Front to endure the winter. On 31 January 14th Gloucesters arrived as part of 35th (Bantam) Division. Trenches had to be manned, but the conditions were so foul that, in places, battalions needed to be relieved every forty-eight hours rather than every four days. In winter, the big difference, apart from more hours of darkness, was the mud, and for battalions arriving as winter set in this was an unforgettable experience.

Men suffered much more from disease, frostbite, and trench foot than they did from enemy action. 12th Gloucesters arrived in France on 22 November 1915 and took over the trenches at Maricourt on 6 December. Captain Henry Colt[1] of 12th Gloucesters recalled:[2]

> The trenches at Maricourt were the worst we ever encountered in the way of mud . . . Just before we went in there had been a week or two of frost, followed by a thaw and simultaneously the trenches had begun to fall in. On top of this came the rain – the result being thick, sticky Somme mud, which meant that to go into the trenches one had to plough through 2½ miles of gluey composition that reached well over the knees. Nor would any description of Maricourt be complete that did not mention the rats. Those beastly rodents simply swarmed! In a very short time all the packs and haversacks had holes chewed into them. One man, determined to safeguard his breakfast, concealed it on his person when he lay down to rest. In about half an hour he was awakened by a struggle on his chest. Two rats had made their way through his greatcoat and were wrestling for his loaf of bread.

Corporal William Ayres, also of 12th Gloucesters, wrote:[3]

> Before entering the trench, every man took from a pile, two thigh length gum-boots – already wet and heavy from previous use, and, so equipped, started on the slow journey to the front line. The mud was thick and

slimy, but, in places, the clay gave it an even thicker, sucking consistency that gripped and held the gum-boot so that it could not be pulled out, and the unfortunate wearer could only lift his leg out of the boot, and go on bare-footed. At the worst periods, some of the troops would be left with one or even no gum-boots. The communication trench was not unduly long, but it would take the whole of the long winter night to complete the relief with the outgoing battalion.

When out of the trenches life was better, as Henry Colt explains:

The 5th Division had created a Divisional concert party with a view to entertaining its troops when the opportunity arose. It was named the 'Whizz-Bangs' and its entourage consisted of men from the units of the Division. The 12th Gloucesters contribution was Pte Bruce Buchanan, a humourist, and Pte Fred Smith, a magician . . . Bruce Buchanan had the men of 'Bristol's Own' in uncontrollable laughter and the men of the other battalions of the Division in a state of confusion with his recitals using Bristol slang.

At irregular intervals, raids on German trenches would be ordered. On 25/26 November 1915 C Company, 1/6th Gloucesters conducted a raid, the first of its kind by the Battalion, on trenches at Gommecourt Wood on the Somme. Five officers and 100 other ranks took part, split into three parties. The plan was for two groups, led by Second Lieutenants Pryce and Badgeley with 25 men in each, to enter the German trenches in two places covered by a barrage, while the remaining 3 officers and 50 men waited in reserve. Norman Edwards, the Maxim gunner, recorded in his diary:[4]

It was typical of Col Micklem to decide to attack the toughest spot on the enemy front, the right hand corner of the wood which formed a small salient. It was not the nearest point to our lines and was reputed to be a regular nest of machine guns an ordinary C.O. would avoid like the plague. But Micklem was no ordinary C.O. and it was the sheer audacity of the scheme that made for its success . . .

A party went out to the Zed Hedge, taking a field telephone with them, and at 11 o'clock the fellows who were actually to make the raid filed out and disappeared. After that everyone 'stood to' keyed up to concert pitch . . . If we were strung up what of the gallant little band of men out in front of the Zed Hedge creeping nearer and nearer to the wood, the outline of which loomed up sinister and ghastly in the moonlight.

Their hands half frozen, their uniforms soaking wet and their nerves strained to breaking point. They waited and longed for the signal that would end the maddening suspense with the visions of death or glory rioting in the brain. Captain Young, who was directing the raid from the hedge, telephoned to the colonel that it was as bright as daylight, and that they would never get in. Micklem's reply was 'Carry on', a command that earned him his DSO. He was taking a great responsibility, for it did seem madness to think that a party could make that final 100 yards dash in bright moonlight without being wiped out, but he backed his judgement that the Hun would never credit us with being such damned fools as to tackle the prickliest point of that immensely strong fortress and he was right.

Just at one o'clock the barrage came down with a crash putting a veritable hail of shrapnel along the edge of the wood. The flash from the bursting shells lit up the trenches and wood with devilish glare that was awe inspiring to witness and meanwhile our gun was rattling away, pumping belt after belt into their lines to the right of the wood. Then the bombs started to go off and we could see the flashes and sparks and hear the shouting.

The right hand party (Pryce) was successful, taking the Germans completely by surprise, bombing shelters and returning with one wounded prisoner. The left hand party found the wire was not cut and the German sentries were alarmed. Despite this, Second Lieutenant Badgeley and ten men got into the German trench and bombed the first dugout but withdrew when Badgeley was wounded. It had been a success: one man was killed, one was missing, and two officers and 18 other ranks were wounded, but none seriously.[5] In a letter to his mother H. Paton Nott wrote:[6] 'Pryce led them brilliantly & they made one prisoner & killed by bombs & bayonets at least 30 men . . . As a result of the fight we hope to get 4 DCM's if not 1 VC & Pryce is certain of the Military Cross if not the DSO.'

Raids could come the other way, too. On the night of 18/19 March 1/6th Gloucesters was attacked by a strong party of Germans, during which time the Battalion was subjected to an intense bombardment including gas. Nevertheless, the attack was repulsed, but 12 other ranks were killed, 3 were missing and 29 wounded or gassed.

On 6 February the General Commanding 1st Division presented DCMs to Company Sergeant Major Crimmins, Sergeant Reece, and Lance Sergeant Needs of 1st Gloucesters. Joseph Crimmins was a Bristolian, who joined the Regiment as a boy soldier aged fourteen. He became a Company Sergeant Major in 1st Gloucesters in December 1914, was discharged in April 1916 but re-enlisted and served as a Company Sergeant Major in 3rd Gloucesters until 1919. Lance Sergeant Needs was awarded the DCM 'for . . . while acting as a stretcher-bearer he dressed and brought in from the front parapet several wounded men under heavy fire.' The Battalion was still in the Loos area and on 25 February was ordered to secure Hart's Crater, which it did brilliantly in extraordinarily severe weather.

12th Gloucesters moved to Arras in mid-February 1916 and on 3 March took over the village of St Nicholas, where the trenches were deep, dry and solidly constructed with timber; they included deep dugouts, which compared to previous positions were comfortable. On the other hand, here the enemy was more active, as described by Corporal Robert Anstey:[7]

> Thankfully the warfare was of that class which was occasionally designated 'peacetime warfare' when there were only snipers to shoot you, if you showed your head, trench mortars and artillery several times a day to worry you, or an underground mine to blow the senses out of you. These simple pleasures were mere trifles, which marred the Arras trenches of 1916.

On 4 March 1916 13th Gloucesters arrived as the Pioneer Battalion of 39th Division. Its role was quite different to other battalions as it was employed on improving defences, digging trenches and constructing or repairing barbed-wire obstacles or building roads. Whenever possible the men worked by day and were back in billets at night, but if the work was at the front then this was reversed. The Battalion's first task was to construct an extensive barbed-wire defence between Gorre, Le Hamel and Les Chaquax to La Bassée Canal in April 1916.

Towards the end of May 1916 2/4th, 2/5th and 2/6th Gloucesters arrived as part of 61st Division. Prior to going to France on 5 May 1916, the Division was reviewed by King George V. Captain Badcock wrote in his diary:[8] 'It was a most impressive sight. Twenty thousand men, hundreds of horses and wagons all moving together in an endless line, under command of a single man – all very fine, fixed bayonets, drawn swords, and bands playing.'

Another raid, this time by 14th Gloucesters on 8 June, led to the death of its Commanding Officer, Lieutenant Colonel Gerard Roberts. Three minutes after the artillery opened up at 9.00 pm in preparation, the Germans responded, and their first shell killed Colonel Roberts. The War Diary records:

> Captain and Adjutant F. H. Toop took control of affairs and did excellent work in getting the raiders out under very trying circumstances. Time Table of Events

9.00pm.	Our artillery opened intense bombardment of enemy Front Line.
9.03pm.	Hostile artillery retaliated on the whole of our Front Line with guns of every description.
9.05pm.	Raiders and covering party left our Front Line and lay out in the middle of 'No Man's Land' . . . commenced cutting operations on enemy wire.
9.20pm.	Artillery lifted to enemy Support Trench.
9.25pm.	Raiders entered enemy trench. Covering party moved up to within 80 yards of enemy trench.
9.40pm.	Raiders evacuated enemy trench.
10.00pm.	Raiders returned to our lines.
10.20pm.	Hostile artillery ceased.
10.30pm.	Situation normal.

The Commanding Officer and one Company Commander, Captain Harry Butt, had been killed, along with 8 other ranks; 3 more would die of their wounds. Captain Toop was awarded the DSO. Meanwhile, other Gloucester battalions and 1/1st RGH were in action elsewhere.

Notes

1. Sir Henry Archer Colt DSO MC Bt (1882–1951) joined 12th Gloucesters in 1914, having previously been a Royal Navy officer. He took over command of 12th Gloucesters (Bristol's Own) in October 1917. He was Area Commander of the Ulster Special Constabulary of County Tyrone 1922–6, succeeded to the title of 9th Baronet Colt in 1931 and was a Squadron Leader in the RAF Volunteer Reserve in the Second War. Many of his recollections can be found in the book on 12th Gloucesters (Bristol's Own) by Dean Marks.
2. Dean Marks, *'Bristol's Own', the 12th Battalion Gloucestershire Regiment 1914–1918.*
3. Ibid.
4. James Bonsor, 'I did my Duty – First World War experiences of H. N. Edwards as seen through his accounts and recent interviews'.
5. Both 2/Lts Pryce and Badgeley were awarded MCs. Thomas Tannett Pryce VC, MC & Bar (1886–1918) was wounded in this raid and evacuated to England. Once fit he joined 2/6th Gloucesters and gained a Bar to his MC. He later transferred to the Grenadier Guards and on 11 April 1918 won a posthumous VC during the Battle of the Lys.
6. Letters of the Nott Brothers.
7. Captain R. H. Anstey MC, *The Raising of the 12th Bn The Gloucestershire Regt 'Bristol's Own' 1914.*
8. A. F. Barnes MC, *The Story of the 2/5th Battalion Gloucestershire Regiment 1914–1918.*

Part V

OTHER FRONTS IN 1916

Chapter 22

Salonika

The Salonika Front in Macedonia was opened as the result of an attempt by the Allies to aid Serbia, in the autumn of 1915, against a combined attack by Germany, Austria-Hungary and Bulgaria. The effort came too late and in insufficient force to prevent the fall of Serbia, while an internal political crisis in Greece caused difficulties for the Allies. Eventually, a stable front was established which ran from the Albanian Adriatic coast to the Struma River, pitting a multinational Allied force against the Central Powers. Although a minor campaign compared to the fighting in France and Flanders, by the spring of 1917 the Allied force on the Salonika Front consisted of 23 divisions: 6 French, 6 Serbian, 7 British, 1 Italian and 3 Greek, plus 2 Russian brigades. The Front remained fairly stable, despite local actions, until the great Allied offensive of September 1918, which resulted in the capitulation of Bulgaria and the liberation of Serbia.

On 25 November 1915 9th Gloucesters disembarked at Salonika in north-east Greece. They were followed on 7 December by 2nd Gloucesters. However, before this, Major Ralph Yorke,[1] who would later command 1/1st RGH, left the RGH in Gallipoli to take command of a composite yeomanry regiment in Salonika. With him to Salonika went other officers from the 2nd Mounted Division on the transport *Japanese Prince*, including Captain Turner of the RGH, who described this encounter:[2]

> We had been joking about the glassy-like sea for submarine purposes when one suddenly appeared 3,000 yards to our starboard after-quarter. She fired three shots, which fell 200 yards aft, and then got the range and started on us. We had no gun and no wireless, so looked in a pretty bad way, as our ordinary steaming was only eight knots. She fired about 20 shots, which all came round us, then she ceased firing and drew in nearer and more on our beam. Then she opened fire again and fired 43 shots from her four-inch guns with shrapnel and H.E. Luckily, although we got a few lumps of shell aboard she never managed a direct hit. Ralph and the captain on the bridge had a pretty thin time, as many of the shells were evidently intended for them. We sent relays of men down into the stokehold and managed to get another three knots out of the old tub, and by keeping her stern towards the submarine gradually crept away

in the darkness, though for a long time we saw the light of her supply ship following in our wake. It was not until 11.30pm that it eventually disappeared.

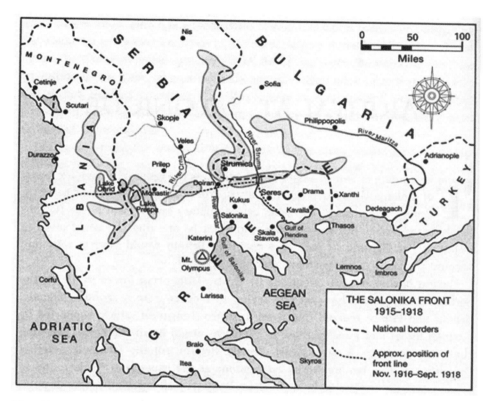

Map 14 The Salonika Front 1915–1918

Private Peck of 9th Gloucesters described the conditions at Salonika when the Battalion arrived:[3]

> The town presented a picturesque appearance from the ship, with its minarets, dark trees, White Tower, and tiers of quaint houses overtopped with the rocky heights in the rear, we got quite a favourable impression. On being marched thro' the town our 'impression' of a nice town was soon dispelled; unkempt streets, rough roads full of 'potholes', and the street corner sightseers laughed at us, pointed at our chins and stroked their black beards; they were remarking of our clean shaven appearance. As we marched on and out of town, we encountered a number of Greek troops coming into town; a rough unkempt lot they looked to us, shoddy

uniforms and a sloppy half-hunched shuffle, instead of marching. We also met some men on ragged ponies, the men's legs a-dangle, dirty white pants enhanced with black garters, black bosses on shoe points and for headgear a black 'monkey cap'. We were amused this time and dubbed them, the 'Nanny Goat Lancers', their rifles looked long and as rusty as old gas pipes. Their tunics were three-quarter length khaki with leather belt, somehow they brought to my mind 'Carl Rosa Opera' troops. They certainly looked a rough swarthy lot and if we had to fight them we didn't think much of their equipment and rifles. King 'Tino' [Constantine] was at this time undecided on which side he should throw in his country's lot with. Later on, after his abdication, Veniselos was made Premier and Greece remained friendly to the Allies. That saved us a lot of bother.

The intensity of action on the Salonika Front was light compared to France and Flanders. On the other hand, it appears from the War Diaries of both 2nd and 9th Gloucesters that there was far less variety in their routine. Spells in the trenches were longer, and there were not the diversions available behind the lines when they were relieved. Disease was more of a threat than the Bulgarians. Private Peck reported:

Lembet, our first camp, was some 4 miles east of Salonika among the hills on the reverse side of the range we had seen, behind the town, from the ship. We seemed out of the world altogether the hills were barren and bleak. The wood built canteen was a busy place at night, our Division seemed to be pretty well 'hunched' together. Biscuits were dear, cigarettes ('Zippettas' Greek) were cheap, poor smokes, I couldn't smoke them (we swore they were made of camel dung) British cigarettes were worth a bucketful of them, beer, frothy stuff, more like aerated water, was in hogsheads, the corks broached in and emptied into baths, ladled out to customers in any receptacle that would 'hold'.

9th Gloucesters worked on the construction of the defences of Tumba and they saw little action in 1916 except in a supporting role in an attack on Horseshoe Hill, which on 15 August 1916 78th Infantry Brigade set out to capture, simultaneously with a French advance. The hill was successfully taken on the night of 17/18th by the 7th Oxford & Bucks Light Infantry without the need to call on the battalions in reserve. From 16 to 19 August the situation remained unchanged, with a few shrapnel shells being dropped on various positions. On 19 August 9th Gloucesters relieved the 7th Oxford & Bucks L.I. over two nights. A feint attack by the Bulgarians on the right flank during the night of 20 August was easily repulsed.

The Allies held a circle round the city of Salonika, through which all supplies came. 2nd Gloucesters' first task, along with other battalions of 27th Division, was to dig miles of trenches in a barren and inhospitable country where disease was a major threat. Meanwhile, roads had to be built. Large amounts of barbed wire were used, and a bastion about 8 miles north of the city was created connecting the Vardar marshes to the west with the lake defences of Langaza and Beshik to the east, then on to the Gulf of Orfano and the Aegean Sea. This area became known as the 'Birdcage' due to the quantity of wire used. At the same time the enemy, the Bulgarians and Austrians, fortified the heights of the hills surrounding Salonika.

Towards the end of June 1916 2nd Gloucesters began a series of moves, until by September they were close to the Struma River, north-east of Salonika. The Allies intended to prevent the transfer of Bulgarian troops to the west by maintaining a continuous offensive, while other nations took on the main battle against the Bulgarians, which culminated in the capture of Monastir in November. The operations involving 2nd Gloucesters were to begin by seizing and holding villages on the northern bank of the Struma. In the early hours of 30 September the Battalion crossed the Struma at Gun Bridge in preparation for an attack on the Karakajois, an area consisting of two villages, Karakajoi Bala and Karakajoi Zir. The Battalion, with 2nd Camerons on their left, attacked Bala. Despite a prior artillery barrage, the Battalion was held up by fire from their right flank, but by 9.00 am the village had been captured; the Battalion had taken 20 prisoners but had suffered 53 casualties, of whom 11 died. The Battalion was attacked on the night of the 30 September/1 October, but by the 5th consolidation was achieved, trenches habitable and wiring complete. It was relieved on 15 October. On 31 October 1916 28th Division attacked Barakli Juma. Although 2nd Gloucesters was in 27th Division it provided support by advancing over 2,000yds from Hormondos north-east across rain-sodden ground. It was shelled continually, but the soft ground meant that the effect of high explosive and shrapnel was very local. Nevertheless, this, together with direct fire and sniping, led to casualties before the Battalion withdrew.

Five days later, 9th Gloucesters, who were still in the Doiran Sector, experienced one of those regular, if infrequent, days of action. The enemy artillery was active and ten high explosive shells fell in the reserve Company's quarters at 1.15 pm, causing heavy casualties. During the day and night work was continued on shelters and trenches, barbed wire entanglements were erected and damage done by enemy shells repaired in anticipation of an attack. A patrol of one officer and twenty other ranks went out in the direction of Hill 380 at 11.00 pm and returned safely at 2.30 am, nothing of note having occurred and no attack having developed.

The last action of 1916 on the Salonika Front was the Battle of Tumbitza Farm, from 17 November until 7 December, which ended in failure for the British. In mid-November 2nd Duke of Cornwall's Light Infantry (DCLI) tried to capture the farm but failed; 10th Camerons were then ordered to do so, supported by 2nd Gloucesters. Rabbit Wood was about 500yds west of Tumbitza Lake, and the farm buildings were some 200yds south of the lake. The plan was for 2nd Gloucesters to take Rabbit Wood, and it advanced at 4.30 am on 6 December and dug in. Then 10th Camerons moved through 2nd Gloucesters and attempted to cross the Tumbitza Stream and assault the trenches on the far bank but was beaten back by rifle and machine gun fire. Any movement in Rabbit Wood now drew shellfire, and casualties began to mount; 10th Camerons withdrew to the wood. At 4.00 pm there was an intense bombardment on the enemy positions which only had a short-term effect. After dark, 10th Camerons were relieved by 2nd DCLI, and 2nd Gloucesters had the task of taking the Farm, supported by 2nd DCLI. At 6.45 am on 7 December, 2nd Gloucesters, followed in support by 2nd DCLI, advanced against the position. C Company and most of D Company succeeded in crossing the Tumbitza Stream under heavy fire and found cover on the opposite bank, but the remainder of the attacking troops were unable to cross owing to the weight of enemy rifle and machine gun fire. At 8.00 am Lieutenant Colonel Kirk of the 2nd DCLI ordered the two companies that had crossed to fall back to the wood. That evening 2nd Gloucesters withdrew back to its billets, having suffered 114 casualties, of whom 34 died. Tumbitza Farm remained in enemy hands.

Notes

1. Ralph Maximilian Yorke DSO CMG (1874–1951) was the son of John and Sophia Yorke of Forthampton Court, Nr Tewkesbury. He was commissioned into the 11th Hussars and fought in the South African War. He commanded D Squadron 1/1st RGH at Gallipoli and took over temporary command of the Regiment when the CO was wounded. He commanded 1/1st RGH from March to December 1916, when he was evacuated to hospital. In 1917 he was promoted to Brigadier-General in command of Western Coastal Defences.
2. Frank Fox, *The Royal Gloucestershire Hussars Yeomanry 1898–1922.*
3. First World War Diary of Private Francis Peck, 9th Gloucesters.

Chapter 23

Protecting the Suez Canal

7th Gloucesters and 1/1st RGH had escaped the misery of Gallipoli and returned to Egypt, where the RGH were reunited with their horses. Egypt had been conquered by the Ottoman Turks in 1517 and become a province of the Ottoman Empire; under Ottoman rule the country went into decline both economically and socially. After Napoleon's invasion in 1798 and his expulsion in 1801 there was a power vacuum, from which Muhammad Ali (Kavali Mehmed Ali Pasha) emerged to be acknowledged by the Sultan in Istanbul as his Viceroy in Egypt. In fact, his allegiance to the Sultan was nominal, and he established a dynasty which ruled the country. In 1869 the Suez Canal was completed by an Anglo/French partnership, but subsequent crippling debt led the Egyptians to sell their share to the British Government. Then in 1882 Britain and France intervened militarily and defeated the Egyptian Army at the battle of Tel-el-Kebir. Egypt was established as a British Protectorate, a status which became official in 1914 when the title of the head of state was changed to 'Sultan' to ensure that any hint of subordination to the Sultan in Istanbul, who had allied the Ottoman Empire with the Central Powers, could be ignored.

With the outbreak of the war, Egypt, and particularly the Suez Canal, were of significant strategic importance for the movement of British Empire troops from India, Australia and New Zealand to the Western Front. By January 1915 the British Suez garrison had increased to 70,000. Then the Turks, encouraged by their German allies, attacked the Canal, which Britain had closed to enemy shipping at the start of the war. The Turks hoped there would be an Egyptian rising once they attacked, but the Turkish Army was spotted moving across the desert and the fighting only lasted a week before they retreated, having seen no Egyptian uprising in support. It was against this background that 1/1st RGH arrived at Alexandria in April 1915, only to depart, as reinforcements, for the ongoing disaster in Gallipoli after three months. The Allies had misjudged the fighting capability of the Turks at Gallipoli. After being forced to withdraw from the Dardanelles they should have known better, but as events would show there were still some harsh lessons to be learnt. For example, the British did not believe that the Turks could bring heavy guns across the desert, but they developed an ingenious way of doing so. They also perfected the ability to 'hide' large numbers of troops in *hods*, groves of date palms in depressions in the desert, where brackish water could generally be found.

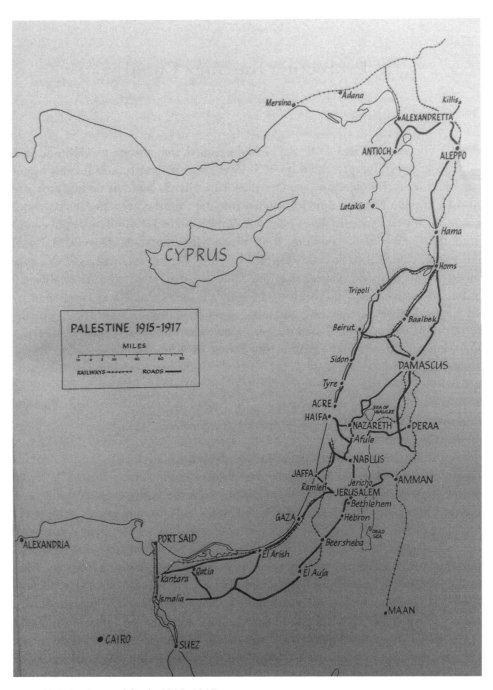

Map 15 Palestine and Syria 1915–1917

Although the main threat was from the east, the British were forced to protect their rear and so formed the Western Frontier Force to deal with the Senussi, a religious sect from Libya who had agreed with the Turks to attack the British in Egypt. The Senussi raised 5,000 men equipped with Ottoman artillery and machine guns and crossed the border into Egypt from Libya on 21 November 1915 to begin a coastal campaign. The British defeated the Senussi at Agagia, where Captain John Bengough, who came from Painswick, was killed. He was not serving with the RGH but was ADC to Major General Peyton, who had loaned him to the Dorset Yeomanry to take part, and he was killed in a charge.

In December 1915 the Turks still occupied the Sinai peninsula, and there was a general recognition that their proximity threatened the Canal. The first task facing the RGH was to rebuild the strength and health of the men after Gallipoli. On 7 December the effective strength of 1/1st RGH was 15 officers, 243 other ranks and 437 horses. By early January, when the Regiment moved by train to Salhia in the desert, this had increased to 17 officers and 316 other ranks, but the horses had been reduced to a more manageable 354. On 10 January Lieutenant General Sir Archibald Murray took over command of the Mediteranean Expeditionary Force. He was facing an enemy whose morale was high after their recent successes and who were well established in the oases between Palestine and the Suez Canal, but he quickly decided that the best way to defend the Canal would be to move its defences forward into the Sinai. A critical factor would be water, and his plan was to advance to Romani and Qatia, where there were good wells, Qatia being some 20 miles east of the canal. To enable these outlying garrisons to be supplied, work began on a railway to link Qatia, Romani and Kantara on the Suez Canal, with the aim of creating a permanent base of 50,000 men at Qatia. Both sides judged that whoever held Qatia and Romani would be able either to protect the Canal or come within striking distance to threaten it.

Although 7th Gloucesters were awarded the Theatre Battle Honour 'Egypt', its involvement was brief. It arrived at Alexandria from Mudros on 23 January 1916 and joined the garrison guarding the Suez Canal until 16 February, when it embarked for Basra with 14th Division.

On 9 March 1916 1/1st RGH marched to Kantara, where Lieutenant Colonel Ralph Yorke, returning from Salonika, became the Commanding Officer. Its role was to patrol, which it did almost constantly. On 1 April intelligence sources reported an enemy force of about 300 Turks and 200 Arab auxiliaries with 4 guns at Bir-el-Abd some 22 miles to the east. The RGH less one squadron, the Worcester Yeomanry less one troop, and camels carrying a field ambulance and ammunition, all under the command of Lieutenant Colonel Yorke, left later that day for Qatia, six miles away, where they spent the night. The next day, they moved on towards Bir-el-Abd, leaving the camels, a detachment of the field ambulance and two squadrons of the Worcester Yeomanry at Hod Negilat on route. Although an enemy outpost was seen at Khirba, they quickly withdrew and Bir-el-Abd was occupied without any fighting; then the column withdrew to Romani. Although the following letter arrived, perhaps there should have been more concern as to where the enemy had gone:[1]

> The Commander in Chief has expressed his pleasure at the activity in reconnaissance recently displayed in the Qatia area and desires his appreciation shall be conveyed to the troops. The Corps Commander has much satisfaction in communicating the above to the GOC 52nd Division, the Gloucestershire Hussars, Worcestershire Hussars, Bikanir Camel Corps, and all who have taken part in the successful little enterprise lately carried out. He recognizes the thoroughness and keenness of all ranks and the excellence of the arrangements made.
>
> C.N.Macmullen, Brig-Gen
> Gen Staff XV Army Corps

On 3 April Brigadier-General Wiggin took over command of all troops in Romani. On 9 April a Worcester Yeomanry squadron found an enemy force just arriving at Bir-el-Abd and killed two of them. A German aircraft bombed Romani and Qatia on 19 April, and on 21 April Romani was attacked before dawn by an enemy patrol.

Note

1. Frank Fox, *The Royal Gloucestershire Hussars Yeomanry 1898–1922*

Chapter 24

1/1st RGH in the Affair at Qatia

The British Army is often as proud of gallant defeats as it is of victory. Qatia Day is the RGH's Regimental Day. The RGH War Diary of 17 April 1916 describes operations:

All stores and water come by rail to Dueidar and then by convoy of camels, on which we entirely depend. Communication is by telephone from Dueidar to Romani and Qatia, by signal and helio to other places. Every day we had outposts out about 8 miles, where they can see a long way and watch. We also have recce patrols out every day, being withdrawn at night. There is water to be found for horses, but you have to dig 5 feet and make it a proper well before it is of any use.

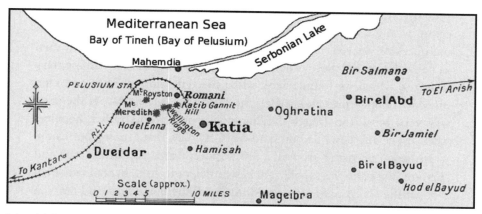

Map 16 Qatia ('Katia' on the map)

When it was learnt in early April that a party of Turks were camping at Mageibra, some 7 miles south-east of Hamisah, a raid in force was planned for Easter morning, 23 April. The day before, two squadrons of Queen's Own Worcestershire Hussars went forward to Oghratina, 5 miles in front of Qatia, to cover the raid on Mageibra, and A Squadron 1/1st RGH, commanded by Captain Lloyd-Baker, relieved them in Qatia, to protect Royal Engineers who were drilling a well.

Michael Lloyd-Baker was forty-three and the son of Granville and Catherine Lloyd-Baker of Hardwicke Court in Gloucestershire; he had been wounded at Suvla Bay in Gallipoli.

Unbeknown to the British, the Turks had assembled a large force under Colonel Kress von Kressenstein, a German military engineer, in the *hods* with the task of delaying the building of the railway. They intended to attack the British bases at dawn on Easter morning, overwhelming Oghratina and Qatia with a force of 2,000 to 3,000 men for each, supported by machine guns and artillery. At the same time, a third force would make a wide sweeping movement and attack Dueidar, a fortified position 12 miles to the rear of Qatia held by the Royal Scots. Thus the Mounted Brigade and units attached to them forward of Dueidar would be completely cut off.

Lieutenant Tom Strickland, a banker who lived on his family estate at Apperley, near Tewkesbury, was wounded and taken prisoner at Qatia. He wrote a vivid account of his captivity, which he survived. He married Lady Mary Charteris, Lord Elcho's sister and died in 1938 of tuberculosis. The following is extracted from his account, written after his release:[1]

In the afternoon of 22 April, A Squadron, RGH, with one machine gun, rode over to Qatia. We found about 40 Worcesters left in charge of the camp, with a small detachment of RAMC in charge of the Red Cross marquee. We arrived there about 4pm and Lord Elcho[2] and as many men as could be spared were ordered to complete some rather rudimentary trenches, which we found there, while the remaining officers and men put down horse lines and settled the horses for the night. As the sand was very loose the trench-digging was arduous and rather hopeless work, especially as we had no sand-bags. By dark that evening our camp, which stood on rising ground, a few hundred yards east of the well and surrounding palm trees, had trenches sufficient to contain about six men each, at the far corners of our position, with the horse lines and tents in the centre . . .

We all stood to arms at 3.30am [on Easter morning] in a thick fog and saddled up the horses . . . At about 5.30am a few vague shapes loomed up in the fog opposite that part of the line where Lord Elcho was and as there was no reply to our men's challenge he ordered the men to open fire and after a few shots these men were seen retiring through the fog. A few minutes after this we heard very heavy rifle fire from Oghratina. At 6.30am our mounted patrol went out and reported seeing nothing on their return. At about 7am we started taking the horses by sections (of about 8 horses) down to the well in the palm grove to water them and officers and men went to breakfast in small parties at a time. At 7.30am we had a last telephone message from Oghratina, which the Sqn Ldr sent on to HQ, saying they were heavily attacked on all sides. Shortly after this message all sounds of firing from Oghratina ceased. At 8.30am as the fog lifted I was sent out with a patrol of five men towards Oghratina to see whether I could discover anything. I rode out about a mile, when my scout in front came galloping back saying he had seen 'hundreds of men advancing towards Qatia'. I climbed up to the top of a ridge and to my surprise saw, about 500 yards off, quite 1,000 to 1,500 men advancing in extended order, the first two lines mounted on horses, after them five or six lines of regular Turkish infantry and behind them Arab camel men. I galloped back to camp and the Sqn Ldr ordered all the men into their positions and the remaining horses back from watering at the well as soon as possible.

The Turks commenced rifle fire at about 9.15am at long range and for some time did little damage. At 9.45am, to our surprise, as we were not aware that the Turks had any guns in the Sinai Peninsula, they started to shell us and our horse lines with shrapnel. The shrapnel very soon began to hit our horses and the Sqn Ldr crawled over to report that he had telephoned Brigade Headquarters asking whether we should retire and fight a rear guard action to Romani as our horses were coming under shellfire, but he was told to 'stay where he was, get as near the guns as possible and he would shortly be relieved'. The message irritated us and we both heartily cursed BHQ because we thought it showed a complete misunderstanding of the situation, to expect our force of under 100 to advance without any cover, nearer to the guns against over 1,000 Turkish infantry, instead of allowing us to sacrifice the tents and camp equipment and while our horses were still available, to fight a rear-guard action back towards our supports, one of the manoeuvres which we had spent many months learning to do . . . At about 10.30am, C Squadron of the Worcester Yeomanry galloped into the palm grove at our rear, dismounted and came into action on the left of our line and very glad we were to see them.

The Turks were all the time advancing by short rushes and taking what cover they could and we could see that the advance was directed by officers who galloped about behind their lines on horseback and who appeared, from their uniforms, to be Austrians or Germans. From this time onwards casualties became more frequent, chiefly from the shrapnel fired by the mountain guns, and the horses tied up in the lines, about 40 to 50 yards behind were in a pitiful state, many of them killed or badly hit. At about 10.45am we could see that our B and D squadrons had come into action about a mile away on our left, against the Turkish right, which held up the enemy's advance for a bit and we heard firing some miles away on our right, which we presumed to be the Warwick Yeomanry, although we could not see them.

During the morning a German aeroplane flew back and forth over our position, directing fire with smoke-bombs which enabled the enemy gunners to finish off the majority of our horses and also to direct fire on to our machine gun, whose crew under Cpl Walwin had a bad time. We saw nothing of our own aeroplanes all day. A shell from the mountain guns hit the hospital tent and set it on fire. Lord Elcho crawled back with a few men to help the Doctor rescue the badly wounded from the tent and make them as comfortable as possible behind some bales of hay near the horse lines . . .

At 2pm we saw that the RGH Squadrons on our left had had to retire and simultaneously the Turks to our front began to advance their infantry and guns until the front line of their infantry was only about 150 yards from our line. Their gunners were now dropping their shells very accurately on us inflicting a good deal of damage . . . Soon after this we saw the Turks fixing bayonets (our own had been fixed shortly before) and the men on my left reported that they could see some of the Worcesters on our extreme left retiring. I was told afterwards that Colonel Coventry had given the order 'Sauve qui peut' [save yourself if you can], but this order never reached us, although it would have been of little avail if it had, as the men in the centre of our line would have had over 200 yards to run in full view of the enemy and would have had little chance of getting away.

Simultaneously with the retirement of the Worcesters, the Turks got up and charged with the bayonet; we kept firing until they were on us and each man was surrounded by three or four Turks. Fortunately some German officers arrived with the Turks and prevented them from bayoneting us . . . The Turks were in a great hurry to get away from the scene of the action . . . We were refused permission to return to our tents to get overcoats and so forth and were hurriedly formed in columns of four, including the wounded who were capable of walking . . . As soon as our papers had been searched and the wounded had received what attention we and the more well-disposed of the Turks could give them, we were marched off towards Bir-el-Abd under escort.

At Dueidar the defenders probably owed their escape from massacre to a little, white dog, which, as the Turks approached, suddenly rushed out into the fog barking viciously. Almost at once a shot rang out and the dog fell dead. The garrison, thus alarmed, sprang to the parapets just in time to meet the first line of Turks, who were almost on top of them. In the subsequent fighting the 1/4ᵗʰ Royal Scots greatly distinguished themselves. Reinforcements rushed up from the rear, and towards afternoon, the Turks fell back.

When the Worcesters withdrew from Qatia about 70 men, including 9 from 1/1ˢᵗ RGH, got away. Twenty were missing, including Michael Lloyd-Baker, all of whom are commemorated on the Jerusalem Memorial; 17 wounded and 63 all ranks were taken as prisoners of war. Subsequently, five MMs were awarded. By holding out all day, A Squadron allowed time for Romani to be strengthened.

Eight years later, in 1922, Lieutenant General Sir Philip Chetwode, who had commanded the Desert Column in Palestine, unveiled the RGH Memorial in College Green, Gloucester. Frank Fox summarized part of his address:

> The affair at Qatia had been much talked about. It was said that the squadron advanced too far and was wiped out. In Egypt, where little fighting took place, the incident aroused a tremendous amount of discussion and a great deal of very wrong criticism. He had made it his business to find out just what did happen, and he could assure them there was nothing to be ashamed of, but everything to make them proud of their regiment.

Notes

1. Published in 'The Donkey Walloper', the 2016 journal of the Royal Gloucestershire Hussars Yeomanry Association.
2. Hugo Francis Charteris, Lord Elcho (1884–1916) was the son of Hugo Richard Charteris, 11ᵗʰ Earl of Wemyss, and Mary Constance Wyndham. He was married to Lady Violet Catherine Manners and the father of two sons. He was killed in this battle.
3. LCpl Walwin commanded the only Maxim gun team in A Squadron. He was wounded but kept the gun firing for seven hours until it jammed because all the water in the water jacket had evaporated. He was taken prisoner but survived. His family ran a photography shop in Southgate Street, Gloucester and after the War he assembled a photographic album of 1/1ˢᵗ RGH, which is now in the Gloucestershire Archives.
4. Frank Fox, *The Royal Gloucestershire Hussars Yeomanry 1898–1922*.

Chapter 25

1/1st RGH Recover to Help Drive the Turks out of Egypt

For 1/1st RGH the aftermath of Qatia was a miserable time. No first-hand account of what had happened was available as all the officers had been killed, wounded or taken prisoner, and in the vacuum rumours and falsehoods abounded. An NCO in the Australian Light Horse who went to Qatia wrote a letter suggesting that the RGH were 'country bumpkins led by privileged toffs'. The Intelligence Summary from GHQ on 26 April includes:[1] 'The day was chiefly spent in endeavouring to counteract the pernicious effect of several "panic" wires sent by officers as regards the Qatia fighting to ladies and friends in Cairo.' One of those killed was Lord Quenington, MP for Tewkesbury and the Adjutant of the Regiment. Exceptionally, his body was taken to Cairo for burial beside his wife, a nursing sister who had died six weeks earlier. Colonel Ralph Yorke wrote:[2] 'The Commander-in-Chief is absolutely furious with us for having sent ten officers to poor Micky's funeral, the reason being that we were able to tell people the truth and put an end to the wild rumours that were going around.' Nevertheless, the Regiment had to sort itself out. Rather than re-create A Squadron immediately, a Composite Regiment, commanded by Ralph Yorke, consisting of B and D Squadrons of 1/1st RGH and a squadron of the Queen's Own Worcestershire Hussars, was formed in 5th Mounted Brigade.

The Battle of Romani in early August was the first large-scale victory by the British Empire in the First World War. A force of 16,000 Turks, Germans and Austrians attacked an Allied Force of 14,000 British, Australians and New Zealanders. Their aim was to occupy Romani and deploy heavy artillery there to harass Allied shipping on the Canal.

5th Mounted Brigade, which included the Composite Regiment, was in the ANZAC Mounted Division. The British had built a strong position in the low sand hills to the east and south of Romani (20 miles east of the Suez Canal). Major General Herbert Lawrence, who was responsible for the security of Romani, planned to lure the enemy into the steep and deep sand up to the Wellington Ridge. At dawn on 4 August, Major Charles Turner,[3] whose D Squadron had been detached to Pelusium Station, 3 miles west, saw a dangerous gap on Mount Royston between the Australian Light Horse Brigade and the Composite Regiment and, using his own initiative, galloped with his squadron to fill it and hold up the Turkish outflanking movement for two vital hours. The Trooper's Diary describes the action:

> Riding out at dawn, Major Turner at once grasped the situation, and quickly returned to call out his Squadron. They were just sitting down to breakfast, when he broke in upon them with 'boot and saddle!' At his 'Make haste boys, or we shall be too late!' they left breakfast to 'waste its fragrance on the desert air' and in the shortest time had swung into the saddle and were speeding across the sand-dunes. Arriving in position, they held the enemy for three hours until reinforced and relieved.

Later in the day, Lieutenant Frank Mitchell's B Squadron[4] combined with the Auckland Mounted Rifles of the New Zealand Mounted Rifles Brigade and took the ridge of Mount Royston at the gallop through deep sand with swords drawn. Brigadier-General Wiggin, who commanded 5th Mounted Brigade, wrote in his official report:[5]

> I went up to the Front, arriving at 4pm, and learnt the situation from Col Yorke. The Brigade Major of the N.Z.M.R. Brigade came up shortly afterwards and asked if we would be ready to co-operate in a vigorous counter attack at 5.00 pm. I replied in the affirmative. Directly we began to put on the pressure the Turks in the valley below put up the white flag and came running in with their hands up. There was a big ridge in front, the southern spur of Hill Royston, on which the enemy had machine guns, which we afterwards took. With the N.Z.s on his left Col Yorke led his two squadrons at this ridge and took it at the gallop. At the same time I ordered the Warwicks to swing forward their right round the end of the spur and attack the enemy's left rear.
>
> When Col Yorke's two squadrons arrived on the ridge they saw below them large numbers of the enemy and four camel guns in emplacements 400 yds in their immediate front. One of his squadron leaders, Lieut Mitchell gave orders to concentrate five rounds rapid at each gun in succession and so knocked out one gun after another by killing or wounding all the gun detachments. I state emphatically that no one took any part in knocking out these guns beyond Lieut Mitchell's squadron of the R.G.H. Many Turks then ran forward towards the ridge with white flags and were told to come up. The total prisoners at this point was 450 and the total for the day 500. On the right the Warwicks had been checked by the fire of well-posted machine guns. I went down to

them myself and pushed two squadrons on round the spur held by the composite regiment. The enemy then rallied a firing line of about 200 men and took up a strong position on a ridge above a *hod*. The move held up these two squadrons, and seeing they were unable to make headway, I withdrew them to the ridge. It was then too late for another thrust.

Frank Mitchell was awarded a MC.

The next day (5 August) the Anzac Mounted Division attacked Qatia, little realizing that 10,000 Turkish troops were carefully concealed in the trenches. When they did, the action was broken off. One officer and four other ranks of 1/1st RGH were wounded. A further, stronger, attack was launched on 6 August, but the enemy had withdrawn to Oghratina.

Brigadier Wiggin, in his report, wrote: 'In action the young soldiers of the latest drafts were as steady as the veterans of Gallipoli, than which no more can be said . . . I cannot impress too strongly the work done by Major Turner's squadron on that officer's own initiative, which proved to be a great factor in the successful issue of the day.'

Romani marked a turning point in the campaign against the Ottoman Empire, whose troops now withdrew across the Sinai to the southern edge of Palestine. 1/1st RGH spent the next four months patrolling. Gradually, the men were becoming more accomplished in the skills needed to operate successfully in the desert. The greatest problem facing all troops, but the cavalry in particular, was water, and during this period long-distance patrols to sink bore holes in likely places had failed to find any. As Frank Fox records, it wasn't all work:

> During this period we were able to visit Port Said, to indulge in the luxury of food variety, and to buy such things as we required for our comfort and entertainment, and we had the convenience of access to our kitbags again. Some there were who found a boat on the inundations, and in an ingenious manner turned it into a sailing yacht, which made many joyful journeys in this miniature sea, and had not a few narrow and exciting escapes from wreckage on uncharted shoals and reefs. No wonder some regret was felt when, after five weeks, the order came to move off up to the front again, but we had a very pleasant destination – pleasant that is as things go in the desert. After a two day journey we found ourselves at and around Hassaniya, for the most part in delightful little *hods* of palm trees, and with the dates just beautifully ripe.

On 7 December, Lieutenant General Sir Philip Chetwode[6] arrived from France to take over the newly formed Desert Column, and his first action was to take El

Arish, the largest village in the Sinai, on 21 December. 1/1st RGH formed the 'advance guard'; setting out from Madan at 2.30 am, they reached Bitta at 5.45 am. Here it was learnt that the Turks had evacuated and left the water supply intact, but it was an indication of the increasing confidence and skill of the Regiment that it had advanced 23 miles over unknown country at night and taken with precision pre-arranged positions surrounding the village before daylight. Two days later, the Desert Column fought an intense battle to capture Magdhaba, but 1/1st RGH was not involved. Construction of the railway and water pipeline continued, with the railway reaching El Arish on 4 January. Now the only Turkish positions left in Egypt were at Rafa and, just to the south, El Magrunein.

It is not entirely clear whether the intention was to mount a strong raid or to capture and hold Rafa on 9 January 1917. Whichever it was, speed and secrecy were essential to prevent the Turks reinforcing what was already a tough position. About 2,000 Turks were dug in behind strong fortifications, with machine guns and field guns, on a little hill with a wide and unrestricted field of fire. General Chetwode led the operation personally, riding with the Anzac Mounted Division and the 5th Mounted Brigade. The approach march went well, with 1/1st RGH leading the advance on the left, and by dawn the enemy position was almost completely surrounded. It then became clear that the ground was entirely open and devoid of cover. Chetwode himself thought 'the task was almost beyond the capacity of dismounted cavalry to carry through'.

1/1st RGH soon came under machine gun fire and, although there was some cover in the sand dunes, these also hid snipers. A general dismounted advance was ordered, with the Worcesters and the Warwicks in support. The squadrons advanced in quick rushes supported by their machine guns in a battle lasting ten hours. When it was reported that Turkish reinforcements were approaching, General Chetwode gave the order to retire, but the commanding officers of the Yeomanry Brigade and the New Zealanders had ordered 'fixed bayonets' and they got into the redoubts, which surrendered; virtually the whole of the Turkish garrison was made prisoner. The Desert Column had 487 casualties, including 71 killed. Once the wounded and dead had been found, in what was by now an extremely dark night, the RGH assembled at Sheik Zowaiid, where the horses were fed and watered before marching back to El Arish, setting out at 1.30 am and arriving at 9.00 am. 1/1 RGH suffered 51 casualties, of whom 14 died, including Major Henry Clifford[7] from Frampton on Severn. The fall of Rafa effectively cleared all the Turkish forces out of Egypt, but they were still in Mesopotamia.

Notes

1. National Archives, Reference WO 157/703
2. Frank Fox, *The Royal Gloucestershire Hussars Yeomanry 1898–1922*

3. Charles Edward Turner DSO CBE TD (1876–1960) had as a young man worked as a tea planter in Rangoon, enlisted in Lumsden's Horse in 1899 and sailed for South Africa. He and his wife, Isabella, lived at Oldown House, Tockington, from where he transferred to the RGH and raised the Oldown Troop, part of D Sqn, RGH, whose Squadron Headquarters was in the Greyhound Pub in Broadmead, Bristol.

4. Francis Arthur (Frank) Mitchell MC (1888–?) was the son of Arthur Michell and Constance Elwes, who was the daughter of John Elwes of Colesbourne Park, Gloucesteshire. He lived at Doughton, near Tetbury. After the War Frank commanded the RGH Armoured Car Company (1931–35)

5. Fox, op. cit.

6. Field Marshal Sir Philip Chetwode Bt, GCB, OM, GCSI, KCMG, DSO (1869–1950) had been commissioned into the 19th Hussars, fought in the Boer War and on the Western Front in 1914/15 before being posted to Palestine in 1916. After the war he eventually became Commander-in-Chief, India. On 29 April 1922 he unveiled the Royal Gloucestershire Hussars War Memorial on College Green in Gloucester.

7. Henry Francis Clifford (1872–1917) was one of a long line of Cliffords who have owned Frampton Court, near Stonehouse, since the eleventh century. He served in the South African War and was Second in Command of the Regiment when he was killed. His grandson, Rollo, commanded the RGH and helped in the production of this book.

Chapter 26

7th Gloucesters in Mesopotamia

The only other 'front' on which the British Army was fighting in 1916 was Mesopotamia, where 7th Gloucesters arrived from Egypt on 18 April 1916. Liddell Hart in his *History of the First World War* describes the campaign in Mesopotomia as 'the site of a fresh diversion of force from the centre of miltary gravity, and one which could only be justified on purely political grounds'. The name Mesopotamia is Greek for 'between the rivers' and refers to the region between the Tigris and the Euphrates. It has been a centre of civilization since earliest times and was also a fertile valley on one of the routes to India. Today it is largely within Iraq, which was not created as a separate state until 1932, although the Arabs called the area 'Al Iraq'. It was loosely part of the Ottoman Empire but became of great importance to Britain when oil was discovered in 1908 on the borders of Mesopotomia and Persia. In 1911 Britain had decided to convert its coal-fired Royal Navy ships to oil and needed a reliable supply. The British Government took a 51 per cent share in a new company, the Anglo-Persian Oil Company (APOC), which would pipe the oil 138 miles to a new refinery at Abadan at the southern end of Mespotamia. Liddell Hart was wrong: with the outbreak of war there was a vital need to secure the oil and its pipeline, as well as to guard the route to India. The domination of the sea by the Royal Navy was a critical part of British strategy, to ensure the safe passage of reinforcements from the Empire and the supply of food and raw materials, whilst denying these to Germany as far as possible; its success made an enormous contribution to eventual victory.

The Persian Gulf and Mesopotamia had been for years the responsibility of the British Raj, and its defence and treaties were overseen by the Commander-in-Chief in India. Shortly after the war started, he sent the 6th (Poona) Division to protect the oil refinery at Abadan in Persia. The Ottoman Fourth Army was based in the region. On 22 November 1914 the British occupied Basra and continued their advance to Qurna which ensured that Basra and the oilfields were protected. On 12 April 1915 the Turks attacked the British camp at Shaiba and were soundly defeated. General Townshend, the commander of the British Force, was then ordered to advance with his small army to Kut, or even to Baghdad. The Turks, concerned about the possible fall of Baghdad, sent more troops to the region. On 22 November 1915 the Battle of Ctesiphon resulted in a stalemate, and Townshend

Map 17 The Mesopotamia Campaign

withdrew his division in good order back to Kut-al-Amara, which the Turks then encircled.

The siege of Kut-al-Amara lasted from 7 December 1915 until 29 April 1916. The 8,000-strong British–Indian garrison was trapped in the town. Two attempts were made to relieve them and both failed; the situation was becoming desperate. At this point, 13th Division, including 7th Gloucesters, sailed from Suez for Basra. In his memoir, Edward Bazeley describes the journey:

> Aboard the S.S. *Simla* on the 13 March, we set out from Port Said along the Suez Canal on our long voyage round three sides of Arabia. At one spot we caught a glimpse from the boat-deck of the tops of the Pyramids far away to the west, lit by the morning sun, and as we passed through the Gulf of Suez, the towering heights of Mount Sinai could be seen in the east. And now we steamed for 1,200 miles through the sweltering heat of the Red Sea – home of flying fish and the dugong or 'mermaid', of which I had seen a stuffed specimen when I was at school in Cheltenham. Turning eastwards near Aden, we collected stores at Bombay, before sailing up the Persian Gulf past Kuwait, and the first oil well at Abadan on the Shatt el Arab. Early in April we landed at Basra, to be greeted with distressing news from the Front.

Suffering badly from fever, 7th Gloucesters were left behind in Basra when 13th Division moved up the River Tigris to Shaikh Sa'ad. This final attempt to relieve the Turkish siege of the 8,000 Allied troops in Kut, whose supplies were almost exhausted, began on 5 April 1916. Initially, things went quite well for the Allies: the Turkish front line was found to be unoccupied and a frontal assault on Fallahiyeh was successful, although it involved a muddy advance and casualties were high. But progress became increasingly difficult and the casualties mounted alarmingly. A decision was therefore taken to change the focus of the attack to the opposite bank, but heavy rain hindered the advance. The attack resumed on 15 April and Beit Asia fell on 17 April, the day before 7th Gloucesters rejoined the Division. The Battalion embarked on 'P Boats', craft driven by stern-wheels, which could pull them off mud banks. As they sailed, they passed herons, hoopoes, crested grebes and kingfishers along the banks, until they reached Shaik Saad, where they disembarked and marched by night into the trenches on the right bank of the Tigris.

Together, with the rest of 39th Brigade, the battalion attacked the Turkish positions at Beit Aiessa the following day across flooded land and under a hail of machine gun fire. Prior to the attack, the Turks fired well aimed shrapnel, which caused about 50 casualties. At 9.00 am C Company was ordered to reinforce the Royal Warwicks and 9th Worcesters, which it did, losing a lot of men in the process. Two days later, the Battalion moved up to reserve trenches and continued digging. A and D Companies attacked but were driven back, having crossed the first line of Turkish trenches; both company commanders were killed, along with three other officers. The next day, the Commanding Officer, Lieutenant Colonel Younghusband, was killed.[1] Captain George Fleming DSO, who was a Staff Captain in 39th Brigade, was promoted to Lieutenant Colonel and took over command of the Battalion. The relieving forces were unable to break through, and the British garrison of Kut surrendered on 29 April 1916 and became prisoners. Altogether, 7th Gloucesters suffered 149 casualties, of whom 76 died. It is clear from the Battalion War Diary that the after-effects of fever were still being felt and morale was quite low, not helped by the loss of their Commanding Officer.

One of the problems identified in the campaign to date was the weakness of the logistic system, and improving this now became a priority for the Allies. Edward Bazeley describes it thus:

> Our own conditions were far from satisfactory. Short of water, vegetables and medical supplies, we all suffered from sores which, like our scratches and wounds, inevitably became septic . . . It is impossible for most people to have any conception of the heat in the daytime during summer in Iraq. It varies according to district between 120 and

130 degrees F. in the SHADE. Even with the protection of a topee, spine-pad and dark glasses, to leave shelter between ten and five was to invite heatstroke and possibly death. Fortunately the Turks were no more immune.

The Battalion War Diary for 27 June records: 'No work is done between the hours of 7 am and 6 pm, the heat being great.'

In July 1916 Lieutenant General Sir Frederick Maude, who had been commanding 13th Division since Gallipoli, took over command of the force; he answered to London rather than to Delhi and was to become the most successful commander in Mesopotamia, much admired by the Arabs. He modernized the port at Basra, oversaw the construction of hospitals and built roads up the Tigris towards Amara, one of which was raised for 36 miles to prevent it being flooded. He acquired 1,000 Ford vans from the USA. Reinforcements arrived, so that by October the Tigris Corps had grown to 150,000, including 45,000 infantry and 3,500 cavalry. He hoped to launch the attempt to recapture Kut before the winter floods. Therefore, after a pause of nearly nine months, the British resumed the offensive on 13 December 1916, advancing up both sides of the Tigris with the aim of recapturing Kut.

The advance began on 30 November, with 7th Gloucesters, consisting of 24 officers and 768 other ranks, as the rear guard to No 3 Column. The Battalion reached the Tigris opposite Sheik Saad on 8 December, when it began to rain heavily. It crossed the Tigris the next day and marched to Twin Canals. On 14 December 7th Gloucesters cleared the right bank of the Hai as far as Nahir Bassouin before crossing it to rejoin the rest of the Brigade. On 15 December the Battalion was suddenly ordered to advance, with two companies of 9th Worcesters on their right and 7th North Staffs on the left. They covered about 1,000yds under some shrapnel fire and dug in. As things remained quiet, a further advance was ordered at 3.00 pm, and 7th Gloucesters advanced a further 1,000yds under shrapnel, high explosive, machine gun and rifle fire of some intensity and dug themselves in again. The night was spent in consolidation of the position and in reconnoitering the enemy's wire. Casualties amounted to 110, of whom 20 died. The Brigade Padre was killed while out with stretcher parties, and Captain Colin Geddie RAMC, the Battalion Doctor, was wounded by shrapnel.

Part of the reorganization had been to 'brigade' the battalion machine gun sections into brigade companies; those serving in them became members of the Machine Gun Corps. Edward Bazeley, who was commanding the 7th Gloucesters Machine Gun Section, was therefore posted to the 39th Machine Gun Company, and his memoir is from then on written from that perspective rather than that of the Battalion:

In November, the main body of the 1st Tigris Corps – the 3rd and 7th Indian Divisions – returned to the Sannaiat front on the left (N.E.) bank of the river. There, its duty was to hold down a large enemy force. Meanwhile the Third Corps – our 13th, and the 14th Divisions, under General Marshall, began the lengthy task of outflanking the Turkish army holding Kut . . . On Christmas morning, in sight of the minarets of Kut, our chaplain celebrated Holy Communion in the trenches, using an altar constructed of boxes of ammunition. Lord Curzon had sent from India a bottle of wine for each officer in the Force, and every soldier received an extra tot of rum.

The year 1916 therefore ended with Kut still in Turkish hands, but the Allies were better organized logistically and ready to achieve more success in 1917. Meanwhile, on the Western Front the Somme offensive had come to an end.

Note

1. Harold Younghusband had been commissioned into the Bedfordshire Regiment in 1900 but had spent much of his service with the King's African Rifles. He fought with 1/5th Bedfords at Gallipoli, where he was awarded the DSO. He took over command of 7th Gloucesters in January 1916, although on the CWGC website he is listed under the Bedfordshire Regiment. He was then thirty-nine, and his wife lived at Beaconsfield.

Part VI

THE SOMME OFFENSIVE 1916

Chapter 27

Preparations for Battle and the Opening Attack

The battle honour 'Somme 1916', covering the period from 1 July to 18 November 1916, was made up of twelve separate battles after the initial assault, which began at 7.20 am on 1 July, when the huge Hawthorn Mine was detonated under a redoubt on Hawthorn Ridge. The British Force, assembled that day to launch the assault across a 20-mile front, contained 20 divisions, most of which were in Fourth Army. Each division consisted of about 18,000 men, of whom about 12,000 were in infantry battalions, with the remainder providing support, including logistics. The majority of these divisions were new to the War. Three had been on the Western Front since the start and one had come back from the disaster at Gallipoli. Of the remainder, four were Territorial and the remaining twelve were 'Kitchener' divisions of citizen volunteers, many organized around 'Pals' or 'Chums' battalions, all drawn from the same towns and for whom the Somme would be their first major battle.

At the end of the disastrous first day, 1 July 1916, five of these divisions had actually got into the German positions; the rest were stopped in no-man's-land. To the north of the road between Albert and Bapaume little ground had been won, and this was where the majority of the British casualties had occurred. South of the road the situation was a little less depressing, as XIII Corps had captured the entire German front line and, although 7th Division of XV Corps had failed to take Fricourt, 21st Division had occupied 1,000yds of the German front line to the north, isolating Fricourt, which the Germans then abandoned. Further south, the French had also had some success. A total of 19,240 British and Commonwealth soldiers were dead and many more wounded. It is impossible to comprehend the scale of this tragedy across communities in Britain and overseas. Almost unbelievably, no Gloucester battalions were involved in the fighting on that awful first day; their turn was to come.

In fact, the action had started long before 1 July. The 'underground battle' began in November 1915 when the Royal Engineers Tunnelling Companies commenced work on nineteen mines. These were to be exploded immediately prior to the infantry attack. Eight were large (over 8,000lbs of explosives), eleven were small. The largest was 60,000lbs. The creation of specialized mining units in the British Army was largely due to 'Empire Jack', Sir John Norton-Griffiths, a self-made entrepreneur, businessman, MP, millionaire and raiser of a Yeomanry regiment. He had served in the Boer War and had subsequently formed an engineering company that worked at home and overseas. He wrote to the War Office in February 1915 proposing the formation of specialist companies that he called 'moles'. When the decision was taken to form specific Royal Engineer Tunnelling Companies, eighteen 'clay kickers' from his own company, which was digging sewers in the clay under Manchester, were enlisted and were in action four days later. Subsequently, he was reputed to have toured the Western Front in a battered Rolls-Royce loaded with fine wines.

The air campaign over the Somme began in April 1916, almost three months before the start of the ground offensive, when General Haig directed General Trenchard, who commanded the Royal Flying Corps on the Western Front, to establish air superiority over the intended battlefield. Trenchard identified six tasks to achieve this: aerial reconnaissance, aerial photography, observation and direction of artillery fire, tactical bombing, 'contact patrols' in support of infantry and air-combat against the Germans. He also insisted that the Royal Flying Corps (RFC), which was part of the British Army until the Royal Air Force was formed on 1 April 1918, should adopt an attitude of 'relentless, incessant offensive action'. As a result, the Corps established air superiority during the early summer of 1916 and then fought a daily battle to maintain it for nearly the entire 5-month ground campaign.

The Allies recognized that the German positions were well dug in behind masses of wire, and that taking these with unprotected infantry would be extremely difficult. It was therefore decided that the ground battle should start with five, later extended to seven, days of shelling on the enemy, before the infantry advanced. The first two days were to be devoted to cutting the German wire. Over the final three days the heavy artillery would destroy trenches, emplacements, strong points and enemy artillery, while field guns would continue attacking the wire. In addition, there would, in places, be a release of gas and smoke to deceive the enemy. Units would fire in 2-hour periods and then rest. Roads and tracks would be shelled at night to hamper supply and prevent relief units getting forward. Each day there would be an intensive bombardment for 80 minutes to make the Germans think an attack was coming, but on the actual day of the assault it would be 15 minutes shorter to enable the infantry to advance whilst the enemy was still under cover. It didn't work. Most of the artillery ammunition available was shrapnel, which was virtually useless against wire or against troops well dug in for that matter; but just as importantly, one third of the 1,500,000 shells fired during the five months failed to explode. The biggest mistake was that so little effort was made to neutralize the German artillery. Thus, when the infantry advanced, if they reached the German lines they were often cut off, as enemy fire prevented reinforcements reaching them or meant they were unable to withdraw.

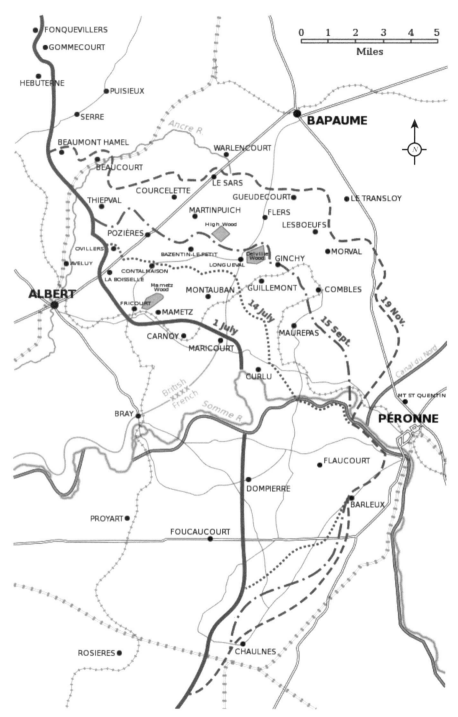

Map 18 Progress of the Somme Offensive Area, 1 July–18 November 1916

There were many reasons why Haig would have preferred the major British offensive of 1916 to have been launched further north. One of these was the logistic demands of fighting in the Somme area. Some 400,000 men and 100,000 horses of the British Army were moved there, and equipment, munitions, rations and supplies all had to be provided. In 1916, and throughout the War, railways were the only effective way of providing logistic support, and 128 supply trains a day were required. The existing railway network was inadequate, and 55 miles of new track were laid. Supply dumps were created but had to be 7 miles from the front to keep them safe from artillery fire. Getting the supplies over those last few miles was extremely challenging. The French and Germans had developed light railways to do this, but until 1917 the British chose to rely on road transport. The Somme was a quiet agricultural area and its roads were quite unsuitable for the heavy traffic that they would be required to bear. At Fricourt in 24 hours in late July 1916, 26,500 men on foot, 3,576 horse-drawn wagons, 5,400 riding horses, 1,238 motor vehicles of various types and 65 artillery guns passed a single point. There was no local stone for road building, so every ton had to be brought in, some even from Cornwall, and the roads could not cope with the demand once the weather deteriorated.

Before 1 July a little-known battle took place on 29/30 June, involving 13th Gloucesters (Pioneers), when the Battalion supported 116 Brigade, made up of three Sussex battalions and 14th Hampshires, in an attack at Richebourg l'Avoue between Béthune and Armentières, in the Pas de Calais. The Battle of the Boar's Head was a diversionary action to make the German Command believe that this area of the Pas de Calais was the one chosen for the major offensive of 1916. It was hoped that this would prevent the Germans moving troops to the Somme area, some 50km to the south. 13th Gloucesters' task was to dig communication trenches in the rear of the assaulting infantry in the dark. The attack was a disaster, 17 officers and 349 other ranks of the Brigade were killed and over 1,000 wounded or taken prisoner. 13th Glosters found men coming back as they tried to dig the trenches going forward; as a result, only one trench was dug. Many of the Battalion were used either to man fire trenches in case there was a counter-attack, to move ammunition forward or to bring back some of the wounded. The Battalion suffered 83 casualties, of whom 22 died. The tragedy on the Somme the following day means that few people are aware of this action.

The attitude of men to the dead may appear callous, but the reality was that there was nothing that could be done for them except record who they were, note where they were buried, write to the family and move on. Looking after the wounded has always been far more important to the British Army, since it is seen as vital for morale. By July 1916 the Medical Services had developed into a highly efficient organization. In extreme cases a man wounded one morning could find himself in hospital in England the next day. The first stage was the Regimental Aid Post. This was close to Battalion HQ and manned by the Regimental Medical Officer, some assistants and usually eight stretcher-bearers, increased to sixteen during an offensive. The greatest challenge was getting the wounded off the battlefield. The stretcher-bearers regularly risked their lives to do so. Some casualties with minor wounds were treated at the Regimental Aid Post and returned to duty; the rest were moved to the Casualty Clearing Station. Each brigade had a Field Ambulance, whose role, as its name implies, was the movement of casualties from the battalions; but it also had the capacity to treat men who could be returned to the front quickly, including the sick. The ways in which a Field Ambulance was deployed varied, but at the Somme most established a number of stretcher-bearer relay points along the casualty evacuation chain from the Regimental Aid Post. The first would have been about 600yds behind, but there were also walking wounded collecting stations – the more of the wounded who could walk the better. Initially, movement was through communication trenches or under cover, but as soon as possible ambulances were used. A Field Ambulance could hold 150 wounded or sick in what was known as an Advanced Dressing Station. Here the wounded were assessed and dressings were adjusted; once the staff were satisfied that the individual was ready he was sent on to the Casualty Clearing Station; there was generally one Casualty Clearing Station per division. Each could hold about 1,000 wounded at any one time and covered a large area sufficiently far from the front line to be safe from enemy shellfire, almost always adjacent to a railway line so that the wounded could be moved back to base hospital by ambulance train. Here major limb and lifesaving surgery was carried out. Others with less serious wounds were treated, so that those who could be were got back to their units as soon as possible. Ambulance Trains were hospitals on wheels. Each could carry 350 patients, and during the Somme offensive 240 were required each week, sufficient for 84,000 to be moved. Base Hospitals were generally located on the coast, as this facilitated movement back to UK; some were in requisitioned casinos. Finally, there were the hospitals and recuperation centres in the UK, the latter generally set up in large private houses and staffed almost entirely by volunteers.

Chapter 28

La Boiselle (8ᵗʰ Bn), Bazentin Ridge (1ˢᵗ & 1/4ᵗʰ Bns) and Fromelles (2/4ᵗʰ, 2/5ᵗʰ & 2/6ᵗʰ Bns)

The Battle of Albert (1–13 July) was the first of the series that make up the Somme offensive and naturally divides into two: the first dreadful day when the British assaulted across the whole front, then the series of smaller attacks that followed, each with more limited objectives. Most of the latter made some progress, without ever achieving all that was intended. In many cases, however, they forced the Germans to counter–attack, which was as costly for them as the British attacks had been for the Allies. The new British plan was to reinforce the success south of the Albert–Bapaume road in preparation for a second general attack on 10 July, postponed to the 14ᵗʰ due to supply difficulties. Meanwhile the French Sixth Army, to the south, was more successful and by 10 July had captured parts of the German third line.

Although 1ˢᵗ, 1/4ᵗʰ, 1/5ᵗʰ, 1/6ᵗʰ and 10ᵗʰ Gloucesters were all awarded the battle honour 'Albert', their participation was limited and involved little actual fighting, but all suffered casualties from shellfire. Meanwhile, 8ᵗʰ Gloucesters was the reserve battalion for an attack at 3.15 am on 3/4 July to capture La Boiselle, which had already been assaulted twice unsuccessfully. Lieutenant Colonel Carton de Wiart, who was commanding 8ᵗʰ Gloucesters, described the battle in his book *Happy Odyssey*:

> In this attack my battalion, the 8ᵗʰ Gloucesters, were in support. The battalion we were supporting soon advanced into a heavy German barrage, and in the noise and confusion imagined they had been ordered to retire. This battalion was retiring through my men, and a retirement is the most infectious disease, there was a moment of desperate chaos, when the issue hung in the balance. The officers and men of the 8ᵗʰ Gloucesters were truly magnificent, and the men rallied and responded to them. They advanced regardless of their appalling casualties until they had fulfilled their appointed task and captured La Boiselle.

The Battalion was relieved on the night of 5/6 July, having suffered 292 casualties, of whom 94 died, including 6 officers. During July 1916 15 platoon commanders in 8th Gloucesters were killed; the Battalion had 16 platoons. The Adjutant, Captain W. Parkes, who was severely wounded, was awarded an MC, and Private W. G. H. Lugg[1] a DCM for going out some 200yds under heavy artillery and machine gun fire to bring back wounded comrades. Carton de Wiart[2] himself was awarded the Victoria Cross:

> It was owing in a great measure to his dauntless courage and inspiring example that a serious reverse was averted. After three other C.O.s had become casualties, he controlled their commands and ensured that the ground won was maintained at all costs. He frequently exposed himself in the organization of positions and of supplies, passing unflinchingly through fire barrage of the most intense nature. His gallantry was inspiring to all.

He had lost a hand the year before, and men of 8th Gloucesters saw their Commanding Officer tearing out the safety-pins of bombs with his teeth and hurling them with his one hand. The village of La Boiselle was 'adopted' in 1920 under the British League of Help Scheme by the City of Gloucester. Funds were raised by the citizens of Gloucester to help re-establish the community, which had been totally destroyed in 1916.

The Battle of Bazentin Ridge was the second of the Somme battles. The front extended from Longueval to Bazentin-le-Petit Wood, and the attack was directed towards High Wood. In a change from previous attacks it was launched at dawn and preceded by a 5-minute 'hurricane' bombardment. Initially, it was successful; Bazentin-le-Grand and Bazentin-le-Petit were both taken within a few hours, and Longueval followed shortly afterwards, although the advance had skirted Delville Wood. High Wood itself was found to be unoccupied, but rather than use troops readily available to seize it, higher command decided to use cavalry, and the delay in moving them forward allowed the Germans to get there first with machine guns, which caused dreadful casualties. Overnight, under heavy German artillery fire, the British tried to establish a position within the wood from which to attack the remainder but were forced to withdraw the next evening; an opportunity had been lost, which was to cost thousands of lives over the next two months. Four Gloucester battalions were involved, although 10th and 14th Gloucesters saw little direct fighting but suffered casualties from intense German shelling; 14th Gloucesters had 119 casualties. 1st Gloucesters moved into the new front line on the night of 14/15 July. So confused was the situation that the battalion HQ they were relieving did not know the location of their companies, and it was dawn before the relief was complete. Patrols quickly discovered that the Germans were some way off, and the Battalion occupied Contalmaison Villa without opposition. It was then ordered to attack the German line that night and set off in driving rain at midnight. The Germans quickly abandoned their position and the Battalion was relieved later that night.

For 1/4th Gloucesters this was its first major battle of the war, and it did well. On 16 July it launched a night attack to capture German trenches near Ovillers and make contact with 7th Worcesters. The attack started at 2.00 am after a 10-minute bombardment, and within 30 minutes the two leading companies had taken the objective but had not made contact with the Worcesters. At 7.00 am contact had still not been made and the two leading companies were being attacked from both flanks. One of the reserve companies, however, had found the Worcesters, and it was ordered to work up the German front line trench with bombing attacks to link the Worcesters with the leading Gloucesters companies. This it achieved by 3.00 pm, having run out of bombs but using captured German ones instead. The next day (18th), the Battalion was ordered to push forward again and did so at 5.00 pm. It had gained the next line by 8.00 pm with few casualties but when it tried to advance again met heavy resistance and was forced to withdraw. It then held the line until relieved on 22 July by 1/6th Gloucesters.

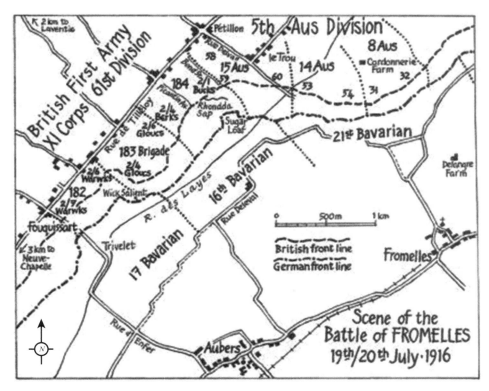

Map 19 The Battle of Fromelles: order of Battle for British and German forces.

61st Division including 2/4th, 2/5th and 2/6th Gloucesters reached France at the end of May 1916 and were sent to the Laventie sector, about 50 miles north of the Somme, and were soon in the front line trenches and conducting raids. A Company 2/5th Gloucesters launched a raid on 20 June which found the wire had not been cut, and the party quickly began to suffer casualties due to effective enemy machine gun fire. Six Other Ranks died and four were missing. Then, on 4/5 July C Company 2/4th Gloucesters conducted a more successful raid led with great dash and gallantry by Captain Frederick (Frank) Hannam, from Bedminster, Bristol, who died of his wounds. He was recommended for a posthumous VC, but this was not awarded. His wife was the tennis player Edith Boucher who won two Gold Medals at the 1912 Olympic Games and was twice a Wimbledon Finalist.

Although it was not a 'Somme battle' the action at Fromelles by 61st Division was an attempt to discourage the Germans from withdrawing troops from a quiet front to strengthen their force on the Somme. The whole operation was badly planned and delayed twice from 17 July because of mist. The attack frontage was only 4,000yds and the ground was flat, waterlogged and easily overlooked by the Germans from Aubers Ridge. In addition to 61st Division the 5th Australian Division, which had only arrived in France a few days before, took part.

The German positions were shelled for seven hours before the assault, but Allied intelligence was unaware that the Germans had abandoned their waterlogged trenches and moved back about 200yds. The delays and bombardment alerted the enemy to the pending attack. In the 61st Division only one battalion reached the German front line and was then forced to withdraw. The Australians did better, in that they did reach the German front line without major casualties, but their efforts to reach the second line were far less successful. They tried to hold on, but at 3.15 am the next morning the Germans counter-attacked. They got behind the Australians, who suffered 5,513 casualties, about 90 per cent of their strength, while the British lost 1,547, about 50 per cent of theirs. A German assessment of the attack was that it had been 'operationally and tactically senseless'. The Australian War Memorial describes Fromelles as 'the worst 24 hours in Australia's entire history' and it did much to sour relations with the mother country.

2/5th Gloucesters were one of the reserve battalions of 184 Brigade and were not therefore involved in the fighting. 2/4th and 2/6th Gloucesters, on the other hand, were the two front line battalions of 183 Brigade. They were bombarded as they tried to leave the trenches and then shot down in no-man's-land.

The Commanding Officer of 2/4th Gloucesters wrote in the Battalion War Diary, 'At the time I considered further attempts to advance in the face of this M.G. fire useless.' The War Diary of 2/6th Gloucesters includes the following:

First wave of two platoons left trenches at 5.40pm . . . Two more waves and part of 4th went out. Men practically blown back as they went over parapet by machine gun and shrapnel. Withdrawn about 7 o'clock. Orders received to attack again at 9 o'clock. 8.20pm orders received cancelling attack. 9pm orders received to prepare for relief by 2/7 Worcesters. Relief completed 2am.

The order at 9.00 pm also included instructions for trying to recover the wounded from no-man's-land.

Most Great War graves were identified in the 1920s, but in 2002 researchers who believed that some of the bodies from Fromelles had never been recovered began work to find them. They were successful: in 2008 the remains of 337 soldiers were found and in the following year a further 250. A new cemetery was created, Fromelles (Pheasant Wood) Military Cemetery. Although there can be no positive identification, it is almost certain that some of those now buried here were Gloucesters.

Notes

1. William George Lugg (1893–1974) was born in Randwick Stroud and worked for Holloway Bros Ltd, wholesale tailors in Stroud, until he enlisted in September 1914. He rose to the rank of Sergeant and after the war returned to live at Cainscross, Stroud.
2. Lt Gen Sir Adrian Carton de Wiart VC, KBE, CB, CMG, DSO (1880–1963) was a remarkable soldier. Born in Belgium of Irish parents, he served in the South African War and both World Wars, during which he was frequently wounded, losing an eye and the fingers of one hand. He survived two plane crashes and tunnelled out of a PoW camp. He was Adjutant of the RGH before the Great War, so that he could hunt with the Beaufort, and commanded 8th Gloucesters 15 June–22 July and 12 September–26 October 1916.

Chapter 29

Delville Wood (12th Bn) and Pozieres (1/4th, 1/5th & 1/6th Bns)

Inevitably, the various Somme battles do not fit into a neat sequence but overlap one another. By mid-July further progress was impossible until Delville Wood, High Wood and Pozières had been captured. It would take seven weeks of fierce fighting to achieve this.

Previously, Delville Wood had been bypassed, and now, together with Longueval, it threatened the salient that the Allies had captured. It soon became known as 'Devil's Wood'. The initial attack by the South African Brigade lasted for six days, during which those killed outnumbered the wounded by four to one. Most of the wood was captured, but German counter-attacks were continuous, at one point supported by 400 shells a minute. The trees were uprooted or reduced to stumps, and the rain turned the ground into a quagmire. The South Africans who were left were relieved on 19/20 July. Another attempt, this time by 2nd Division, was launched on 27 July, and this was followed on 4 August by 17th Division. Finally, 24th Division captured the whole wood on 3 September.

The only Gloucester battalion involved was 12th Gloucesters (Bristol's Own), who fought at Longueval rather than in the wood itself. Here the Battalion was more heavily shelled, with HE, shrapnel and gas, than at any other time in the War and suffered a large number of casualties. It occupied the front line at Longueval from 23 to 26 July. When it went back to the village on the 28th, the front line had moved forward a little and the enemy shelling was even heavier. At 6.00 am the next morning the CO, Lieutenant Colonel Archer-Shee DSO, MP, visited all the trenches. Lance Corporal Robert Anstey recalled:[1] 'I shall not easily forget the thrill I received as I saw the CO running across open ground, utterly unconcerned in the midst of some very heavy shelling, in order to move B Company to a less exposed position.'

That afternoon the Battalion launched a successful two-company attack against strongly held positions, which they held until relieved on the 30th. In a subsequent letter to the CO the Brigade Commander wrote:[2]

I have much pleasure in asking that you will have recorded against the names of the NCOs and men not only my admiration but also the admiration of the 95ᵗʰ Brigade and the 5ᵗʰ Division for the splendid courage and devotion to duty which they displayed on 29, 30 and 31 July in holding on to the advanced post at Longueval, in a very critical situation. I know you must be proud to have men of this stamp in your battalion, equally I am proud to have them in my Brigade.

The village of Pozières and, in particular the ridge behind, provided an excellent observation post and needed to be captured before further advances could be made. The task was allocated to the 1ˢᵗ ANZAC Corps, supported, on the left, by 48ᵗʰ (South Midland) Division, which included 1/4ᵗʰ, 1/5ᵗʰ and 1/6ᵗʰ Gloucesters, attacking towards Ovillers. The 1ˢᵗ Australian Division captured the village of Pozières within the first 24 hours, but there then followed a struggle for the ridge itself. In seven weeks of continuous fighting the three Australian Divisions suffered 23,000 casualties, of whom 6,800 were killed or died of wounds. Charles Bean, Australia's official war historian, wrote that the ridge 'is more densely sown with Australian sacrifice than any other place on earth'.

The three Gloucester battalions (1/4ᵗʰ, 1/5ᵗʰ and 1/6ᵗʰ) had an equally frustrating time attempting, often unsuccessfully, to take German positions and generally being shelled. The significant actions were:

20 July – 1/5ᵗʰ Gloucesters attacked German trenches unsuccessfully; 114 casualties.

21 July – 1/6ᵗʰ Gloucesters launched a three-company attack which failed but was described by Wyrall as 'a very gallant failure'. Lieutenant Colonel Micklem in his report wrote:

> The cause of the failure was, in my opinion, the lack of artillery preparation. None of the machine guns previously reported had been knocked out and the enemy line had hardly been shelled at all . . . Reliable information is difficult to obtain now the officers and nearly all the N.C.O.s of the leading companies are casualties.

Norman Edwards wrote an account of his personal involvement:[3]

> Just after midnight we got our stuff together and joined up with 8 Platoon . . . We moved slowly up the trench, we knew not where but about 2.15am we reached our starting point. At this moment one of our Stokes Mortars commenced rapid fire and one of their pellets must have fallen on a bomb store in the German lines, for about twenty went off like squibs . . . I took a bearing on the North star and 'Gunboat' gave the

order for us to advance. I crawled over the parapet telling the chaps to follow . . . we had hardly gone 20 yards when three or four machine guns opened fire on us. From then it was undiluted hell. We crawled forward taking cover in enemy shell holes . . . The fire had become so intense by this time that it was almost impossible to move, but we made another 10 yards and found a deep shell crater and hung in there . . . By the light of the flare I saw the gallant figure of 'Gunboat' Smith walking about rallying the men and as I watched I saw him stagger and fall in a heap. A few minutes later he came crawling towards us aided by young Watts, his batman, so I helped him over the last few yards. He had no idea where our line was and taking a back bearing on the pole star I put him on the right track and they crawled away into the darkness. We hung on as it was useless going forward until the men in front had moved on. A feeling of impotence gave way to fuming blazing anger fed by primitive emotions . . . We could not fire because of the two waves of men in front but action of some sort was essential . . . I had crawled about 20 yards when I slid into a deep shell crater and found an officer applying field dressings to two wounded men. 'Gunboat' Smith and Watts his batman, who was badly wounded, were also there. The officer told me to try to get him back to our lines. He could just about crawl and we started. We hadn't gone five yards when 'Gunboat' was hit again . . . Then what felt like a blow from a sledgehammer hit me and I rolled into a crater. Vic appeared and tied up my wound and we did what we could for 'Gunboat', dragging him back to the deep crater. The officer then ordered me to try to get a stretcher . . . Somehow I reached our front line alive, but to my dying day I shall always wonder how.

He told two men where the wounded men were lying before the Medical Officer saw his arm and ordered him back to the dressing station. He was eventually evacuated to England. 2nd Lieutenant Arthur R. Smith ('Gunboat') died of his wounds the following day; he was twenty-three. Private Watts survived.

23 July – 145 Brigade mounted unsuccessful attack; 156 casualties in 1/5th Gloucesters, who were relieved at 3.30 am. Relieving battalion launched a fresh attack and 120 Germans surrendered.

24 July – Germans attacked 1/4th Gloucesters but kept back by artillery and mortars.

25-27 July – Whole division withdrawn to rest and reorganize. Returned on 13 August.

16 August – 1/4th Gloucesters launched attack on German trenches at 2.00 am but met by hail of fire making it impossible to advance. Seventy killed, wounded or missing. Battalion relieved later in the day and withdrawn. Private Owen Hunt of Cheltenham, serving with 1/5th Gloucesters, was killed, leaving his widow and their eight children. She received no pension and always kept the back door unlocked for him to come home.[4]

18 August – 1/5th Gloucesters supported attack by 143 Brigade which took 400 prisoners.

21 August – 1/4th Gloucesters attacked successfully trenches on Leipzig Redoubt and took 150 prisoners. The Battalion resisted three counter-attacks successfully.

25 August – 1/5th Gloucesters launched a two-company attack on German trenches which was successful after a fierce battle. Cyril Winterbotham, who had frequently in his letters expressed doubts about his own courage, was killed leading one of these companies. His Company Sergeant Major, William Tibbles described him as 'that gallant leader'. He was buried along with the other officers of the company, who had all been killed in the German trench they had captured. His brother Percy, the Adjutant of 1/5th Gloucesters wrote to their mother:

> Don't worry about the poor old man being buried in a Hun trench. It's only his body and his big heart and soul have gone where there's no more war or worry . . . I went up to the trench where poor Cyril lies and put up a big white cross which the Regt Pioneers had made.

Sadly, after the War, Cyril's body could not be identified so he has no known grave and is commemorated on the Thiepval Memorial. On 3 September the Battle of Pozieres was over.

Cross of Wood

God be with you and us who go our way
And leave you dead upon the ground you won.
For you at last the long fatigue is done,
The hard march ended; you have rest today.

You were our friends; with you we watched the dawn
Gleam through the rain of the long winter night,
With you we laboured till the morning light
Broke on the village, shell-destroyed and torn.

Not now for you the glorious return
To steep Stroud valleys, to the Severn leas
By Tewkesbury and Gloucester, or the trees
Of Cheltenham under high Cotswold stern.

For you no medals such as others wear –
A cross of bronze for those approved brave –
To you is given, above a shallow grave,
The Wooden Cross that marks you resting there.

Rest you content; more honourable far
Than all the Orders is the Cross of Wood,
The symbol of self-sacrifice that stood
Bearing the God whose brethren you are.

Lt Cyril Winterbotham 1/5th Gloucesters
Killed in Action 27 August 1916[5]

Notes

1. Dean Marks, *'Bristol's Own'*, *the 12th Battalion Gloucestershire Regiment 1914–1918*.
2. Ibid.
3. James Bonsor, 'I did my Duty – First World War experiences of H.N.Edwards as seen through his accounts and recent interviews'.
4. J. Devereux and G. Sacker, *Leaving All That Was Dear – Cheltenham and the Great War*
5. *Poems by Cyril William Winterbotham* was printed in 1917 by J. J. Banks & Son of Cheltenham for private circulation. The first poem included was written when Cyril was a small boy. *Cross of Wood* was written shortly before he was killed.

Chapter 30

Captured

Throughout the war soldiers on both sides were taken prisoner. During the fighting at Pozières, F. W. Harvey, the poet, who was by now a Lieutenant in 1/5th Gloucesters, having won a DCM as a Lance Corporal the previous year, was captured.[1] In his book *Comrades in Captivity* he describes being taken prisoner in a German trench where he had gone alone prior to leading a reconnaissance patrol that evening; it provides an unexpected insight into both the man and life at the front in August 1916, in the midst of the Somme Offensive:

On August 17 it occurred to me during my 'rest period' that, as I knew nothing of the ground we were to patrol that night, I might as well go out and have a look at it. Long unburned grass between the trenches afforded plenty of cover, and it is common knowledge that the hours between two and five were the quietest period of the day alike for German soldiers and English. During that period everyone except the sentry was asleep . . . It has been a practice of mine, ever since I was made responsible for patrols, personally to examine the ground before I took my men over it, and this seemed a good opportunity . . . I decided to go alone . . .

After leaving the trench, I went crawling along in the shadow of the hedge, which ran through our lines and terminated just in front of the enemy parapet, at this point about three hundred yards off. I carried an automatic pistol.

When the hedge ended the grass became short, and before leaving I lay and listened for about ten minutes . . . there was no sound of digging, talking, or firing . . . If I had had a man with me I should now have gone back, but I was beginning to be rather pleased with myself, and, there being no other life than mine at stake, crawled forward out of cover.

Shell-hole by shell-hole I worked my way cautiously to a little ditch or drain which ran through a gap in the German wire and on to the parapet.

Along this drain, carefully edging my way, I came at last to the projected shadow of the parapet, where I lay (holding my breath) to listen. There was not a sound. I twisted my head sideways, and looked up. Nowhere along the parapet, which here jutted out into a point, was there visible either head or periscope.

I wriggled a little higher and looked quickly over the top of the trench. There was nobody there.

Reason told me at this point that it would be better to go back . . . 'Be damned if I go back!' said I, and slipped straightway over the top into the trench beneath.

It is easier to get into a German trench than to get out. I had barely reached the next bay, which was also empty, when I heard footsteps, and a good many of them, coming along behind me. If I turned back to find my hole in the wire I ran the risk of meeting those feet before I got to it. It seemed better to go on. The trench was good deal deeper than ours but I expected to find holes through the parados such as our own trench possessed in large numbers. Through one of these I could creep, finding cover in the long grass behind, and a place where I could watch what was going on around me . . .

But my luck was out. Nowhere in the parados was there any sign of an exit. The feet were getting nearer. I continued to walk down the trench before them, looking for cover. Then at the end of the bay, I caught sight of a small iron shelter. It was the only place. I approached it swiftly, and was hurrying in when two hefty Germans met me in the doorway. I was seized. My pistol wrenched away. There was no escape possible . . .

It is a strange thing, but to be made prisoner is undoubtedly the most surprising thing that can happen to a soldier. It is an event which one has never considered, never by any chance anticipated . . .

Yet now I was dumbfounded . . . one of them looked so ridiculously like a certain labourer I had left working on my father's farm in Gloucestershire that I simply burst out laughing – which possibly saved my life.

Another of those taken prisoner at Pozières was Valentine Fry of Cheltenham. In the *Graphic* of 5 August his photograph appeared with the caption 'Missing with no hope of being found alive'. He was therefore included on the Cheltenham War Memorial, but in fact he did not die until June 1977, aged eighty-one.

Note

1. Frederick William Harvey DCM (1888–1957) was born in Hartpury near Gloucester and was a poet, solicitor and broadcaster. After the War he lived in the Forest of Dean, working largely to defend individuals, often for no fee, believing as a result of his own experience that imprisonment was pointless. His books include *A Gloucestershire Lad at Home and Abroad*, *Gloucestershire Friends*, *Poems from a German Prison Camp* and *Ducks and Other Verses*, as well as *Comrades in Captivity*. There is a memorial to him in Gloucester Cathedral.

(*Above*) New recruits for 1/5th Gloucesters in August 1914, possibly in Cheltenham. They travelled by train to the Regimental Depot at Horfield Barracks in Bristol, where they were enlisted.

(*Right*) The cobblers and tailor of 1/4th Gloucesters. Keeping boots in good order was vital, and when uniform was torn on barbed wire it either had to be replaced or repaired. The tailor would also affix badges of rank and medal ribbons when required. The boots had iron toe and heel plates and leather soles studded with nails, making them hard-wearing rather than comfortable.

(*Above*) 13th Gloucesters were a Pioneer Battalion and therefore their training was quite different to that of other battalions. Here they are learning bridge-building at Wensley in the Yorkshire Dales in 1915, before becoming the Divisional Pioneer Battalion of 39th Division in France in March 1916.

(*Below*) New recruits for 1/5th Gloucesters learning how to dig a trench at Chelmsford in 1914. Trench-digging was an essential part of training before battalions left for operations. Being able to take cover in well built trenches saved many lives during artillery bombardments. It was some time before there was sufficient uniform for the thousands who joined up.

(*Above*) Families outside the Sergeants' Mess tent, 1/4th Gloucesters, Danbury, Essex. The Battalion had moved to Essex in mid-August 1914, and the wives had probably travelled by train from Bristol for the day, before the Battalion departed for France at the end of March 1915.

(*Below*) 13 Platoon, D Company, 2/4th Gloucesters in 1915. Every platoon contained a mix of individuals, some of whose humour lightened the darkest of days. 2/4th Gloucesters reached France in May 1916 and the Battalion's first battle was on 19/20 July at Fromelles, where they were bombarded as they tried to leave the trenches and then shot down in no-man's-land. The Commanding Officer wrote in the War Diary: 'At the time I considered further attempts to advance in the face of this M.G. fire useless.'

(*Above*) 1ˢᵗ Gloucesters Vickers machine gun team, 1915. The machine guns of both sides, together with artillery fire, led to the stalemate on the Western Front. Until the advent of the tank, any movement led to casualties.

(*Below*) 2ⁿᵈ Gloucesters Regimental Aid Post at Armentières, July–September, 1915. The RAP was the first stage in the casualty evacuation chain to which stretcher bearers brought those that had been wounded. It was also where those who were sick were initially treated.

(*Right*) A rickety bridge across a gully in Macedonia in 1916 where 2nd and 9th Gloucesters were fighting from 1915 to 1918. There were few roads in Macedonia, making movement of supplies extremely difficult.

(*Below*) Officers of 2nd Gloucesters, shortly after their arrival at Salonika in December 1915. Most had fought with great gallantry at the Second Battle of Ypres earlier in the year. The group includes A. C. Vicary (middle row, second from right), who would become the Commanding Officer in 1918 and whose horse, 'The Sphinx', accompanied him throughout the War, and George Power (at the left of Vicary at end of row), whose amusing letters provide a valuable insight into life at the Front.

(*Above*) Trench life. 1ˢᵗ Gloucesters, 1915.This shows how unpleasant life in the trenches in winter could be, which meant that companies were often rotated every 48 hours. At the same time the difficulties for the Germans attacking this position are clear.

(*Left*) Company Sergeant Major (CSM) William Bizley MM, who commanded the snipers in 1/4ᵗʰ Gloucesters, spotting for a sergeant colleague. He was born in St Paul's, Bristol in 1872, joined the Volunteers in 1892 and by the outbreak of the War had already been awarded theTerritorial Efficiency Medal and reached the rank of Sergeant. He had also been summoned for 'furiously and recklessly riding a bicycle' in Bristol in 1895 and been fined 5 shillings. Severely wounded at Ovillers on 15 August 1916 and taken prisoner, he was released on 17 November 1918, six days after the Armistice.

The funeral cortège of Private Alfred George Potter of 14th Gloucesters, who died of wounds and gangrene on 18 May 1915, aged twenty-two, on its way to St Michael's, Two Mile Hill, Bristol. The contrast with the burials on the Western Front is striking. He was an only son with eight sisters.

Private Francis George Miles VC being 'chaired' by a crowd on his return in 1919 to Clearwell, Forest of Dean, which is believed to have sent more men to the War than any other village in proportion to its size. He was a miner who in December 1914 enlisted in 9th Gloucesters and went with the Battalion to Macedonia, from where he was evacuated with a poisoned foot and was then posted to 8th Gloucesters. While attached to the Royal Engineers he was the only survivor of 50 men buried by a mine. Once recovered, he was posted to 1/5th Gloucesters, with whom he won the VC. After the war he returned to become a 'free miner' in the Forest of Dean. He was invested with the VC at Buckingham Palace by King George V on 13 May 1919, and the villagers of Clearwell presented him with a gold watch.

Company Sergeant Major William Biddle MC, DCM, MM of 1st Gloucesters and family at his investiture with the MC at Buckingham Palace in 1920. He had been awarded it for action in June 1918, but the investiture was delayed because he was severely wounded in hand-to-hand fighting on 18 September 1918, receiving twelve wounds and losing a finger. He was killed by a German bomb at Clacton-on-Sea in September 1941.

(*Above left*) The Rigby brothers, from 63 Clegan Road, Gloucester. William (left) enlisted in 1/5th Gloucesters in August 1914, was badly wounded in August 1916 and, once he had recovered, joined 2/4th Gloucesters. John (right) enlisted in 1/1st RGH in May 1915 and served with them for the rest of the War. A third brother, Archibald, was killed with 1st RWF in May 1917.

(*Above right*) Private William Biddle in India in about 1906, with both Queen's and King's South African Medals (few soldiers were awarded both). He was to become one of the most decorated Other Ranks in the Great War. He had been court-martialled in 1903 in South Africa for 'Conduct to the Prejudice of Good Order and Military Discipline' and sentenced to '84 Days Hard Labour'.

Lieutenant Colonel Dan Burges VC, DSO, Gloucesters, was awarded the VC whilst in command of 7th South Wales Borderers for his action at Jumeaux (Balkans) on 18 September 1918. When the battalion came under severe machine gun fire he himself, though wounded, kept moving to and fro encouraging his men. Finally, as they neared the enemy's position, he led them forward through a decimating fire, until he was again hit twice and fell unconscious. He lost a leg as a result of his wounds. He was later President of the Society of Bristolians and Master of the Society of Merchant Venturers.

Second Lieutenant Hardy Falconer Parsons of 14th Gloucesters, who was awarded a posthumous VC for his action on 21 August 1917 on the Somme, when the Germans attempted to recapture the Knoll with flame-throwers. Although severely burnt, he remained at his post holding the enemy up with bombs (grenades) long enough for the Battalion to organize reinforcements that drove the Germans back. He had been educated at Kingswood School, Bath and at Bristol University, where he was studying medicine in preparation for missionary medical work. He was twenty. His VC was said to have been one that King George V most admired.

Captain Manley Angell James VC of 8th Gloucesters was born in 1896, educated at Bristol Grammar School and played rugby for Bristol. He was commissioned into 8th Gloucesters in 1914 and was severely wounded at La Boiselle, spending five months in hospital. In 1917 he was wounded again, Mentioned in Despatches in June and was in heavy fighting at Wytshaete and Messines Ridge, for which he was awarded an MC. On 21 March 1918 his company was fighting near Velu Wood. Although wounded, he refused to be evacuated and helped repulse three enemy attacks the next day. Although the Germans eventually broke through, the company made a determined stand; wanting to buy more time for the brigade to escape, he led his company in a fierce counter-attack and was again wounded. Single-

handedly he took control of a machine gun and kept the enemy at bay until he was wounded for a third time and eventually captured; he was awarded the VC.

A sergeant of 1/4th Gloucesters wears a gas mask and goatskin jerkin. The Allies were completely unprepared for the use of gas during the Second Battle of Ypres, with devastating consequences, and initial protection was generally inadequate. Gas hoods with mica eyepieces, such as this one, were introduced in July 1915.

"Any more for any more"
HGB. June. 15.

Our Washing apparatus in a Dye Works
at N—

SMOKING PROHIBITED

ALL BOOTS MUST BE PLACED IN THE RACKS.

Bathhouse scene drawn by Lance Corporal Henry Buckle of 1/5th Gloucesters who was a whitesmith from Tewkesbury before the War. His writings and drawing from the trenches have been published as *A Tommy's Sketchbook* by The Soldiers of Gloucestershire Museum.

Captain J. C. Proctor of 13th Gloucesters produced a series of memorable sketches and drawings that capture much of the horror of life on the Western Front. The tank 'Crème de Menthe' was commanded by a Gloucester, Captain Arthur Inglis, and had penetrated the German lines successfully on 15 September and brought back a German general as a prisoner. On 9 August 1918 at Amiens Inglis was severely wounded and was evacuated to his brother's nursing home in Cheltenham, where he died.

A soldier of 1/4th Gloucesters writing home. The postal service to and from the Western Front was efficient and quick, less so from other fronts. All letters home had to be censored, principally by platoon commanders.

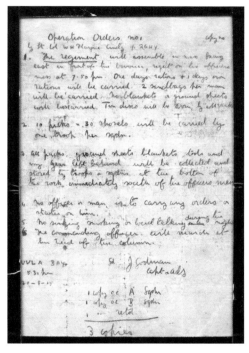

(*Above left*) Lieutenant Colonel Adrian Carton de Wiart VC, DSO was a cavalry officer who had already fought in the South African War and with the Camel Corps in Somaliland, where he lost an eye, before he was given command of 8th Gloucesters, with whom he won a VC in 1916. He had also been Adjutant of the RGH before the War. During the capture of La Boiselle on 3/4 July 1916, after three other COs had become casualties, he controlled their commands and ensured the ground won was held. Earlier he had lost a hand, and men saw him tearing out the safety pins of grenades with his teeth and hurling them with his one good arm. To his friends he said of his VC that 'it had been won by the 8th Gloucesters, for every man in the Battalion had done as much as I had.'

(*Above Right*) 1/1st RGH Operation Order No 1 for the dismounted attack on Scimitar Hill on 21 August 1915 during the Gallipoli Campaign, Written in pencil, it is a model of brevity, unlike many infantry Operation Orders, and amounts to little more than 'Follow me', as it includes 'The Commanding Officer will march at the head of the column'.

(*Above*) Corporal Hugh Walwin (right) of 1/1st RGH manned A Squadron's only Maxim gun team at Qatia on 23 April 1916. Despite being wounded he kept the gun firing for seven hours until it seized, when all the liquid in its water jacket had evaporated. He was taken prisoner by the Turks along with 62 other members of the Squadron and began a terrible march across the desert to Jerusalem and on to Damascus. Hugh Walwin's family owned the photographer's in Southgate Street, Gloucester, which he took on after the War.

(*Below*) A bridge of boats near Kut-el-Amara. The Siege of Kut lasted from 7 December 1915 to 29 April 1916. 7th Gloucesters arrived in Mesopotamia from Egypt suffering badly from fever and did not join the battle until 18 April. This photograph was taken by Private Alfred Blake from Hotwells, Bristol, who had worked for the Bristol Docks Company. He joined 7th Gloucesters as it arrived in Mesopotamia in 1916, was probably evacuated to India suffering from sickness and, once he had recovered, transferred to another regiment, since he took part in the Third Afghan War between May and August 1919.

(*Above*) In early May 1918 1/1st RGH took part in the raid on Es Salt. Having reached the town the Regiment was sent to seize the Howeij Bridge but found it was strongly held by the Turks, who were also occupying the high ground shown on either side of the road in this photograph and making any movement hazardous. After two difficult days the British force withdrew. When criticized, General Allenby dismissed the notion of failure, convinced that the operation had misled the Turks into believing the British intended to strike in the west and deploying their forces accordingly.

(*Below*) Sport was important, partly to keep everyone fit but also to provide a diversion and some fun. On 28 July 1917 1/1st RGH held a sports day, which inevitably included horsemanship and, as this photograph, shows a 'harem race'.

In October 1916 Lieutenant Robert Wilson (centre) of 1/1st RGH commanded this ambush party in Palestine which engaged an enemy patrol of twelve men. He wrote afterwards, 'We played Merry Andrew with a few of their cavalry and pinched some lances and brass stirrups, irons and bits besides a lot of other stuff which I had to hand in to HQ.' He was awarded an MC and the two sergeants, MMs. His father owned a farm at Bishopstone, near Shrivenham, which Robert took on after the War with his wife Edith, always known as 'Paddy', a VAD nurse whom he had met in Cairo.

1/1st RGH on the move along the Old Roman Road through the Sinai north of Bir-el-Abd following the victory at Romani in August 1916.

(*Above*) In December 1917 1/1st RGH and an Indian cavalry regiment escorted captured Turks into Jerusalem. Lieutenant Robert Wilson commanded the RGH escort and can just be seen on the far left of this photograph.

(*Below*) The horse lines of 1/1st RGH camped outside Aleppo. Only two English cavalry regiments fought the whole way from Egypt to Aleppo in Syria, 1/1st RGH and the Sherwood Rangers Yeomanry. The others in 5th Cavalry Division were from the British Indian Army. Between 19 September and 26 October 1918 the Division covered 500 miles and captured over 11,000 prisoners and 52 guns, while losing only 21 per cent of its horses, which caused General Allenby to comment, 'The 5th Division were as good horse-masters as fighters.'

(*Above*) On 18 Dec 1918 Tpr Edward Forrest of B Squadron 1/1st RGH spotted an enemy column retreating north and galloped alone to stop it. It surrendered, and he found he had captured an ammunition train consisting of thirty-seven wagons, four officers and 100 men. He was awarded a well deserved DCM.

(*Below*) The final cadre of 1/1st RGH to be demobilized, consisting of 8 officers and 19 other ranks, under the command of Colonel Turner, arrive at Gloucester Station on 15 August 1919 for an official welcome. 1/1st RGH were at Bileraman near Aleppo in Syria on 11 November 1918, and although the first demobilization party left on 13 January 1919, the closing day of the campaign for the Regiment was not until 24 June 1919.

Chapter 31

High Wood (1ˢᵗ, 8ᵗʰ & 10ᵗʰ Bns)

Ligh Wood lies on high ground with observation south, east and north-east, sitting between Delville Wood and Pozières. During the period from 20 July to mid-September six British divisions, 1ˢᵗ, 5ᵗʰ, 7ᵗʰ, 19ᵗʰ, 33ʳᵈ and 51ˢᵗ (Highland), took part in the fighting at High Wood. 1ˢᵗ, 8ᵗʰ and 10ᵗʰ Gloucesters were all involved at some stage.

20–22 July – 1ˢᵗ Gloucesters held the front line.

22 –26 July – 10ᵗʰ Gloucesters captured and held Point 17 south of Martinpuich, which gave the British observation over the German line. The Battalion was then withdrawn until 17 August.

22 July – 8ᵗʰ Gloucesters moved into the front line at Bazentin-le-Petit and attacked unsuccessfully position north of High Wood. The Battalion launched another attack, which failed on 30 July, and was then withdrawn.

17/18 August – 10ᵗʰ Gloucesters returned to the front and immediately provided bombing support to an unsuccessful attack on a line in front of Martinpuich during which the Battalion suffered 72 casualties.

19 August – 10ᵗʰ Gloucesters provided similar support to another unsuccessful attempt to take the line in front of Martinpuich by 1ˢᵗ R Berks and suffered another 72 casualties.

8 September – 1ˢᵗ Gloucesters, whose strength was now only 17 officers and 302 other ranks, launched an attack as part of 3ʳᵈ Brigade.

In 1969, over 50 years after the event, Donald Baxter, who commanded A Company, 1ˢᵗ Gloucesters wrote a letter describing the battle to the editor of the Regimental magazine, *The Back Badge*:

> I have just celebrated my golden wedding, and it brought home to me very forcibly the gallantry of the 'Gloucester Soldier'. I would not have been celebrating my golden wedding had it not been for their gallantry.
>   The order of battle was as follows:

The frontal attack on High Wood by the four companies of the Battalion, A Company (my company) on the left, B, C and D Companies on the right. The plan was a slow bombardment until 12 noon when the Battalion would jump out and begin the attack.

There were several incidents before the attack. We had to walk along a communication trench for about half-a-mile to the jumping-off trench. To my surprise and consternation when I started to walk up the trench, I found the Padre standing at the entrance, shaking hands with the men as they advanced and saying 'Good-bye, Boys'. If he had thought for six months he could not have done a worse thing for morale. The leading man of No 1 Platoon (and one of the original reservists left) said, 'Wow, we are going into some battle if the Padre says this.'

Having lined up in the jumping-off trench, the artillery fired short, and hit some of the men in the trench. Colonel Pagan got on to Brigade HQ and stopped the shelling of our own men.

As we waited for 12 noon, Private Alder, who was an original reservist and who had not particularly shone as a soldier, said to me, 'I wish to come with you as your orderly.' I was delighted to accept. The left flank of my company was in the air, but it was well known that there was a little nest outside High Wood of enemy machine guns and the artillery had orders to silence these guns. Unfortunately, during the operation they did not do this. The whole of my No 1 Platoon were casualties, including a fine young officer named Edwards, who had only been with us for 48 hours. As far as I can recollect, he came from 'Prince Edward's Horse'. The only instructions I gave my company were to run as fast as possible to the enemy line on the edge of the wood, as it was the safest place to be. The distance was approx. 150 yards. The other companies being on my right had a shorter distance. It was hard work running across 'No Man's Land' pitted with shell holes, so half way across I threw my rifle away and reached the first objective, the trench at the edge of the wood. Presumably we surprised the enemy, as I collected about 20 prisoners there. Up to then, the only casualties were No 1 Platoon. Here begins a real good scrap.

The soldiers were magnificent. When they saw I was being attacked, a voice on my right said, 'Leave him to me, I'll settle him.' Having gained the first objective I was crawling under a cavalry trench bridge when a wounded 'Hun' got up and clutched me by the throat; I managed to shake him off. The next moment, I suddenly saw Colonel Pagan staggering along in pain. He told me he had two spent bullets in his stomach. Looking around, I found my orderly was still with me, so I told him to help Colonel Pagan back to Battalion HQ. I was informed afterwards that the Colonel was in the Welch Lines and was cheered all along their lines. We gained our second and final objective, and fought off a counter-attack by the enemy.

Before starting the attack, I filled my water bottle with half whisky and half water. I was standing by the trench after the defeat of the counter-attack, when my water bottle was hit, which sent me to the ground. I thought a drink wold be a good idea, when I found a spent bullet had penetrated the bottle and it was empty! Just at that moment the CSM came up to me and, standing straight up, he gave a perfect salute and said, 'I beg to report, Sir, that I have killed my eleventh German with my revolver.'

We held on to this position until dusk, when I received a message from the Adjutant that I was to withdraw my troops to the jumping-off trench. In the early morning I assembled the whole Battalion, being the senior officer left. I found that myself (a captain) and 3 subalterns were the only officers left out of the whole battalion. This really was a soldier's battle. I cannot ever repay the debt to my own Company for the valour they displayed on that day.

After more than 50 years this is a remarkably accurate account of what must have been similar to many other battles in the Somme Offensive. According to the Battalion War Diary, the Battalion actually attacked with two companies in front (A and B Companies) and two in reserve. The attack was launched at 6.15 pm; the Battalion began the move up to the jumping-off trench at 12 noon. The shelling by our own artillery of the Gloucesters went on for about two hours before it was stopped. There was no officer by the name of Edwards killed or wounded; this was probably Second Lieutenant Alan Francis Brown, whose mother lived at Libertus Villas, St Marks, Cheltenham. At 7.40 pm Captain Baxter requested reinforcements to enable the company to hold the ground captured, but the reserve companies had lost too many men to artillery fire and so the two leading companies had to be withdrawn.

It was during this fighting that William Biddle, who was to become one of the most decorated NCOs in the whole Army, won his DCM. William had enlisted in the Regiment in March 1900 and joined 2nd Gloucesters in South Africa, where he was sentenced by a Court Martial to 84 days hard labour. Fourteen years later, by now in 1st Gloucesters, his disciplinary record was woeful, but he was about to prove that as a fighting soldier he was a huge asset. One of the most dangerous jobs in an infantry battalion during the War was Signals Sergeant, which he had become in November 1914. Communication from battalion headquarters both forward to the companies or back to brigade was by telephone or runner. The telephone wire was regularly cut by shellfire, and the signals sergeant would go out to repair it. By the time of High Wood he had already been Mentioned in Despatches in June 1915, awarded the MM in April 1916 and won the Bar to his MM in July 1916, on both latter occasions for repairing telephone wires under heavy shelling. He was wounded in August 1916 and the citation for his DCM states: 'He commenced to lay a telephone line but finding part of the enemy's trench still occupied, he collected four men and led an assault, capturing eight prisoners.'

C. A. Wilson[1] in his memoir wrote:

> At High Wood in September '16 he [Biddle] had discarded his rifle and gone on with a couple of Mills bombs, one in each pocket. During the battle he was intent on this repair work when he suddenly came face to face with a trench full of Germans and then followed something to which it is impossible to find a reasonable explanation: by threatening the Germans with his bombs he succeeded in marching about thirty of them back as prisoners. Some time after the High Wood show I was talking to Biddle about this and then he told me that he'd been very lucky to get away with it for one of our men had come up behind him when he was trying to persuade the Germans to give themselves up and wanted to shoot at them. Biddle told him to clear off and find some other Germans to kill if he wanted to, and this is what the man did.

Three officers of 1st Gloucesters were killed and 2 subsequently died of wounds. In addition to Colonel Pagan, 3 company commanders and 4 subalterns were wounded, 84 other ranks died and 125 were wounded. The Battalion was reduced to 4 officers and fewer than 100 other ranks. Patsy Pagan refused to be evacuated until the battalion was ordered to pull back. He was subsequently sent to hospital in London but got back to his beloved Battalion on 10 November. Among those killed was Sergeant B. J. Gray. He was the Sergeant of the Scout Section, in which he had done exceptional work and had been recommended for a commission.[2]

The next day, 9 September, 10th Gloucesters was attached to 3rd Brigade and only just got into position in time for an attack, which failed. Then, on 21 September, 10th Gloucesters took over the front line and discovered the German line opposite had been evacuated so took possession of it. High Wood was, at last, in Allied hands. On Christmas Eve 1916 10th Gloucesters' survivors held a service at High Wood and erected a wooden cross dedicated to their lost comrades. In 1927 the cross was retrieved and placed in Christ Church, Cheltenham, where it remains to this day.

Notes

1. C.A.Wilson, *Recollections of the 28th at War 1914–1918*
2. The Grays were a Regimental Family. B. J. Gray was the son of Beresford Gray, who was RSM of the 28th during the South African War and died at Ladysmith. Beresford's brother Robert rose through the ranks of the 28th to become RSM and then be commissioned Quartermaster in 1895. He, too, was at Ladysmith. Although he retired in 1910 he rejoined in 1914 and served as the Quartermaster of the Regimental Depot at Horfield Barracks. He must have made a lasting impression on many recruits. Robert's father, James, fought with the 28th in the Crimean War; he married one of Florence Nightingale's nurses. James was almost certainly the son of William Gray, who served in the 61st and whose Punjab Medal is on display in the Soldiers of Gloucestershire Museum.

Chapter 32

Guillemont and Morval (12ᵗʰ Bn)

A fter the War, five separate battles were identified as taking place in September 1916 as part of the Somme Offensive, although to the soldiers on the ground these distinctions were certainly not obvious. With the exception of 12ᵗʰ Gloucesters, the part the Gloucester battalions played in these five battles was limited; they spent much of the time either in reserve or out of the line completely, resting and absorbing reinforcements.

The Battle of Guillemont was the culmination of the fighting that had begun on 22 July. The Germans, occupying the village of Guillemont, had repulsed repeated British attacks but on 3 September 5ᵗʰ Division, which included 12ᵗʰ Gloucesters (*Bristol's Own*), succeeded against the odds. The 12ᵗʰ Gloucesters War Diary is succinct: 'S of GUILLEMONT 3ʳᵈ Sept –12 noon – Bn took part in general attack on German trenches carried out by XIVth and XVth Corps and the French. Final objectives taken.'

In his book ('Bristol's Own'. *The 12ᵗʰ Battalion Gloucestershire Regiment 1914– 1918*) Dean Marks provides a more detailed description:

The British barrage opened up at 8.30am and the attack began at midday. The men advanced behind a creeping barrage advancing at the rate of 50 yards per minute. They were instructed to keep within 25 yards of the landing shells! On high ground, above and to the right of the ground over which the two Companies attacked, was a German fortified position known as Falfemont Farm. In front of the position was a cliff above a chalk pit, directly overlooking the Battalion's objectives, on the edge of which were sited several machine guns. It was clearly realized that unless these positions were neutralized, the attack of 95ᵗʰ Brigade would be under severe threat. The problem was artillery or, more to the point, the lack of it . . . The threat represented by the existence of the Falfemont Farm positions was intended to have been eliminated before the attack of the 95ᵗʰ Brigade began. Due to the shortage of guns the French agreed to provide the necessary artillery support. And so the Falfemont Farm positions were attacked at 8.50am on the 3ʳᵈ by the 2ⁿᵈ KOSBs but the gallant attempt was an utter disaster. [Unbeknown to the KOSB, the French artillery was diverted to another task] . . . Falfemont Farm remained intact . . . The first objective for 12ᵗʰ Gloucester was a sunken lane followed by several dugouts in an embankment and a machine gun covering the dugouts. The initial obstacle to be dealt with was easily overcome and the dugouts 100 yards further on were found to be unoccupied. But off to the right was a lone machine gun, which did some damage. It had to be neutralized. A section of A Company, with Capt E. A. Robinson present, rushed it. Six pals, who had joined together in September 1914, were brought up against the gun at close quarters. They rushed it and were all killed in the space of a moment. Capt E. A. Robinson was hit in the chest and his trusty batman, Pte Percy Edwin Fisher, killed. The gun was put out of action but at a cost.

Percy Fisher was thirty-eight and before the War had been employed by Pleasance and Harper, Jewellers, of Wine Street, Bristol.

The second objective for 12th Gloucesters was the German line between Wedge Wood and the south of Guillemont Village, and this was taken without too much trouble. The third objective was the sunken lane running north from Wedge Wood toward Ginchy. The landmarks, after so much fighting, were not as clear as they are on the map, and C Company mistook Lenze Wood for Wedge Wood and went too far, whereupon they were caught by their own artillery fire. The War Diary records this shelling, but the entry has been crossed through. Dean Marks quotes Sergeant Norman Pegg[1] frequently:

It is the recollection of scenes witnessed at Guillemont which causes me to read, or listen to, with a deep sickening feeling some of the glib descriptive writing or public speaking, official and unofficial, which have from time to time thrust themselves on the people who have stayed at home. To the men who underwent the experience, a battle is not gay, glorious or frivolous, but devilish and murderous.

No Gloucester battalion took part in the capture of Ginchy on 9 September, another location fiercely defended by the Germans which could only be taken once Delville Wood and Guillemont were in British hands. This now cleared the way for the British to launch the next major offensive.

The Battle of Flers-Courcelette (15–22 September) was an attempt by Fourth Army, with eleven divisions, to achieve a major breakthrough. It saw the first use of tanks in battle. There were some minor successes, but the principal objectives of Lesbeoufs and Morval, from which the breakout could take place, were not captured. 1st, 10th and 12th Gloucesters were all awarded the Battle Honour 'Flers-Courcelette' but none played a significant part in the battle and were either in reserve or holding and occupying trenches. One of the tanks, however, 'Crème de

Menthe' (each was called after a French drink), was commanded by a Gloucester, Captain Arthur Inglis.[2] He was awarded an immediate DSO, the first for action in a tank:

> For leading 'C' Section tanks in C5 (Crème de Menthe) during the major Allied advance on the Somme, 15th September 1916. He advanced his tank in company with the 2nd Canadian Division, and, despite losing a wheel, Crème de Menthe led the way to the objective, clearing the German redoubt of depleted machine gun nests and what remained of the enemy garrison. Inglis returned in Crème de Menthe to Allied lines with a thoroughly disorientated captured German general, who would never forget his enforced ride to captivity over no man's land in the depths of a British land-ship.

Morval and Lesboeufs were now taken after an intense barrage of unprecedented ferocity, but the weather had deteriorated and a combination of tiredness and lack of reserves meant that this success could not be exploited. 1st, 10th and 12th Gloucesters were awarded the Battle Honour 'Morval'. 1st Gloucesters was in reserve and took no part; this was the end of its involvement in the Somme Offensive. 10th Gloucesters were at High Wood. 12th Gloucesters, despite reinforcements, was only 300-strong and was in reserve when the attack began at 12.35 pm on 25 September. Once the leading battalions had taken their objectives, it and 2nd KOSB moved through and captured part of Morval. The whole of 5th Division now left Fourth Army.

Notes

1. Norman Pegg DCM was born in New Jersey, USA and came to Britain in 1896, when he was three. When the *Titanic* sank in 1912, he was a junior reporter for *Berrow's Journal* in Worcester. Sent to do legwork on the disaster, he uncovered that a teenager, Kate Phillips, had run off with her boss, a married man, Henry Morley. He drowned, she was saved. Pegg enlisted in 12th Gloucesters (Bristol's Own) in September 1914 but appears to have remained a journalist for the *Bristol Evening News*, sending them the odd report.
2. Arthur McCulloch Inglis DSO (1884–1919) was born in India and educated at Cheltenham College. He was commissioned in 1906 into 2nd Gloucesters and was later ADC to the Governor of Gambia Colony in West Africa. He fought his tanks in subsequent battles but on the first day of the Battle of Amiens (9 August 1918) he was severely wounded. He was evacuated to the UK and died in his brother's nursing home in Cheltenham in May 1919; he is buried in St Mary's Churchyard at Prestbury.

Chapter 33

The End of the Somme Offensive at Ancre Heights and Ancre (8th & 13th Bns)

By late September the British had abandoned the aim of breaking through the German lines and merely wished to capture high ground from which to renew the offensive in 1917. Thiepval was on the German front line and had defied all attempts to capture it since 1 July. The Battle of Thiepval (26–28 September) was the first to be fought by the Reserve Army, shortly to become the Fifth Army, under General Hubert Gough. British successes earlier in September meant that it was now possible to attack from the flanks, and this led to success. The only Gloucester battalion that might have been involved was the Pioneer Battalion of 39th Division, 13th Gloucesters, but they were working on restoring and improving Chord Trench, which according to the Battalion War Diary was a reserve trench. In a letter to his father dated 2 October J. C. Procter wrote:[1]

> The work at present is very interesting. The wretched infantry have been having an awful time, and our men too, but to a lesser extent. This is more or less compensated by the fact that the division, an unlucky one up to now, has had two big successes both connected with redoubts to the east of the place which fell on my last day at home. This has bucked everyone up very much and it is pleasant to see the little batches of prisoners go past every day. These latter vary very much in quality, owing I expect to what unit they come from. The other day I saw some very sturdy ones. Yesterday 40 went past our camp of a very miserable description and woebegone to the last degree. Some were bent and bearded, others mere boys. All were covered with trench mud, and perfectly green in the face. Our barrages are so terrific now, that attacking has been a simple affair as far as the enemy infantry is concerned. They come out & put up their hands as soon as our first wave goes over in many cases. Some come over without any action taking place at all. Most of our casualties are shellfire at the moment, a rather healthy sign, I think . . . We have had a lot of Tanks past us lately. They come in the night or early morning and sneak into a wood nearby for the day. The more I see of them the more I like them, and whatever else they do, they buck the men up no end. Apart

from this, I think they are good things, shouldn't wonder if they're not money better spent than Zepps. If only we could invent one that would do 20, and leap 50 yards at a time when so inclined!

By the beginning of October German forces had been reorganized with reserves taken from the Verdun front. The German Air Service had been centralized and new fighter aircraft acquired, which gave them air superiority. September had been the worst month for German casualties in the whole Battle of the Somme; their losses in October were fewer. The weather was foul, and as the Germans were driven back they got closer to their logistic bases and re-supply became easier across ground that had not been fought over. For the British the reverse applied: re-supply became harder. The Battle of Transloy Ridges (1–18 October) was the last of the Somme battles to be fought by Fourth Army. The aim was to straighten out the line as far as the village of Eaucourt l'Abbaye, and the Flers line of defences as far as the village of Le Sars. Initially, some objectives were captured but by no means all. However, by 7 October most had been taken, and the next eleven days were spent creating a straighter front line. No Gloucester battalions were involved.

The Battle of Ancre Heights, which lasted for over forty days from 1 October, was fought to secure the whole of the Thiepval Ridge, in order to obtain observation over the upper River Ancre. This meant capturing the Schwaben Redoubt and the Stuff and Regina Trenches, which were so well defended that they had repeatedly blocked previous attempts to take the high ground. The weather got steadily worse and the start had to be delayed. The battle consisted of a series of large attacks on 1, 8, 21 and 25 October and 10/11 November, with smaller actions in between. Stuff Redoubt fell on 9 October, the last German position on Schwaben Redoubt on 14 October, and by 21 October the British had advanced 500yds. All that remained was a last German position in Regina Trench. Bad weather now forced the postponement of further action, until a surprise attack at midnight on 10/11 November by 4th Canadian Division took this remaining position.

8th and 13th Gloucesters were awarded the Battle Honour 'Ancre Heights'. 8th Gloucesters had spent August and September training and absorbing reinforcements, while occasionally going into the line. On 27 October General Sir Herbert Plumer, the Commander of Second Army, inspected a parade of 57 Brigade and presented Colonel Carton de Wiart with the ribbon for his Victoria Cross; it was customary for medal ribbons of gallantry awards to be presented at a parade in the field by a senior officer, while the medal itself was presented later at a formal investiture. Six days later, the Brigade was inspected by the King of the Belgians. Then, on 24 October, after much of the Ancre Heights had been captured, the Battalion went into the line east of Thiepval, where it was heavily shelled. Colonel Carton de Wiart was wounded again, but the expected counter-attack never materialized.

13th Gloucesters, the Pioneer Battalion of 39th Division, had been employed since August mainly on defence works near Beaumont Hamel, but it was back on the front line near Thiepval in early October. As the Schwaben Redoubt fell and then the Stuff Trench, the battalion constructed new communication trenches between old and new positions and strengthened the new front line, vital tasks to enable the British to defeat German counter-attacks. Typically the men worked through the night, with a platoon of the battalion allocated to a Royal Engineer Section, often under heavy shellfire, either digging or wiring.

All the previous battles fought by the Reserve Army, which had now become the Fifth Army, were preliminaries to this last major battle of the Somme offensive, the Battle of Ancre (13–18 November). It had originally been intended to launch it on 15 October as part of the Battle of Ancre Heights, but the weather and appalling conditions, deep mud, poor visibility and waterlogged roads forced it to be postponed repeatedly, and as a result the objectives were modified and less ambitious. Commentators vary in their assessment of the battle: 'A feat of arms vying with any recorded. The enemy was surprised and beaten' (Edmund Blunden). 'The objectives of the battle were not achieved, only in the marshy lowlands near the river were gains made, and these at great cost' (Commonwealth War Graves Commission). 'The attack was a relative success. Beaumont Hamel and Beaucourt were captured, but Serre and the northern part of the German line remained untouched' (J. Rickard in *History of War*). 'A limited success' is probably a fair summary.

Two Gloucester battalions, 8th and 13th, were awarded the Battle Honour 'Ancre'. The 8th Gloucesters War Diary for 18 November states: 'Formed up in Artillery formation preparatory to attack on W. outskirts of Grandcourt. 6.10am. Attack launched. First objective reached and carried . . . Casualties: 12 officers, 283 ORs.' 13th Gloucesters repaired the road from Hamel to St Pierre Divion as soon as the Division attacked the Hansa Line on 13 November. The next day, the Division, with 13th Gloucesters, left the Somme and by 20 November was at Ypres.

The Somme Offensive, planned as a battle of enormous proportions to end the war on the Western Front, failed on the first day and then became a battle of attrition. It seems unlikely that the sort of gains envisaged by the Allies were ever realistic, given that the German defences were so well constructed that the men occupying them could survive artillery barrages; and once these were lifted, it was a case of men protected only by cloth uniforms advancing against dug-in machine guns. Any assessment of the battle will always be concerned with casualties, which were horrendous and to twenty-first century thinking unbelievable. What is often overlooked is that the German casualties were just as terrible. The Allied casualties totalled 623,907: 419,654 were from Britain and its Empire of whom 95,675 died; 204,253 were French, of whom 50,756 died (these figures exclude the French losses at Verdun). The German casualties were about 465,000, of whom 164,055 died and about 38,000 were made prisoner, and these also exclude Verdun, which was a German failure. The major difference between the two sides was that the Allies had a far larger pool of manpower from which to draw.

One of the outcomes was that as early as September the Germans decided to build a new, shorter defensive line to the rear as a precaution, called by the British 'The Hindenburg Line', to which the Germans were forced to withdraw in the following March. During the four and a half months of the Somme Offensive the British were able to rest divisions for long periods. The Germans were seldom able to do this. For the British, what had been a largely volunteer Army with no fighting experience in July 1916 had become 'battle hardened' and much more skilled and effective. Conscription had been introduced by Parliament in January 1916 without which it would not have been possible to replace the losses on the Somme. Two other important developments had taken place: airpower had been shown to be significantly more valuable than had previously been thought, and tanks had been used for the first time. Although unreliable, tanks had demonstrated that with improvements they could overcome machine guns and wire obstacles while crossing trenches. On the other hand, the British reliance on road transport for logistic re-supply proved totally inadequate, particularly as the weather worsened and the roads became virtually impassable.

During the period 1 July to 19 November 1916, 1,813 members of the Gloucestershire Regiment died in France. Not all of these died on the Somme; some were involved in action elsewhere, particularly the 2/4th, 2/5th and 2/6th Battalions at Fromelles. Some succumbed to wounds received before 1 July, while others wounded on the Somme will have died after 19 November or back in England.

Note

1. Captain JC Procter MC was the Adjutant of 13th Gloucesters but was also a talented artist who produced some powerful sketches and drawings of life at the Front which are in the Soldiers of Gloucestershire Museum.

Part VII

OTHER FRONTS IN 1917

Chapter 34

7th Gloucesters at the Capture of Kut and Baghdad

In Mesopotamia, 1916 ended with Kut still in Turkish hands but the British Army far better organized and poised to recapture the town. Progress was slow, partly because of the rains; although the British had a numerical advantage of 20:1, the Turks were extremely well dug in. At least no one was now under any illusion about the Turks' fighting ability. It took two months of strenuous combat to clear the west bank of the River Tigris below Kut, during which 7th Gloucesters, like most of the battalions in 13th Divsion, suffered severely. Initially, the Battalion either manned lunettes (crescent-shaped defensive structures facing in at least two directions) and redoubts or provided working parties day and night to construct new trenches prior to an attack on 25 January. During this the Turkish trenches were captured and then lost to a counter-attack, but gradually, over the following few days, the British prevailed.

On 2/3 February the Battalion was again in action, establishing a line of picquet posts closer to the Tigris. The first three were successfully positioned, but when two platoons of C Company advanced to form the fourth, the Turks opened fire, and in a fierce action 3 officers and 16 other ranks were killed and 4 officers and 44 other ranks wounded. On 10 February the Battalion sent out a strong party to reconnoitre and capture an enemy trench that was believed to be lightly held. A Company advanced but 400yds from the objective were fired on from the 'unoccupied' trench and both flanks. They were forced to dig in until darkness before retiring but had suffered 73 casualties, of whom 49 died. The Company Commander, Lieutenant F. L. C. Hodson , was awarded an MC. Company Sergeant Major Dommett,[1] who organized parties to drive back the enemy and went back alone to personally lead stretcher parties and bring in the wounded, was awarded a DCM, and Corporal Sanders and Private T. Baker won Military Medals. One of the wounded may have been Harold Lusty.[2] When another attack was launched the next day, the enemy had withdrawn, and several of the dead Gloucesters were found close to the enemy's parapet.

On 17 February the British crossed the Shumran bend to the right of the Turkish forces, who, recognizing that they were overwhelmed, undertook a skilful retreat from Kut a week later, pursued by a flotilla of naval gunboats. 7th Gloucesters did not cross the Tigris until 25 February, when the Battalion was quickly in action against the Turkish rearguard. It advanced over 1,500yds of open ground under

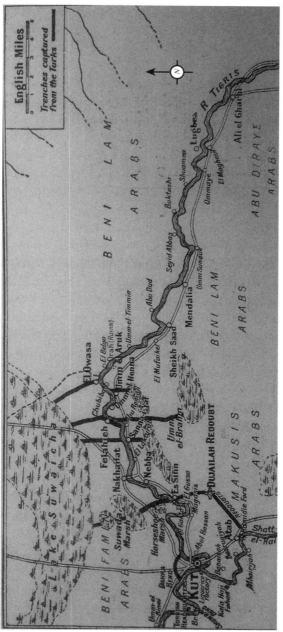

Map 20 Operations around Kut, 1916/17

heavy fire, took the position and captured 300 prisoners. Two days later, the *Basra*, a Turkish Red Crescent ship, was captured and three missing Gloucesters were recovered; three more were rescued by the cavalry on 1 March. Kut, which had been the scene of such a disaster, was at last back in British hands, and although the British and Battalion casualties appeared heavy, the Turkish losses in their repeated counter-attacks had been far heavier.

The British advance petered out after some 60 miles beyond Kut on 27 February, by which time, according to their War Diary, 7th Gloucesters 'rested in bivouac at Ruins. Iron rations were consumed.' The effective strength of the Battalion was now half what it should have been, 15 officers and 464 other ranks. The British were quickly re-supplied and the advance towards Baghdad began again on 5 March, with 7th Gloucesters marching 20 miles one day and 15 miles the next. Ctesiphon is one of the great cities of ancient Mesopotamia, 22 miles south of Baghdad on the junction of the Diyala River with the Tigris. Edward Bazeley in his memoir describes his first sight of it:

> Ten miles south of the river Diyala, we were startled to see on the horizon the majestic ruins of the great Palace of Ctesiphon, rising starkly above the flat plains of Mesopotamia to a height of 100 feet. Many of us would have welcomed a chance to examine in detail this remarkable ancient monument of mellow brown brick that has withstood the ferocity of sand-storms for 1,700 years; but now we had news that the Turks were making a stand, and we must prepare for battle. The position in which they had decided to defend Baghdad is one of great natural strength, for here the Diyala, 120 yards wide flows into the Tigris between high, steep cliffs. For us there were two alternatives: to march many miles upstream towards the Nahrwan Canal (constructed by Nebuchadnezzar) or to launch boats down a ramp where the Turks had recently destroyed the only bridge. In either case surprise was impossible.

On 9 March 30 men of 7th Gloucesters volunteered to row 38 Brigade across the Diyala, but the Turks resisted this assault. The British then moved the majority of the Corps north, and the Turks responded by following the British move on the other side of the Tigris. This left just one enemy regiment holding their former position which enabled the Battalion to cross the Diyala on 10 March and remain in action until it was dark. The Turks now withdrew to Baghdad, but the British, following up swiftly, took the city without a fight on 11 March; two days later, 7th Gloucesters 'searched the southern half of city on left flank of Tigris'.

On 19 March General Maude issued 'The Proclamation of Baghdad', which began:

> In the name of my King, and in the name of the peoples over whom he rules I address you as follows. Our military operations have as their object the defeat of the enemy, and the driving of him from these territories.

In order to complete this task, I am charged with absolute and supreme control of all regions in which British troops operate; but our armies do not come into your cities and lands as conquerors or enemies, but as liberators. Since the days of Halaka [Jewish Law] your city and your lands have been subject to the tyranny of strangers, your palaces have fallen into ruins, your gardens have sunk in desolation, and your forefathers and yourselves have groaned in bondage. Your sons have been carried off to wars not of your seeking, your wealth has been stripped from you by unjust men and squandered in distant places. Since the days of Midhat[3] the Turks have talked of reforms, yet do not the ruins of today testify the vanity of these promises? It is the wish not only of my King and his peoples, but it is also the wish of the great nations with whom he is in alliance, that you should prosper even as in the past, when your lands were fertile, when your ancestors gave to the world literature, science, and art, and when Baghdad city was one of the wonders of the world.[4]

The capture of Baghdad was not quite the victory that the Allies had hoped for. The Turks had escaped and remained a threat; there were 10,000 Turkish troops to the north and a further 15,000 on their way from Persia. To ensure Baghdad remained in British hands Maude needed to force the Ottoman Sixth Army north, prevent the Ottoman 8th Corps advancing from Persia, capture the rail yard at Samarrah and secure the dams around Baghdad to prevent the Turks breaking them and flooding the area.

7th Gloucesters began moving north on 24 March. Five days later, having marched about 30 miles, the Battalion deployed with 39 Brigade against a Turkish position on the Marl Plain north-east of Marah. The men advanced at 7.00 am over about 500yds of 'ground as flat as a sheet of glass' under heavy shellfire throughout and then assaulted and captured the enemy position together with some Turkish prisoners. They suffered 47 casualties, of whom 11 died. The next day, the Battalion withdrew to bivouac at Jedidah after a 6-hour march, as the War Diary records: 'The men being, in many instances, very much exhausted from fatigue, heat and a long dusty march. The Battalion is still in serge service dress and has had no protection from the sun which during the past fortnight has become exceedingly hot.' The Battalion strength was now 13 officers and 417 other ranks.

On 7 April 7th Gloucesters began moving north again and on the 11th reached Chaliya, where both 39th and 40th Brigade met a large enemy force moving down from Kifri. Initially, the Battalion took up a position in the firing line while 40th Brigade advanced, but on the order to retire the Battalion covered the withdrawal; in doing so six other ranks were killed, including Private Albert Timmins, who had won a DCM at Beit Aiessa on 21 March 1916.[5] In addition, there were nearly thirty cases of heat stroke evacuated to the Field Ambulance. For a few days the two brigades remained ready for further action, but patrols on the 14th found that the enemy had withdrawn.

Meanwhile, other British forces had advanced in different directions and on 21/22 April defeated the Turks at the Battle of Istabulat, forcing the enemy to abandon the Samarrah rail yard. With this, General Maude decided to halt; British casualties in the offensive are estimated to have been about 18,000, with a further 37,000 suffering sickness, principally heat stroke. He was concerned that his supply lines were being overextended. Baghdad was secure, and the risks of an Ottoman attack significantly reduced. 7th Gloucesters spent the rest of 1917 training, improving defences, going on leave and generally rebuilding their strength. In the eight months from 1 May to the end of December just 20 men of the Battalion died, mainly from disease, while its strength increased from 13 officers and 417 other ranks to 28 and 916. General Maude himself died of cholera in November.

Notes

1. Sidney Emmanuel Dommett (1877–1940) was born in Stroud. He enlisted in the Gloucesters in 1894 and served in the South African War with 1st Gloucesters. His CO refused to sanction his marriage in 1903 to Jane Pitts of Bristol until he could confirm that he had £5 in a savings bank and a clergyman or JP could confirm the good character of Jane Pitts, possibly because they already had a son, born in 1896. He had a poor disciplinary record and was still a private soldier at the outbreak of the Great War. Thereafter his promotion was rapid: he was Mentioned in Despatches at Gallipoli, where he was wounded, and became the RSM of 7th Gloucesters in April 1917. He was discharged in September 1919 and lived in Bristol. His first wife died of cancer in 1917, he remarried in 1921 and they lived in Stoneleigh Road, Bristol.
2. Harold Lusty (c.1887–1917) died on 15 February. He came from Springfield, Thrupp, Stroud, and it was a remark by his great-nephew to the author that was partly the inspiration for this book (*see* Introduction).
3. Midhat Pasha (1822–1883) was a leading Ottoman statesman appointed Governor of Baghdad in 1869. His three years in the City are recognised by some authorities as the most stable and secure period of Ottoman rule in the region.
4. In 2003 this same text, with minor amendments, was used by Colonel William Mayville, US Commander 173 Airborne Brigade in Kirkuk (Emma Sky, *The Unravelling – High Hopes and Missed Opportunities in Iraq*).
5. Albert Timmins DCM, who came from Birmingham, had been awarded the DCM; while 'acting as orderly to the Commanding Officer he continually carried messages across open ground under heavy machine gun and rifle fire and unhesitatingly exposed himself to ensure quick delivery of the messages.' He had also been Mentioned in Despatches.

Chapter 35

1/1st RGH and the Eventual Capture of Gaza

By January 1917 the British were ready to continue their advance north into Palestine from Egypt. The first task was to take Gaza. Prior to the battle, the 5th Mounted Brigade, which included 1/1st RGH, became part of the Imperial Mounted Division, which was part of the Desert Column under Lieutenant General Sir P. Chetwode. At the same time they received one Hotchkiss gun for training prior to the issue of twelve on 1 April.

At Gaza the plan was a repeat of action at Rafa, but on a larger scale. The town was to be captured from the south by 52nd (Lowland) Division. The Turkish garrison consisted of some 4,000 men, but they had much larger forces 10 to 20 miles to the north-east. Speed was therefore essential, and the two Mounted Divisions moved round the town to prevent any enemy reinforcements reaching it. 1/1st RGH, however, had been removed to support 2/4th Royal West Kents in 53rd Division and crossed the Wadi Ghuzze at daybreak under cover from the infantry. B Squadron acted as the advance guard with a patrol on the beach. About 2.00 pm the Royal West Kents advanced and 1/1st RGH conformed to their movements. When, later in the afternoon, the Battalion began to fall back it left a gap between itself and the RGH. At 5.00 pm the decision came to break off the battle when the British were on the verge of victory. The Commanding Officer of 1/1st RGH went forward and found D Squadron some distance in front of the infantry and under heavy fire. He ordered its reinforcement with the reserve squadron and told them to hold on until dusk, before retiring south of the *wadi*. This they did. Gaza had not been captured, and Sergeant William Nash, a Bristolian from Palmyra Road, Bedminster, had been killed. The Commander-in-Chief wrote in his despatches:

> The Gloucestershire Hussars, with a battalion and a section of 60pdrs, crossed the *wadi* near the sea coast, and for the remainder of the day succssfully carried out their role of working up the sand-hills to cover the left of 53rd Division, and to keep the enemy employed between the villages of Sheik Ahmed and Gaza.

Almost a month later, the Second Battle of Gaza began, by which time the town's defences had been strongly reinforced. Whilst the first battle of Gaza was nearly

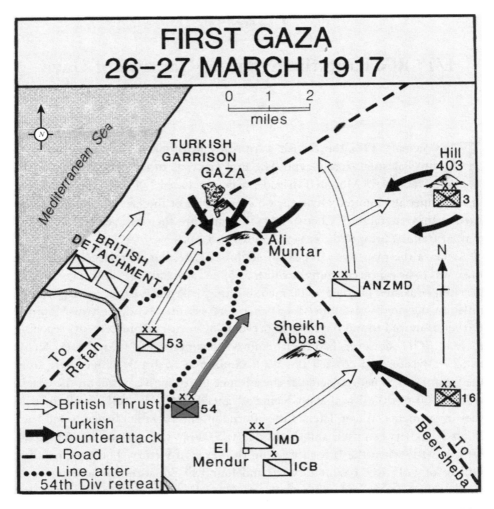

Map 21 First Battle of Gaza. 'British Detachment' is 2/4 Royal West Kents and 1/1ˢᵗ RGH.

a costly victory, the second was an even more costly total defeat. This time the British attack consisted of three infantry divisions, supported by two mounted divisions. The number of guns had been greatly increased and gas was used for the first time in the theatre, but the supply of shells and gas was inadequate. Generals Murray and Dobell intended it to be a Western Front-type battle, and it was, but not in the way they had hoped. There was no surprise, and every attempt by the infantry to reach the enemy's trenches failed. The strength of the defending entrenchments and supporting artillery completely repelled the attacking infantry

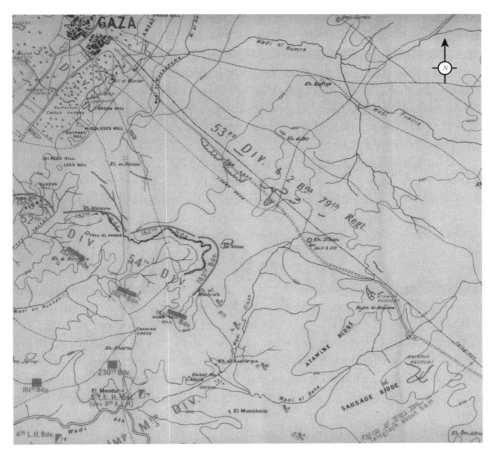

Map 22 Second Battle of Gaza

and casualties approached 50 per cent for only slight gains. On the evening of 19 April the British withdrew.

The role of the cavalry was to protect the right flank and 'contain' any reinforcements coming from Beersheba, some 40 miles south-east of Gaza. 5th Mounted Brigade, which included 1/1st RGH, were ordered to march to El Mendur on 17 April, turn down the Wadi-El-Sharia and clear out enemy from El Munkheilah to Khirbet-Um-Rijl. Large numbers of enemy were seen all day, and the regiment was shelled, but without loss. That evening it was relieved and remained in reserve. On 19 April the Brigade returned to the battle line with RGH on the right. It advanced up the Wadi al Baha under heavy fire, much of it coming from Sausage Ridge. Despite the enemy fire, the dismounted yeomanry reached and attacked along the Gaza to Beersheba road with little cover. By noon the line had swung to the left, leaving the right flank exposed, and the reserve squadron came forward to protect it. In the afternoon more cavalry reinforcements came forward, but although the enemy was checked, Sausage Ridge could not be cleared. By early evening orders were given for a complete withdrawal; three other ranks had died. One positive outcome of the battle, according to Anglesey, was that 'the Yeomanry at Second Gaza truly came into their own. From now onwards the Australian jeering ceased.' He quotes Trooper Ion Idriess, an Australian, in his book *Desert Column*, who said that the yeomanry 'fought in a way that has made the crowd accept them as brothers'.

A month later Lieutenant Robert Wilson[1] of the RGH wrote:[2] 'Cavalry warfare is about over I think . . . They can't say we haven't done our share – we have taken every inch of ground this side of Kantara . . . and I should think I have ridden on an average the whole distance at least three times – the infantry have simply followed us up.' Wilson was wrong: there was much more for the cavalry and 1/1st RGH to do in this campaign. There was a fear that the Turkish success would encourage them to go on to the offensive again, and the role of the mounted troops was to maintain observation of the enemy's outpost line and report any unusual activity. This was made more hazardous because the enemy enjoyed air superiority. There was a shortage of water, which meant none for washing, and in the hot weather the sick rate began to rise, often due to septic sores. There was little fighting, and on 8 May 1/1st RGH moved to a new camp on the coast at Tel-el-Marakeb, where the opportunity to swim in the sea and wash made a great difference to morale and general wellbeing. Towards the end of May the Regiment played a minor role in a successful operation to destroy the enemy railway line between Asluj and El Auja.

Meanwhile, the setbacks at Gaza led to the replacement of General Murray by General Edmund Allenby[3] in June 1917. He soon set about boosting morale, not least by visiting front line troops, something Murray rarely did. He moved his headquarters from Cairo to near Rafa and was ruthless in getting rid of any officer who he considered too old or unfit. At the same time he demanded and got three more squadrons of Bristol Fighter aircraft, two more infantry divisions with artillery, a further 5,000 men to bring his existing force up to strength and anti-aircraft guns. Robert Wilson described Allenby's first formal review of the RGH:[4]

> It meant a lot of spit and polish . . . We sat on our horses for three hours without moving an eyelash with drawn swords that ultimately weighed five tons . . . whilst he rode round. This was after three hours of forming up and getting into shape – a battle is a picnic compared to a show of this sort.

At least every officer, NCO and trooper knew he had a new commander, and one who would be inspirational in what followed.

Allenby decided to delay another attack until the end of October, while the additional forces arrived, air supremacy was established and the necessary logistic preparations were put in place. Meanwhile, he was determined to deceive the Turks as to his intentions. 1/1st RGH continued much as before, with the Regiment taking on the duties of the outpost line in turn with others. Five posts were thrown forward during the day and withdrawn at dusk behind the barbed wire, leaving six standing patrols out beyond the wire at night. Occasionally the Turks were observed harvesting barley and were dispersed with machine gun fire at a range of 3,000yds, but otherwise there was no action. There were opportunities for relaxation, and on 28 July the RGH held a regimental sports day which included wrestling on horseback, a V.C. race, a mule race for officers and a 'harem race'. When the RGH took over the outpost line duties in October, a patrol of 4 men was lured into a trap by a Bedouin and 3 were taken prisoner. Two days later, the regiment sent out two ambush parties under cover of darkness, one of which, commanded by Robert Wilson, engaged an enemy patrol of twelve men. He wrote on 19 October:

> I was in charge of a little ambush a few nights ago and played Merry Andrew with a few of their cavalry and pinched some lances and brass stirrups, irons and bits besides a lot of other stuff which I had to hand in to HQ. [This was followed up on 26 October by:] You will be very surprised to hear that I have been 'awarded the Military Cross' . . . I expect it is something to do with the ambush business I told you about in another letter – the Sergeant and Corporal I had with me both got Military Medals.[5]

Allenby's plan for taking Gaza was based on first capturing Beersheba. In preparation for this the mobility of the mounted troops was increased. Each man was issued with saddle-wallets, in which he carried three days' rations as well as a few clothes. Two nosebags on each saddle carried sufficient grain for two days, and a third day's forage was carried in wagons. To lighten the load, blankets and greatcoats were dispensed with. When 1/1st RGH moved into postion on the 23 October A Squadron clashed with an enemy squadron, pushed it back and made good the El Buggar ridge. A troop of A Squadron then moved to occupy Hill 720, where it was charged by enemy cavalry and forced to retire, losing one man, whose horse fell; he was taken prisoner. D Squadron, who were in reserve, then moved to support A Squadron and occupied Hill 720. B Squadron, meanwhile, made good Hill 630, with the enemy retiring, but the Berkeley troop had a fierce battle against an enemy squadron, holding on until the Warwickshire Yeomanry arrived in support. Later, B Squadron was shelled and five men were wounded. The fighting

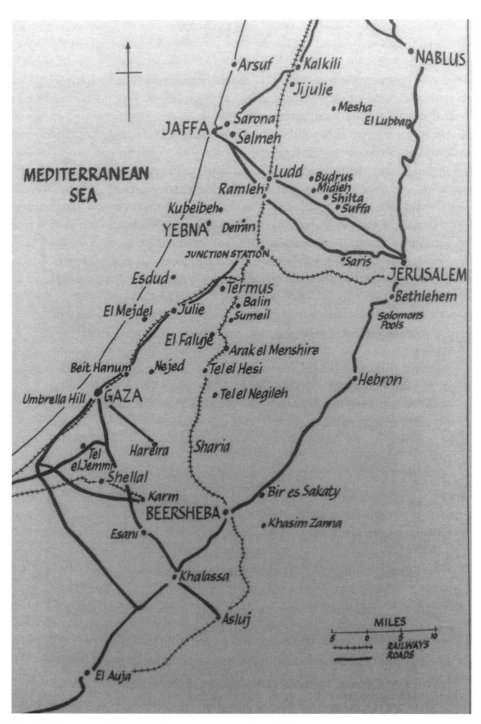

Map 23 Capture of Gaza and Pursuit to Jerusalem, 1917

was not over, but eventually the outpost line was established and handed over to the Warwickshire Yeomanry.

Allenby intended to make the Turks expect an assault from the sea by making enquiries in Cyprus about supplies for a substantial force, as well as sham preparations for a coastal landing. This convinced the Turks that the attack on Beersheba on 31 October, which was completely successful, was merely a more comprehensive reconnaisance, when in fact its capture was Stage 1 in the Third Battle of Gaza. The RGH were part of the Corps Reserve and, had it not been for two Turkish aeroplanes attacking the brigade transport column towards dusk, would have suffered no casualties.

Prior to 31 October Gaza was shelled, including by naval gunfire, in what was the heaviest bombardment carried out by the British outside the Western Front throughout the war. 1/1ˢᵗ RGH was under the Anzac Mounted Division, who were protecting the British right flank. On 4 November, when the RGH had just handed over their section of the outpost line to the Worcestershire Yeomanry, the Turks counter-attacked and 1/1ˢᵗ RGH returned at the gallop to relieve the situation. Two officers and 12 other ranks were wounded, 2 of whom died. When XXI Corps attacked Gaza itself on 7 November they found the enemy had evacuated the city during the previous night.

Allenby's original plan was to have the cavalry fresh for a decisive pursuit, but this was no longer possible. Of the eleven brigades of the Desert Mounted Corps only six were available for the exploitation, and none of these was fresh after a week of fighting and marching. A pursuit, nevertheless, began. The initial strategic obective was Junction Station, since if this could be taken the way would be open to Jerusalem. The first action was at Huj, where the RGH was in reserve, while two squadrons of the Warwicks and one of the Worcesters took the Turkish position in an unstoppable charge, although 75 of the 170 who took part were killed or wounded. When the Turks tried to mount a counter-attack, however, this was stopped by a section of RGH machine guns under Captain Herbert.[6] He dismounted and turned the Turkish machine guns on the counter-attack. He was killed four days later, on 12 November.

In his diary Tim Cripps records:[7]

9 November – I am sitting on a stone grinding floor in a village in a valley (Huj). It is mid-day and the horses have not been watered for thirty-six hours, poor brutes; we are waiting our turn. They haven't had water oftener than that for three or four days. We left Beersheba three nights ago and marched out at 1.30 am, and got to where the fight was going on at dawn and had a harassing day, though no actual fighting . . . Lost our way and the show fizzled out. It was an impossibility in the

dark anyhow, so just as well. Had an awful night at Sheria. Water very scarce – thousands trying to water – and eventually each Squadron got parted and lost. By 12.30 I had watered, and after wandering about a bit I pegged down where we were, slept in my saddle, and found the Regiment in the morning.

Notes

1. Robert Henry Wilson (1894–1980) was born in Shrivenham, where his father farmed. He first joined the Wiltshire Yeomanry but was commissioned into the RGH, whom he joined in June 1916 in Egypt. After the War he returned to the family home, Prebendal Farm at Bishopstone, near Swindon. Helen D. Millgate has edited and published his recollections and letters in *Palestine 1917*.
2. Robert Wilson, *Palestine 1917* (ed. Helen D. Millgate).
3. Edmund Henry Hynman Allenby GCB, GCMG, GCVO (1861–1936) had been commissioned into the 6th Inniskilling Dragoons. He fought in the South African War and was nicknamed 'The Bull' due to his size and violent temper. He commanded the Cavalry Division in the B.E.F., and, when the B.E.F. was expanded he led the Cavalry Corps. He then commanded V Corps and subsequently Third Army but lost Haig's confidence at the Battle of Arras and was replaced. He was surprised to find himself sent to command the Egyptian Expeditionary Force, but it was an inspired selection. After the War he became Viscount Allenby and was High Commissioner for Egypt and Sudan until he retired in 1926. His only son was killed on the Western Front.
4. Wilson, op. cit.
5. Ibid.
6. Captain the Hon Elydir John Bernard Herbert JP (1881–1917) was the son and heir of Major General Ivor Herbert, 1st Baron Treowen, and the Lady Treowen of Llanarth Court, Raglan, Monmouthshire. A copy of the action, painted by Lucy Kemp-Welch, hangs in the Soldiers of Gloucestershire Museum. Prior to the War he was a barrister at the Inner Temple.
7. Frank Fox, *The Royal Gloucestershire Hussars Yeomanry 1898–1922*.

Chapter 36

1/1st RGH in the Pursuit to Jerusalem

The Turks retreated north, but it became apparent that they were going to try and make a stand to cover the Jerusalem branch line connecting to the main railway north. On 10 November 1/1st RGH was ordered to Arak-el-Menshiye, where an enemy counter-attack was threatened, but this did not develop in any strength. The next day, although a large number of sick men and horses were evacuated, the pursuit went on. At 6.30 am on 12 November 5th Mounted Brigade assembled at Arak Station, and the Regiment formed the advance guard with orders to march via Summeil on Balin. It occupied a hill to the north of Balin, from where a very large number of men could be seen advancing. More enemy were detraining from El Tine station, and the Worcestershire Yeomanry, less a squadron, came up in support. The enemy were engaged by the Honourable Artillery Company (HAC) guns, attached to the Regiment, and by the machine guns, but this did not impede the Turkish progress significantly and some fierce fighting developed.

What happened next is described in *The Diary of a Yeomanry M.O.* by Captain O. Teichman DSO, MC, RAMC, the Medical Officer of the Worcestershire Yeomanry:

Our regimental dressing-station was established in a stone-walled camel-yard in the highest part of the village and soon contained many wounded. After a time we noticed that all troops were coming down from the northern slopes and were streaming away to the north-east. From our position in the village we at the dressing-station could see through our glasses considerable numbers of the enemy detraining at El Tine station, and realized that very strong reinforcements were coming up against us. This seemed to be the great danger, as we, a weak brigade, were ahead of our main body, while the Turks, with a working railway behind them, could bring up large reinforcements and guns at short notice. Our battery shelled these reinforcements from the north of Balin, but were completely outgunned by the enemy's heavy artillery. On one occasion our HAC battery galloped into the open to the left of the hills, and came into action in full view of the enemy.

After being busy in our dressing-station for some time we came to see how things were going, and were horrified to see strange-looking turbaned troops coming down over the ridge, which a short time ago had been occupied by our yeomen. In the distance we could see our men retreating on the right. The enemy, who were beginning to descend the steep declivity, were only some 300yds away. Luckily we had kept the horses on which the wounded had been brought in, so, realising that escape was a matter of seconds, we hastily mounted all our casualties and galloped them out of the rear of the yard. There were, however, not enough horses to go round, and some of us had to escape on foot. Some horses were shot and came down, but luckily all the wounded managed to escape after galloping about two miles, the horses bearing the serious casualties being led by men who were slightly wounded. This was an occasion when we profited from the many practices and competitions we had carried out in carrying wounded out of action by various methods. Some of us who had no horse to ride had a strenuous and exciting time on foot. As we looked back we could see that some Turkish cavalry were following the infantry, and we knew that when the former got to the bottom of the declivity and were able to gallop they would easily catch us up. As we ran we felt that we were under heavy rifle fire, and more horses were hit. After running about a mile two of us came across a couple of riderless horses, mounted and managed to gain the crest of the hill held by our own men and comparative safety. There were some fine rescues that day.

Before the action had commenced in the morning a troop of the Gloucester Yeomanry, with a Hotchkiss gun, had reconnoitred near El Tine station, and taking cover behind a thick cactus hedge, had watched the enemy detraining. While so engaged a large Turkish staff motor-car containing two Turkish generals had passed within about 50yds of the yeomen's hiding place, and the latter had riddled car and Generals with their Hotchkiss gun. Needless to say, after this performance the yeomen rejoined their regiment as fast as possible.

The RGH had 7 killed and 13 wounded in the action.

The next day, 13 November, the Action at El Mughar, which Allenby described as a 'fine feat of arms' but did not involve the 5th Mounted Brigade, meant that the British were now only 5 miles from Junction Station, which they took the next day. These were exciting times for the cavalry, as Allenby writes: 'If Qatia was the nadir of the yeomanry's performance in the campaign, El Mughar nearly reached the zenith, with Huj, perhaps half way between. El Mughar was a model of what could be achieved by cavalry charging in extended formation, its objectives pointed out on the ground supported by both artillery and machine gun fire.'

Algar Howard[1] was one of the few officers to serve with 1/1st RGH throughout the Great War, rising to the rank of major, and was awarded the MC in Palestine. He kept a diary, which is in private hands but is an invaluable source of information about the Regiment. 1/1st RGH had only played a supporting role at Huj and El Mughar but their time would come. In the meantime, the routine needed to continue, and in his diary Algar Howard writes:[2]

November 13 – Horses are nearly done [watering]. Men hungry and tired but cheerful as usual. Half rations yesterday, none today. Open, rolling country, rather hot. Flies bad round the villages. A yeoman observed he couldn't see 'why the Bible made such a rattle about this country'. I haven't seen my feet for days and have not had my clothes off for a week.

November 15 – We spent all day yesterday watering ninety horses. Only one bucket apiece. The night before last they had their first watering for 56 hours. Horses have gone for three days without water. It is a wonderful sight to march along a line the enemy has retired upon. Dead men, aeroplanes, burnt guns, ammunition lying about.

Having taken the Junction, Allenby's next objective was Jerusalem. Jaffa surrendered, without a fight, on 16 November, after Ramleh and Ludd had been taken the previous day. The mounted troops had been marching and fighting continuously since 31 October, had advanced about 75 miles as the crow flies, and, despite the constant struggle for water, two major actions had been fought. Re-supply was a constraint; the railway was being pushed forward as rapidly as possible and every opportunity to land stores on the coast was being taken, but this was dependent on the weather. The Turks were split in two, and the nearest line where the two halves could link up was from Tul Keram to Nablus. Allenby, while recognizing that a pause was necessary, judged that he needed, if possible, to maintain momentum while the Turks were disorganized and demoralized. Advancing across the Philistine Plain was one thing, however. Quite another was the route through the Judean Hills which the British faced to reach Jerusalem. There was only one good road which traversed the hills from north to south, from Nablus to Jerusalem. The remaining 'roads' were little more than goat tracks through narrow defiles dominated by the hill fort of Nebi Samwil (the Tomb of Samuel), a strongly held position and known as 'The Key to Jerusalem'. The Judean Hills surrounding Jerusalem had prevented Napoleon, the Crusaders, the Romans and others from reaching the Holy City, but the British pressed on. To add to their difficulties, the winter rains were imminent and most of the men were in summer kit. This was a foul piece of country: roadless, rocky hills with steep ravines which could suddenly become raging torrents filling the valley bottoms with thick black mud. The supply problems were exacerbated by the difficulties faced by the camels, who often fell and broke their legs. The situation was saved by acquiring donkeys, known to the troops as 'Little White Mice'; by mid–August every regiment had been issued with 22 donkeys.

The RGH did not take part in the direct assault and capture of Nebi Samwil, which fell on 23 November. The Regiment was replaced in 5ᵗʰ Mounted Brigade by the 10ᵗʰ Australian Light Horse, as Allenby wished Australian forces to be involved in the capture of Jerusalem. The Regiment did, however, play a vital role in repelling the Turkish counter-attacks as they tried to recapture the high ground. On 16 November 1/1ˢᵗ RGH moved to the banks of the Wadi Sukarier, 15 miles north of Askalon, and took up the observation line Termus to Tine to Kezaze. The next day, the Regiment was attached to XXI Corps but its task remained substantially unchanged. Then, on 28 November, the Regiment less one squadron moved as part of 3ʳᵈ Mounted Brigade to El Burj. Here it prepared for dismounted action, sending the horses back to Deiran; El Burj lay on the road from Jaffa (modern Tel Aviv) to Jerusalem. The Turks were desperately trying to drive the British off the high ground north and north-east of Jaffa. About 1.00 am on 1 December the Turks attacked the 3ʳᵈ Australian Light Horse Brigade, and 1/1ˢᵗ RGH found itself in fierce fighting. Had El Burj fallen to the Turks, the British would have lost the road from Berfilya. The left flank of the British advance on Jerusalem would have been exposed and the enemy would have been able to site their guns so as to enfilade the Jaffa–Jerusalem road, thus denying the supply of rations, materiel, etc. An infantry company arrived as reinforcement, but the Turkish attacks continued unsuccessfully until dawn, when they found it impossible to retreat. Over 100 were taken prisoner plus 19 wounded, and 200 bodies were found in front of the ALH, 1/1ˢᵗ RGH and 4ᵗʰ Bn Royal Scots Fusiliers. The Turks continued to shell the position during the day, and that evening 1/1ˢᵗ RGH was withdrawn to the support line. One officer and two other ranks had been killed, and two wounded.

Although Nebi Samwil had been taken, the British were unable to continue immediately and capture Jerusalem. A pause was now essential because the British XXI Corps was exhausted and needed to be replaced. Supplies of ammunition, food and fodder were extremely short, and the men and animals were wet, cold and becoming casualties. The lines of communication, however, had been so improved that it was now possible for XX Corps to relieve XXI Corps and continue the action, and this was completed by 2 December. On the evening of 8 December the Turks withdrew from Jerusalem, and the city surrendered the next day. Out of respect for its status as a Holy City, important to Judaism, Christianity and Islam, Allenby dismounted and entered Jerusalem on foot on 11 December.

Notes

1. Sir Algar Henry Stafford Howard KCB, KCVO, MC, TD (1880–1970) from Thornbury transferred to the RGH from the Carmarthen Militia Artillery in 1908 and was mobilized in 1914. He had joined the College of Heralds in 1911, where he subsequently had a distinguished career, becoming Garter Principal King of Arms in 1944. The records of the College of Arms were stored at Thornbury Castle during the Second World War.
2. Frank Fox, *The Royal Gloucestershire Hussars Yeomanry 1898–1922*.

Chapter 37

A Quiet Year in Macedonia for 2nd and 9th Gloucesters

Turning to the Balkans, the situation on the Salonika Front appeared to have been changed by the fall of Monastir in November 1916 and the prospect of Bulgaria ordering a ceasefire; but this didn't happen. The first four months of the new year saw little change, except that the Allied Army of the Orient, as the force was called (although it wasn't drawn from the Orient or fighting there), had grown to 24 divisions: 7 British, 6 French, 6 Serbian, 3 Greek and 1 Italian, together with two Russian Brigades, the army thus contaiing representatives of six of the ten Allies.[1] It must have been a challenging command, with plenty of opportunity for misunderstanding in so many different languages. The Serbian Army included the only British woman officially to serve as a soldier in the First World War.[2]

Greece was only informally part of the Alliance. There were two main factors dictating Greek behaviour. The first was an ancient enmity with Turkey which influenced most of her actions. The second was an internal political division: on one side were the monarchists, who desired a neutral role for Greece although some preferred an alliance with Germany, as King Constantine was married to the Kaiser's sister. They were opposed by the nationalists, led by Eleftherios Venizelos, a charismatic and influential personality who had grand notions of Greek expansion and looked to the parliamentary democracies of France and Britain as role models for good governance. This mattered because Salonika, through which all supplies and reinforcements came, was in Greece. In a letter home dated 7 January George Power wrote: 'Goodness only knows what Greece is going to do. Without knowing anything of the inside of the show, the allied action seems rather provocative.' Two days later he wrote: 'Things seem to have settled down here as far as Greece is concerned. I don't know that, even now, anyone will trust the devils further than they can throw them.' Eventually, in June, King Constantine went into exile and his son Alexander became king. The new government immediately declared war on the Central Powers.

Meanwhile, the British faced the Bulgarian Second Army from the mouth of the River Struma along the Tahinos–Butkova–Doiran lakes to the River Vardar, a distance of about 90 miles. This meant that there was little opportunity to take battalions out of the line or from close reserve, and their endurance was further tested by the winter weather and high rainfall that made re-supply over the mountain roads extremely difficult. The 2nd Gloucesters' War Diary reveals that on almost every day over the three months from January to the end of March the Battalion was employed on 'work on Battalion defences'. This monotony was relieved on 14 January, when D Company 'in conjunction with yeomanry and cyclists occupied Beglik Mah and held it all day with no opposition', and on 18 March, when 2nd Gloucesters beat the Lovat Scouts 15-8 in a rugby match. In addition, there was some occasional contact with the enemy. The other diversion was described by George Power in one of his letters:

> I am seized with grave misgivings about the hearts of my officers here! A tremendous entente between the 1st Canadian Hospital and M.G.C. [Machine Gun Corps] has sprung up. Certainly they are charming people and were awfully kind to us at Christmas. The amount of work those girls get through is really wonderful and yet they are always cheery. [A month later he reported:] One of my subalterns has gone and got himself engaged to one of the sisters at the hospital. They seem very happy. He walks five miles in the rain regularly every evening when his work is done to see her.

By contrast, 9th Gloucesters ran an extremely active patrolling programme at night. In January the Battalion sent out eighteen patrols, generally of an officer and about eight men. When they identified enemy activity they called for artillery fire on their return. On 31 January the Battalion mounted a raid which drove the enemy from their position; there were no British casualties. During February there was less patrolling and more work on defences. A far less successful raid was mounted on 6 March, during which the Battalion suffered 12 casualties, 5 of whom died.

The main fighting in the spring took place around Lake Doiran, when the British attacked and gained a considerable amount of ground, although 9th Gloucesters' part in this was unsuccessful. The First Battle of Doiran in 1917 took place from 25 April to 7 May. 9th Gloucesters was one of the battalions ordered to launch an assault at the Jumeaux Ravine. The Battalion had just arrived at the assembly point at 9.05 pm when the enemy put down a heavy barrage of high explosive. 11th Worcesters suffered severe casualties and first A Company, under Captain Fawcett, was sent to reinforce them; but they also took heavy casualties, so B Company, under Captain Griffiths, was despatched as well. At 5.15 am he reported that the position was strongly held by the enemy and his Company had great difficulty in deploying from Ravine XI, which they were holding pending receipt of further orders, owing to heavy rifle and machine gun fire. It was now getting light and at

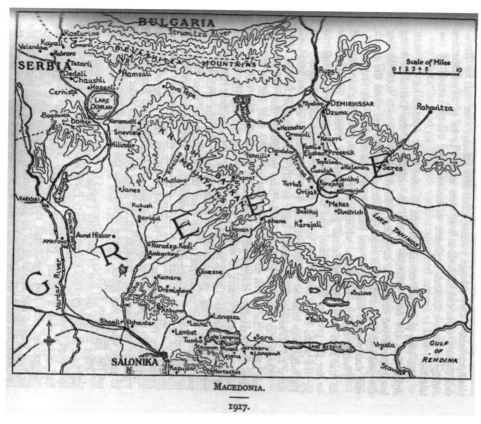

Map 24 Macedonia, 1917

4.35 am he was ordered to retire to the Trench Line, which they reached at 5.00 am. Stretcher-bearers went out without arms or equipment to endeavour to bring in the wounded. That evening, rifle fire broke out and it was reported that the enemy was attacking an adjacent battalion; B Company was ordered forward to support it. Captain Walter Griffiths, who came from Somerset Square in Redcliffe, Bristol and had a BSc from Bristol University, was about to lead his Company out when he was killed. He had been commissioned into the Regiment in October 1914.

After criticism from High Command, a further unsuccessful breakthrough was attempted on 8/9 May 1917, the Second Battle of Doiran. 9th Gloucesters was in reserve to 77th Infantry Brigade and at its Assembly Position on Hampshire Ridge Camp at 11.15 pm. At midnight the Battalion was ordered to support 10th Black Watch, who were preparing to attack through 12th Argyll and Sutherland Highlanders, but before this could happen the enemy had counter-attacked and retaken the latter's position. At 2.00 am a three-company attack was ordered, with 12th Argyll and Sutherland Highlanders on the left and two companies of 9th Gloucesters on their right, protected by bombers and Lewis machine guns. The Highlanders were not able to reorganize in sufficient time, so I Company, Royal Scots Fusiliers was substituted, and this caused the attack to be delayed until 5.50 am, by which time it was light. It never really got going due to machine gun fire from both flanks, and soon the assaulting troops retired. 9th Gloucesters had suffered 65 casualties, 15 of whom died; nothing had been achieved.

Meanwhile, life in 2nd Gloucesters continued much as before, although now it was much warmer, and malaria, spread by mosquitoes, became almost more of a hazard than the Bulgarians. The Battalion trained, winning the Divisional Wiring Competition, played sport, patrolled, and occasionally mounted raids that were quite exciting and sometimes led to the capture of prisoners. In mid-October 1917 a major raid on Homondos involving 2nd Gloucesters was ordered. The Battalion, together with 10th Hampshires, the Lovat Scouts and a section of 82nd Machine Gun Company, was divided into two columns. The aim was to kill or capture the garrisons in three villages, Sal Mahale, Kispeki and Ada, which formed the enemy outpost line; the Gloucesters were in Column A. At 10.00 pm on 24 October they set out and initially made good progress, but then the ground became very difficult, with numerous ditches and thick undergrowth which made keeping in touch in the dark almost impossible. At 5.00 am the leading company made contact with the enemy outside Ada, but an attempt to rush the post was hampered by effective supporting fire from other enemy posts. Nevertheless, Ada was taken at about 7.15 am, but by then the majority of the Kispeki and Ada garrisons had withdrawn. Column A began to withdraw at 8.50 am and they were back in their own lines by 12.30 pm. One officer had been wounded, 5 other ranks killed and 22 wounded.

In effect, 1917 in Macedonia ended as it had begun. The troops were probably still being referred to as 'The Gardeners of Salonika' as Georges Clemenceau had christened them, due to their reluctance to break out from that city. All this would change dramatically in 1918. One change took place in December, when Alexander Craven Vicary, whom we first met as Adjutant of 2nd Gloucesters in 1914, took over command of the Battalion. He was the owner of The Sikh, the horse he was still riding.

Notes

1. At the beginning of 1917 the Alliance consisted of the French, British and Russian Empires and Italy, Japan, Belgium, Serbia, Montenegro and Romania; the USA joined in April 1917.
2. Flora Sandes (1876–1956) had travelled to Serbia in August 1914 to join the Serbian Red Cross. She was separated from her unit during a difficult retreat and enlisted in the Serbian Army. She rose to the rank of corporal but was wounded by a grenade in hand-to-hand fighting. She ran a hospital, was promoted to sergeant major and commissioned after the War.

Part VIII

THE WESTERN FRONT IN 1917

Chapter 38

Winter on the Western Front and the Advance to the Hindenburg Line

Back on the Western Front, the winter of 1916/17 was one of the coldest on record. The gains made at such huge cost needed to be held, so 1st, 1/4th, 1/6th, 8th and 12th Gloucesters remained in and out of the Somme trenches. When out of the front line, several of the battalions spent time in tents at Mametz Wood, a pestilent spot in bitter weather and soon knee-deep in mud. Here they spent the days road-making, returning each evening with sodden clothes to cold, clammy tents – a real test of grit, pluck and humour. When their turn came to occupy the front line, the trenches were only reached after a long trek either above ground or through communication trenches full of deep, sticky mud which were little more than man-traps. Men who attempted the latter route often became stuck in the mud and had to be pulled out, sometimes leaving their gumboots behind.

In November 61st Division was transferred from First to Fifth Army, and so 2/4th, 2/5th and 2/6th Gloucesters joined the others in the Somme area. A. F. Barnes described the horror:

> The contrast between the sectors in front of Laventie and the Somme crater fields was striking. Here were primitive conditions – men clinging to shell holes, mud deep enough to submerge a gun team and limber, masses of unburied dead strewn over the battle fields; no sign of organized trenches joined up to one another – and, last, but by no means least in importance, no landmarks anywhere. The whole scene was one bleak wilderness of death.

The routine continued for much of the winter. Every battalion managed to hold some sort of Christmas festivities, and these were generally supplemented by food parcels from families and friends in England. The postal service to and from the Western Front was excellent. Meanwhile, reinforcements arrived. During November 1917 8th Gloucesters received 236 other ranks reinforcements, just over a quarter of their full strength. All needed to be absorbed into platoons and trained, and this dominated activity.

Charlie Wilson,[1] who was a Company Quartermaster Sergeant (CQMS) wrote in his 'Recollections':

> The normal routine for the C.Q.M.S.s was to draw the rations and divide them up for platoons in proportion to their strengths. The meat, milk, butter and jam would all be put in tins but the tea and sugar was issued loose and used to be put into clean sandbags – a horrible arrangement because one got bits of sandbag in one's tea. The mail too would be sorted out into platoons at the Ration Stand and we would be given orders for the time of parade for taking rations up to the companies. This would be fixed to suit various conditions, one of which would be the avoidance of the enemy's regular shelling periods. How fortunate it was that the German was so regular in his habits! He would 'strafe' at fixed times with the greatest regularity. Having arrived at the Ration Point we would hand over the rations and mail – and sometimes hot-food containers. But often there would be a hitch in the proceedings and the platoon rations would get held up. Meantime the regimental transport and the C.Q.M.S.s would have departed and one would be left with a lonely trudge back on one's own. During the day there were certain routine things for a C.Q.M.S to do such as preparing Acquittance Rolls for paying-out when the companies came out of the line. Then there were all the problems connected with men's pay such as Separation Allowances for men's wives, etc; 'Boards' on losses 'due to enemy action' and such like.

In October 1916 5th Division, which included 12th Gloucesters, had moved to Béthune, where the situation remained comparatively quiet for the Battalion over the next six months. On 25 February 1917 Colonel Archer-Shee, who had commanded the Battalion since July 1915 and remained a Member of Parliament, resigned. He had found that commanding the battalion whilst carrying out his parliamentary duties was too much, but the experience he had gained must surely have brought a touch of realism to the House of Commons when he spoke there. His successor was Lieutenant Colonel Robert Rawson.[2]

39th Division, including 13th Gloucesters, moved north to the Ypres Sector, and for the first few months of 1917 the Battalion constructed and improved trenches and carried out other defence work in the divisional area. There was a trickle of casualties from shelling or sniping.

By March there were rumours that the Germans were about to withdraw, and on 12 March 1/5th Gloucesters War Diary records: 'Weather very good and dry. In the evening many fires could be observed in front but still no signs of an enemy retreat; can't be long delayed now!' It wasn't: on 16 March the Germans began their retreat to the Hindenburg Line. The Allies' sacrifice on the Somme had not been entirely in vain. German losses had been so great that they needed to move to positions that could be held with fewer troops. Initial impressions were deceptive, however; although the Germans were giving up ground they were moving to a stronger position. The new German doctrine was to occupy the front line with the minimum of force but with counter-attack divisions just beyond the range of the Allied artillery. The Allies were to discover these new tactics in the future. Their immediate task was to occupy the ground vacated.

1/5th Gloucesters raided La Maisonette on 17 March and got quickly into the German trenches; patrols pushed forward into and through the buildings of the village. By the evening it had reached the Péronne–Éterpigny road, finding everywhere that the Germans had gone. The War Diary records: 'We were the first Battalion in the Brigade and all divisions in 3rd Corps to discover the enemy retreat and follow up.' It moved to Peronne three days later and found hardly a house left standing and many still burning. The Battalion spent the next two days extinguishing fires and clearing the streets of bricks and rubbish. It then marched to Cartigny and Catelet, where it continued to clear up, filling craters in the roads. On 5 April 145 Brigade attacked Lempire with Ronsosoy and Basse Boulogne. Zero hour was 4.55 am, and by 6.00 am the Battalion was through Lempire and consolidating on the far side of the village but had suffered 56 casualties, 15 of whom died.

The 10th Gloucesters War Diary records:

> 17 March 1917. Further patrols succeeded in entering the German line between 8 a.m. and 9 a.m. those on the left meeting no opposition while those on the right were at first prevented from entering . . . The patrols pushed down to the SOMME at BRIE and remained there till dark . . . Casualties – 1 man killed.

On the same day, 17 March, 1/4th Gloucesters sent out a patrol which reached the banks of the Somme without meeting the enemy. Three days later, the Battalion crossed the river and on 29 March it reached Villers-Fauchon; the next day it attacked St Emilie at 4.00 pm without artillery support, as orders did not reach the Gunners. The Germans fought hard and with considerable gallantry, but eventually the village was captured and the surviving Germans retreated towards Epéhy. The Battalion suffered 58 casualties, of whom 7 died.

On 18 March 2/5th Gloucesters followed up the Germans moving to Vermandovillers, where they too discovered how methodical and thorough the enemy had been. Villages were devastated, and in an act of wanton destruction all the fruit trees had been cut down. The Battalion spent the next 10 days mending the roads. On 31 March it occupied Vermand. Here Ivor Gurney,[3] the poet serving with 2/5th Gloucesters, wrote:

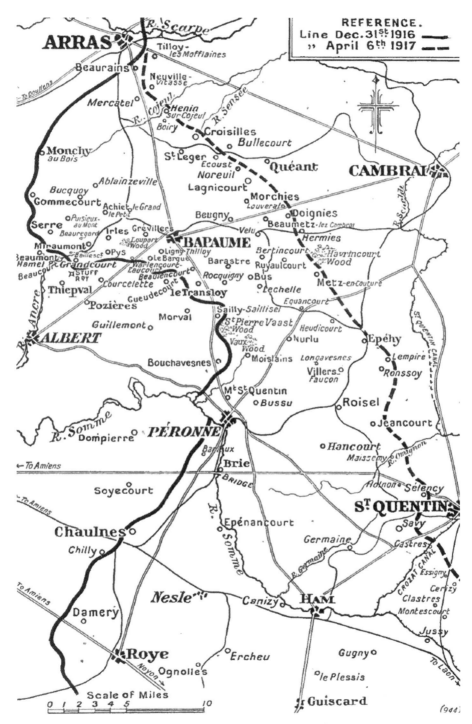

Map 25 The German Withdrawal to the Hindenburg Line, 1917

Near Vermand

Lying flat on my belly shivering in clutch frost,
There was time to watch the stars, we had dug in;
Looking eastward over the low ridge; March scurried its blast,
At our senses, no use either dying or struggling.
Low woods to left, (Cotswold spinnies if ever)
Showed through snow flurries and the clearer star weather.
And nothing but chill and wonder lived in mind; nothing
But loathing and fine beauty, and wet loathed clothing.
Here were thoughts. Cold smothering, and fire-desiring,
A day to follow like this or in the digging or wiring.

Worry in snow flurrying and lying flat, flesh the earth loathing.
I was the forward sentry and would be relieved
In a quarter or so, but nothing more better than to crouch
Low in the scraped holes and to have frozen or rocky couch –
To be by desperate home thoughts clutched at, and heart-grieved.
Was I ever there – a lit warm room and Bach, to search out sacred
Meaning; and to find no luck; and to take love as believed.

When 2/5th Gloucesters went into action again, taking part in the assault and capture of Bihecourt in early April, Ivor Gurney was among the 7 officers and 27 other ranks wounded; 15 other ranks died in the fierce battle.

2/4th Gloucesters followed up the German withdrawal, advancing to Kratz Wood, Maissemy and Bihecourt. In one village all the houses had been blown up from their cellars. On 6 April the Battalion relieved 2/6th Gloucesters west of Fresnoy and at 9.10 pm attacked and captured much of the village under an artillery barrage in conjunction with 2/8th Worcesters. The companies were held up in the village by wire in front of trenches and by heavy rifle and machine gun fire, so a line was consolidated in the village during the night about 300yds from the enemy trenches. One other rank was killed and 13 wounded in the action.

In January 1917 1st Division, with 1st and 10th Gloucesters, had been transferred to the Barleux sector of the Somme front. Here both battalions took their turn in the front line. During the German retreat to the Hindenburg Line they patrolled but did not take a significant part in the action. Thus by April 1917 the Allies had advanced to the new German line, but now the task was to break it, and this was to prove extremely difficult.

Notes

1. Charles Alexander Wilson (1892–1978) had transferred to the Gloucesters as a CQMS in 1916 from the Corps of Army Schoolmasters. He was the son of a Gloucester who had been RSM of 5th Gloucesters in 1908. He was commissioned into the 1st Battalion but after the War, realizing his prospects were not good, transferred to the new Army Education Corps, with whom he served for 33 years, retiring as an Honorary Brigadier in 1953. His brother Frank also joined the Gloucesters.
2. Robert Ian Rawson (1875–1944) was commissioned into the Regiment in March 1894. Prior to taking over 12th Gloucesters, he had commanded 6th Battalion, Argyll & Sutherland Highlanders for over two years. He remained with 12th Gloucesters until August 1918, when he was promoted Brigadier-General to command 103 Brigade. He retired in 1923. He achieved a lasting legacy in the Regiment by presenting a silver cup to be competed for annually in a gruelling inter-platoon march and shoot competition. This ensured that his name was remembered long after those of other First World War Commanding Officers was forgotten.
3. Ivor Bertie Gurney (1890–1937) was born in Gloucester. He became a chorister in Gloucester Cathedral and won a scholarship to the Royal College of Music in 1911. He enlisted in February 1915 and joined 2/5th Gloucesters. He returned to the Battalion after recovering from his wound and was gassed in September 1917. After the war he suffered a mental breakdown and spent the last fifteen years of his life in mental hospitals, where he continued to write poetry, music and plays. He is one of the sixteen 'Great War Poets' listed in a memorial in Poet's Corner in Westminster Abbey and is buried at Twigworth, near Gloucester.

Chapter 39

12th Gloucesters at Fresnoy during the Battle of Arras

The Allies now launched a combined operation to break through the German line. The British attacked, in the Second Battle of Arras, to prevent the Germans diverting troops to counter the French Nivelle Offensive 50 miles to the south. The British assault on 9 April was initially successful: within hours they had penetrated between 1 and 3 miles, taken 9,000 prisoners and suffered few casualties. But yet again the British inability to exploit success rapidly meant the opportunity for a dramatic breakthrough was lost, and a battle of attrition and heavy casualties followed.

12th Gloucesters (Bristol's Own) was in reserve to the Canadian Corps for its brilliant capture of Vimy Ridge on 9 April and then fought at Fresnoy in the Third Battle of the Scarpe. For a tired and under-strength 12th Gloucesters Fresnoy was probably the most desperate battle this gallant Battalion would fight in the whole war.

Over the night of 4/5 May 95th Brigade relieved the 3rd Canadian Brigade, who had captured Fresnoy. 12th Gloucesters had only three companies, but two companies of 1 DCLI were under command when it took over the wood to the north of the town. Colonel Rawson's report, written in his own hand, describes the ebb and flow of battle and the demands placed on a Commanding Officer and his men:

The following is my report on the enemy's attack on Fresnoy:

1. During the whole of the 7th inst he had barraged our lines very heavily all day during which time I constantly called for artillery support but got practically none.
2. During the previous day enemy aeroplanes had been all over our lines at a height of 200 feet as reported previously; our aeroplanes did nothing to prevent this.
3. During afternoon of the 7th enemy laid down a barrage on front, close support, support and HQ lines practically obliterated our trenches, especially the front and support lines. The men were put into shell holes during the day.
4. During the night 7th–8th I relieved my two front line companies & my dispositions then were A Coy on right, C Coy on left, B Coy in support; D Coy

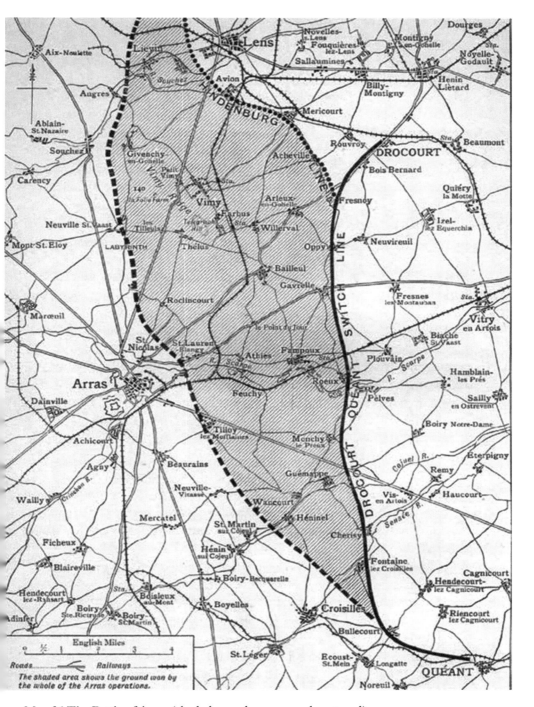

Map 26 The Battle of Arras (shaded area shows ground captured)

1 DCLI in reserve in T30C, C Coy 1 DCLI in ARLEUX LOOP in T29, both about 60 strong. D Company of this Battalion arrived in ARLEUX LOOP & Sunken Road at Battn HQ at 2.45am on relief, having been 3 nights in front line previously.

5. On evening of 7th I had asked Brigade to warn Corps & Divisional artillery to be ready for an S.O.S. & was assured by Brigade that this had been done & we would get every support.

6. About 3.06 am, a very heavy barrage was laid on Battalion HQ & at same moment the Battalion's observer reported one red rocket but that smoke, dust & mist made it impossible to see lights or anything. I myself at once sent through the S.O.S. on all lines & on Artillery Line by the Liaison Officer.

7. The barrage put up by us was practically NIL. No heavy shells were heard passing over & the Field Artillery barrage was very thin & slow. I called on the Brigade for more but was told they could do no more & the Artillery was not responding.

8. We could hear Lewis Gun & Rifle fire continuously up in front but could see nothing owing to the fog & dust etc. It was also raining hard & the ground very muddy.

9. Scouts were sent up to try & get information. The two companies of DCI & D Coy 12/Glouc stood to & M.Gs fired on barrage lines.

10. About 4am or a little after having a report from a wounded Sergeant that the enemy was attacking our front line in force & that support company had moved up under Captain PARR & was holding them I ordered D Coy DCLI under Capt KENDALL to move up in support & if necessary counter attack. I also ordered C Coy DCLI to move to the position vacated by D Coy & to be ready to support my left flank.

11. About 4.30am Capt KENDALL reported to me in person that C Coy 12 /Glouc & a mixed crowd of Canadians were back on top of him & he had formed them in the SUNKEN ROAD running North from 29 by 9c to 29 by 9.5. I ordered him to counter attack with his company (D) & my own C Coy & to regain the front line.

    2 wounded officers of my C Coy came in & reported the Canadians on their left had fallen back carrying some of C Coy with them & gradually the whole Coy had come back. Casualties were heavy.

    I could get no information about my right except that when last seen by wounded men the O.C. A Coy had been seen lying very badly wounded and had asked how things were going & that Capt PARR was up & fighting on the front line.

    I moved 2 Platoons of C Coy DCLI into the Sunken Road left empty by Capt KENDALL. Many Canadians were passing through Battn HQ saying they had been relieved & were going out. My Adjutant held them up with his revolver & eventually they went back towards their own front.

My own D Coy under Major Allison was now refreshed and I warned it to get ready.

12. At 6.35am I received a message from Captain KENDALL saying that front line was retaken (message untimed) & we were holding. Situation on left clear & Canadians holding on but situation on right not clear. The counter attack had been held up for a time by machine gun fire from FRESNOY [*sic*] PARK, which I could not understand as E Surreys were reported to me by Col Fargus as still holding the front line. I thought it likely that enemy had got through the gap left by C Coy. I sent Capt Leicester, Batt Signalling Officer, with two runners to scout the right & report the situation of Capt Parr.

13. About 7am I rec'd a message from Captain Kendall 'our line is now roughly from T30 central running North. They have been blown out of the trenches occupied. Parties of Canadians kept retiring through us & bring our men back too. Casualties are getting heavy. Germans appear to be sniping us from FRESNOY WOOD about T30 to 9.8. There do not appear to be many Germans in front of us but artillery fire is very heavy. There are plenty of men for continuing action.'

Almost on top of this message Capt Kendall himself came in & reported all his people back in the SUNKEN Road he started from. He had enough men to carry on with & it was hopeless counter-attacking without a barrage which we could not get.

14. Capt Kendall reported about 7.30am that casualties were very heavy & his men shaken & asked for another company.

I ordered Major Allison with D Coy 12/Glous to advance to SUNKEN road & make ground to the front, & join his front on the left to Canadians at T30 b 9.8 as I now had the Canadian dispositions from their C.O.

This was done, & at 9.45 Major Allison reported his Company held up by Machine Gun fire on line H & south through T30 & heavily barraged.

15. At 8am all wires were cut & position seemed very serious as I was informed the E Surreys had fallen back on ARLEUX, I had no news of my own right except that they had been surrounded where they stood by both flanks.

I sent a runner message to Col Fargus asking for all possible assistance & the heaviest possible barrage on FRESNOY WOOD & North of it.

I also sent off a Pigeon Message, which unfortunately was not addressed but understand it got through in 40 Minutes.

It had no result as regards any artillery fire.

16. I received a reply from Col Fargus around 8.20am to say my message rec'd & I Coy of Devons were behind me in ARLEUX LOOP & request for barrage had been passed.

17. At this time there were about 130 wounded in the Regt Aid Post and Batt H.Q. including 30 stretcher cases.

18. About 11.30 Major Allison, having been previously wounded, my D Company began to fall back & arrived mixed up with DCLI & Canadians in the SUNKEN Road running through T29d central in which HQ was.

   I had now no one in front. I ordered Capt Kendall & his company who had rested while my D Coy were in front to hold the SUNKEN Road from T29 b 9.5 to b 9.0 40 strong now & C Coy DCLI from there to T29d central with strong point at the latter place, while I re-organized the remains of 12th Glouc & got their rifles clean as they were clogged with mud & were very shaken.

   One company of DEVONS in ARLEUX LOOP behind Batt H.Q. & 8 Bde M.G.S along the ARLEUX LOOP.

   Shelling was now quieter though it never stopped. By 3pm we had about 150 of 12 Glouc re-organized in 6 platoons with 3 Lewis Guns our line was firmly established & my left flank joined up and right flank well-guarded provided the road at Batt H.Q. was not enfiladed from ARLEUX.

   There was not a single Company officer left in 12/Glouc & the Signals Officer was also killed about 11am.

   Major Colt arrived to assist me & we were able to rest a little.

   The position remained thus until evening when Col Blunt of 1 DEVONS arrived to take over.

   An S.O.S. was sent up by the Canadians on our left who reported 600 enemy north of FRESNOY WOOD. This time we got a good barrage which broke up any attack. The barrage was discontinued at 9.15 and at 10pm the remains of 12/Glouc were relieved by 1/Devons.

19. Before the enemy's infantry attack most of the Lewis Guns in front line had been blown up, but two were kept going, in each case the No 1 being the only men remaining of the team. 1 gun claims to have wiped out 4 waves of German with 15 drums firing point blank at 50 yards.

   The German losses are stated by my men to have been very heavy & they were piled in lines on the ground.

   Our men's rifles being clogged with mud from being buried they pulled the pins out of their rifle grenades & used them as hand grenades, doing much damage.

   There is no doubt that A & B Coys on the right were surrounded, stood their ground & fought to the last.

   Taking known casualties & men returned & allowing for a number of killed from shellfire, there could not have been more than an odd unwounded prisoner. A Coy had practically ceased to exist before the Infantry attack began & the brunt was borne by B Coy.

Capt Parr was never heard of again but was last seen surrounded & fighting with a shovel.

10.5.17   RJ Rawson Lt Col Comd 12/Glouc Regt

The Lewis gun that Colonel Rawson refers to was operated by Corporal Harry Civil, who remained at his post when others withdrew and, when he did go back himself, organized an improvised counter-attack. The Bavarian Division suffered 1,585 casualties. The Gloucesters suffered 389 casualties, of whom 94 died. One officer and 39 other ranks of 1 DCLI also died. A Canadan officer later said:[1] 'We are full of praise for the English Bristol lads, who held on despite frightful fire, served their machine guns to the last and only fell back from their advanced lines when Fresnoy village, by then a heap of ruins, became a death trap in which no man could stay alive'. Despite the gallantry displayed by the Battalion, no awards were made. Harry Civil received a Certificate of Honour!

Note

1. Dean Marks, '*Bristol's Own*'. *The 12th Battalion Gloucestershire Regiment 1914–1918.*

Chapter 40

Battles, Gallantry and 'Hush Camp'

The Second Battle of Arras ended on 16 May 1917. A New Zealander, Lieutenant Roy Fitzgerald MC of 12th Gloucesters, had been wounded and captured at Fresnoy. Later he recalled:

> I was cut off with a number of others, all of whom were wounded. I must have been rendered unconscious as the next thing I remember is coming round and being in the enemy's hands. I was taken to a German field dressing station where bullets were removed from my arms and shrapnel from my face without anaesthetic. But this was due to the rush and any suffering was not intentional. From here I sent a postcard to my wife back at Warmley, Bristol, which reached her through the Red Cross about six weeks later. On May 11th, I arrived at hospital at Rastatt in Germany, where my wounds were seen to. I had been hit nine times. They took X-ray photographs and I really do believe they did their best for me. By June 8th I was considered well enough to move and was transferred to Strohen prison camp.[1]

Elsewhere in France, 1/4th Gloucesters and 7th Worcesters attacked Queuchettes Wood in the early hours of 13 April, and by 4.00 am all the objectives had been taken. An immediate counter-attack by the enemy was driven back. During the day the Battalion was heavily shelled, until relieved that night by 1/5th Gloucesters. One officer and 9 other ranks were killed or missing. The three Gloucesters TA battalions (1/4th, 1/5th and 1/6th) were in almost continuous action and relieving one another as operations continued. Early on 24 April 1/6th Gloucesters tried, unsuccessfully, to take the Knoll. 1/4th Gloucesters, together with 4th Berkshires and 7th Worcesters, were then ordered to attack the Knoll at 11.00 pm. Major Parkinson, who was commanding 1/4th Gloucesters, was killed just before zero hour, and although one company reached its objective, two others pushed too far forward. These two were forced to withdraw to avoid being surrounded, and the Battalion was relieved during the night by 1/5th Gloucesters.

On 18 April disaster struck 1/6th Gloucesters and the Nott family in particular. The Germans had mined with a delayed action fuse the cellar selected for Battalion Headquarters at Villers Faucon; when it exploded, the Commanding Officer,

Thomas Nott, his brother Louis, who was his Adjutant, and five other officers, including the Medical Officer and Chaplain, were all killed. The Notts came from Stoke House in Stoke Bishop, Bristol, and their other brother, Henry, had been killed almost exactly a year earlier. Such was the resilience of battalions by this stage of the war that the routine of 1/6th Gloucesters appeared to survive this shattering blow. Captain John Crosskey from 1/5th Warwicks took over temporary command, a new doctor arrived later the same day, and the following day the Battalion took over the outpost line from 1/5th Gloucesters. For the Nott parents and their two daughters, Jeanette and Dorothy, life could never be the same, as was the case for so many other families. The Notts had all the letters from their three sons bound in twelve leather volumes, which are now in the Soldiers of Gloucestershire Museum.

In April 1st Division moved to Péronne, where both 1st and 10th Gloucesters were employed repairing the railway. The weather was glorious and the countryside was green. Eventually, on 26 May, after a pleasant interlude, 1st Gloucesters, who were once again a fit and well-trained battalion, moved to the Ypres Salient.

The aim of the Battle of Messines (7–14 June 1917) was to capture the ridge that overlooked Ypres from Ploegsteert ('Plugstreet') Wood through Messines and Wytscharte to Mt Sorrel, in preparation for the Third Battle of Ypres later in the year. After a 17-day preliminary bombardment, 19 mines that had taken months to put in place were detonated under the German lines with a devastating explosion that was audible in Downing Street. Some 10,000 Germans are thought to have been casualties of the mines, killed, wounded or so dazed that they were unable to resist the Allied attack. 8th Gloucesters moved up on the night of 6/7 June and successfully attacked Black Line in front of Onraet Wood at 8.10 am. At 3.10 pm they launched a further successful attack against the village of Oosttaverne and the Odonto Trench. When the Battalion was relieved during the night of 8/9 June it had taken 200 prisoners, 11 field guns and 20 machine guns, and had suffered 108 casualties, killed, wounded or missing. 8th Gloucesters went back into the line on 15 June for four days. Subsequently, members of the Battalion were awarded 1 DSO, 2 MCs, 2 DCMs and nine MMs.

A month later, 8th Gloucesters took over the front line and on 9 July attacked Druid's Wall and Wall Farms east of Oosttaverne. Two officers and 12 other ranks were killed. The Commander of 19th Division issued a Special Order of the Day:

I have decided to award the BADGE OF HONOUR to 'A' Company 8th (S) Bn. Gloucestershire Regiment, for its gallant conduct during the capture of DRUID'S and WALL FARMS on the night 9/10 July, and for the part it took in beating off by heavy rifle fire the attack of a hostile storm troop which entered our line on the night of 27/28 July. In these two affairs the Company lost 5 officers and 32 other ranks killed and wounded. This honour is awarded in recognition of the fine soldier-like spirit displayed by all ranks on these occasions and of the good fighting record of 'A' Company and of the Battalion to which it belonged.

The 19th Division Butterfly Badge of Honour was awarded for conspicuous bravery by complete units. The Battalion went back into the line on 23 July at Oosttaverne, where 2 officers and 32 other ranks died, principally when the Germans raided the line on 28 July. During this raid CSM Tye 'twice passed through a heavy barrage to ascertain the situation and returned with accounts and valuable reports. He showed complete disregard for his personal safety and by his coolness and splendid example rendered valuable assistance in repelling the attack.' He was awarded a DCM, and Second Lieutenant Gordon le Brun won an MC.

Only ten men in the whole British Army won two Bars to their DCM; one was Company Sergeant Major (CSM) Stanley Phillips from Drybrook in the Forest of Dean. His DCM was gazetted in June 1917 while serving with 10th Gloucesters – 'He has consistently shown a fine example when under fire, and has done splendid work throughout.'

The two Bars to his DCM were won as a CSM with 10th Worcesters. On the first occasion, 'When his company was almost surrounded, CSM S Phillips with a handful of men took up a position to cover the withdrawal and held back the enemy by fire while the survivors of the company made their way back through the burning village to the fields behind. Then he withdrew and took over command of the company.' The second Bar was awarded for his action on 14 October 1918: 'It was only due to his great gallantry in taking his company commander's orders along the line to withdraw that the remainder of his company, amounting to about 20 per cent, were saved.'

1st Division was in reserve for the Messines Battle and 1st Gloucesters was employed carrying stores, mainly trench mortars and bombs, up to the front, suffering no casualties. On 15 June the Battalion began a series of moves towards the coast, and at St Idesbald 3rd Brigade held a race meeting, which the Prince of Wales attended on 1 July 1917, exactly a year after the start of the Battle of the Somme. On 17 July the whole of 1st Division moved to 'Hush Camp' at Le Clipon on the coast, where it trained for an amphibious landing behind the German lines. The German submarine threat had increased considerably, and a plan was developed to establish heavy guns that could subject the submarine base at Zeebrugge to continuous fire, while at the same time destroying the German heavy batteries at Raversyde. The selected landing area was shallow, so each brigade was to be transported on a pair of monitors steaming abreast, with a pontoon 200yds long and 10yds wide lashed between them. The guns' stores, hand-carts for stores and ammunition, three tanks and the two leading battalions of each brigade were to be on the pontoons, and the remainder of the troops on the monitors. The latter were shallow-draft and not very seaworthy craft, mounting a heavy gun and typically 320ft long by 90ft wide, drawing 9ft of water. The idea was for them to be pushed up against the sea wall during the night. The wall itself sloped to a height of 30ft and was surmounted by a 4ft vertical wall, so fully laden men needed to be very fit to climb it. The training for both 1st and 10th Gloucesters was designed to be both interesting and demanding, and they had also played hard to get fit. 1st Gloucesters won the Brigade rugby and the long distance running competition. The operation was, however, dependent on Fifth Army reaching Staden during the Third Battle of Ypres; this they failed to do. On 20 October the decision was made to cancel what would surely have been an extremely risky enterprise. Instead, 1st Division was sent into the mud and morass of Passchendaele.

When the Third Battle of Ypres began on 31 July, 14th Gloucesters (Bantams) was still in the Arras area at Aizecourt-le-Bas where it received orders to prepare for an attack on the Knoll near Lempire. At 4.00 am on 19 August 105 Brigade, including 14th Gloucesters, attacked and captured the Knoll. One other rank was killed and four wounded. At 4.00 am on 21 August the Germans attempted to recapture the Knoll. The Battalion War Diary states: '21/8/17. At 4am, the enemy attempted to recapture the KNOLL. The attack was made at three separate points, assisted on the right by *flammenwerfer* [flame-throwers]. The enemy was repulsed at all points . . . Casualties: Officers 1 killed, 1 wounded. O.R. 3 killed, 1 died of wounds, 16 wounded.' The citation for the award of the Victoria Cross to Second Lieutenant Hardy Parsons[2] reads:

> For most conspicuous bravery during a night attack by a strong party of the enemy on a bombing post held by his command. The bombers holding the block were forced back, but Second Lieutenant Parsons remained at his post, and single-handed, and although severely scorched and burnt by liquid fire, he continued to hold up the enemy with bombs until severely wounded. This very gallant act of self-sacrifice and devotion to duty undoubtedly delayed the enemy long enough to allow of the organization of a bombing party, which succeeded in driving back the enemy before they could enter any portion of the trenches. The gallant officer succumbed to his wounds.

Notes

1. Roy Fitzgerald was an engineer in Nigeria when war broke out and was commissioned into the Gloucesters in early 1915. From Strohen prison camp he and another officer, Lieutenant Harding of the Cheshires, escaped in early 1918 dressed as private soldiers and

reached the Dutch frontier after seven days. After a short leave he transferred to the Royal Flying Corps, which became the Royal Air Force on 1 April, and he was shot down and killed in aerial combat over Morlancourt on 1 July 1918; he was twenty-seven.

2. Second Lieutenant Hardy Falconer Parsons VC (1897–1918) was the son of the Revd and Mrs J. Ash Parsons of Redland, Bristol. His father was a Wesleyan minister, and Hardy was born in Rishton, Lancashire. He was educated at Kingswood School, Bath and had been at Bristol University, studying medicine in preparation for missionary medical work. He was twenty. His VC was said to have been one that King George V most admired. Hardy's brother, Ewart, a pilot in the RAF, was killed in a flying accident on 17 June 1918.

Chapter 41

The Third Battle of Ypres (Passchendaele)

The Third Battle of Ypres was and remains to this day controversial and notorious. It is also commonly referred to as Passchendaele, after the village and ridge that was its ultimate objective. While the British were fighting the Battle of Arras, the French were engaged in the disastrous Second Battle of the Aisne, which led the French Army to mutiny and General Nivelle to be replaced by General Pétain. As a result, by the latter part of 1917, any significant action on the Western Front had to be initiated by the British. It is easy with hindsight to view what happened critically, but at the time there appeared to be a 'window of opportunity'. The Russian Revolution had begun in February, and if this led to the end of hostilities on the Eastern Front, which seemed likely, then Germany would be able to move whole armies to France and Flanders. Meanwhile, the German U-boat campaign had gathered momentum during 1917 and was causing a crisis at home; the Allies needed to damage Zeebrugge, where the U-boats were based, or at least threaten it. This is a brief background to the Third Battle of Ypres which culminated at Passchendaele, of which Lloyd George wrote 'Passchendaele was indeed one of the greatest disasters of the war . . . No soldier of any intelligence now defends this senseless campaign.' But Lloyd George had been against it from the start, eventually giving way to Field Marshal Haig, whose plan it was. Haig had wanted for many months to use the Ypres salient as the starting point for an offensive that would not only break the German line but also clear the coast and counter the U-boat threat.

The problem with Haig's plan was that the Ypres Salient had been fought over continuously since 1914 and was a ghastly place, particularly in bad weather. It is low lying and boggy, because the soil structure does not allow water to drain away. Before the war there was a system of ditches and waterways which drained the land, but these had been destroyed by three years of shelling. Furthermore, by 1917 it was covered in shell holes and craters and without any real distinguishing features. Manning the trenches was bad enough; trying to advance and attack was a great deal worse, although what is often forgotten is that any German counter-attack had to cover the same awful ground. A. F. Barnes recounts an apocryphal story which sums up the combination of horror with the humour vital to maintaining morale:

A British Tommy was picking his way along a duckboard track when he espied an Australian hat lying in the mud. Stooping to pick it up, he was

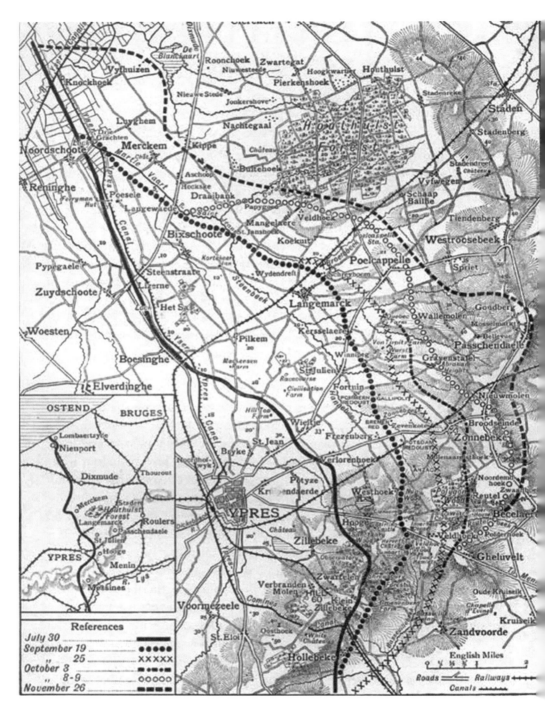

Map 27 The Third Battle of Ypres, 1917

surprised to find it resisted his efforts: the reason, he soon discovered, was that it was held down by the strap, which went under the chin of its owner, whose eyes were just visible above the slush. Getting a firm foothold, he dived his arms into the mud and under the other's armpits and tried to drag him out. 'Steady does it, Tommy,' spluttered the Australian, 'I'm on a horse.'

It was almost impossible to dig deep dugouts in the muddy ground. The Germans had therefore constructed, in the ruins of farms and other buildings, strong points built of reinforced concrete often many feet thick, similar to the pillboxes that still can be found in many parts of England from the Second World War. These were difficult to assault, being heavily armed with machine guns, manned by men determined to hold out at all costs and sited in depth so that they supported one another. Although the Allies made gains, they did not achieve the desired breakthrough, which might just have made the loss of life more acceptable. To some extent, the decision to launch the battle was based on the misapprehension that the morale of the German Army was close to collapse; it wasn't. Despite all these factors, the battle began on 31 July 1917 and lasted until the village of Passchendaele was captured on 6 November.

The Allied Plan was a series of offensives on all fronts, so timed as to assist each other by depriving the enemy of the opportunity to reinforce any one front, as this would mean weakening another. It was meticulously planned as an 'advance in stages', thus allowing tactics to be changed as events unfolded. It began with a 15-day bombardment during which 4m shells were fired (1.5m were fired before the Somme Offensive). At first things went well and the ground was dry, but it wasn't long before communication with the artillery broke down; then the Germans counter-attacked and stopped the British where they stood or drove them to flight. Then it rained hard for the next three days, which made movement almost impossible, and Haig was forced to halt the offensive on 4 August. Fifth Army had lost 7,800 dead or missing, which, compared to the 20,000 lost on the first day of the Somme, seemed bearable in 1917. Although the Germans had lost similar numbers, the first few days undoubtedly belonged to them. The Third Battle of Ypres might then have been stopped, but Haig's persistence ensured that it went on. On 24 August he transferred responsibility for the campaign from General Gough's Fifth Army to General Plumer's Second Army. Plumer called a halt and dictated a change of tactics to a step-by-step approach, which would lead eventually to the capture of Passchendaele. Like other major battles on the Western Front the Third Battle of Ypres in fact consisted of a series of individual battles: Pilckem, and the subsequent capture of Westhoek; Langemarck; Menin Road; Polygon Wood; Broodseinde; Poelcappelle; and the First and Second Battles of Passchendaele. Eleven Gloucester battalions took part in at least one of these actions.

Chapter 42

13ᵗʰ Gloucesters at Pilckem and the Territorials at Langemarck

13ᵗʰ Gloucesters, the Pioneer Battalion of 39 Division, was the only Gloucester battalion involved in the Battle of Pilckem Ridge (31 July–2 August). The Battalion spent much of July preparing for it, and their War Diary records: '1/29 July Bn employed on completion of assembly trenches, maintenance of C.T.s [communication trenches] and fire trenches, construction of trench tramways and dug outs with a view to offensive operations.' Once the battle started, the Battalion moved forward behind the assaulting troops clearing roads and tracks so that artillery and supplies could get forward. One company was given the task of maintaining light railways. During the month the Battalion suffered 96 casualties. At the same time, the gallantry of some other ranks was recognized by the award of 7 MMs in July and August. 13ᵗʰ Gloucesters was withdrawn for a week on 8 August to rest and then took over similar duties at Vierstraat for the remainder of the month and most of September.

The Battle of Langemarck was the second attack of the planned sequence, and although the official dates of the battle are 16–18 August the actual fighting continued until virtually the end of the month. Eight British and two French Divisions were committed and all the Territorial Force battalions of the Gloucesters were involved: 1/4ᵗʰ, 1/5ᵗʰ and 1/6ᵗʰ in 48ᵗʰ Division and 2/4ᵗʰ, 2/5ᵗʰ and 2/6ᵗʰ in 61ˢᵗ Division. Altogether, 6 Gloucester officers and 279 other ranks died, the majority from 1/5ᵗʰ and 2/4ᵗʰ Gloucesters.

48ᵗʰ Division moved up to the Ypres sector on 22/23 July. 1/5ᵗʰ Gloucesters then took over the front line at Ypres itself on 5 August. The Battalion War Diary records: 'Hostile shelling very heavy and continuous – a good many casualties'. Then 145 Brigade was the leading brigade in the attack by 48ᵗʰ Division at 4.45 am on 16 August. In comparison with what was achieved elsewhere, 48ᵗʰ Division was successful: 1/5ᵗʰ Gloucesters advanced in four waves, the leading companies each forming two waves in 'artillery formation' under an artillery barrage. The Battalion captured Border House and 'Gun Pits' on the south and north side respectively of the St Julien–Winnipeg road, but then machine guns in Janet Farm and elsewhere prevented any further advance, although one house containing a machine gun was dealt with using rifle grenades. By now the barrage, which moved at a pre-planned rate, had left the Battalion behind, and it was taking increasing casualties so dug in where it was. A German counter-attack at about 10.00 am was repulsed but, as the War Diary records, 'During the day enemy snipers were very active and caused us more casualties.' Altogether the Battalion suffered 217 casualties. It was a gallant action, particularly as nearly an inch of rain had fallen on 14/15 August which made the already sodden, low-lying ground a considerable obstacle to any movement. When relieved, the battalion still held the ground it had captured initially. The Gloucesters withdrew to reorganize and, as the War Diary records, 'Many new NCOs had to be made.' 1/4th and 1/6th Gloucesters were not involved in the attack but subsequently held the front line.

Action continued for the rest of August, and one of the divisions involved was 61st Division with 2/4th, 2/5th and 2/6th Gloucesters. It had gone into reserve at Arras in mid-May 1917 with all the battalions significantly under strength, but this changed in July when new drafts arrived. On 15 August the quiet life the Division had been enjoying, training interspersed with sports meetings and horse racing, ended as it moved to the Ypres sector. On 17 August 2/4th Gloucesters went into the line in the Wieltje sector. Two days later, in conjunction with 48th Division on their left, B Company attacked Pond Farm Galleries but met strong resistance together with uncut wire, and withdrew. The Battalion was relieved on the 21st but returned to the line on the 23rd.

Meanwhile, 2/5th Gloucesters, which had seen plenty of fighting, was about to gain its first Battle Honour and to do so in some style. On 22 August 184 Brigade attacked Pond Farm, a grim and giant concrete fortress manned by 50 Germans with 5 machine guns which had resisted the assaults of no fewer than five divisions in previous fighting. 2/5th Gloucesters were due to be in support, but at the last moment the orders were changed and two companies deployed at zero hour (3.00 am) behind 2/4th Oxfords and two behind 2/1st Bucks. Both the leading battalions advanced to a point where their losses were so great that they could not hold their furthest objectives. At 12 noon two platoons of D Company 2/5th Gloucesters attacked Pond Farm after a hurricane bombardment but were unsuccessful until joined by two platoons from C Company; together they then stormed the fortress and killed or captured its entire garrison. The Battalion losses were heavy: 2 officers and 16 other ranks were killed, 1 officer was missing, and 1 officer and 51 other ranks were wounded. On 23 August 2/5th Gloucesters was relieved by 2/6th Gloucesters. On 23 August Lieutenant Pryce won a Bar to his MC when he led his company to recapture a postion lost to the Germans: 'He set a magnificent example, and by his good leadership and personal influence, the fighting of his company was never impaired'. He would later win a VC with the Grenadiers.

The fighting continued when 2/4th Gloucesters launched an attack on 27 August as part of 183 Brigade. The report of the Commanding Officer, Colonel

Boulton, written the next day, is a reminder of just how difficult the conditions were and of the resilience and leadership these demanded. The following is précis of his report:

> The task of assembly for the operation proved a difficult one owing to the very dark night and heavy rain which had made the going very bad. For the attack A Company was left forward, C Company in the centre and D Company right forward.
>
> On the way up to my battle headquarters, I learned that the left company had become split into two parts owing to heavy shelling and casualties. I saw the Company Commander at Battalion HQ of 2/6th Gloucesters and he told me that he would have no difficulty in getting the rear half of the company into position and that the front half were already up in the line in their place. Soon after the Company Commander – Lieut HALL – reported with one of his platoon commanders, 2/Lt. HADLEY. I understood from what he said that he had found the rear half of his company and I sent him off at once to put them into position. From that time onwards I received no communication from the left company at all. This was because a large swamp separated us and it was impossible to get runners through. It came to light after the operations that the two platoons of this company referred to either went astray again or were never found by Lt HALL. At any rate they did not take part in the action and appear to have been in the support battalion's lines the whole time.
>
> The other companies got into position well. One platoon of my reserve company (C Company) was attached to the left A Company as I thought that their task would be the most difficult.
>
> The state of the ground was very bad indeed and the men had to be in shell holes up to their knees in water. I considered that the going would be so bad as to necessitate a slower rate of advance of the barrage but was informed that it could not be changed. Our barrage was put down at 1.55am and appeared to be very accurate. The men advanced closely under it but it was obvious that they were experiencing great difficulty in keeping up with it owing to the mud. The going was so bad in some places that it was a matter of dragging each leg out with the hands after each step. Rifles and machine guns became clogged and rendered useless.
>
> At 3.30 am I received a message from D (right) Company stating that they were held up by machine gun fire and were unable to advance. I immediately sent a message ordering them to push on at all costs in order to support flank companies and detailed one of the reserve platoons to go to their support.

At 4 am B Company (the centre company) reported that they had failed to take their objectives owing to machine gun fire and the mud and had been forced to withdraw with heavy casualties. I therefore ordered the supporting platoon, which was about to move forward to support D Company, to stand by and I sent a message to Brigade stating that centre & right were forced to withdraw and had suffered heavy casualties and asking for instructions.

At 4.30 am a message was received from the Brigade asking for a situation report and instructing me to man new line and old line. A reply was sent that right & centre were held up.

At 5 am a message was received by runner timed 4.05 am stating that artillery was being turned on again and ordering the line to be established firmly South of Scholer Galleries. As this crossed my last message I ordered Companies to consolidate on present ground.

At 6 am the situation was unchanged and there was still no report from my left company. A message was received from Brigade HQ ordering reorganization and another attack, calling on the Support Battalion to take over the old line.

At 6.15 am this message was cancelled and an order was received ordering me to dig in from where we were in touch with left the Division on our left to Pond Galleries.

At 6.40 am the company commanders of B (centre) and D Company (right) reported to me stating their strengths were then 12 OR and 30 OR respectively. At the same time brigade ordered me to establish myself in Hindu Cott calling on one or two companies of 2/6th Gloucesters and working in conjunction with left Division to establish myself on the line Winnipeg – Hindu Cott. I therefore sent a message to 2/6th Gloucesters asking for one company to reinforce A Company (left) and one company to come to Capricorn Keep as reserve. At the same time I ordered my three reserve platoons to reinforce my centre and right.

From 7.30 approx to 9 am there was artillery barrage fire on both sides. At 10 am an order was received that 2/6th Gloucesters would take over night 27/28, 2/4th Gloucesters having established the line Hindu Cott to left Division. A post was established at Hindu Cott and orders to the above effect sent to left A Company (left) by runners and patrols who however failed to find them owing to the swamp referred to above.

Centre & right companies were relieved but two platoons of B Coy were unable to get out before dawn and are still at POND GALLERIES. No officers or men of the D Company of supporting platoon attached to us have returned. This Company as stated above never received it's relief orders and must be still in the line.

I consider that the failure to take the objectives was chiefly due to the mud and to the men having to lie in water for 12 hours prior to the attack . . . The men are very much exhausted and in need of a hot meal and dry clothes, especially socks.

R.E.BOULTON, Lieut.Col.,

Commdg. 2/4 Glosters. 28/8/17.

The Battle of Langemarck was over, and it is easy to conclude that not much had been achieved at a considerable cost in casualties, but the First World War was one of attrition and the German Army recognized that their losses were unsustainable. The British could take some encouragement from the development in tactics but above all from the fact that, despite the appalling conditions, good leadership meant morale was still satisfactory.

Chapter 43

8th Gloucesters at Menin Road and 1/5th & 12th Gloucesters at Broodseinde

No one who was not present at Passchendaele would ever be able to grasp fully how ghastly it was. Most people wonder how on earth the men went on. Everard Wyrall writes: 'The thing which kept the British soldier going was first his indomitable pluck and then his extraordinary optimism, his never failing cheerfulness under the most appalling conditions'. There was another factor, 'regimental pride', reflected in this poem published in the *Fifth Glo'ster Gazette*:

> We know of the Anzacs, the Highlanders, the Guards.
> Their names are gilded gloriously, and sung by many bards.
> But we know – and THEY know – of other men as fine –
> The good old County Regiments – the Regiments of the Line.
>
> For them no vivid writer lets loose his fluent pen;
> For them no correspondent tells where, and how and when;
> Of their glory, in story, they write the tale anew –
> The old County Regiments, that fight along of you.
>
> The Worcesters, the Gloucesters – they've done their bit.
> The Warwicks and the Berkshires, as fighting men they're IT;
> They show it, we know it; they've marched and fought like Hell
> Those old County Regiments and dozens more as well.
>
> The Oxfords, the Bucks, and the Lancashires are fine.
> But if they fight for days and nights we never read a line.
> The Surreys, the Hampshires, the Devons too can fight;
> And surely they might have SOME of the glory that's their right.
>
> They've no one to boom, they do not advertise;
> Just in Battalion orders their hidden glory lies,
> They have no Agent-General to star them in the Press,
> But ask the foe! The Germans know – and we, well, we can guess.

In lofty dim cathedrals their battle standards blaze,
Enscrolled in gold with fights of old, and, after many days
They shall return and claim them, and newer names shall shine
More proudly yet on the Colours of the Regiments of the Line.

Drink to the gallant Anzacs, drink to the kilties too!
They're bonny fighters – we know them and it's true.
Toast them, and all their valour! and then I'll give you mine –
The old County Regiments – the Regiments of the Line.

After the Battle of Langemarck, 61st Division, with 2/4th, 2/5th and 2/6th Gloucesters, was in and out of the front line and occasionally took part in some minor actions until 18 September, when they left the mud of the Ypres Sector and moved to near Arras. Meanwhile, the British were preparing for the next sequence of battles, Menin Road, Polygon Wood and Broodseinde, and were also introducing the new tactics dictated by General Plumer. Developing new tactics was one thing, but time was needed to disseminate the changes and practise them. There was therefore a lull in the fighting until 20 September.

The British plan depended upon giving priority to heavy and medium artillery in order to destroy the German concrete pillboxes and machine gun nests and for counter-battery fire, i.e. engaging German artillery positions to reduce the fire on our own troops. There were also changes in how air observation was to be used to concentrate on identifying movement of German troops. For the infantry, the plan was to have a limited objective for each attack and then to dig in quickly, ready to repel the inevitable German counter-attack. Then, once the new line had been established, another assault would be launched to do the same again. There was another important change: the weather was much better. The Menin Road battle began at 5.40 am on 20 September and by mid-morning had taken most of its objectives to a depth of nearly a mile. German counter-attacks in the afternoon all failed, and minor action went on for the next four days.

Then, on 25 September, two German regiments recaptured pillboxes at the south-west corner of Polygon Wood in a major counter-attack. This proved costly for both sides and led directly to the Battle of Polygon Wood, which began the next day and continued until 3 October.

It is often suggested that battalions were launched into attacks with little preparation, but one of the other reasons that morale remained high was that preparation for new attacks was as thorough as possible, something which inspired confidence. There was also a feeling that lessons were being learnt, but this applied to both sides. 8th

Gloucesters War Diary records the preparations for the Menin Road battle and the action itself, as well as other events including the arrival of reinforcements:

Place	Date	Summary of Events and Information
Strazelle	Sept 1	D Coy had use of ranges at Noot Boom. Battalion bathed at Baths near Strazelle
	2	Divine Services for all denominations
	3	Tactical Scheme exercised
	4	New formation for Attack practised
	5	Brigade exercised in new Formation for attack. 2/Lt C.P.Fleming joined Battalion for duty
	6	Battalion marched to Mont Noir area and camped
Mont Noir	7	Training under Company arrangements. Special training for Rifle Grenadiers. CO and 3 officers visited line to be taken over.
	8	Draft of 59 Other Ranks joined
	9	Major D.J.B.McMahon proceeded to 10th Battn Gloucestershire Regt for duty. Battn practised new formation for attack
	10	Training as on 9th inst
	11	Battn moved to Forward Area at Bois Confluent. Transport to Siege Farm.
Bois Confluent	12	Draft of 144 Other Ranks joined for duty.
	13	6pm. Moved into the Line and took over the left sector of the Div Front in relief of 8th N Stafford Regt and 10th Worcester Regt.
Klein Zillebeke	14	Enemy moderately quiet. Relieved at night by 13th Battn Rifle Brigade and came out to Beaver Corner.
Beaver Camp	15	Day spent cleaning up
	16	New Attack Formation exercised
	17	Brigade rehearsal for new Attack Formation. 2 Lt G.S.Le Brun awarded MC & C.S.M Tye awarded D.C.M. in connection with operations on 28 July.
	18	3 coys proceeded by bus to St Eloi and relieved 13th Battn Rifle Brigade. 1 Company at Camp.
Klein Zillebeke	19	Enemy fairly active

Place	Date	Summary of Events and Information
	20	Battalion participated in an offensive. Zero hour 5.40am. First objective J 31 d 48 to J 31 d 15 reached with considerable ease and this line consolidated. On advance to final objective strong points and snipers dealt with. Objective at J 32 c 25.35 to P 1 b 85.80 was eventually reached at 7am. Enemy artillery barrage on original front & support lines very heavy. Casualties 2nd Lt R. E. Kimber & 2nd Lt J.M.Humphrey killed. Lieut F. J. Nicholas & 2nd Lt T.M.Colcutt wounded. Other Ranks 9 killed, 126 wounded & 25 missing.
	21	Posts and new front line bombarded at intervals. Held line until evening when Battalion was relieved by 7th South Lancs Regt and returned to Beaver Corner
Beaver Camp	22	Cleaning up, etc
	23	Divine Services for all religions held in Camp.

No other Gloucester battalion was involved in the Menin Road battle, and although 1/5th, 8th and 12th Gloucesters were awarded the Battle Honour for Polygon Wood (26 September–3 October), their involvement was limited. 1/5th Gloucesters sent two companies to be at the disposal of 175 Brigade during the battle but made no attack. On 27 September, however, the whole battalion relieved 2/10th London Regiment in the line, where it was heavily shelled the next day. Sixteen all ranks were killed. The Battalion was relieved by 1/4th Berkshires on 29 September, giving them three days to prepare for the next battle. 8th Gloucesters manned the front line trenches from 27 September until 1 October. 12th Gloucesters was not involved until 1 October, when it relieved 11th West Yorks in reserve. Heavy shelling, particularly at night, resulted in 4 officers and about 130 other ranks being gassed; 19 other ranks died.

Overall, both the battles of Menin Road and Polygon Wood had been successful. The Allies had taken their objectives and resisted German counter-attacks as intended. The third in this sequence of 'bite and hold' battles, Broodseinde, was slightly different because both sides were planning to attack on 4 October. The Allied preliminary bombardment therefore caught a number of German units out in the open preparing their own attack. 1/4th, 1/5th, 1/6th, 8th and 12th Gloucesters were all awarded the Battle Honour 'Broodseinde', but only 1/5th and 12th Gloucesters played a significant role. Both 1/4th and 1/6th Gloucesters provided support, such as stretcher parties, and 8th Gloucesters held the front line but appear to have suffered no casualties. This was considered the most successful of the sequence of battles for the British and caused a crisis among German commanders and a severe loss of morale in the Fourth German Army. It was not a success for 1/5th Gloucesters, however. The Battalion moved up on 3 October, in readiness for the attack, which was due at 6.00 am the next morning. At 5.00 pm on 4 October the Battalion attacked Adler Farm, Inch Houses and Vacher Farm, with a company allocated to each. Conditions were beastly, with heavy rain. The barrage was too far ahead of the advancing troops and the German machine guns were free to fire on the companies as they struggled forward. All they could do was to consolidate after advancing about 300yds, which they did. The Battalion Diary states, 'Casualties were light', but in fact the figure was 131, of whom 25 died.

Broodseinde was also a severe test for 12th Gloucesters, in reserve to 1st East Surreys for the attack by 95th Brigade which began at 6.00 am. At 6.40 am the Battalion, less A Company, moved forward to occupy the line that had been held by the East Surreys, during which time they suffered heavily from German artillery. Later in the morning, C Company was sent to reinforce 1st Devons, and this led to more casualties. During the following day the Battalion held the line and were again heavily shelled before being relieved that night. Overall during the period 1–12 October 1917 there were 359 casualties in the Battalion (150 from gas), of whom 88 died.

All these casualties might not have been in vain had the weather not turned foul. The Germans made preparations for local withdrawals and began considering a greater withdrawal, which would have meant losing the Belgian coast and ceding the Allies a strategic objective. However, the heavy rain worked to the advantage of the Germans, who were pushed back on to less damaged ground, while the Allies struggled to bring forward artillery. Restricted routes provided easy targets for German artillery. The Allies had already suffered heavily, although they had had considerable success. Things were about to get a whole lot worse.

Chapter 44

Poelcappelle and the Capture of Passchendaele

Three victories, Menin Road, Polygon Wood and Broodseinde, seem to have encouraged the Allies to believe that a breakthrough was possible; but the return of the rain changed everything. Over an inch fell during the two days before the next attack, the battle of Poelcappelle, and as a result the outcome of the fighting was completely different. Only in the north did the Allies achieve a substantial advance, and the German counter-attacks were generally successful. 1/4th, 1/5th, 1/6th and 12th Gloucesters were all involved in some way.

1/5th Gloucesters remained at Dambre Camp throughout, but the Battalion supplied large parties for carrying duties, escorting prisoners and stretcher-bearing, tasks that were themselves hazardous in the prevailing conditions. Meanwhile, at 5.25 am on 9 October, 144 Brigade advanced up the Poelcappelle Spur towards Westroosebeke, with 7th Worcesters on the right, 1/6th Gloucesters in the centre and 1/4th Gloucesters on the left. 1/4th Gloucesters was supposed to be guided to the start line, but when no guides appeared, the Commanding Officer, Lieutenant-Colonel John Crosskey,[1] decided to lead them himself. In doing so he 'lost' three companies and another platoon due to the enormous difficulty of moving on a pitch black night. Runners were sent to look for the missing men and by 4.30 am the Battalion was complete. When the attack began, the leading companies were able to get within 50yds of the barrage before it lifted; but thereafter the rate of advance assumed by the gunners was unrealistic given the sodden nature of the ground, and the barrage fell further and further in front of the advancing infantry. Soon German machine gun fire, combined with snipers, was delaying the advance, and the Battalion was held on a line up about 150yds east of the County crossroads. At 5.00 pm two companies of 8th Worcesters attacked Oxford Houses but were unable to capture them. The leading companies of 1/4th Gloucesters then withdrew about 100yds and subsequently handed that line over to the Camerons, having suffered 177 casualties, of whom 69 died. In his lengthy, detailed report Lieutenant Colonel Crosskey concluded:

> In my opinion, the reasons why we failed to take our objectives were: the exhaustion of the men, most of whom had been tramping over the heavy ground for the greater part of the night; the sodden condition of the ground; and that the barrage was lost after the first lift and never again caught up.

John Crosskey, who was seriously wounded, was awarded the MC and evacuated to England.

1/6th Gloucesters do not appear have had the same difficulty in getting into position for the attack. By 2.30 am the first wave was in a line along the front tape, the remainder of the Battalion in section columns 300yds behind. As it advanced behind the barrage, German machine guns opened up. A Company, on the right, were fired on from a trench, but two platoons entered it, capturing 20 prisoners and 4 machine guns. Meanwhile, B Company, on the left, had cleared the Cemetery, which was held by snipers and a machine gun team. They then encountered machine guns sited in shell holes, but when they charged the Germans threw up their hands. About 20 prisoners and 3 machine guns were taken. The Battalion second wave then pushed through. In C Company the rear platoons lost contact with the leading ones, but they probably reached a point about 200yds north-east of the Burns Farm–Vacher Farm road. On the left, D Company advanced against a strongly held pillbox, but when they got close, the Germans surrendered. Three German counter-attacks were driven back, and by nightfall the line of 1/6th Gloucesters closely followed the Vacher Farm–Burns House road. Some 70 prisoners and 12 machine guns had been taken, but losses in this gallant battle amounted to 242 all ranks, of whom 87 died. The Battalion was relieved on the next night.

Prior to the battle, 12th Gloucesters was in Sanctuary Wood, which was by now an unimaginably foul and miserable place. There were no trees, and the 'Battalion was in shell-holes, dugouts and shelters. Movement by day was very limited as same could easily be observed by the enemy. Duck-boards and tracks in the vicinity of Sanctuary Wood constantly shelled during the day.' On 8 October the Battalion was split: two companies remained, forming carrying parties, while the other two took over the Support Line behind 1st Cheshires from 1st East Surreys. The War Diary records: 'Rain fell very heavily during the night and the ground very muddy. It was also very dark and the companies found great difficulty in getting into positions. Consequently the relief was not completed until early morning.' When the attack was launched, 12th Gloucesters was heavily bombarded, and later the two companies in Sanctuary Wood provided both carrying and burying parties. The two forward companies were relieved on the night of the 10/11th with difficulty, due to the state of the ground and an enemy barrage, which forced the companies to remain in position until it was over.

Four days later, one imagines to everyone's surprise and delight, 48th (South Midland) Division were ordered to Italy. As a result, 1/4th, 1/5th and 1/6th Gloucesters withdrew to prepare for the move, which began on 21 November.

The battle for the village of Passchendaele itself was fought twice. The first attempt, on 12 October, failed. The Allies gained a little ground but a German counter-attack took most of it back again. 8th Gloucesters took over the front line

(Belgian Wood–Hessian Wood–Canal) during the night of 11/12 October and was relieved on 14 October but appear to have suffered no casualties. No other Gloucester battalion was involved on 12 October.

In the interval between the first and second battles of Passchendaele 14th Gloucesters arrived from the Somme and by 21 October were at Houlthulst Forest preparing for action. Prior to the attack by the Canadian Corps on 25 October, Fifth Army maintained pressure on the Germans, and on 22 October 14th Gloucesters, as part of 105 Brigade, launched an attack at 5.35 am under a creeping barrage which was completely successful. All objectives were taken and a counter-attack in the afternoon repulsed. Over 40 prisoners were taken, but the cost was great; the Battalion War Diary does not report the casualties so the number of wounded is unknown but 75 died, all of whose names are recorded on the Tyne Cot Memorial. The German artillery, assisted by aeroplane observation, did most of the damage. The Battalion Headquarters suffered two direct hits and 'the Regimental Aid Post was also shelled continuously all day'.

The second attempt to capture Passchendaele took place from 26 October to 10 November, when the Canadian Corps finally took the village and the ridge, thus ending the Third Battle of Ypres.

12th Gloucesters remained out of the line after Poelcappelle, recovering and receiving some reinforcements and training. On 28 October it moved forward to relieve 16th R Warwicks in the front line, which it held until being relieved on the night of 1 November having suffered light casualties. Sergeant Norman Pegg recalled:[2]

> During our adventure here it poured with rain most of the time and, what we referred to as trenches, were in fact inland waterways. In these circumstances there was no chance of drying your feet, which stayed wet the whole time. The result of this was that when we were relieved, we were able to march out at a rate of around one mile per hour . . . Despite these disadvantages there was still time for a laugh occasionally.

The men went back into the line on 5 November for two more nights, by which time the Third Battle of Ypres was nearly over, at least as far as 12th Gloucesters was concerned, because it, too, was now sent to Italy.

Elsewhere, it was clear that the amphibious landing that had been the purpose of 'Hush Camp' was not going to happen; therefore 1st Division with 1st and 10th Gloucesters arrived to take part right at the end of the Passchendaele battle. On the night of 7/8 November 1st Division took over the front held by 63rd Division and part of the Canadian Corps. 1st Gloucesters was in reserve. On 8th November orders were given for an attack to capture the Goudberg Spur running south-west from the Passchendaele–Westroosbeke road and to secure more of the Ridge itself. 3rd Brigade, with 1st Gloucesters in reserve, was to attack. The troops, moving forward to assembly positions, had to walk on duckboard tracks across a sea of mud and water. On the afternoon of 9 November the two attacking battalions, 1st South Wales Borderers and 2nd Royal Munster Fusiliers, began their move to their forming up positions; one took 11 hours, the other rather less. The attack began at 6.05 am, and the South Wales Borderers never reached their objective; the Munsters got to theirs but were unable to hold it. This was partly because the Allied counter-battery fire was unable to move up to within range because of the state of the ground. By 9.30 am the attack had failed and there was a danger that the Germans might even occupy the Brigade front line. 1st Gloucesters went forward and by the evening was holding the whole Brigade front, rather in advance of the original line, with the Munsters and South Wales Borderers in the rear. During the night of 11/12 November the Battalion was relieved. Colonel 'Patsy' Pagan, who been in command of 1st Gloucesters since May 1915, was in temporary command of 3rd Brigade for this attack and on 10 November was wounded in the eye when he went forward to see what was holding up the Munsters. At the Casualty Clearing Station he learnt that he was destined to be evacuated to England for treatment; but he felt his Battalion needed him so made some excuse and, hatless, wearing a dressing gown and canvas shoes, hitched lifts back to 1st Gloucesters. The Battalion was delighted, and although he was required to attend an interview with his divisional commander (the hospital had posted him as an absentee), everyone knew that the morale of 1st Gloucesters would be increased by his reappearance in such circumstances. A Regimental legend was born.[3]

This account of Third Ypres would be incomplete without mention of 13th Gloucesters (Pioneers). On 29 September 39th Division was withdrawn from the line and 13th Gloucesters went with them, having lost a further 8 other ranks killed and 35 wounded. Two officers gained MCs. They were back at Vierstraat on 16 October working on 'Northern Track' and then 'Plumer's Drive' for the rest of the month. In November the War Diary records 'work on Mole Track called Gloucester Drive', and later in the month they were 'extending forward roads towards Passchendaele'.

The Third Battle of Ypres was over, but for those that had taken part on both sides it would remain in their memory for the rest of their lives. Most found it impossible to describe the conditions, or if they did, their audience were unable to comprehend what it had been like. It was only amongst themselves that there was an understanding of the courage, tenacity and humour that had enabled them to keep fighting.

Notes

1. John Henry Crosskey MC (1892–1951) was born in Edgbaston and was studying medicine at Birmingham University when he decided to enlist in 1914. He was commissoned into the Royal Warwicks and served with 1/5th R. Warwicks. In April 1917 he took over temporary command of 1/6th Gloucesters when Lt Col Nott and other officers were killed by a delayed-action mine in Battalion HQ. He joined 1/4th Gloucesters in June 1917 and took over command in August. Although found fit again in January 1918, he was allowed to resume his medical studies. He subsequently became a GP in Birmingham but remained a Territorial Force officer in the Royal Warwicks until 1922.
2. Dean Marks, *'Bristol's Own', the 12th Battalion Gloucestershire Regiment 1914–1918.*
3. Peter Rostron, *Gloucestershire Hero – Brigadier Patsy Pagan's Great War Experiences.*

Chapter 45

2/4th, 2/5th & 2/6th Gloucesters at Cambrai, 1917

It may seem extraordinary that nine days after the end of the ghastly Third Battle of Ypres and the capture of Passchendaele itself the British should have launched another attack. There were good reasons for this, however. Russian participation in the War was clearly about to cease, and the Germans would then move troops from the Eastern Front to the West. The Battle of Cambrai (20 November–6 December) was a British attempt to break through the Hindenburg Line before this happened. The battle is often described as being the first use of tanks. This is wrong: tanks were initially used in 1916 on the Somme at the Battle of Flers-Courcelette. It was, however, the first time that the real potential of the tank as an offensive weapon, capable of achieving 'shock action' and overcoming machine guns and barbed wire obstacles, was demonstrated. In addition, the effectiveness of the British artillery was much improved by radio in aircraft that speeded up the passage of information, more reliable fuses on the shells and better survey, which led to greater accuracy.

The Allied plan was for 381 tanks, accompanied by 8 infantry divisions and supported by 1,000 guns, to attack the German trenches without any preliminary bombardment on a front of 10,000yds. There were three successive lines of German trenches nearly 4 miles in depth, and the intention was to break through all three on the first day. The Germans were completely unprepared for the assault, and in many places the attackers advanced 4 miles in 4 hours with few casualties. There was a problem in the centre, where the 51st Highland Division had, on the orders of their commander, followed at a few hundred yards behind the tanks instead of advancing with them. Unsupported by their infantry, the tanks were knocked out one by one. Nevertheless, in England the bells rang out for victory; the *Daily Mail* called it a 'splendid success' and on 23 November ran the headline 'HAIG THROUGH THE HINDENBURG LINE'. Such euphoria was understandable following the heartbreak of Passchendaele, but it was premature.

Once again, the Allies failed to capitalize on their success. The Germans, whose first reaction was to execute a major retreat, sensed the opportunity for a counter-attack and assembled 20 divisions, quickly turning what might have been a major Allied success into a virtual disaster. On 30 November the Germans, supported by a barrage of gas shells, attacked and advanced 3 miles in 2 hours, at one point threatening to envelop several Allied divisions.

61st Division, which included 2/4th, 2/5th and 2/6th Gloucesters, played no part in the initial attack. It had been moved from Ypres to Arras in mid-September and thence to the Cambrai front at the end of November, and was now with XVII Corps in Third Army. It was only when the Germans launched their counter-attack that 61st Division was ordered to reinforce the battalions under attack in the area of La Vacquerie.

Initially, only 2/4th and 2/6th Gloucesters were used. On 1 December both battalions moved into the line in the Havrincourt Wood sector. It was a difficult relief as the Front Line was held by the remnants of battalions and had only been retaken the previous day. There was no wire in front of 2/4th Gloucesters, and two 'communication trenches' led from the German lines into the Battalion's. On 2 December bombing fights took place intermittently, and in the early afternoon the enemy attacked 2/6th Gloucesters on the left, driving them back and leaving a gap of about 300yds, with the enemy in the same trench as 2/4th Gloucesters. A counter-attack failed and there was intermittent bombing and fighting all night. On 3 December the Germans attacked the 2/4th Gloucesters in large numbers after a heavy barrage. The line held for a time, but eventually the German bombing parties moved along the communication trenches and gained the upper hand. The Battalion was forced to retire. The right hand company was virtually cut off, while the centre and left companies began to withdraw in confusion. Lieutenant Colonel Donald Barnsley, the Commanding Officer, managed to gather a number of men to hold new positions, although casualties were heavy. Meanwhile, the support company reinforced with cooks, signallers and sanitary men who had occupied the reserve trenches were hopelessly outnumbered and forced to withdraw. The Germans had also suffered heavily and when they at last halted to consolidate their gains, 2/4th Gloucesters were able to reorganize. There was no further attack on 4 December. On the 5th the Battalion was relieved, and by the 6th the Battle of Cambrai was over. The battalion lost a total of 145 killed and missing and 90 wounded, and 4 MCs, 1 DCM (Private R. Force), 15 MMs and 1 Bar to a MM were awarded.

Over the same period 2/6th Gloucesters War Diary records:

2 December 1917. Enemy made an attack on one of our saps about 6 a.m. (part of Hindenburg Line) with a large party. He drove us back twice, but local counter attacks re-captured the ground. About 6.30 a.m. the enemy attacked again with a larger party, gained and held the sap owing to our supply of bombs running out. About 2 p.m. after a heavy barrage the enemy attacked with large forces on a fairly wide front, bombing down trenches and attacking across the open. We were forced to retire about 300 yards. Counter attacks were made to drive the enemy back,

but without success. Battalion H.Q. was captured during this attack, the Commanding Officer being hit near Battalion HQ & believed to have been taken prisoner [Major William Ruthven of the East Yorkshire Regiment, who had only taken over command of 2/6th Gloucesters on 21 November, died of his wounds]. At night several attacks were made on our new positions, but all were repulsed.

3 December 1917. At dawn, the enemy continued his attack (under an intense bombardment), up trenches and over the open. The main attack was made on our right flank but small bombing attacks were made on the ground held by the remaining officers and men of the Battalion which at times were partially successful, but finally the enemy was driven back to his original position. The attack on our right flank was successful, the enemy finally occupying the village of La Vacquerie.

Five officers and 168 other ranks were killed or missing and 12 officers and 140 other ranks were wounded.

On 3 December, two days after the Germans had broken through 2/4th and 2/6th Gloucesters, 2/5th Gloucesters moved to Gonnelieu to support 3rd Guards Brigade, who had been fighting continuously for 8 days. After spending 24 hours in close support, the Battalion was ordered to move through Villers Plouich to a position behind Welch Ridge. A night-flying aircraft dropped a bomb that hit an ammunition dump near D Company, awaiting orders in a sunken road; 16 other ranks were killed and 1 officer and 53 other ranks were wounded. Recognizing that this was a dangerous position, the Battalion moved rapidly into position in inky darkness, without guides. At dawn the Germans attacked La Vacquerie. On 5 December the Germans broke the line in the Warwicks area. A. F Barnes describes what happened next:

> Captain Dudbridge, who was on the right, organized, on his own initiative, counter bombing attack and succeeded in re-establishing the line. This little action proved that D Company, under the inspiring leadership of Captain Dudbridge, had lost none of its morale, in spite of the disaster of the sunken road, which might well have shaken the Company to pieces.

On 5 December 2/5th Gloucesters moved through Villers Plouich, which was a shambles and soaked with phosgene gas, so gas masks had to be worn constantly. Two days later, it moved into the line near Corner Work and was eventually relieved on 10 December and occupied huts at Havrincourt Wood. The Battalion remained in the area in and out of the line until 24 December, when it moved again by train to Cappy behind the Somme front.

Two months later, a court of enquiry was convened to examine what had gone wrong at Cambrai when the Germans counter-attacked. At the same time the Germans appear to have judged the tank to be of little use and to have no future. As a result, the Allies adopted fresh tactics, which they were able to use in 1918, whilst the Germans failed to develop a tank of their own. On 15 December an Armistice was signed between Russia and Germany.

Part IX

OTHER FRONTS IN 1918

Chapter 46

Italy 1918 with 1/4th, 1/5th, 1/6th and 12th Gloucesters

Because Italy fought against Britain in the Second World War many people assume it was among our enemies in 1914–18. In fact, it was an ally. Although a member of the Triple Alliance with Austria-Hungary and Germany, Italy did not declare war in August 1914, arguing that the Alliance was defensive in nature and therefore Austria-Hungary's aggression did not oblige Italy to take part. Italy, moreover, had a longstanding rivalry with Austria-Hungary, dating back to the Congress of Vienna in 1815. In the early stages of the war Allied diplomats courted the Italians, attempting to secure their participation on the Allied side. This culminated in the Treaty of London of 26 April 1915, by which Italy renounced her obligations to the Triple Alliance. On 23 May 1915 Italy declared war on Austria-Hungary, and by July 1917, when Germany sent troops to reinforce the Austrians, Italy and its Allies had been fighting the armies of Austria-Hungary and Germany for two years in Northern Italy. Now the situation changed dramatically. In October 1917 the Italians were routed at the Battle of Caporetto and lost about 300,000 men, 265,000 being taken prisoner. French and British divisions were sent urgently by train from France and Flanders to assist the Italians. They included 48th Division with 1/4th (City of Bristol), 1/5th and 1/6th Gloucesters in early November, and the 5th Division, with 12th Gloucesters (Bristol's Own) on 1 December.

Northern Italy in the winter is cold and inhospitable; soldiers who thought, as they left the Western Front, that they would find sunshine were bitterly disappointed. The Italian Army's retreat had been arrested on the River Piave, but its leadership wasn't at all sure that it could hold firm. The British and French offered to hold the line for them, but the Italian higher command thought otherwise, reasoning their Allies' lack of winter clothing would result in frostbite and heavy losses. The British therefore took over the Montello sector, further east and not so high in the mountains, and their presence allowed the Italians to withdraw and refit. The 48th Division was not in the front line over this period. It held reserve positions around Montello and commenced training in mountain warfare, but 12th Gloucesters manned the line between Nervesa and Palazzon. On 26 January, when the Battalion relieved the 215th Italian Infantry Regiment, it was decided that every man should wear an Italian helmet to deceive the enemy into thinking that the

Map 28 The Campaign in Italy, 1918

British had not taken over the line. As Norman Pegg commented,[1] 'A very comical effect was produced. It was questionable as to whether the CO or his orderly, Cpl Hudson, produced the most comical effect.' The Battalion was engaged in several fighting patrols until 18 March 1918, when 5th Division was relieved and ordered back to France; the situation there had become precarious after the Germans launched their 'Grand Offensive'. Norman Pegg recalled:

> The patrols we carried out nightly with the greatest impunity would not
> have been possible against well trained Germans. The Hungarians, who
> we were up against, however, were a very inferior crowd. They struck us

as being slip-shod soldiers . . . Against them we could not help but have a good time, and it was therefore, with feelings of great regret that we heard at the end of March that we were to leave Italy, for the nightmare of France.

Norman was awarded a DCM for his action on the patrols he describes above. On one night commanding a patrol of four men he discovered an enemy post and captured two of the enemy. The next night he accompanied an officer on a similar mission and took two more prisoners. After the War he became a journalist and racing correspondent.

The three Territorial Gloucester battalions in 48th Division went into the line for the first time at the end of February at Nervesa on the southern bank of the River Piave and immediately commenced patrolling, a very different proposition to patrols on the Western Front. The distances involved were greater, and to cross the Piave they had to wade across 60ft of freezing water, 4ft deep in places. The Italians were right: it was intensely cold and the ground was deep in snow. In March they moved to the Asiago Plateau on much higher ground to the west, which was quiet. There were few trenches as such, the defensive positions usually being constructed from rocks and clinging precariously to ledges on the steep mountainsides.

In June the Austrians launched an offensive aimed at breaking the Piave River defensive line and inflicting a major defeat on the Allies. It failed, and they suffered some 175,000 casualties, but 1/5th Gloucesters, who were in the front line on the Assiago Plateau, fought a desperate battle. On 15 June 23rd and 48th Divisions were attacked by four Austrian divisions. 23rd Division were able to repulse the assault but the Austrians penetrated 3,000yds in the 48th Division sector. 1/5th Gloucesters was in the front line holding the right sub-sector. Their strength was about 490 men, 30 per cent of all ranks being in hospital with influenza. The brigade commander was doubtful whether they should go into the line at all, but two of his other battalions, the 1/6th and 1/7th Royal Warwickshires, were down to even fewer men. The main line held by 1/5th Gloucesters was immediately south of the winding Ghelpac stream. The line itself was no more than a string of scattered posts, placed as high as possible and overlooking the forest but not necessarily affording a clear field of fire. Four outposts were also positioned north of the stream in no-man's-land, although still 1,000yds or so from the Austrian lines. The 1/4th Battalion, Oxfordshire and Buckinghamshire Light Infantry were on the Gloucesters' right. The boundary between them was a 400yd stretch of railway line running north-south that connected Canove di Roana behind the Austrian lines with Cesuna behind the British line.

At 2.45 am on 15 June the Austrian bombardment commenced. Some of the firing was erratic, but on the Gloucesters' front a number of their posts were specifically targeted and two were completely obliterated, leaving a gap in the line. An ammunition dump at Handley Cross, behind the 48th Division's front, was also hit, and this hampered the bringing up of reinforcements. It was a misty, damp morning and the large quantities of smoke, gas and dust thrown up by the bombardment further reduced visibility. Many posts could see nothing at all but heard rifle and machine gun fire going on all around them as the Austrian infantry advanced at 4.00 am. B Company, in the outpost line, retired at 4.30 am to positions just north of the Ghelpac in accordance with a predetermined plan. At about 6.30 am they drove off the first Austrian scouts who approached them but still risked being outflanked and cut off, so withdrew to the Battalion's main line. The Austrians relied on sheer weight of numbers to maintain their advance and they had no shortage of manpower. Shortly after 10.00 am the Austrians succeeded in breaking through where the railway line divided the Gloucesters and the Oxfords. A Company was in danger of being surrounded and so retired, covered by twenty-one-year-old Private Gilbert Oliver of 28 Albert Place, Cheltenham, who sacrificed both his Lewis gun and himself to allow the rest to escape. The Gloucesters' Battalion Headquarters had been organized by the Adjutant, Captain Basil Bruton,[2] and put up a determined resistance but was overrun in hand-to-hand fighting, during which he was killed. Lieutenant Colonel Adam, the CO of 1/5th Gloucesters, wrote to Basil's wife, Isabel:[3]

> It might be truly said of him that he came nearest to that ideal type of British officer that every man ought to get for himself. Courage and ability, generosity and kindheartedness, mixed with a sense of fairness and the discipline which is necessary, never sparing himself, but always working for the good of the Battalion – these were the qualities that those who worked with him always recognized he possessed.

The remaining men, perhaps 100 or so, were forced back into an 'S'-shaped defensive line along Ghelpac Road. There they held the Austrians until about 8.15 am but were then outflanked and had to retire again in two further stages to behind the railway line. A critical situation was saved by a counter-attack by 1/7th Warwicks, which stabilized the line. Eleven officers and 138 other ranks were killed or missing, and 9 officers and 64 other ranks were wounded. The Battalion was awarded 1 DSO, 2 MCs, 1 DCM and 5 MMs. At 5.30 pm 145 Brigade, including 1/6th Gloucesters, launched a counter-attack but was forced to withdraw; at 7.30 pm it attacked again but was forced back; a further attack the next morning found, however, that the Austrians were withdrawing. 1/4th Gloucesters had remained in reserve throughout.

There was then a lull in the fighting in Italy. The Italian Commander-in-Chief declined to launch an attack until he was assured of success, despite pleas from the Allies to do so. On 13 September 1/5th Gloucesters returned to the Western Front, where it fought in some of the final battles of the war. Meanwhile, 1/4th Gloucesters carried out successful raids by the whole battalion on 28 August and 23 October (the day before the Battle of Vittoria Veneto), and 1/6th also carried out raids on 8/9 August and on 24 August. The final major offensive was a large-scale Allied attack on the whole of the Austrian line by nine armies against four Austro-Hungarian armies. 48th Division's role in this was to hold its front while two Italian divisions drove a wedge into the Austrian line. The Battle of Vittorio Veneto began on 24 October. In general it went extremely well, but in front of 48th Division the enemy clung to the mountains. On 1 November 1/4th and 1/6th Gloucesters were ordered to attack at 5.45 am. Both battalions encountered heavy resistance and failed to make much progress. On 2 November the attack was resumed and they reached the summit of Mount Interotto; the Val d'Assa was forced and the Austrian Army faced defeat. The advance continued on 3 November, but the two Gloucester battalions had seen their last fight. The Armistice in Italy came into force at 3.00 pm on 4 November. This had been no easy battle. Sergeant C. Bees and Corporal G. J. Fry were both awarded DCMs for gallant conduct during a raid on Ave on 23/24 October. Sergeant Bees was 'in command of a platoon and rushed a party outside a dugout causing several to surrender and went on to his final objective capturing a machine gun.' When Corporal Fry's section was held up by an enemy machine gun, 'he rushed it single handed . . . he set a magnificent example and throughout the operation showed great determination and courage.' In addition, the gallantry of 1/4th Gloucesters was recognized by the award of 1 Bar to MC, 4 MCs, and 13 MMs or Bars to MMs.

Notes

1. Dean Marks, '*Bristol's Own*', the 12th Battalion Gloucestershire Regiment 1914–1918.
2. Basil Vassar Bruton (1878–1918) had been a partner in Bruton Knowles & Co of Gloucester, having been educated at the Crypt School, King's School Gloucester and Bromsgrove. He had been Mentioned in Despatches earlier in the Italian Campaign. His uncle was Sir James Bruton, Mayor of Gloucester from 1900 to 1918, and he himself was City Councillor for the Allington Ward. His son-in-law, Digby Grist, grandson (the author of this book) and two great-grandsons all served in the Regiment.
3. Letter in the author's possession.

Chapter 47

The Impact of the Russian Revolution on Mesopotamia and on 7th Gloucesters

It is time to return to the adventures of 7th Gloucesters in Mesopotamia. At the beginning of 1918 the strength of the Battalion was 28 officers and 916 other ranks. Remarkably, it was still commanded by Lieutenant Colonel Richard Jordan, who, it may be remembered, had raised the Battalion in 1914 and been badly wounded in Gallipoli in August 1915. Although he rejoined on 20 January 1916 he tore his Achilles tendon after just three days, was evacuated to hospital and did not return for a further year until 15 January 1917, when he resumed command for the rest of the War. He must have known his men extraordinarily well, and they him. At the beginning of 1918 his greatest concern was almost certainly smallpox. Five other ranks had died of the disease the previous month and A Company was in 'isolation' at Sadiyeh.

The campaign in Mesopotamia halted after the capture of Baghdad in April 1917, while the Allies coped with the incredible heat of summer. An attempt to take Ramadi, 70 miles west of Baghdad, in July failed largely due to the heat, but a second, better organized assault in September succeeded, and Tikrit, 90 miles north-west of Baghdad, was captured in November without a fight. Twelve days later, General Maude, who had made such a difference to the campaign, died of cholera. 7th Gloucesters had not been involved in either of these actions and had been relatively static for nine months; the men spent their time training or improving the defences under the direction of the Royal Engineers. An entry in the Battalion War Diary for 17 January 1918 records: 'Lance-Corporals Peters, Dunn & French left camp en route for BAGHDAD to join as Instructors to the Armenian Army.' On 21 March, the Gloucesters' Regimental Day (known as Back Badge Day), 7th Gloucesters held a holiday with sports in the afternoon and a concert in the evening.

Towards the end of March an advance party departed for Abu Saida to set up a 'summer camp' for the Battalion, but on 9 April the Division began to move north and by the 29th had marched 84 miles without any fighting and reached Tuz Khurmatli, where the Column it was part of was ordered to engage the Turks. The fighting began at 5.00 am and lasted for about five hours; the Battalion suffered no casualties, although nearly 1,000 Turks were taken prisoner. There was then a pause until 4 May, when the advance continued towards Kirkuk, starting each day before dawn and halting about 10.00 am as it began to get hot. The Turks abandoned Kirkuk without a fight and 7th Gloucesters formed part of the garrison, providing a Guard of Honour for the Corps Commander's official entry to the city on 9 May. The Battalion left Kirkuk on 14 May to march to their summer camp at Abu Said, which they reached on 29 May. The War Diary records:

> End of march – Battalion having marched 265 miles since evening of April 22nd. Casualties during that period were seven O.R. (by bomb accident) and four officers and ninety-five other ranks to field ambulance. Nine of these having rejoined before the march was completed.

Regimental Quartermaster Sergeant George Turle noted in his diary on 28 May:

> Got quite a surprise. Had a gift from the Lord Mayor and Mayoress of Bristol, a box containing pipe, tobacco and cig papers . . . On half rations – ½ lb Bread; 2 oz sugar; 2 oz bacon; 1 slice cheese; 1 bottle of water for 24 hours; 4 oz biscuit.

The Battalion remained at Abu Saida until being sent to reinforce Dunsterforce in the Caucasus in August.

Until the Russian Revolution, Tsarist Russia had been an ally and had fought the Germans and Austrians on the Eastern Front and the Ottomans in the Caucasus. But Bolshevik Russia had signed a peace treaty and ceased fighting, leaving a vacuum in the Southern Caucasus. This might not have mattered, except that Britain had long feared attempts to destabilize India's North-West Frontier through Afghanistan and so had established, early in the war, the East Persian Cordon to prevent attempts by enemy agents to stir up trouble in the region. Of more immediate strategic importance was Caucasian oil, which was refined at Baku on the Caspian Sea, and the cotton crop of Turkestan across the Caspian.

The Government in London now saw the need to organize local forces in Northern Persia and the Southern Caucasus to replace the Russians and oppose the Turks. Dunsterforce[1] was formed in December 1917 by volunteers who needed to be 'men of strong character, adventurous spirit, especially good stamina, capable of organizing and eventually leading irregular troops', and its initial mission was 'to gather information, train and command local forces, and prevent the spread of German propaganda'. At the start it consisted of 100 officers and 250 men in a column of armoured cars. In the spring of 1918 the Germans began to push forward to Baku from Eastern Ukraine, whilst the Turks advanced across the Caucasian border. Dunsterforce left Baghdad on 27 January 1918 and reached Enzeli (Anzali) in Northern Persia on the Caspian Sea, nearly 200 miles south of Baku, on 17 February. Here they found Russian regular forces, who withdrew on 1 April to be replaced by a Bolshevik Committee, whom the British arrested in

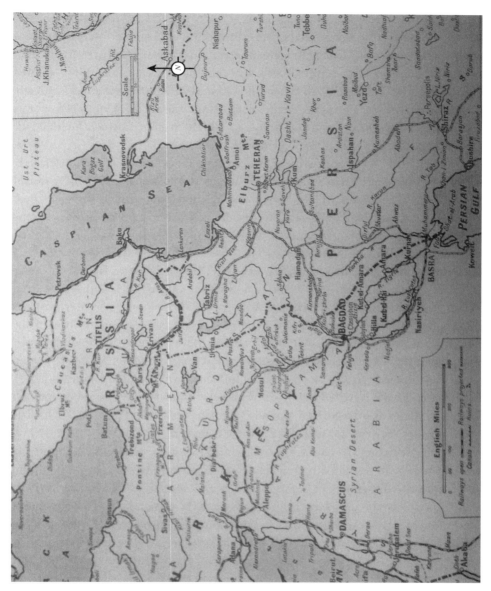

Map 29 Western and Southern Russia, 1919

August. Meanwhile, German and Turkish forces had begun to advance into the South Caucasus on a different axis, and the objectives of Dunsterforce changed: it had now grown to about 1,000 strong and become an expeditionary force. On 4 August it reached Baku, where the Bolshevik Government had been replaced by the Central Caspian Dictatorship, and began trying to organize the defence of the city against the advancing Ottoman Islamic Army of the Caucasus, about 14,000 strong, 70 per cent of them Azerbaijanis. In addition to Dunsterforce, there were about 6,000 troops, principally Armenians, defending Baku. The Turks attacked on 26 August and by 14 September it was clear that the battle was lost; Dunsterforce withdrew on 14/15 September. What followed in Baku was the last major massacre of the War, several thousand Armenians being murdered. Dunsterforce was disbanded two days later and the troops in Northern Persia, which included 7th Gloucesters, became part of the North Persian Force.

On 18 August 7th Gloucesters, less D Company, had set out to join Dunsterforce, initially by train and then by motor lorry. They arrived at Hamadan, having travelled over 200 miles, on 25 August. On 16 September, when Dunsterforce was disbanded, 7th Gloucesters along with the rest of 39 Brigade, 36 Brigade, supporting arms and the remnants of Dunsterforce, became the NORPERFORCE with the task of preventing the Bolsheviks reaching North Persia. The situation changed dramatically two days later, when Allenby began his brilliant rout of the Turks in Palestine. By 25 September it was clear that Ottoman rule of the region was at an end; their withdrawal from Persia was anticipated and the various Arab tribes, whose loyalty had been suspect, quickly became allies. There is no evidence of 7th Gloucesters being involved in any fighting, but the Battalion was constantly on the move as the small force attempted to dominate the huge area. By 30 September most of the Battalion was in the Zinjan area, where in early October an epidemic of influenza broke out and four men died. A month later, having travelled hundreds of miles by train and lorry as well as on foot, 7th Gloucesters was concentrated around Qazvin in north-west Persia on 31 October 1918, at which date the war with Turkey came to an end.

That the British and Indian armies took so long to achieve success in Mesopotamia was due mainly to the climate; Iraq is one of the hottest places in the world, quite apart from the difficulties of communication and the size of the country. At the same time it was not a priority for the Allies once the oil supply had been secured. Nevertheless, for those battalions like 7th Gloucesters who were deployed there it demanded resilience to cope with the heat and disease. The tragedy was that, having defeated the Ottoman Empire, the Allies reneged on promises they had made to the Arabs, the consequences of which are haunting us a century later.

Note

1. Major General Lionel Charles Dunsterville CB CSI (1865–1946), who commanded Dunsterforce, was the model for Rudyard Kipling's 'Stalky' in *Stalky & Co*; they were at school together. He had been commissioned into the British Army but later transferred to the British Indian Army and had served on the North-West Frontier, Waziristan and China, so was well suited to the task.

Chapter 48

Palestine – 1/1ˢᵗ RGH in the Raid on Es Salt

In Palestine, 1917 ended with the fall of Jerusalem. The signing of the Armistice between Russia and Germany was to have a major impact on Allenby's ability to continue the capture of Palestine. He was forced to release significant numbers of seasoned men to Europe to deal with the German offensive in March 1918. Many of these were replaced by Indian troops, some of them with little training. In addition, the weather made road and rail construction extremely slow, and in any case a period of prolonged rest was needed, not least to nurse the exhausted horses back to health. These factors meant delaying any significant advance against the Ottomans in Palestine for nine months, until September 1918. Allenby, in the meantime, decided that when the British did advance they would do so up the coastal plain, where he could use his cavalry to greatest effect. Before this, it was essential to protect the right flank by driving the Turks across the River Jordan; additionally, any operations in the Jordan Valley might lead the Turks to expect the main advance to be made there. Jericho was taken on 21 February, and a main crossing point over the Jordan was secured in mid-March. After the first attack on Amman at the beginning of April had failed, a second action was launched by the Desert Mounted Corps supported by the 60ᵗʰ (London) Divsion on 30 April; this is known as 'the Second Action of Es Salt'.

1/1ˢᵗ RGH left El Burj on 1 January and reached a rest camp north of the lagoon at Deir-el-Belah eight days later. Here it received reinforcements and conducted musketry and machine gun training. Some leave was possible, there were sporting competitions and on 14 March the Regiment was inspected by HRH the Duke of Connaught and Strathearn, who presented decorations. The Duke, who was the third son of Queen Victoria and Prince Albert, had been a career soldier, rising through the ranks to become a Field Marshal and Inspector General of the Forces from 1904 to 1907, so his visit must have been a major event. It was during this period that the Regiment established the 'RGH Hounds', consisting of a single couple: 'Tripe', who had a brilliant nose and drive, and 'Onions', who preferred to stay in camp and deserted when the Regiment moved. Other regiments also hunted, principally jackals, and according to an article published in February there was normally a field of about 100.[1] A steeplechase meeting was held on 7 March, and in early April the Regiment moved to Selmeh, from where the men were able to visit Jaffa and there were some opportunities to go to Jerusalem. It was also during this period that Robert Wilson fell in love with a VAD nurse, Edith Ross, always known as Paddy, while on a course in Cairo in January. He wrote home on 25 February: 'I met a topping little VAD whilst I was there. She used to go to church with me and sometimes lunch or dinner. There was nothing much in it, but you get so fed up with soldiers' company that it's a nice change – she is an Irishman.' He had in fact asked her to marry him, which she did in October 1919.

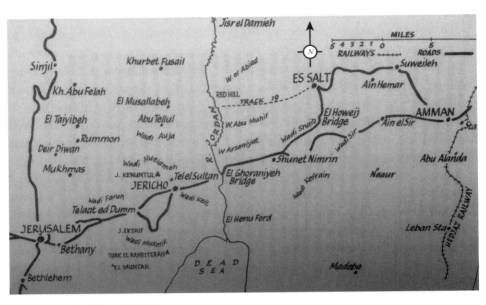

Map 30 The Raid on Es Salt

On 24 April, rest and recuperation over, 1/1ˢᵗ RGH began to move towards the Jordan Valley to take part in the fighting for Es Salt. Algar Howard recorded the journey in his diary:[2]

> Friday, 26 – We leave Enab at 7pm and trek 21 miles through Jerusalem by moonlight, which was very impressive, and we halted at midnight two miles beyond Bethany in the country known in the Bible as the Wilderness, where we off-saddled and had tea. We arrived at Telaat-ed-Dumm at 3am, April 27, very tired and dirty. This place is half way between Jerusalem and Jericho, and there is plenty of water, otherwise there is nothing to say about it. The country is a veritable wilderness; not a tree, not a crop, not a blade of grass, not an animal except scorpions, snakes, vultures and hawks (the latter most consistent camp followers now). Forty days and forty nights here would indeed have been a penitence . . . Telaat-ed-Dumm

appeared to us to be a most beastly place, nothing but dust and stones, but we little knew how delightful a spot it was, compared to the valley below.

April 27 – We moved at 2pm to the Jordan Valley. We went down the old road, which was very rocky, rough, and precipitous, while the wheeled transport went by the new road, recently made by the Turks, very much longer, but with good gradients . . . The modern Jericho is on a flat plain, with a long avenue of poplars running north-west, and many gardens of apricots, bananas, grapes, oranges and tomatoes . . . We turned north and went up the valley till we came to our camping ground, which was nothing but rocks. We had no idea what the position of affairs was, where our outpost line was, or where the Turks were.

On 29 April the Regiment crossed the Jordan by the Ghoraniyeh Bridge, then turned north to the Wadi Abu Muhir. The enemy were astride the Jericho–Amman road, with detachments of cavalry on both flanks. For the attack the cavalry, less one regiment, was to move along the east bank of the Jordan to Umm-el-Shert and Jisr-el-Damieh and then turn up through the hills on two tracks and capture Es Salt. The Sherwood and Worcestershire Yeomanry led 5ᵗʰ Mounted Brigade, with 1/1ˢᵗ RGH in support. Having gained the plateau above the Jordan Valley, the force encountered even more difficult mountainous country and in many places it was essential to dismount and lead the horses in single file along precipitous bridle paths; on occasions it was impossible to lead the horses, so men hung on to their tails and were pulled up. The camels, who were included to evacuate the wounded, could not cope and were sent back. The Turks fired on the column in the late afternoon some miles south of Es Salt, and it was decided to wait until dawn to attack the town. By now, however, an Australian Light Horse Brigade which had advanced on an easier route had reached Es Salt and captured the town itself.

On 1 May 1/1ˢᵗ RGH had a precipitous ride down into Es Salt. Having watered the horses and filled their water bottles, the Regiment was sent through Es Salt to seize El Howeij Bridge. Headed by D Squadron, they proceeded down the main Es Salt–Jericho road, which followed the bottom of a steep ravine with a rushing stream beside it. After about four miles the Squadron was held up by rifle and machine gun fire a mile north of the bridge and so took up an outpost position astride the road. It was a difficult situation: the enemy were holding the high ground on both side of the ravine, which was too steep to climb. There was no means of attack except down the road, which was blocked at the bridge and covered all the way by machine guns. The obvious thing to do appeared to be to block the road and wait for the infantry to drive the Turks on to the Regiment. However, when the Division was informed of the position it ordered that the bridge should be taken.

Communications to Division were difficult, but the order to attack was countermanded and 2nd Brigade, which had been sent to Ain Hemar, instead of holding the road there was withdrawn to attack the El Howeijh Bridge the next day. Meanwhile, D Squadron 1/1st RGH remained in observation all day under under heavy and accurate shellfire from a 4.5-in gun and from a few machine guns. D Squadron had four casualties – two killed and two died subsequently of wounds. The latter had been sent back to Es Salt in a captured German ambulance. Finally, it was decided that the Regiment should withdraw to a stronger position about 3 miles back for the night. D Squadron got back about 8.00 pm with orders to move out again to the same position at 4.00 am the next day.

The next morning, 2 May, D Squadron found their position from the previous day held by the Turks, who had to be driven out. The 5th Mounted Brigade was ordered to attack dismounted, with 2nd Light Horse Brigade in reserve. At 8.00 am 1/1 RGH moved down the road. In 1928, Brigadier PJV Kelly,[3] the commander of 5th Mounted Brigade, recalled the events of that day:[4]

> We were on low ground. The enemy had an artillery OP on top of the high ground overlooking us and the Huweij [sic] Bridge. No movement on our part was possible without heavy shelling from an invisible howitzer battery. We had already experienced the accuracy and deadly effect of this fire in various reconnaissances which had taken place. The attack was carried by elements of 2 regiments (Gloucester and Notts Sherwood Ranger Yeomanry) and a very weak 3rd regiment in reserve. The only covering fire was that of a mountain pack artillery battery, which had accompanied me. Machine guns and Hotchkiss had to be quite early in the advance left behind, as the ground was found quite impassable to any pack. The attacking regiments had no opportunity of ever firing a shot, nor did we ever see any of the enemy . . . The advance, over a distance of about 1 mile from the point of assembly to the hill domineering and commanding the Huweij Bridge, took between 6 & 7 hours . . . There was no question of breaking off the attack, it simply spent itself.

Towards evening the Worcesters and Sherwoods returned so exhausted that they had to rest, and 1/1st RGH were left to hold the line, with D Squadron still at the front. By this time Es Salt was being severely threatened by Turkish reinforcements.

Despite the situation at Es Salt, 5th Mounted Brigade remained ready to continue the attack the next day once fresh troops arrived. Little action happened;

a donkey convoy with ammunition arrived towards evening; B Squadron were able to relieve D Squadron; and Captain Vines of the RGH discovered a track out from the road. Elsewhere the situation was becoming more and more critical, but 1/1st RGH settled down for another night. Just before the Regiment was able to eat its meal it received orders 'to move in half an hour'. Everyone ate quickly, left the fires burning and withdrew at 2.30 am down the track discovered by Captain Vines, followed by the rest of the Brigade; the column was nearly 5 miles long. Eventually, the Regiment reached the Jordan Valley and arrived in camp at 12 o'clock after a 36-mile trek, exhausted. Five other ranks had died and 8 had been wounded. Altogether, 1,000 Turkish prisoners had been taken.

The Marquess of Anglesey wrote:

> The taking of Es Salt was the sole tactical success of the operation, which otherwise proved to be the biggest failure of the whole of Allenby's campaign. This was because the information on which the plan had been based was perilously defective and in some respects erroneous.

Allenby, however, dismissed the notion of failure, convinced that the operation had misled the Turks that the British intended to strike in the west and deployed their forces accordingly.

Notes

1. *The Field*, 24 February 1917.
2. Frank Fox, *The Royal Gloucestershire Hussars Yeomanry 1898–1922*.
3. Brigadier Sir Philip James Vandeleur Kelly KCMG, DSO had been commissioned into the 3rd King's Own Hussars. He commanded 5th Mounted Brigade from 4 December 1917 until 22 July 1918, when it became the 13th Cavalry Brigade, which he commanded until 7 October 1918.
4. Brigadier Kelly's papers are held in the Imperial War Museum (Documents 19655).

Chapter 49

Palestine – 1/1ˢᵗ RGH Endure the Jordan Valley in High Summer

Algar Howard wrote to his family after two days in the lower Jordan Valley:[1]

Of all the cursed spots of filthy, hideous, dusty country give me the banks of the Jordan. Why John the Baptist ever selected such a God-forsaken, horrible spot I don't know. The flies are simply unbearable. There is no air, and it is deadly hot. Killed a large scorpion this morning and a snake. It is a loathsome spot.

He was not exaggerating, yet this is where the British spent the summer of 1918. Allenby's strategic plan demanded that the troops had to stay in this Valley of Death, as he explained:[2]

It is the best line I can hold. Any retirement would weaken it. My right flank is covered by the Jordan; my left by the Mediterranean Sea. The Jordan Valley must be held by me; it is vital. If the Turks regained control of the Jordan, I should lose control of the Dead Sea. This would cut me off from the Arabs on the Hedjaz railway; with the result that, shortly, the Turks would regain their power in the Hedjaz. The Arabs would make terms with them, and our prestige would be gone. My right flank would be turned, and my position in Palestine would be untenable. I might hold Rafa or El Arish; but you can imagine what effect such a withdrawal would have on the population of Egypt, and on the watching tribes of the Western Desert. You see, therefore, that I cannot modify my present dispositions. I must give up nothing of what I now hold. Anyhow, I must hold the Jordan Valley.

There may have been little fighting, but the suffering of the men and horses was immense. The valley is generally abandoned in these months, even by the majority of the Arab population, and the official military handbook stated: 'Nothing is known of the climate of the lower Jordan Valley in summer-time since no civilised human being has yet been found to spend a summer there.' The maximum temperature in July averages 113.2°F (45°C) in the shade and can reach over 120°F (49°C). The bottom of the valley, which was once under the sea, is covered in a white clay dust several feet deep, impregnated with salts. Each morning as the sun rises the wind gets up and blows this dust into acrid clouds. If this was not enough, there are scorpions, tarantulas, centipedes and snakes, particularly the horned viper, to contend with. Furthermore, the men were not only required to be present, but to work, digging trenches, patrolling and generally making their presence felt. As Fox wrote, 'That they went through all this to the triumphant end was, on the whole, the greatest achievement of courage, discipline and endurance of the whole campaign.'

A day after their succesful but demanding withdrawal from Es Salt, on 5 May, 1/1st RGH were ordered to the Wadi Auja to relieve the 4th Battalion of the Imperial Camel Corps Brigade. Algar Howard wrote in his diary:

> Sunday, 5 May – We got orders at 2pm to move in three quarters of an hour. Everything seemed to be in a fearful hurry, and we all thought there was another attack on. The CO goes on and I follow with the regiment as fast as possible. We arrive at Wadi Auja and are then guided up along to Wadi Mallaleh, where we eventually arrive at 5pm. I have to drop guides at every turn to bring on our rear parties to Wadi Mallaheh and put down horse lines for the night. The three squadrons are to take over from the ICC at 3am next morning.
>
> Monday, 6 May – Three squadrons go into the line at 3am, the camels remaining till night to come out. I take the led horses back to Wadi Mallaheh and pick a camp. The 9th and 18th Bengal Lancers arrive at 3pm. The Turks are very active, and altogether the positions are not satisfactory.

He was right. The position they took over was overlooked by the Turks and any movement by day drew fire. Twice the enemy attacked but were held off, and eventually it was agreed that the Regiment should move back to the old line during the night. As D Squadron was about to move they came into contact with the enemy and their pack horses went astray, so that when they withdrew they had to carry everything. Enemy attacks were constantly expected but did not materialize, although the defences needed to be strengthened. Working hours were 4.15 to 7.15 in the morning and 6.00 to 9.00 at night. Before the Regiment was relieved on 14 May the effects of the climate were being felt: 21 men had been evacuated to hospital, principally with diarrhoea or septic sores, and 4 days later this number rose to 42. After 12 days out of the line the Regiment returned on 26 May. By now the composition of 5th Mounted Brigade had changed: the Worcesters and

Sherwoods had been replaced by 9th Hodson's Horse and 18th King George's Own Lancers from 3rd (Ambala) Cavalry Brigade of the British Indian Army.

June was like May, except that it was hotter and there was an increase in enemy air attacks and long-range shelling. Some of the tedium was relieved by patrolling, but meanwhile work continued on the defences. At last, on 23 June, 1/1st RGH moved well out of the line to a camp that was 1,000ft higher and significantly cooler. The relief only lasted a week before the Regiment moved back as an immediate reserve at one hour's notice. July and August are the hottest months in Palestine, and on 1 July two parties left for rest camps in Port Said and Jerusalem and the remainder of the Regiment moved well away from the Jordan Valley to recuperate. On 17 July they began to move back into the valley and resumed the old routine. During July Major Gerald Horlick died of malignant malaria; he had moved from the Regiment some time before to command a Machine Gun Section.[3] 1/1st RGH spent August out of the Jordan Valley training, in preparation for the new offensive. By now the Great German Offensive on the Western Front was over, and some reorganization in Palestine led to the 2nd Mounted Division being renumbered as the 5th Cavalry Division on 22 July 1918 and the brigades as 13th, 14th and 15th (Imperial Service). 1/1st RGH was in 13th Cavalry Brigade and, with 1/1 Sherwood Rangers in 14th Brigade, were the only English regiments in the Division; the remainder were from the British Indian Army. They were all poised to drive the Turks out of Palestine and win the war on that front.

Notes

1. Frank Fox, *The Royal Gloucestershire Hussars Yeomanry 1898–1922.*
2. Mathew Hughes, *Allenby in Palestine. The Middle East Correspondence of Field Marshal Viscount Allenby June 1917–October 1919.*
3. Gerald Nolkin Horlick (1888–1918) was the son of Sir James and Lady Horlick of Cowley Manor, Gloucestershire. James and his brother William were born in Ruardean in the Forest of Dean and went to America, where they developed Horlicks, the malted milk drink. Gerald was born in Brooklyn and was working as an Assistant Manager at Horlicks before the War. His parents restored the glorious organ loft in Gloucester Cathedral in his memory.

Chapter 50

Palestine 1st RGH Capture
Nazareth in a Cavalry Charge

egiddo (19–25 September 1918) was the final and decisive battle of the Palestine campaign. Although Allenby's intention was to launch his main attack up the coast he had been determined to mislead the Turks throughout the summer and this tactic continued until the last moment. The Arab Northern Army therefore began an attack on the railway junction at Daraa on 16 September to interupt the Ottoman lines of communication. Then, on 18 September, two divisions of XX Corps launched an attack in the Judean Hills, partly to confirm Turkish expectations but also to block the Ottoman withdawal route from Nablus across the Jordan and if possible to capture the Ottomans' Seventh Army Headquarters in Nablus itself. With the stage set, the main attack could then be launched on the coast by four infantry divisions of XXI Corps across an 8-mile front on 19 September. As soon as the breakthrough was achieved, the Desert Mounted Corps with its three mounted divisions, which was poised behind the division of XXI Corps closest to the coast, was to move as quickly as possible to seize the passes through the Carmel Range and the communications centres of Al-Afuleh and Beisan, which were 60 miles away; this was the maximum distance that the cavalry could cover before needing to halt for rest and to water and feed their horses.

There were two other forces in Allenby's plan. Another division of XXI Corps was to launch a subsidiary assault 5 miles inland of the main attack and, once the breakthough here had been achieved, 5th Light Horse Brigade was to capture the Headquarters of the Ottoman Eighth Army at Tulkam and the lateral railway line by which both Ottoman armies were supplied. Finally, a mixed force of 11,000 men, which included the Anzac Mounted Division and known as Chaytor's Force, was to capture the lines of communication between the Ottoman Fourth Army at Es Salt and the other two Ottoman armies.

It was vital to continue to mislead the enemy while preparations were made, so the holding force in the Jordan Valley was exceptionally active and dummy camps were built, while on the western flank concentrations of troops and cavalry were assembled and kept under cover in daylight hours, during which the strengthened Royal Air Force had achieved air superiority and prevented enemy aircraft from observing what was happening. All these efforts worked: the enemy were completely deceived and taken spectacularly by surprise.

1/1st RGH, meanwhile, had been brought up to full strength, and training focused on the task ahead. During the night of 17/18 September the Regiment moved up with the rest of 5th Division to a concealed position in orange groves at Sarona, near Jaffa, and rested. At 4.30 am on 19 September 385 guns opened up a devastating 15-minute bombardment enhanced by naval gunfire, then the infantry advanced. By 6.00 am, 4 hours earlier than expected, the infantry had broken through, allowing the cavalry, with the RGH the only British unit in the vanguard, to pass through the gap they had made. What followed was the sort of action that cavalrymen dreamt of but few had ever experienced, particularly in the First World War. Initially, they rode up the beach, which was heavy going for the horses, but once they cleared the beach they were on the Plain of Sharon, which was perfect cavalry country taken at the canter. 13th Brigade encountered minor opposition, which added a frisson to the morning, and two incidents involving the RGH illustrate this. At about 10.00 am shellfire led to a patrol of five men, under Corporal Wiseman, being sent out to reconnoitre the position of the guns. They found two enemy guns limbering up, so charged immediately, and the officer in charge surrendered with 20 men. In a separate action, Trooper Edward Forrest[1] saw a large column of trucks moving to the north from Nahr-el-Falik; drawing his sword he galloped toward the column, which halted on his approach and surrendered; it consisted of 37 wagons, 4 officers and 100 men. Forrest was awarded the DCM.

By 11.30 am 13th Brigade had advanced 15 miles and reached Liktera, where it captured a large number of prisoners and more materiel, including a transport and supply depot largely manned by Germans. At 11.50 am it halted at El Hudeira and rested, while the remainder of the Division moved up to join it. Many of the horses were now exhausted; 5 had to be destroyed and 17 others evacuated.

The next phase for 13th Brigade was the advance on Nazareth some 40 miles away. It began at 6.00 pm that evening and was a complete contrast to the morning's excitement. 1/1st RGH was behind 18th Bengal Lancers. The going was extremely difficult over rough and rocky country. Often the whole Brigade was in single file. The Indians had trouble with their pack animals, which were inclined to lag behind. When the Indians halted it became clear that they had lost touch with their column; in fact, they were hopelessly lost. Algar Howard wrote in his diary:

> I discovered to my horror that the Indians in front of me, whom I was following, had lost touch with the main body at the critical moment when the mountain track divided into four different well worn paths across the vale in four different directions. This was a terrible affair, and I pictured

myself lost at the head of the regiment, and I saw Gen Kelly, the Brigade Commander, with the 18th Bengal Lancers in their glory, advancing on Nazareth. I was furious with the Indians in front of me, and cursed them up hill and down dale. That being of no avail I settled down, halted, and dismounted. There were a lot of Bedouins' shacks about but having no interpreter it was useless to ask them, and probably impossible to drag them out of their shacks. One path led eastwards, which appeared to be the wrong way, as I knew one objective was to blow up the railway which runs to Haifa and that could only go east and west along the valley somewhere. I sent a scout up the path, but he returned saying that he heard and saw nothing. Another scout reported the same of a path running eastwards. I had meanwhile made up my mind that one of the two paths leading across the valley must be right. A scout up one of these solved the situation by picking up a packman, who had fallen out of the troop ahead. We went along and soon came up with Major Mills, the 2nd in Command of the Lancers, whom I was delighted to meet – until he told me that he had also lost the Brigadier and staff, who had gone on in front. Another halt and more scouts sent out, and after half an hour we found the Brigadier near the railway, much to everyone's relief. Being late we hurried on, leaving the R.E. officer with a specially trained demolition officer to blow up the line, which he did.

On reaching Mejeidil, the RGH took over as advance guard and moved on at a sharp trot. At 4.25 am on 21 September the column sighted Nazareth; the Regiment drew swords and galloped into the little town. The enemy were taken completely by surprise. Hundreds of them surrendered and the German GHQ was captured, although General Liman von Sanders had either escaped the previous evening or was hiding successfully. Robert Wilson decided to search the upper storey of the Turkish barracks:

I hurled myself at the first door and was confronted by a smiling, bowing officer who immediately proffered his revolver and sword. I thanked him very much and told him to go downstairs where Hargreaves was waiting. After hurling myself at two or three more doors and being received in the same gracious manner I simply walked into the remaining rooms . . . In each room the occupant went through the same procedure . . . Eventually I came to the last door, which was very firmly bolted and barred. I thought of doing the 'Western' stunt of shooting the lock off but didn't know how to do it. It all seemed ominous as I could hear movement and whispering going on inside and thought I had reached the hornet's nest.

I flung all my weight at the door, which crashed open. I was prepared for anything – except the tableau which confronted me. On the floor on his knees, with hands clasped in prayer was an officer and, on the bed with no blankets or anything, a woman and her baby – born only a few seconds earlier – which had yet to offer its first squeak. This had me beaten, of course, so I just shook hands with the officer, patted the woman on the head and left them in peace.

Eventually, some of the enemy rallied and heavy street fighting ensued, but within an hour the complete town had been captured and 1,500 prisoners taken. At 8.00 am enemy on high ground to the west of the town made a determined counter-attack. D Squadron and part of B Squadron pushed forward and inflicted heavy losses. The Regiment then came under machine gun fire from high ground and was ordered to fall back into a reserve position on the Nazareth–Jaffa road and take up a line of outposts on high ground from the El Alfule–Nazareth road. The next day, it was decided to re-occupy Nazareth; 1/1st RGH led and reoccupied the town with little opposition. Squadron Sergeant Major William Price from Corsham in Wiltshire, who had previously won the MM, and Sergeant R. G. Thompson were killed along with 28 horses, and 1 officer and 10 other ranks were wounded.

Note

1. Edward Forrest DCM (1896–1982) was born in Horfield, Bristol. He was with the party left in Egypt to look after the horses while the Regiment sailed for Gallipoli. He was one of the few officers and men who had mobilized with the Regiment in 1914 to take part in the major parade on entering Aleppo on 27 October 1918. After the War he returned to the family business as a baker. Remaining in the RGH, he gained the Territorial Efficiency Medal in December 1927.

Chapter 51

1/1ˢᵗ RGH Advance into Syria

The Seventh and Eighth Ottoman Armies, west of the Jordan, were no longer effective, although there was a great deal of 'mopping up' required. The Ottoman Fourth Army, east of the Jordan, was still in existence and had yet to be defeated. On 24 September Es Salt was taken and the Turks retired to Damascus. On 23 September 5ᵗʰ Cavalry Division, including 1/1ˢᵗ RGH, set out from Nazareth to take Acre and Haifa. Algar Howard's diary records events in more detail:[1]

> September 23 – Reveille at 2.30am. Dress, cook and eat breakfast in the dark. Everybody being hidden under a separate fig tree, it was difficult to get collected. However, we got off somehow to the starting point, which we passed in good time. The 18ᵗʰ Bengal Lancers were doing advance guard today . . . By 10 o'clock we reach a large village, called Seframa . . . We feed horses and have lunch . . . After half an hour we went on again . . . Acre is surrounded by tall palm trees. Close to it is a mound, which obviously the enemy would hold, as it was the only tactical position anywhere near. On the other hand, we had a huge flat plain to move over in order to approach the town. The Brigadier did the obvious thing, which was to make a large detour round to the east and north side of the town. While doing this they fired a few shells at us, but the armoured cars got up to the town and reported no resistance. The 18ᵗʰ Bengal Lancers then galloped to the mound and captured two field guns, which had been left there. We also captured 150 men.

On 27 September 1/1ˢᵗ RGH left one squadron to garrison Acre until the infantry arrived and began the long journey towards Damascus. The going was tough: in places the horses had to be led and some died during the march. Algar Howard adds detail:

> Friday, September 27 – We move off (5ᵗʰ Cavalry Division) at 2.40am for Tiberius. The road is good, and as soon as day breaks one wakes up and feels quite fresh again. At 9am we arrive at Tiberius, a squat, thickly housed town on the very edge of the Sea of Galilee, the road leading to

it going down a steep hill. The last of the Australians were just leaving as we arrived, and as they were held up at the Jordan crossing we were given two hours to off-saddle, water, and feed. This we did on the edge of the lake, and of course we all bathed. It is a delightful sea with a very stony bottom. We had a good meal and plenty of tea . . . At 1pm we move off around the edge of the lake by Capernaum, of which there are few signs left. The road seems unending, but after a long, stiff climb we finally reached a spot near Kasra Atra in the dark, where we lay down just as we were.

Saturday, September 28 – Reveille at 4am and we move off at 9am for El Kunitra. On arrival at the Jordan crossing we have to set to work to make a road near a ford to get our guns over. This we do with brushwood and stones . . . At 5.30pm we set off along a road with very rocky country on each side and eventually arrived at El Kunitra at 11pm, where we camped for the night. Found lots of hay in the village, which we borrowed, as the inhabitants were very hostile Circassians.

Sunday, September 29 – We had all day to rest. The country round is rocky, with a good deal of short grass. It lies below Mount Hebron, and is cold and desolate . . . We are now 3,000ft up and the nights are very cold. We have only our drill jackets and no coats, but use horse blankets by night as well as our own. At 6.30pm we move off again, but do not get very far as the Australian Division is held up at Sasa and take a long time to get on. We are kept waiting on the road, shivering with cold, for 4½ hours. No orders came down, and we had to be ready to move at any moment. It was the coldest night we have yet experienced. Many slept on the road. Others walked up and down to keep warm. I did the latter, as it was too cold to sleep. It was a really miserable night, but finally we moved on at 4.30am on Monday, September 30.

When 1/1st RGH reached Sasa on 30 September there were signs of recent fighting all round them, including wounded Turks waiting for ambulances. At 1.00 pm 1/1st RGH moved off as the leading regiment of the brigade towards Kaukab, which had already been taken before they got there. Captain Lord Apsley[2] was sent with two troops to capture the high-powered Kadem wireless station near Meidan on the road to Damascus, which was transmitting a great deal of German propaganda. When they reached Kadem they saw the equipment being destroyed by about 500 Turks and Germans. The patrol formed up and charged. The enemy offered no resistance and between 150 and 200 were captured, but after going a short distance the prisoners refused to accompany their captors, and fire was now coming from all directions. Outnumbered by about twelve to one, the patrol was again ordered to charge; 3 Germans and 12 Turks were killed with the sword and many more wounded, while one RGH NCO and 2 horses were wounded. More Turkish and German reinforcements were then seen to be advancing, and the patrol was forced to withdraw. Captain Lord Apsley was awarded the DSO.

The Desert Mounted Corps advanced on Damascus in two columns. One, the 4ᵗʰ Cavalry Division, moving via the south side of the Sea of Galilee, Irbid and Derma, had encountered considerable opposition but had pushed on and eventually linked up on 28 September with the Arab Army, which had played a significant part in attacking the retreating Turks and Germans. 1/1ˢᵗ RGH was in the second column, consisting of 5ᵗʰ Cavalry Division and Australian Mounted Division. By midday on 30 September all the exits from Damascus had been closed, and the next morning it was occupied by the Desert Mounted Corps and the Arab Army. The capture of 20,000 prisoners meant that the remnants of the Turkish armies in Palestine and Syria were no longer an effective force but a mass of individuals fleeing north without organization. 1/1ˢᵗ RGH reached the outskirts of Damascus in the early hours of 2 October but was on the move again at 8.00 am for a triumphant march through the city. Despite the dust, which meant the men could see little, they received a great welcome from the European and Syrian inhabitants. After marching all day the Regiment eventually camped in a forest of orange trees, beautifully shaded and well-watered. As Major Howard recorded in his diary, 'From 5.30am on September 29 to 8pm on October 2, I and the rest of the squadron had only slept nine hours in a total of 110 hours. So you can imagine we needed rest.'

Having taken Damascus, Allenby now needed to capture Beirut to provide a port and a much shorter line of supply. Once this was achieved, the Desert Mounted Corps moved on to Rayak and Zahle, which were occupied on 6 October. On 9 October the Corps took Homs. The next objective was Aleppo, over 200 miles from Damascus, where there were said to be 20,000 of the enemy. This task was given to 5ᵗʰ Cavalry Division, supported by the Armoured Car Batteries.

1/1ˢᵗ RGH rested for six days until 5 October, when the Regiment led 13ᵗʰ Brigade the 25 miles to Khan Meizelun, where it found abandoned the sword of Captain Lloyd-Baker, who had been killed at Qatia. The next day it moved on to Rayak, where A Squadron, who had been left to garrison Acre, rejoined the Regiment. It was here that Trooper William Kendall, born in Poole, was killed in a bombing attack by a single enemy aircraft flying very high. One horse was also killed and two wounded, a reminder that the war was not over.

Once again, Algar Howard adds contemporary detail:

> We moved across a rough mountainous ground till we struck the main road at Rayak. Here there were many signs of the retreating Turk. Dead

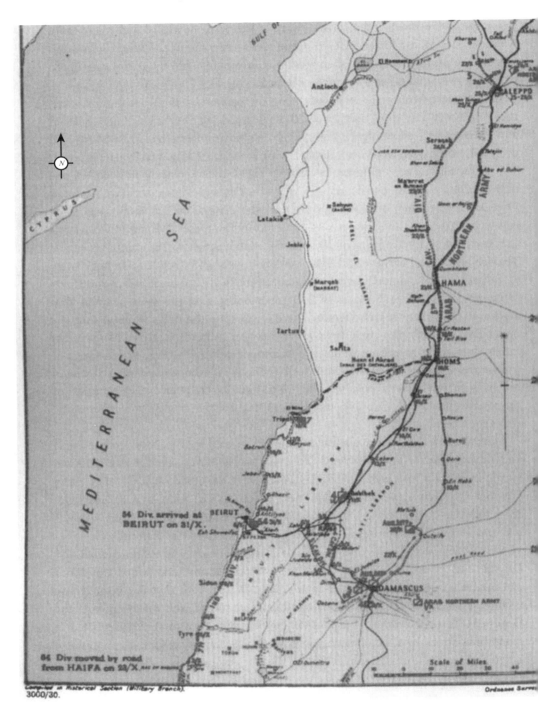

Map 31 Damascus to Aleppo

men, horses, and camels everywhere . . . We moved via Khan Dimez to Khan Meizelun, where we arrived at 2pm . . . During the march from here to Aleppo we fed entirely on the country except for sugar, milk, and bacon, which we got where we could. Before starting, a party of about six men went in advance with the supply officer, who had to requisition mutton or beef, barley and wood, at or near each camp. The sheep were driven in, killed, and butchered, and, if we had time, we always boiled the mutton overnight and ate it cold the next day, otherwise each man had to fry his own. On arrival in camp 75 per cent of the men had to go off with sacks and blankets to fetch barley for the horses; others were sent to gather green millet stalks; others to forage for wood, to obtain which was always the greatest difficulty. We often had to pull down doors and windows of houses to get enough for our cooking. After a 15 or 18 mile trek the real day's work was only begun, and everybody was busy until dark. Hardly a horse was groomed. Each regiment took it in turn to do advance guard and outposts for the night.

October 6 – Move off at 6.30am, preceded by 14ᵗʰ Brigade. After a long trek through waterless country with deep ravines and gorges in any of which we might have been held up by a few Turks, we arrive at the beautifully cultivated and rich valley of Nahr Zaarn, between the Lebanon and anti-Lebanon hills . . . We got good water and proceeded on to Rayak, the important railway junction between Aleppo, Beirut and Damascus. Here the broad gauge from Aleppo shifts into narrow gauge to Damascus and rack railway to Beirut. It was used as a centre by the Turks for repairs and making engines, also an aviation park. The machinery captured here was worth over a million pounds . . . On approaching Rayak an immense fusillade was going on, and I thought we were in for another battle, but it turned out to be only the inhabitants, all of whom were armed with Turkish rifles taken from the retreating Turks, who were showing their joy by letting off in every direction. The ride through the narrow streets was most dangerous, little boys of seven or eight letting off rifles about two feet from one.

Monday, October 7 – Had a day of rest and gave the horses some good grazing. One Taube aircraft came over us.

Tuesday, October 8 – During breakfast over comes a Taube, this time with bombs, of which we get three. One signaller, Pte Kendall, was blown to pieces, and I had two horses killed and one wounded. We were lucky to get off so cheap.

Malaria and the need to look after prisoners were becoming considerable problems for the Desert Mounted Corps. The Australian Division had been left in Damascus dealing with prisoners. On 9 October it was decided that the 4th Division was too weak and should remain at Kahle, which left the 5th Division, including 1/1st RGH, to continue to Homs and then on to Aleppo via Baalbek. The Regiment moved 8 miles north to Tel-es-Sherif and then, on 11 October, led 13th Brigade to Baalbek, where it received a great reception. Two days later it advanced another 18 miles to Lebwe. A further 16 miles took it to El Kaa, and the next day 18 miles to Kussier, which it reached on 15 October. 1/1st RGH led into Homs on 16 October, when it paused for four days; men were being evacuated daily to the Field Ambulance, and keeeping the horses fit placed a considerable burden on everyone. When 1/1st RGH left Homs on 21 October its strength was only about one third of that at the start of the march. On 24 October the Division reached Maarit el Namaan, where the villagers were hostile. On 26 October 1/1st RGH entered Khan Tuman, where it heard that the Turks had withdrawn from Aleppo and the Allies had taken the city, the strategic centre of the Ottoman Empire in Asia. On 27 October the Regiment moved past Aleppo to Bileramun, where it remained until it heard at 11.50 on 31 October that an Armistice had been signed with the Turks. Between 19 September and 26 October the Division had covered 500 miles, which probably meant about 700 miles for individuals. It had captured over 11,000 prisoners and 52 guns and had lost only 21 per cent of its horses, which caused General Allenby to comment, 'the 5th Division were as good horsemasters as fighters.'

Notes

1. Frank Fox, *The Royal Gloucestershire Hussars Yeomanry 1898–1922.*
2. Allen Algernon Bathurst, Lord Apsley DSO, MC, TD, DL (1895–1942) was the eldest son of the 7th Earl Bathurst of Cirencester Park, who had commanded 4th Gloucesters during the Boer War. Allen Bathurst won the MC in 1917. He remained a Territorial Officer between the Wars and was MP for Southampton from 1922 to 1929 and for Bristol Central from 1931 to 1942. In the Second World War he served in the RGH and the Arab Legion. He was killed in a plane crash in Malta in 1942. His wife won Bristol Central in the by-election following his death but lost it in the General Election of 1945. Allen Bathurst was killed before his father died and his son therefore inherited the title and became 8th Earl Bathurst in 1943.

Chapter 52

2nd & 9th Gloucesters in Macedonia

It is difficult to escape the conclusion that Salonika was the backwater of the First World War, despite the fact that it involved more Allied nations than any other front. The Spring Offensive of 1917 had failed and both sides had returned to static warfare, with disease, principally malaria, a major threat. The routine was unlike that on the Western Front. 9th Gloucesters generally held the front line for about 15 days at a time, during which there was always an active programme of patrols either aimed at reconnaissance or designed to capture enemy soldiers. It was, however, rare for these either to report anything or come into contact with the Bulgarians, who were the enemy. During early 1918 9th Gloucesters was almost at full strength of about 1,000, although sickness always reduced the effective numbers by nearly 100.

By contrast, at the start of 1918 the strength of 2nd Gloucesters was about 75 per cent of what it should have been. The Battalion had enjoyed free beer on Christmas Day and plum pudding on Boxing Day, provided by the wives committee back in England. Much of the effort in January and early February was spent on improving roads and railway lines, when the snow permitted. From 17 February until 30 April 2nd Gloucesters occupied a sub-sector of the Front. The Battalion War Diary includes an account of this period:

> The period in trenches has been marked with no incident of great importance, but there has been plenty to do and the Battalion has left its mark on the line and the strength of the position has been considerably increased.
>
> As the trenches run along the crest of the first ridge on the Left bank of the STRUMA there is no depth to the Bridge head positions at all and should the enemy penetrate and capture our one line of trenches, the garrison, if any were left, would unquestionably have to retire across the river. To counteract the lack of depth in the position, as far as the nature of the ground permitted, a strong advanced line was constructed, as it was not possible to make a support line close in rear of the main trenches. The existing line of Night posts was chosen for this line and the posts were strengthened, good dug outs for the garrisons were made and the wire in front of them considerably thickened. The key to the advanced line is SNIPERS KNOLL, a hill about 400 yds in front of the left sphere in the main line. This hill was tunnelled through and a Lewis gun position made

which sweeps the whole of the front of the advanced line [the tunnel was 200yds long and dug by hand by the Battalion without assistance]. Finally, another line of wire was run out from SNIPERS KNOLL, Northwards to the river across the DRAMA Road, and a post made on the DRAMA Road where this wire crossed it. This completed the strengthening of the advanced line, and it can safely be said, that such a line would give great annoyance to an enemy attack and quite possibly stop it altogether.

Having strengthened the advanced line and provided a certain amount of depth to the position, the main line of trenches had to be considered. There being only 4 Vickers guns which could fire across the front of the position, a barrage of Lewis Guns was arranged . . . Accordingly, it was decided to make tunnels cut under the parapet and strike up from them to selected positions, whence a good field of fire could be obtained. This was done with 8 gun positions and proved very successful. A mounting was devised and night lines laid out, for the guns to sweep the whole front very thoroughly. The main line of wire was then increased and some tactical switches run out. The main wire is now about 25 yards thick and presents an almost impassable obstacle.

Having provided for the defence of the position more securely, the protection of the garrison during bombardment was considered and galleries cut out into the rock of the hill were made for the entire garrison . . . It is not known what stopping power they have as no direct hit on top of them has yet been obtained, but as they are at least six feet thick in the roof, nearly all of which is rock, they should keep out shells up to 3.9 howitzers. In view of the coming fever season, the mosquito proofing work was pushed on with and all the galleries and many selected dugouts were made mosquito proof . . . The sickness has not been excessive, an average of 35 a day from the Battalion and of these, an average of 9 go to hospital each week.

Occasionally things went wrong. On 18 May a patrol of 9th Gloucesters was surprised by the enemy, and once the contact was over three other ranks were missing. On the Western Front 'missing' generally meant killed, but there is no record of these three dying or returning to the Battalion, so they were probably prisoners of the Bulgarians, which must have been tough.

On 30 April 2nd Gloucesters moved out of the line into Bluff Camp, a collection of bivouacs and dugouts, where it remained as Brigade Reserve until 11 June, training and playing sport. The weather was getting hot, so sun hats and shorts were worn, and a rifle club was established. After twelve days back in the front line the Battalion went by train to a rest camp at Vrasta on the coast. It was only there until 7 July, because the whole of 27th Division then relieved a French Division in a new area west of the River Vardar. Here the Battalion remained throughout the rest of July and the whole of August. By 13 July the fighting strength was reduced to 438 all ranks, mainly due to sickness, but those with three years overseas service were allowed to go on leave to England.

Meanwhile, in early July, Allied losses during the German Offensive on the Western Front meant that additional battalions were needed from Macedonia. Unusually, this was not done by brigades but by individual battalions. 9th Gloucesters began a move to France on 4 July, leaving only 2nd Gloucesters in Macedonia.

In early August Colonel Alec Vicary, who had taken over command of 2nd Gloucesters in December 1917, was told that a major assault across the whole Salonika Front was planned for 15 September; but there would be a preliminary assault by 27th Division to capture the Roche Noir Salient, in which the Battalion was to play a leading role. The strategy was to deceive the Bulgarians into thinking the main attack was to be up the Vardar valley, and so draw off their reserves. The Battalion's task was to capture and hold the Tr. du Yatagan and the Mamelon aux Buissons, which was 50ft higher than any other part of the Salient and therefore the key to the position. The Battalion practised and trained in great detail, not least because their strength was so low that they had to adopt new formations. The War Diary gives some idea of the preparation:

> Each company practised their share of the attack over ground on which a model of the trenches had been marked out . . . The attack was practised daily by all companies in fighting order, each man carrying his haversack and small kit on his back, four sandbags rolled in his belt, two bombs, 170 rounds SAA.

Colonel Vicary said later:

> By the end of August the Battalion was probably at a higher scale of efficiency, especially in the handling of light automatics, than it had been since 1914. In spite of secrecy, it was obvious that all ranks were convinced that the Battalion was to carry out an important attack. It was almost unbelievable that after nearly four years of war officers and men could have been so extraordinarily keen.

2nd Gloucesters moved forward on 31 August, and the attack began at 5.30 pm on 1 September, in order to allow consolidation of the captured positions before darkness fell. The attack relied on speed and surprise, so there was no Allied artillery fire until 5.36 pm. All the meticulous preparation paid off and the objectives were captured without a check, but the Gloucesters now found themselves in an exposed position, with only shallow trenches in which to try to consolidate. The Battalion suffered 89 casualties, of whom 14 died, but held the captured positions until relieved on 12 September; it was shelled intensely at times, which led to a further 9 other ranks being killed or mortally wounded. The Battalion was awarded 1 Bar to a DSO (Lieutenant Colonel Alec Vicary), a Second Bar to an MC (Lieutenant John Vicary),[1] 1 MC and 6 Military Medals.

2nd Gloucesters then provided support to the major Franco-Serbian assault and on 22 September began to advance in pursuit of the enemy. By 27 September it had reached Dedali. There, 82nd Brigade amalgamated its three weakened battalions into one composite battalion, which was about to attack the enemy rearguard when the Bulgarians sued for an Armistice and hostilities ceased. The war in the Balkans ended officially on 30 September 1918.

Seven officers of 2nd Gloucesters commanded other battalions in Macedonia. One of these was Lieutenant Colonel Daniel Burges,[2] who was commanding 7th South Wales Borderers, with whom he won a DSO and a VC. The citation for the latter states:

> For most conspicuous bravery, skilful leading and devotion to duty in the operations at Jumeaux (Balkans) on 18 September, 1918. His valuable reconnaissance of the enemy first line trenches enabled him to bring his battalion without casualties to the assembly point, and from thence he maintained direction with great skill, though every known landmark was completely obscured by smoke and dust. When still some distance from its objective, the battalion came under severe machine gun fire, which caused many casualties amongst company leaders. Lieutenant Colonel Burges, though himself wounded, quite regardless of his own safety, kept moving to and fro through his command encouraging his men and assisting them to maintain formation and direction. Finally, as they neared the enemy's position, he led them forward through a decimating fire, until he was again hit twice and fell unconscious. His coolness and personal courage were most marked throughout and afforded a magnificent example to all ranks.

Notes

1. John Vicary (1884–1967) was the younger brother of A. C. Vicary. He was articled as a solicitor in Exeter before the War and obtained a Regular Commission in the Gloucesters in May 1915. He joined the 2nd Battalion and was awarded the MC during the second battle of Ypres and a Bar to his MC at the Bala. On the outbreak of the Second War he was given command of the newly formed 7th Glosters and in 1942 was appointed Commander of 184 Brigade. He was, however, unable to persuade the authorities to allow him to see active service and spent most of the war in Northern Ireland.
2. Daniel Burges VC, DSO (1873–1946) was a Bristolian who joined the Regiment in 1893 and served in the South African War. He commanded C Company 2nd Gloucesters in the early stages of the Great War and was wounded in May 1915. He commanded 10th East Yorks before taking command of 7th South Wales Borderers in Salonika, with whom he won the VC and lost a leg. He retired in 1923. He was the Major of the Tower of London 1923–33, President of the Society of Bristolians and Master of the Society of Merchant Venturers. There is a memorial to him in the Arnos Vale Crematorium in Bristol. His medals and gold watch were donated by his family and are on display in the Soldiers of Gloucestershire Museum.

Part X

THE WESTERN FRONT IN 1918

Chapter 53

Reorganization and Disbandment

I t is now necessary to go back nine months to events on the Western Front at the beginning of 1918. The Russian Revolution and the collapse of the Tsar's army had recreated the situation that the Germans had envisaged when they invaded Belgium and France in 1914: a strategic moment without any threat from the East, leaving the Central Powers free to concentrate all their remaining strength on the West and capture Paris. It is estimated that they moved 19,000 officers and 600,000 other ranks from the east to the west and were able to deploy 192 divisions, including all their elite ones, against the Allies' 178 divisions. The Germans believed that the British were exhausted and demoralized by the major battles of 1917, but recognized that they needed to move quickly before the Americans arrived later in the year. America had entered the war on 6 April 1917 but the US Army was only 108,000 strong, so the Germans calculated that it would take the US at least a year to recruit and train more soldiers before sailing to Europe. The Great German Offensive, as it became known, therefore depended on speed; and had they not neglected the development of the tank, probably because they had been concentrating so exclusively on defence, the outcome might have been different. It was launched on 21 March, known to all Gloucesters as 'Back Badge Day'.[1]

There had also been significant changes in the British Army. By March 1918 there were just four Gloucester battalions in France and Flanders. Four had gone to Italy and four had been disbanded. The decision to start disbanding battalions may seem odd, as the War was far from won; indeed, there was still some desperate fighting to come. Britain was, however, running out of men to join up, and it was therefore decided to reduce each brigade from four to three infantry battalions and to use the extra men to bring other battalions up to strength. Surplus men went to Entrenching Battalions, which were temporary units that provided pools of men from which draft replacements could be drawn.

It might be assumed that this major change in the organization of brigades would have created difficulties for commanders used to being able to plan on two battalions in front and two behind; but the truth was that by this stage of the War everyone had become used to being far more flexible, as the strength of each battalion ebbed and flowed due to casualties and reinforcements. There is little doubt that three full-strength battalions were preferable to and more efficient than four under-strength ones. On the other hand, disbanding a battalion brings many problems for individuals. Commanders who are trusted and respected disappear, opportunities for promotion are reduced and friendships are broken up; although every effort was made to keep platoons and sections together, the unique spirit that each battalion develops and makes it believe it is better than others is lost.

2/4th and 2/6th Gloucesters had fought their last battle as battalions of the Gloucestershire Regiment. On 9 December 1917 2/4th Gloucesters reorganized into two companies and celebrated Christmas on 28 December. By the end of the month 61st Division was occupying the line around St Quentin. On 18 January 1918 the much reduced Battalion moved to Holnon Wood and the Enghien Redoubt. The Battalion was disbanded on 20 February 1918. Many of those remaining joined 2/5th Gloucesters in the same Division, and the others went to form part of 24th Entrenching Battalion. A total of 275 officers and other ranks of 2/4th Gloucesters had died, the majority during the last few months of 1917.

By February 1918 2/6th Gloucesters were at Vaux. Here the Battalion was disbanded, parading for the last time on 6 February 1918, in front of the Brigade Commander. The next day it began to disperse, most of its surviving members going to join either 2/5th Gloucesters or 24th Entrenching Battalion. By 20 February 1918 all its equipment had been got rid of and the 2/6th Gloucesters no longer existed. Since arriving in France and Flanders in May 1916, 329 of its officers and other ranks had died.

10th Gloucesters had also fought its last battle. When the seaborne invasion for which 1st Division had trained during the summer of 1917 did not materialize, the Battalion moved back to the Ypres sector in November but did not take part in either the Third Battle of Ypres or Cambrai. The Battalion was disbanded on 19 February 1918. Five officers and 100 other ranks were transferred to 1st Gloucesters, 7 officers and 150 other ranks went to 8th Gloucesters and the remainder became the 13th Entrenching Battalion. Lieutenant Colonel James Kirkwood, a New Zealander with a distinguished record, had taken over command of 10th Gloucesters in March 1917 and he transferred with his men to command 13th Entrenching Battalion. A total of 37 officers and 625 other ranks had died, principally at Loos in September 1915 and on the Somme in 1916.

The action at Passchendaele on 22 October 1917 was virtually the end of fighting for 14th Gloucesters (Bantams). The Battalion remained in Houthulst Forest until 1 November, suffering 4 other ranks killed by artillery fire and 1 officer and 16 other ranks wounded. Most of November and December was spent out of the line, and the Battalion War Diary records a mixture of training, sports and 'divine services'; 6 other ranks were wounded. On 16 January 1918 14th Gloucesters took over the front line until 20 January ('ground still impossible'), and 2 other ranks were wounded. It went back into the front line for the last time on 1 February and on 4 February raided Gravel Farm in the Langemarck Sector, where a raiding party of 38 other ranks led by Second Lieutenant Rundle DCM and Second Lieutenant Denby killed over 30 Germans. Four other ranks were wounded, as were a further 10 in the retaliatory bombardment of the Battalion position. Among the messages that the Battalion received was:

> The Corps Commander wishes you to convey to Brig Gen Marinidin DSO and all ranks . . . his congratulations on successful raid carried out last night. I am particularly glad that the 14th Gloucesters had the opportunity of finishing as it began its career in France, by carrying out a successful raid.

The Battalion was relieved on 5 February, a final divine service was held on 10 February and the following day 12 officers and 250 other ranks transferred to 13th Gloucesters and the remainder went to Surplus Wing, II Corps Reinforcement Camp at Bollizelle. 14th Gloucesters were no more. Eleven officers and 378 other ranks had died and one (posthumous) Victoria Cross had been won, together with many other awards for gallantry.

The Gloucester battalions that remained in France and Flanders to fight for the rest of 1918 were 1st, 2/5th, 8th and 13th (Pioneer). After Passchendaele 1st Gloucesters remained in reserve until 5 December 1917, moving regularly from camp to camp. It then moved up to the line until 16 December; active patrolling was carried out on most nights. January to April 1918 was spent in and out of the line in the Ypres Salient; there was heavy snow, the weather was bitter and the countryside desolate. Then on the night of 6/7 April 1918 the whole of 1st Division moved south of La Bassée Canal. At about 4.00 am on 9 April the German guns began a bombardment of great intensity. This was the start of the second phase of the Great German Offensive of 1918.

In January and February 1918 2/5th Gloucesters was in position around Fresnoy, receiving substantial reinforcement through the disbandment of 2/4th and 2/6th Gloucesters. In preparation for an expected German offensive in the spring 1918, 2/5th Gloucesters was in the second line of defence, the Enghien Redoubt behind Holnon Wood, when the Germans launched their attack.

After Passchendaele 8th Gloucesters moved on 12 November 1917 to Blaringhem, where it trained until 29 November, moving to Wardrecques for more training before entraining and marching to Etricourt on 6/7 December. It moved into the line at Ribecourt for ten days from 8 to 18 December and was back in the line 20–23 December and 28 December–5 January. One officer was mortally wounded on 4 January. This routine continued through January until mid-February, when the battalion was withdrawn for training.

13th Gloucesters (Pioneers) was committed to building plank roads and other improvements to routes in the Ypres sector after Passchendaele, but in early December it was withdrawn to a rest camp near Boulogne. This rest ended on 24 December, when it moved up again, and by January it was busy on a number of tasks in the Ypres Sector, living at Siege Camp revetting trenches and generally improving the defences. Given the nature of the ground, this must have been a miserable task. Towards the end of January the Battalion moved to the Somme. The Allies had learned lessons and changed their defensive tactics, adopting a 'defence in depth' arrangement rather than a continuous line of trenches. The new system was made up of three zones. The Forward Zone was about 3,000yds deep and consisted of a line of outposts with strongly fortified redoubts on the rising ground behind; they were not connected by any trench system but by a single line of barbed wire. The Battle Zone was also a line of redoubts but without outposts. The Rear Zone was a double line of trenches some 2 miles behind. 13th Gloucesters spent the whole of February 1918 and until 21 March helping to construct these new defences, at which point the whole situation changed dramatically.

Note

1. On 21 March 1801 at the Battle of Alexandria the 28th (North Gloucestershire) Regiment reacted to a critical moment in the fighting when the French cavalry broke through the British lines. The rear rank of the 28th turned about (a drill movement never practised) and, holding their fire until the French were almost upon, then fired a devastating volley, which led directly to British victory. The Regiment began wearing a badge in the back of their head dress as well as the front, and this unique form of dress continues to this day.

Chapter 54

The Gallantry of the Gloucesters during Operation Michael

T he German Spring Offensive, or *Kaiserschlacht* (Kaiser's Battle), was a series of major assaults designed to win the War before the US Army arrived. The first was Operation Michael in the area of St Quentin on the Somme, launched on 21 March 1918. The British Front was held here by Fifth Army, the weakest of the British Armies on the Western Front, holding the longest section, where the defences were described as 'sketchy'. Fifth Army had also suffered more from the reorganization of the infantry than others, and this was hardly complete when the German launched their onslaught. It began with a heavy barrage on positions south-west of the town; five minutes later it became an artillery bombardment across a 50-mile front in which mustard, chlorine and tear gas were mixed with high explosive on the forward positions, while heavy artillery concentrated on the Allied artillery and supply lines to the rear. The infantry assault began at 9.40 am and by midday the Germans had broken through in many places and large numbers of British infantry had been taken prisoner. The Allies had little alternative but to conduct a fighting retreat and use it to buy time by delaying the Germans where they could. On 24 March Bapaume was evacuated, and over the night of 26/27 March Albert was also given up, but by now Allied reinforcements were arriving in numbers at Amiens and the rate of the German advance was slowing. Operation Michael ended on 5 April 1918, by which time the Germans had advanced 20 miles on a front of 50 and were within 5 miles of Amiens. However, as they advanced deeper and deeper into Allied territory other factors began to count against them, as Sir John Keegan describes:[1]

> The accidents of military geography began to work to the Germans' disadvantage. The nearer they approached Amiens, the more deeply did they become entangled in the obstacles of the old Somme battlefield, a wilderness of abandoned trenches, broken roads and shell-crater fields left behind by the movement of the front a year earlier. The Somme may not have won the war for the British in 1916 but the obstacle zone it left helped to ensure that in 1918 they did not lose it. Moreover, the British rear areas, stuffed with luxuries enjoyed by the army of a nation

which had escaped the years of blockade that in Germany had made the simple necessities of life rare and expensive commodities, time and again tempted the advancing Germans to stop, plunder and satiate themselves.

He might have added the gallantry of many British battalions, as exemplified by what happened to the 2/5th, 8th and 13th Gloucesters.

General Gough was replaced on 28 March as Commander of Fifth Army. For many commentators, and certainly to most of those who knew him in Fifth Army, this was a grave injustice. There are, of course, others who disagree, but the reason that the Germans did not take Paris was that Fifth Army under his leadership fought a 38-mile withdrawal in which they contested virtually every yard of ground; their heroism was outstanding, and it was undoubtedly the right strategy. Lloyd George, and to some extent Haig, however, needed someone to blame and divert attention to from their own failings. Gough was the victim.

On 18 March 2/5th Gloucesters took over the Battle Zone positions at Holnon Wood, which is where it was when the Germans launched their attack. When the mist and smoke cleared at about 1.00 pm the Battalion discovered the enemy had got through the Forward Zone and were about 500yds away but unable to make further progress in daylight. There was some fighting during the night, but when the mist cleared on the 22nd the Germans had infiltrated forward, and by midday the situation was desperate; the Battalion was ordered to withdraw to Beauvois and D Company was tasked with covering the move of the rest of the Battalion. Their action was described by Sir Arthur Conan Doyle:[2]

> The defence of the line in front of Beauvais was kept up with remarkable tenacity by 150 men of the 2/5th Gloucester battalion performing what was an extraordinary feat, even in this war of miracles, for they held on to a line 2,000 yards in length until 3.30 in the morning of March 23, holding up the whole German advance. All night the enemy tried to rush or to bomb this thin line of determined men, but it was not until the cartridges ran low that the British made their retreat, sneaking round the outskirts of the village which blazed behind them, and making their way to Longuevoisin where they joined their comrades who had already given them up as lost.

8th Gloucesters was not in the front line when the German attack began on 21 March. It 'stood to' at 5.30 am and moved to an assembly area at 1.00 pm, prior to counter-attacking the village of Doignies at 7.00 pm. It was during this fighting that Major Manley James[3] won a Victoria Cross. His company was fighting near Velu Wood to the east of Bapaume and captured 27 German prisoners and 2

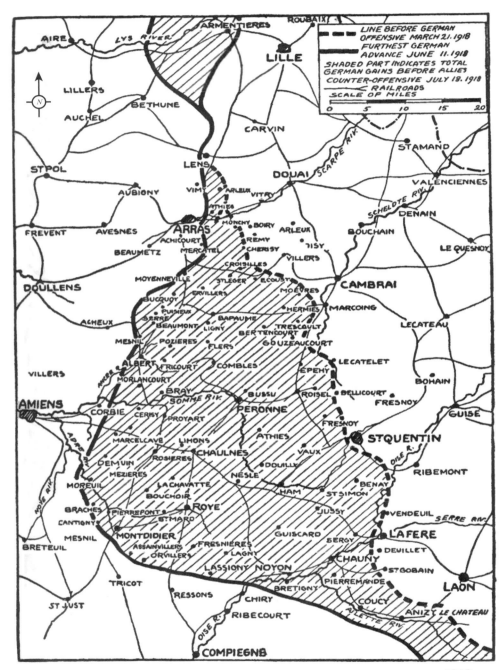

THE GERMAN OFFENSIVE FROM ARRAS TO THE OISE, MARCH-JUNE, 1918

Map 32 The German Great Offensive, Operation Michael, 1918

machine guns. On 22 March the Germans made three separate attempts to retake Doignies but were beaten back with heavy losses on each occasion by machine gun and rifle fire. Wounded, Major Manley James refused to be evacuated and helped repulse the enemy attacks. Although the Germans eventually broke through, his company made a determined stand, and to buy more time for the brigade to escape he led his men in a fierce counter-attack and was again wounded. Single-handedly he took control of a machine gun and kept the enemy at bay, until he was wounded again for a third time and eventually captured. He spent the rest of the war in a PoW camp. The Germans shelled the Battalion with well-directed fire and enemy aeroplanes flew low over the Battalion using their machine guns, but there was no response from Allied artillery despite urgent calls for support. Seven officers and 200 other ranks were casualties by now. On 23 March the troops on the left of 8th Gloucesters withdrew quickly at 7.30am, and 8th Gloucesters was forced to do the same, fighting a rearguard action. The threat of the brigade being captured was averted by rushing up a composite company from the Gloucesters and Worcesters to the rear of Velu Wood, where they stopped the Germans and saved a battery of 18-pounders which were firing over 'open sights'. Later, 8th Gloucesters withdrew to Bancourt. All the wounded, except those who could walk, were taken prisoner.

The situation was now so desperate that the next day (24 March) 8th Gloucesters, despite their losses, took part in the Battle of Bapaume. The Battalion left camp at 5.00 am to hold a Reserve Line astride the Bapaume–Cambrai road. They withdrew about 8.00 pm, 'closely pressed by the enemy', and reorganized at Grevillers. Four times the next day the enemy attacked 19th Division, who fought a rearguard action from Grevillers through Irles and Miramount to a line Puisieux to Achiet-le-Petit. The next day (26 March), the retreat continued to a line Hebuterne to Bucquoy. Three days later, a battered 8th Gloucesters left the battle by train. On 31 March the Battalion took over the front line at Messines, little knowing that this was where the second phase of the German Spring Offensive would be launched seven days later.

13th Gloucesters (Pioneers) ceased work on defences on 22 March and became line infantry occupying the Green Line east of Templer La Fosse. The Battalion fought a rearguard action, retiring through Peronne and Cléry to take up a position near Herbécourt.

By 26 March the overall situation had become even more alarming. The Germans were exploiting the gaps that appeared as the Allies fell back. One of these allowed them to infiltrate the Rosières–Bray line. Here six British Divisions were attacked from the front, flank and rear by eleven German divisions. In some bitter fighting, in which both 2/5th and 13th Gloucesters took part, Rosières was held, at least temporarily. 2/5th Gloucesters occupied a position on the canal at Breuil on 25 March and moved to Roye that night. At 6.00 pm on 26 March it moved to Quesnel, where the Battalion dug in, before being ordered to move to Marcelcave and take part in an attack by 183 and 184 Brigade on Lamotte. 61ˢᵗ Division argued against this, but Corps Headquarters insisted it should go ahead without artillery support as there were supposed to be few enemy in the village. The attack was launched at 12 noon, the enemy was stronger than expected and the Battalion withdrew at 3.40 pm, having suffered 200 casualties in this failed operation. The Battalion was now reduced to 150 tired men holding a thin line at Marcelcave, 10 miles in front of Amiens. Fortunately, the Germans did not attack. The Battalion was relieved on the 31ˢᵗ by Australians. For ten days 2/5ᵗʰ Gloucesters had been continuously in action; they had lost 20 officers and about 550 other ranks; 4 officers and 37 other ranks had been killed; but the planned German breakthrough had been thwarted.

Meanwhile, 13ᵗʰ Gloucesters occupied a line south of Cappy on 26 March and, fighting a rearguard action, retired on to the Provart–Framerville Line. The next day it moved to Morcourt and reoccupied the ridge between Morcourt and Provart, where it was heavily attacked and forced to retire. It took up fresh positions south-east of Marcelcave on 28 March, when it was attacked twice but drove off the enemy on both occasions. The next day it moved to trenches north of Demuin. On 30 March 13ᵗʰ Gloucesters held off another German attack before being eventually relieved. During the month the Battalion had suffered 326 casualties.

For the Gloucester battalions the First Battle of Somme 1918, which ended on 5 April, was over. On 4 April 2/5ᵗʰ Gloucesters moved to Warlus near Arras. The Battalion consisted of Headquarters, 6 company officers and about 150 men, so the first task was to receive reinforcements and train them up to the same high standard that the Battalion had achieved by 21 March. The Brigade Commander was now Brigadier General 'Patsy' Pagan, who had commanded 1ˢᵗ Gloucesters. It was not, however, allowed much respite, as the Germans were about to break through on the Lavantie front.

Notes

1. Sir John Keegan, *The First World War*.
2. Sir Arthur Conan Doyle, *A History of the Great War: The British Campaign in France & Flanders, Volume V, Jan–Jul 1918*
3. Manley Angell James VC, DSO, MBE, MC, DL (1896–1975) was educated at Bristol Grammar School and played rugby for Bristol. Commissioned into the 8ᵗʰ Gloucesters in 1914, he was severely wounded at La Boiselle. In 1917 he was wounded again in heavy fighting at Wytshaete and Messines ridge for which he was awarded an MC. In January 1939 he commanded 1ˢᵗ Royal Sussex and in February 1941 took over 128 (Hampshire) Brigade in North Africa, where he was awarded the DSO for stopping the attack at Beja. His brigade was assault brigade of 46 Division at Salerno, where he was wounded again. At the end of the war he joined the RAF Regiment and was Director General Ground Defence at the Air Ministry. He retired in March 1951 and worked for the Bristol Aeroplane Company. He was made an MBE (Civil) in 1958. His son, Peter, served as a National Service officer in the Gloucesters.

Chapter 55

More Required of the Gloucesters in the Battle of the Lys

The Great German Offensive was not over – only the first round. On 7 April, two days after the end of Operation Michael, the Germans launched Operation Georgette, this time in the north. The Allies had sent troops south and the Germans saw an opportunity to capture Ypres and break through to the sea. Operation Georgette was smaller than Operation Michael, but two German Armies, Sixth and Fourth, attacked the British First Army, which was now relatively weak. Once again the Germans broke through the Allies and there was some desperate fighting, not least by the Gloucesters.

After the War the Battle of Lys was divided into eight individual battles:

Estaires	9–11 April	1st Gloucesters
Messines	10–11 April	8th Gloucesters
Hazebrouck	12–15 April	2/5th & 12th Gloucesters
Bailleul	13–15 April	8th Gloucesters
First Kemmel	17–19 April	8th & 13th Gloucesters
Béthune	18 April	1st & 2/5th Gloucesters

No Gloucester battalions were engaged in Second Kemmel (25–26 April) or Sherpenberg (29 April).

1st Gloucesters had spent January–April 1918 in the Ypres Salient, where the state of the countryside after four years of war, combined with heavy snow and bitter cold, was a real test of their resilience. Then, on the night of 6/7 April, 1st Division moved south of La Basée Canal. Early on 7 April the German guns opened Operation Georgette with a bombardment of great intensity. They then attacked on 9 April in thick fog and soon made progress. At 10.00 am 1st Division was told that the enemy had taken parts of Givenchy, and shortly afterwards 1st Gloucesters began to move, principally to the bridges over the La Basée Canal, where it remained until the night of 15/16 April, when it relieved the Liverpool Scottish of the 55th Division at Festubert. The position was 1¼ miles wide and included the village itself, but on the left flank there was a gap of some 600yds. On 17 April the Battalion captured a German sergeant major, who provided valuable

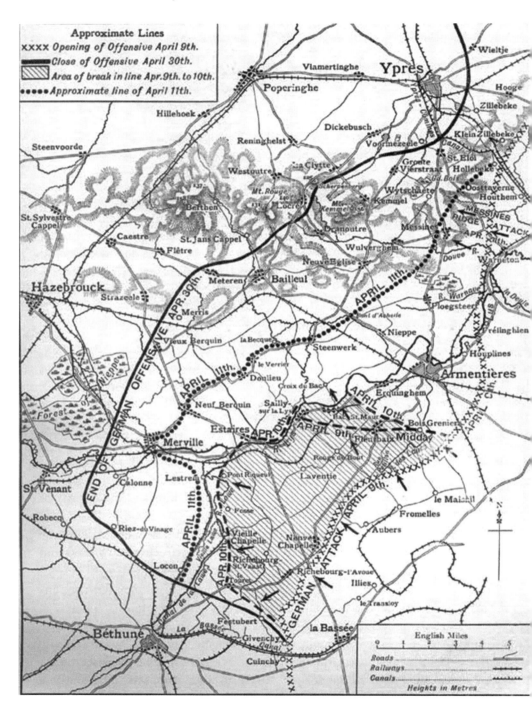

Map 33 The Great German Offensive, Operation Georgette, 1918

information about the intended attack on the 18th against the southern flank of the British position. Previous attacks had been directed towards the centre.

It is difficult, with the benefit of hindsight and our knowledge of the outcome of the War, to capture the real fear among the Allies at this time that they might be defeated. On 11 April Field Marshal Haig issued an Order of the Day:

> Many of us are now tired. To those I would say that victory will belong to the side which holds out longest . . . There is no other course open to us but to fight it out. Every position must be held to the last man: there must be no retirement. With our backs to the wall and believing in the justice of our cause, each one of us must fight to the end. The safety of our homes and the freedom of mankind alike depend upon the conduct of each one of us at this critical moment.

1st Gloucesters were about to turn Haig's words into action at Festubert (after the War the fighting at Festubert was included as part of the Battle of Béthune). The Germans attacked the Battalion at 8.15 am on 18 April with 4 regiments of infantry (12 battalions), having first subjected it to heavy artillery fire for 3½ hours. The main waves of the enemy were held but they were able to get through the gap on the flank. Every platoon was soon engaged in the fight. The sole reinforcements available were 12 men from Battalion Headquarters, cooks, batmen and drivers, who joined the battle. As the enemy threatened the rear, platoons faced about, and, fighting front, flank, and rear, the Battalion held them off. It was a critical battle, vital to the whole British position. The Germans tried in every way to annihilate 1st Gloucesters. They climbed into ruined houses to snipe the men in the trenches; they brought up field guns and fired over open sights. But by noon the enemy was weakening and began to withdraw; as the afternoon wore on, the line was re-formed on its original position. The brigade commander signalled:

> I wish to express my admiration for the gallant defence put up by your Battalion yesterday. The tenacity with which they held their position when attacked in front, flank, and rear by four Regiments has earned the praise of commanders of all grades . . . All ranks fought as though mindful of the emblem[1] they wear, and fully justified the wearing of it.

There were 184 casualties, and 25 Military Medals were awarded, believed to be a record for the decoration to a battalion on a single day, as well as a Bar to a DSO, 4 MCs, 2 DCMs and 2 Bars to DCMs. Company Sergeant Majors Bill Reece and William Biddle both won Bars to their DCMs. The latter, no longer the Signals Sergeant, was now a Company Sergeant Major:

When all communications failed with Battalion Headquarters, and the enemy were working round the rear of his company, he attacked with a dozen details and drove them back. He did the journey (1,200 yards) between his company and Battalion Headquarters under heavy bombardment three or four times during the day when runners failed to get through.

William Biddle's successor as Signals Sergeant was Henry Coles, the son of Mr and Mrs William Coles of 6 Parson St, Stapleton Rd, Bristol, who was killed in the same battle. He had been awarded the DCM in 1917 for 'repairing and maintaining lines under heavy fire'.

8th Gloucesters, having already been involved in desperate fighting to deny the Germans in Operation Michael, now faced doing the same again. The Battalion arrived from the Somme on 29 March and took over the line in front of Messines which it held for ten days, an indication of how few reserves were available. On 10 April the Germans launched an attack after a 5-hour bombardment and outflanked the Battalion, forcing them to fall back to a line near Stinking Farm. On 11 April 19th Division counter-attacked, and on 12 April 57 Brigade was relieved, taking up a position between Daylight Corner and Neuve-Église, from where 8th Gloucesters withdrew on 14 April. On 16 April the Battalion occupied reserve trenches near Beaver Corner, where it suffered 'slight shelling' before withdrawing two days later to near Abeele and a few days later to Proven to begin reorganizing and training.

Meanwhile, 2/5th Gloucesters, who had lost so many men during Operation Michael, were training intensely as reinforcements arrived. It seems somewhat surreal to read in the Battalion War Diary for 9 April: 'Officers riding class at 3.30pm under C.O.' This period of rest did not last, as 61st Division was soon in action, under command of First Army. The Battalion reached Steenbeque at 5.00 am on 12 April and was ordered to move to St Venant 'as soon as possible' as the Germans had broken through at Merville. By 3.00 pm it was bivouacked north-west of St Vincent, where 190 reinforcements arrived and were immediately posted to the rifle companies. Assuming these reinforcements were distributed evenly, it meant more than 10 men to each platoon. Platoon commanders would not have had time to learn any of their names before they were in action. That same evening (12 April), the Battalion took over the forward trench system, and the next morning the Germans advanced in small parties and gradually the shelling increased. At 10.15 am C Company's HQ was knocked out and all communication lost; the company was attacked three times during the morning but the enemy were repulsed on each occasion. At 3.30 pm the Battalion HQ was heavily shelled and at 5.30 pm B Company was forced to evacuate its forward posts. The Battalion was relieved that evening and three days later moved into the front line in the

Baquerolles Farm Sector. Here on 18 April the Germans attacked south towards Béthune and took East Baquerolles Farm; a counter-attack by D Company failed to regain it. At dawn the next day the Germans got between A and D Companies, but a successful counter-attack by a platoon of A Company under Sergeant White and 16 men drove them back (in this action the Gloucesters captured a German machine gun which was subsequently presented to the City of Gloucester, although its present whereabouts are not known). Sergeant White was awarded the DCM. The same day, a large reinforcement of 6 officers and 348 other ranks from 24 Entrenching Battalion arrived. Another attack on the farm by the Battalion at 8.30 pm was not successful, and on 19 April it was relieved but was then ordered to attack German positions from La Pierre Au Beure to beyond Baquerolles on 23 April. This attack, launched at 4.33 am, took all its objectives by 5.15 am; the Germans then bombarded the Battalion from from 12 noon until 5.00 am the next morning before counter-attacking, but were repulsed. Overall in April 2/5th Gloucesters suffered nearly 250 casualties, and 108 members of the Battalion died. The Battalion was relieved on the 25 April, and moved to Laleau, but was back in St Venant 4 days later. It was in and out of the line for the next two months, when it was at last granted a period of 'rest' in a variety of locations until 5 August.

One of the striking things about the First World War is the way in which Divisions were moved rapidly by rail, not just between parts of the Front but also from one Front to another. 12th Gloucesters started back from Italy on 2 April 1918. Ten days later, it was in action, taking up a position from the Lys Canal through Nieppe Forest to La Motte Chateau. When the Germans advanced, the Allies had to cope with refugees, as Private Bruce Buchanan recalled:[2] 'We marched up to the Forest of Nieppe, passing on the way various refugees who had been driven from Merville and its neighbouring villages.' On 13 April the Germans launched an attack on the Battalion which was repulsed with 76 casualties, including 18 killed. Another attack on 15 April was also thrown back, as by now everyone was well dug in. 12th Gloucesters was relieved on 16 April, but was back in the front line on 21 April. The next day it captured Le Vert Bois Farm, subsequently known as 'Gloucester Farm', under a creeping barrage without serious opposition, but it took all day to overcome Le Vert Bois itself. Three German machine guns were captured and 39 prisoners taken.

On 10 April 13th Gloucesters (Pioneers), which was still on the Somme, was ordered to provide three companies to form two Composite Battalions of 39th Division Composite Brigade, with 13th Battalion, the Sussex Regiment. The Battalion HQ of 13th Gloucesters then formed a cadre for training American troops. Meanwhile, on 11 April, the Composite Brigade entrained for Vlamertinghe to join the Battle of Lys, and on 16 April became part of 62nd Brigade of 9th Division. That evening, it took part in a counter-attack to re-occupy Medelstede Farm and

Wytschaete Wood, an action which earned 13th Gloucesters the Battle Honour 'Kemmel'. Ten days later, at 5.00 am on 26 April, the Germans attacked 2nd Composite Battalion as it was holding the line Bus House to the Bluff and got through, forcing the battalion to withdraw. A platoon of 13th Gloucesters was surrounded and fought their way out, although only 1 officer and 17 men reached safety. During the month 13th Gloucesters suffered 299 casualties, including 118 taken prisoner.

No Gloucester battalions were involved in any further major actions. The Germans abandoned Operation Georgette on 29 April.

Notes

1. The 'emblem' referred to is the unique Back Badge (a badge worn in the back of the head-dress) adopted initially by the 28th (North Gloucestershire) Regiment after the Battle of Alexandria in 1801, when they had fought back-to-back to defeat a French attack; it was subsequently worn throughout the Gloucesters.
2. Dean Marks, *'Bristol's Own', the 12th Battalion Gloucestershire Regiment 1914–1918*.

Chapter 56

The Beginning of the End

The Germans' Great Offensive was still not over. There were three more major assaults for the Allies to deal with, all in the south against the French and the Americans, who by now were beginning to make a difference. The Germans launched Operation Blücher-Yorck on 27 May. It lasted for eleven days until 6 June and four British Divisions were sent to reinforce the French, among them 19th Division, which included 8th Gloucesters; this meant that the Battalion had fought in the first three of the German Offensives. From 9 to 11 June the Germans attacked towards Paris in Operation Gneisenau and broke through the Allied defences, causing panic in the French capital. Their final effort was Operation Friedensturm, from 15 to 18 July, by which time they had lost far more men than they could afford if they were to defend Germany when the Allies returned to the attack.

The German objective in the Battle of the Aisne (27 May–6 June), as the German offensive Blücher-Yorke was known, was to capture the Chemin des Dames Ridge, taken by the French the previous year. In addition to the French Sixth Army and the four British Divisions attached to it, this was also the first action by the American Expeditionary Force. Taken by surprise, the Allies were unable to prevent the Germans breaking through and advancing to the Aisne in six hours. Eventually, however, the Germans found they had insufficient reserves to cope with Allied counter-attacks and on 6 June halted their offensive.

On 28 May 8th Gloucesters moved to Chambrecy, arriving at 4.30 am on 29 May, and was immediately sent out to cover the village 'while the rest of the Brigade had breakfast.' The Brigade then advanced to occupy the line of the road from Lhery to Tramery, but came under fire before it reached it. By 2.00 pm 57 Brigade formed the front line as other troops withdrew, and the next morning the enemy attacked in force and the whole line withdrew about 1,000yds in good order; but this position became untenable when the Germans got into Romigny, and the Brigade then withdrew to the high ground overlooking Chambrecy. 8th Gloucesters had lost 3 officers and 45 other ranks killed, and many more wounded. On 1 June the Germans attacked a French division on the left of 8th Gloucesters, forcing it to withdraw before turning on 57 Brigade. Just as it appeared certain that 8th Gloucesters would have to retreat, B and C Companies rallied, counter-attacked and, supported by a French Regiment, drove the enemy back. It was another gallant action by a battalion that had been fighting almost continuously since March. Although the Division was heavily shelled on 6 June it was not attacked again, and the offensive was over.

No Gloucester battalions were involved in the final two German offensives in the south, but there was still fighting further north, where the epidemic of 'Spanish' flu began to assert itself. Military censors restricted news of this violent influenza outbreak, which would cause five times more deaths across the world than the War, but newspapers were free to report deaths in neutral Spain, which is how it got its name. There are many theories as to its source, but none include Spain.

1st Gloucesters spent four months in and out of the trenches after Béthune. When they were 'out' they played games and trained. When they were 'in' they often conducted raids. On 4 June D Company, consisting of 3 officers and 100 men supported by 12 Royal Engineers with mobile charges for destroying bunkers, carried out a successful raid on the enemy outpost and support lines west of Auchy. The company suffered 10 casualties, 3 of whom died. CSM William Biddle was awarded an immediate MC, which with his MM and Bar and DCM and Bar meant he became one of the most decorated NCOs of the War, as well as showing that soldiers with a poor disciplinary record in peacetime often perform exceptionally in war.

After the bitter fighting of the Battle of the Lys had ended and the German Army had failed to break through at Hazebrouck, the front line was re-established on the eastern fringe of Nieppe Forest. On 20 June 1918 5th and 31st Division were ordered to attack on a 6,000yd front east of Nieppe Forest to advance the British lines away from the edge of the wood, where they made an easy target for German artillery. 12th Gloucesters was tasked with capturing Le Cornet Perdu and moved forward during the night to launch the attack at 6.00 am on 28 June. All objectives were taken by 9.30 am, although a few German machine guns caused 164 casualties, of whom 45 died. One officer reported killed on 25 June was William Abbott, who had joined the Battalion just eleven days previously. He was the son of William and Kate Abbott of 11 Grove St, Gloucester and had enlisted in August 1914 in 1/5th Gloucesters, was wounded in the knee in November 1916 and evacuated to a hospital in Bristol. On discharge he was posted as an officer candidate and joined 12th Gloucesters on 14 June 1918 as a Second Lieutenant. He was not in fact killed but taken prisoner, although his family only learnt of this when he was repatriated in November 1918. In his Statement of Capture he wrote:

> At 5.45 pm I left our trenches and accompanied by 2nd Lt. R.W. Drew and an NCO [Corporal George Henry Greening from 47 Marle Hill Parade, Cheltenham] to reconnoitre a house in enemy lines, known to be

held at night, but uncertain as to whether held by day . . . In crossing the exposed portion of the ground the NCO was hit. I ran forward from the wheat and with Mr Drew got the wounded NCO as far as possible under cover close to the house. As the house was apparently deserted and the NCO was confident the shot had entered his back, Mr Drew returned to our lines, to ascertain if anyone had fired from our lines and to bring back stretcher-bearers. I stayed to protect the NCO who was shot through the lungs and in very serious condition. I then observed an advanced enemy post on the left side of the house, the sentry of which having fired at and hit the NCO, had run along the trench to warn the remainder of the garrison . . . As our position was perilous the NCO endeavoured to crawl back to the wheat from which position I could have got him back to our lines. I covered his retirement. He only moved about 5 yards and then lay motionless. I moved back towards him when heavy rifle fire opened up from the hostile post. Rolling into some broken ground, I lay motionless . . . about 20 minutes elapsed and Mr Drew returned and hailed me cautiously from the edge of the wheat field. I commanded him to keep out of sight, but it was too late and fire was opened again, Mr Drew being hit through the head and killed instantly. I decided that my best chance was to wait until dusk and then get back, as the NCO was dead. It was then about 6.45 pm. About 30 minutes elapsed when, to my great dismay, I glanced up and saw Germans not 3 or 4 yards away. They had come around the house to get the bodies in. They saw me and covered me and I was taken back to their trench. I was kept in this post until dusk . . . At night I was taken to the rear of enemy lines and from there to a village near Lille, where I had the usual examination by enemy intelligence officers, afterwards being sent to Lille.

2/5th Gloucesters were about to be relieved and given a six-week break out of the line on 24 June, when their Commanding Officer, Lieutenant Colonel A. B. Lawson,[1] was killed as he walked into a German patrol while inspecting his line before handover. Brigadier-General 'Patsy' Pagan wrote: 'This officer was only approached by one other as a battalion commander among the many I met in France. He was absolutely fearless, very able, and was devoted to the welfare of his men. He was always unruffled, whatever the circumstances, and was a very fine leader of men.' Although he had only commanded the Battalion for three months, such was his character that as A. F. Barnes wrote, 'To 2/5th Gloucesters it felt like a personal bereavement.' The Battalion was withdrawn to Linghem near Aire, which was where Spanish influenza reached 184th Brigade. Within two weeks 250 men were in hospital.

In May 1918 the two Composite Battalions of which 13th Gloucesters had formed a part were disbanded, and the survivors of 13th Gloucesters re-joined their Battalion. From these a Cadre Battalion (known as 13th Gloucesters) and a Demonstration Section were formed, and the remainder were drafted to other units. In June and July 1918 13th Gloucesters trained 105th Engineer Regiment of the American Expeditionary Force. Thereafter it prepared camps and administered reinforcements as they arrived, until the Armistice was signed in November.

Two other changes in the Gloucester battalions took place in this period. The 9th Battalion, which was in 198 Brigade in 66th Division, arrived back on the Western Front from Macedonia on 14 July. More surprisingly, a new battalion, 18th Gloucesters, was created at Clacton-on-Sea on 20 June 1918. It was to join 49 Brigade in 16th (Irish) Division. The Division had been formed in 1914 and had fought with distinction on the Western Front. However, in June 1918, having suffered heavy casualties, it was decided to withdraw it back to England and completely reconstitute with new battalions, of which 18th Gloucesters was one. The Division returned to France on 1 August 1918. Thus, by the beginning of August 1918, 1st, 2/5th, 8th, 9th, 12th and 18th Battalions of the Gloucestershire Regiment were on the Western Front, ready to end the War in the '100 Day Offensive'.

Note

1. Lieutenant Colonel Arthur Bertram Lawson DSO & Bar (1882–1918) was educated at Winchester and commissioned into the 11th Hussars in 1901. He commanded A Squadron, 11th Hussars before being appointed to command 2/5th Gloucesters on 17 March 1918, just three months before he was killed.

Chapter 57

The 100-Day Offensive, Advance to the Hindenburg Line

The '100-Day Offensive' was a series of attacks by the Allies, begun on 8 August and lasting until the Armistice on 11 November, by which time the Allies included the nearly 2m soldiers of the American Expeditionary Force (AEF). The first stage was to regain the ground taken by the Germans earlier in the year and advance to the Hindenburg Line.

The four-day battle of Amiens, which began on 8 August, was the first of the Allied attacks and was a resounding success. The British advanced 7 miles on the first day, and although thereafter they slowed down as they got beyond the support of their artillery, its impact on the morale of both sides was huge; the Allies were now convinced they would win the War, most Germans that they would lose.

There were no Gloucester battalions involved, but further north 2/5th Gloucesters participated in an attack by 61st Division close to the Belgian border. The Battalion took over the line near Lille on 8 August. The line at this point ran along the Plate Becque, a muddy stream varying in width from 15 to 25ft and of uncertain depth, with enemy posts on the far bank. On the night of 9 August the 9th Northumberland Fusiliers tried and failed to establish a bridgehead across the river. 2/5th Gloucesters was given the task the next night, using eight bridges, each 25ft in length and supposedly light enough to be carried by two men. A. F. Barnes describes what happened:

> The operation was entirely unsuccessful. Of the bridges two were too short; two broke, precipitating some Lewis gunners into the river, where their guns were lost; the bridges, requiring six men to carry them, were observed; the enemy was on the alert and brought the advancing troops under a merciless machine gun fire, so that, although they succeeded in crossing the stream, little progress was made when the further bank was reached. The artillery barrage was inaccurate and ineffective, one heavy battery having mistaken Itchen Farm, which was inside the British lines, for an enemy position.

It might have been funny had not 12 other ranks died and 2 officers and 38 other ranks been wounded. When his company was held up by machine gun fire,

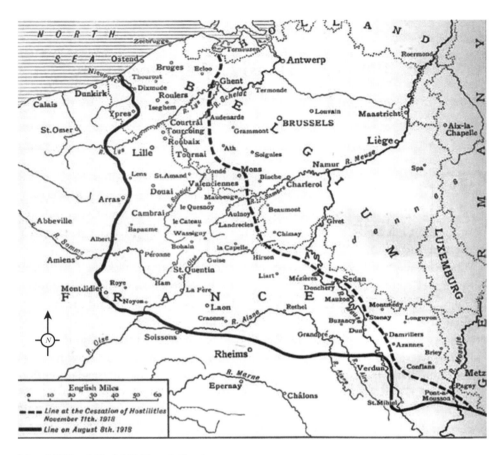

Map 34 The Allied 100 Day Offensive

Corporal Terrett[1] advanced with his section of six men as far as he could and then dug in. He and his section maintained their position all day inflicting considerable casualties and then skilfully withdrew. The citation for his DCM states that 'he rendered splendid service'. Privates Livings and Barrett, who were part of the same section, were awarded MMs. The Battalion was relieved on 14 August.

Although Marshal Foch, the Allied Supreme Commander, wished the British to continue the Battle of Amiens, Haig decided that it would be more effective to launch the next British offensive in the Somme area. The 'Second Battle of the Somme 1918' began on 20 August and lasted for 14 days, during which the Germans were pushed back over a 34-mile front. Albert was captured on 22 August and Bapaume on 29 August. 12th Gloucesters had been relieved by 2/5th Gloucesters on 7/8 August, and along with the rest of 5th Division became part of the GHQ reserve. This gave the Battalion the opportunity to rest, clean up and retrain, although it was regularly on the move. By 20 August it was in the Somme area and about to take part in what became another major battle for the Battalion. On 21 August a three-phase attack was launched, led initially by 37th Division, which captured its objectives without much trouble. 5th Division then pushed through 37th Division, with 95th Brigade leading and 12th Gloucesters in reserve. The next objectives were also taken without significant opposition; the thick mist was causing more problems than the enemy. 12th Gloucesters and 1st E Surreys now took over and reached the Arras to Albert railway line, meeting rather more resistance; according to the War Diary, 'Owing to the mist which considerably hampered artillery and tanks it was impossible to continue the advance to the final objective.' One officer and 11 other ranks had died and nearly 100 were wounded, so the fighting was fiercer than the War Diary suggests. 12th Gloucesters spent the next day reorganizing and resting, but at 5.30 pm, following enemy shelling, the Germans were seen advancing to mount a counter-attack. Two platoons of A Company under Second Lieutenant R. H. Anstey[2] were sent out to enfilade the advancing enemy and captured 180 prisoners and 5 machine guns. The German counter-attack broke down, but a further 5 other ranks had died.

The following day, 23 August, 12th Gloucesters launched an attack at 11.00 am behind a creeping barrage to capture the railway line itself. The Germans had constructed machine gun nests along it and these caused numerous casualties before they were overwhelmed. The Battalion losses over the previous days meant that it had been reinforced by two companies of 1st DCLI, but even so it was unable to advance beyond the ridge in front of Irles and asked for reinforcements. Before these arrived, however, the Commanding Officer, Lieutenant Colonel Colt, led a charge with the remainder of 12th Gloucesters and the DCLI companies and captured the village. Losses were heavy. Thirty other ranks died and 9 officers, including Lieutenant Colonel Colt, and 170 other ranks were wounded. Captain J. H. Maywood DCLI, the Battalion Adjutant, was killed. The Battalion was left with just one captain and two second lieutenants at the front and was withdrawn into reserve, where it remained until the 29th, when it took over 'assembly positions' from 13th Brigade, ready to attack Beugny village, 9 miles east of Irles the next day. Once again, 12th Gloucesters was in reserve for this attack, but overnight on 31 August/1 September took over part of the front line. The Second Battle of the Somme 1918 was over, but not until 4 September was 95th Brigade relieved, whereupon 12th Gloucesters could at last spend ten days resting and reorganizing. Lieutenant Colonel Colt was awarded the DSO, and three officers, including Second Lieutenant Anstey, MCs; it had been another gallant action by Bristol's Own.[3]

There were also a number of subsidiary actions. The only one relevant to this story is the Battle of the Drocourt–Quéant Line. The stationary warfare in which First Army had been engaged changed towards the end of August as the enemy was driven back. Earlier in the month, 1st Gloucesters had lost the final of the Divisional Rugby to 6th Welch, but the final of the 3rd Brigade inter-company football had been between two Gloucester companies, which C Company won. The Battalion was nearly at full strength, with 32 officers and 871 other ranks, as the Canadian Corps launched an attack on 26 August. By early September the Allies were within assaulting distance of the powerful trench system known as the Drocourt–Quéant Line, the breaking of which would turn the whole of the Germans' positions on a wide front. 1st Division was tasked with supporting the Canadians, and 1st Gloucesters was in reserve to a Canadian Division, which attacked at 5.30 am on 2 September. The Canadians broke the Drocourt–Quéant Line and by nightfall had pushed forward 3 miles and reached the outskirts of Buissy. Eight thousand prisoners were taken and many guns captured. 1st Gloucesters, who had remained in reserve throughout, rejoined 3rd Brigade the next day and took up a position in front of Vis-en-Artois behind Rémy. Here it remained until 8 September, taking no part in any action. It suffered occasional casualties from enemy shelling, but no deaths. On 11 September the Battalion moved by train to Villers-Brettoneux as 1st Division became reserve for the Australian Corps.

The newly formed 18th Gloucesters had arrived in France on 1 August 1918, spent time training and moved up to the front. By 9 September it was occupying the line in the vicinity of Loos. On 11 September the Battalion attacked as part of a Brigade plan and captured its objectives without difficulty; but during consolidation the enemy emerged unexpectedly from cellars and dugouts and regained the position, driving the Battalion back to the start line. The Battalion attacked again at 5.45 pm and this time took and held the objective; by the next day the Germans had abandoned the village. In the fighting 23 other ranks had died, including 2 Company Sergeant Majors.

2/5th Gloucesters found itself back for another tour at Plate Becque on 25 August being heavily shelled. On 31 August it began to advance towards the Lys. A. F. Barnes wrote:

> Words give but a feeble impression of the strenuous nature of these four days. With only a skeleton of Battalion Headquarters, an insufficiency of runners, an inadequate supply of wire, and a constantly moving line, there was the utmost difficulty in obtaining information and transmitting it to Brigade. The whole tour provided a most useful initiation into the conduct of a moving battle after the long period of stationary warfare.

The War Diary of 8th Gloucesters is frustratingly succinct and contains no detail of any action. The Battalion rotated between occupying the line in the La Couture sector and billets at Locon. There must have been some fighting, as 1 officer and 21 other ranks died in the first nine days of September, and although some deaths may have been as a result of wounds received earlier, 12 of the dead have no known grave and are commemorated on the Loos Memorial.

Notes

1. Henry Terrett DCM, from Gloucester, had been a coach builder for Messrs Collett & Sons before the War. Prior to winning a DCM he had been evacuated to hospital five times, twice with influenza, once with scabies, once with eczema and once with bullet wounds to arm, shoulder and hand. In 1922 he married Hilda Flora Howell, also of Gloucester, and when she died in 1932 he married her sister Dorothy in 1934.
2. Robert Harold Anstey was born in Bishopston, Bristol and enlisted in September 1914 in 12th Gloucesters (Bristol's Own). He was commissioned into the Regiment in October 1917 and was initially posted to 2/5th Gloucesters, with whom he was wounded in March 1918 and evacuated home. On his recovery he joined 12th Gloucesters and was wounded again in the action described above. After the War he spent 25 years employed by Messrs T. H. Downing & Co Ltd, Hosiery Manufacturers, principally as their representative in Kent and East Sussex.
3. Dean Marks, *'Bristol's Own', the 12th Battalion Gloucestershire Regiment 1914–1918*.

Chapter 58

The 100-Day Offensive, Breaking the Hindenburg Line

The enemy had fallen back to the Hindenburg Line. Breaking through the Line was the objective of the next series of battles, which lasted from 12 September to 9 October. In front of the Line the Germans held strong positions at Havrincourt and Epéhy, which had to be taken first. Havrincourt was captured by Third Army on 12 September.

1st Gloucesters moved to Tertry on 12 September and marched to Villeveque to relieve 16th Lancashire Fusiliers. On 14 September it attacked and captured Maissemy Ridge, which it held against a counter-attack, although the much-decorated Company Sergeant Major William Biddle was severely wounded. The next day it attacked again to seize higher ground and was successful, earning praise from the Corps Commander but suffering 63 casualties, 16 of whom died. The Battalion was relieved and moved back into reserve. The positions now gained along the front made it possible to launch a major attack on 18 September on Epéhy. 1st Division was part of the attack, but 3rd Brigade was in reserve and 1st Gloucesters saw none of the fighting. It moved up to the Maissemy Ridge in support of 1st Brigade and remained there until 23 September, when it was ordered to capture Fresnoy-le-Petit as part of a 3rd Brigade attack. This was to prove yet another test of the Battalion's resilience and effectiveness. The advance began at 5.00 am on 24 September, under a creeping barrage. D Company, on the right, went straight through to its objective. The two platoons of 'moppers-up' from B Company clearing the southern side of Fresnoy surprised a German Battalion Headquarters in some deep dugouts in the cemetery and captured 4 officers and about 160 other ranks. On the left, the advance made little headway due to uncut wire and some cleverly concealed machine guns, which opened a deadly fire on A Company from a strong point on the north-east side of the village. Once it was light no further movement was possible. The company was pinned down all day and after dark was withdrawn man by man. Meanwhile, the two mopping-up platoons of B Company took over from D Company, who side-stepped to the left, and by midday they had secured the objective. The Battalion was then ordered to take and hold the Alcace and Beauvrainges Trenches. This attack, at 5.30 pm, was entirely successful, and a German counter-attack was defeated. Some 60 Germans were captured. Meanwhile, the strong point in the north-east corner of Fresnoy was inflicting casualties. All attempts by two platoons of C Company to attack the strong point from the east and then the north failed. German soldiers trying to surrender were shot by their own officers. A plan was made to storm the strong point, but there was concern about the fate of wounded Gloucesters being held by the enemy, so a trench-by-trench approach was adopted, which was successful. By 10.20 pm the strong point had been taken and 4 wounded Gloucesters rescued.

After the War, 12th Gloucesters was also awarded the Battle Honour 'Epéhy', but it suffered no casualties. The shelling continued, however, and the Battalion War Diary records that on 23 September C Company trenches were heavily shelled and 4 other ranks were wounded. The transport lines at Ytres were also shelled and 22 animals killed.

8th Gloucesters continued to be in and out of the Line in the Lacatour (La Couture) sector. Here 11 other ranks were killed on 22 September; all are commemorated on the Loos Memorial. Again, the Battalion War Diary makes no mention of what happened, except to record that the Battalion was in the Front Line; so the cause of death of these men remains a mystery.

Elsewhere, 12th Gloucesters was in action. The construction of the Canal-du-Nord, begun in 1913 to link the River Oise with the Dunkirk–Scheldt Canal, had been abandoned on the outbreak of war, but the Germans had made the whole area virtually impassable by damming and flooding it. It was therefore a formidable obstacle. At 5.20 am on 27 September four Allied divisions attacked and took the Germans completely by surprise. 95th Brigade was the reserve brigade of 5th Division for the first phase on 27 September. During the night the Brigade moved forward and relieved 15th Brigade. Initially, 12th Gloucesters was in reserve but was ordered to capture an objective the next day. These orders were subsequently altered, which created difficulty in getting companies into the correct positions in time for their tasks; in fact, they only arrived at their assembly positions as the barrage started at 3.30 am, so the attack began in some confusion. At 4.30 am it was reported that the objective had been captured, but this was later found to be incorrect and as it became light the Battalion came under intense machine gun fire, especially from Gonnelieu. At first both flanks were open, until 1 DCLI came up on the left, but the right flank remained exposed. Isolated German machine gun posts remained a threat and had to be dealt with using rifle grenades. The Battalion was relieved on 30 September having suffered 52 casualties, 24 of whom died, but about 120 prisoners had been taken.

There was little time for 1st Gloucesters to recover from capturing Fresnoy-le-Petit before the Battalion was back in action. The Allies now planned a final all-out assault to end the war, consisting of four simultaneous offensives by the Americans, French, British, and Belgians. The British offensive was on the

St Quentin–Cambrai front in the general direction of Maubeuge and against the most highly organized of the enemy's defences and the greatest density of his troops. The Hindenburg Line itself, just to the east of the St Quentin Canal, was a major obstacle. Fourth Army launched its attack at 5.55 am on 29 September. 1st Division was to form a defensive flank north-east of Ste Helène, while 1st Gloucesters were given the task of taking Faucille Trench, Foreats Trench and Frofait Allet and Glu Trench as far south as the junction of Forestier and Fumistes Alley. It was a fine but foggy morning, and when all the 1,500 Allied guns began firing at 5.55 am the noise was deafening. Due to the fog, 1st Gloucesters did not advance until 11.40 am, but the enemy shell and machine gun fire was terrific and no advance on a general front was possible. At 3.00 pm the front line troops were held up 250yds from the first objective, but a platoon from B Company worked round the left flank, where the South Wales Borderers had begun their attack, and gained their first objective with little opposition. This gave the platoon the opportunity to work up Faucille Trench and bomb the German machine gun at the top of the ridge. The Germans then withdrew and by nightfall on 29 September 1st Gloucesters had captured all its objectives. Eight other ranks had been killed and 48 wounded.

2/5th Gloucesters moved on 7 September to Estaires, which the Germans had left full of delayed explosive charges. On 27 September the Battalion received orders to occupy Junction Post, a key position on the divisional front, early on 29 September. This it did without trouble, but the enemy were still holding the ground to the west and so threatening the position. At 6.30 am on 30 September C Company, with two platoons of B Company, attacked and took the German position, but 2 officers, including a company commander, and 14 other ranks died.

On 21 September 9th Gloucesters became the Pioneer Battalion of 66th Division. This was not simply a change of title; it meant a change of organization to three companies, training in new skills and adopting a different routine. It was not until 9 October that the Battalion War Diary records the Battalion being engaged in its first pioneer task: 'Work was carried out on the repairing of roads and making of tracks.' By then the Hindenburg Line had been broken and it was time for the pursuit.

Chapter 59

More Gallantry in the Pursuit from the Hindenburg Line

Although the German Army was retreating, there remained proud, determined individuals and groups who would fight to the last. The Allied pursuit was vigorous, and it was often impossible for the guns and other equipment to keep pace with the infantry. By early October commanders thought one more determined attack by Fourth Army would turn the enemy's defences. It began at 6.05 am on 3 October. 1st Division made no direct attack but kept in touch with the left flank of the attacking divisions. 1st Gloucesters therefore moved in stages to a position in front of Preselles. Then, at 6.00 am on 5 October, the Battalion was ordered to attack Mannequin Hill, some 2,200yds east of Preselles, which had been taken but lost in a German counter-attack. It attacked with three companies in the front line and one in reserve. A and C Companies reached the objective, but D Company on the left was heavily enfiladed by machine gun fire and had to withdraw. Nevertheless, the Hill was taken with 17 casualties, 3 of whom died. The Battalion was relieved that night.

25th Division had withdrawn to England in June 1918 but returned to France in September, reconstituted with battalions withdrawn from Italy. 1/5th Gloucesters was one of these and joined 75th Brigade on 17 September 1918. By 3 October the Battalion was at St Emilie and was about to be thrown into intense action for the next three weeks. The Battle of the Beaurevoir Line had started, and 75th Brigade was ordered to capture Beaurevoir and the high ground between La Sablonnière and Guisancourt Farm on 5 October. 1/5th Gloucesters dumped greatcoats and packs and set out in fighting order to march the 4 miles to Lormisset. The attack began at 6.30 pm. West of Beaurevoir there was a railway embankment, and at zero hour the Battalion moved quickly, so the leading companies reached the embankment before the barrage had lifted. It suffered some casualties from British fire, but surprised a German nest of 11 machine guns, who were still taking cover. It continued into the village, where the only opposition was from isolated machine guns and snipers. The Battalion had soon established a line 200yds beyond the village. There were 54 casualties, of whom 11 died, in what was judged a highly successful operation. The Battalion was relieved on 7 October but, prior to this, a platoon of C Company attempted a raid on an advanced enemy post but were met by heavy machine gun fire and had to retire. The Battalion reached a position north of Estrées on the 8th, just as the Second Battle of Cambrai began. It moved forward during the afternoon and received orders for an attack the next day on Maretz and Honnechy at 5.20 am, to be made under a creeping barrage. The Battalion met no resistance until it reached Maretz because, on its left, the troops of 66th Division had a different zero hour and their barrage therefore started at 5.45 am, overlapped and caused some casualties in the reserve companies of the Gloucesters. By 6.30 am a mist had fallen over the battlefield but it did not impede progress, although the barrage supporting 66th Division did. Once in Maretz, the Battalion met stubborn resistance, but eventually the village was secured. At 5.20 am the next day, 10 October, 75th Brigade continued to advance. One mile east of Honnechy resistance stiffened and eventually 1/8th Warwicks halted, whereupon B Company, 1/5th Gloucesters moved through the Warwicks but met heavy enfilade fire from machine guns. When all the officers and many of the NCOs had been wounded, the company was forced to withdraw.

1/5th Gloucesters left Honnechy on 12 October but returned five days later, as 75th Brigade was in reserve to 50th Division for an attack on German positions on the River Selle. On 18 October the Battalion moved across the river under hostile shellfire to Benin. 50th Division now launched an attack, the second phase of which was for 75th Brigade to capture the line of the Bazeul–Baillon Farm road, with 1/5th Gloucesters on the left. The first phase went well, and at 8.45 am 75th Brigade pushed through and took their objectives but suffered from machine gun fire and sniping for the rest of the day. On the 19th an attempt to occupy the line of the Richemont stream failed due to heavy machine gun fire but succeeded the next day after stubborn fighting. The Battalion was relieved later that day.

There was still more for 1/5th Gloucesters to do. On 24 October 75th Brigade set out to capture a line from the north-eastern edge of L'Évêque Wood to the western edges of Bousies to the north-west of Landrecies. After advancing some 300yds the Battalion was halted by fire from machine gun nests, and for five hours heavy, stubborn fighting ensued, until Private Francis Miles[1] made his way forward alone and shot one machine gunner, putting the gun out of action. He then advanced on another, shot the gunner and captured a team of eight, before beckoning the company forward; it duly followed, capturing 16 machine guns, 1 officer and 50 other ranks. Miles was awarded the Victoria Cross. 1/5th Gloucesters was now able to continue forward, meeting strong resistance, which it gradually overcame. The final attack at 4.45 pm was successful, and the Battalion was relieved on 24 October, having been in almost continuous action for three weeks.

The Germans were expected to try to hold the River Selle, and the plan was for Fourth Army to attack on 17 October on a front of about 10 miles from Le Cateau southwards. The attack was led by 46th and 6th Divisions, with 1st Division passing through 6th Division to capture the villages of La Vallée Mulatre and Wassigny. 3rd Brigade, including 1st Gloucesters, was initially in reserve but was brought into action on 18 October, with 1st Gloucesters in reserve. B Company formed a defensive flank and at 6.30 pm was ordered to clear Ribeauville, where opposition was weak. 3rd Brigade attacked again on 19 October and by nightfall was within 800yds of the Canal de la Sambre. On 20 October they pushed forward again closer to the Canal, and the situation was now quiet. Nine other ranks had been killed.

The War Diary of 8th Gloucesters for the first half of October seems remote from the action going on elsewhere. On 12 October the Battalion was in the south of Cambrai, where 'Companies were at the disposal of company commanders for saluting drill up to 12 noon'. The next day being Sunday, divine services were held, the one for Roman Catholics in Cambrai Cathedral. The contrast between these activities and what was to follow must surely have prevented anyone becoming bored. By 18 October the Battalion had reached St Aubert and was in position for a general attack on Aussy on the 20th. This necessitated crossing the River Selle, so each leading company was accompanied by Royal Engineers with bridging equipment for each platoon. The attack was entirely successful. On 23 October the Battalion was ordered to 'make good' another objective, the Capelle–St Martin Road. It was impossible to get orders out to the two foremost companies due to heavy machine gun fire, so B Company was ordered to push through the two leading companies and take the objective. The War Diary states:

> The Company moved up in artillery formation, making use of every possible cover. When our slight barrage opened at 14.26 hours the Company advanced with great determination with the result that the enemy became demoralized and approximately 150 prisoners and 10 machine guns were taken. At about 1600 hours the enemy was reported massing in Q.22 A and B. The Corps heavies and field guns got on to this area very quickly and prevented all chance of any counter-attack developing.

The Battalion was relieved on 24 October.

9th Gloucesters (Pioneers) spent most of October either in the line or repairing roads. During the month they suffered 21 casualties. On 11 November the Battalion marched to Sars Potières, where 'notification [was] received that Hostilities would cease at 1100 hours. Work carried out in the filling in of mine craters, and on the maintenance of roads.'

2/5th Gloucesters' involvement in the Battle of the Selle was brief and confused. They left Estaires on 3 October and by the 14th were at Proville. On 24 October the Battalion was bivouacked in a sunken road when at 2.00 pm it was ordered to attack the village of Vendegies and the high ground north-east of Écaillon. In contrast to previous operations, there was little time for detailed preparation. The Battalion reached Bermerain at 5.00 pm after a rapid march and attacked almost immediately, with few maps and little idea of the ground or the position of the enemy and other troops. Despite these difficulties it was successful, suffering just 27 casualties.

The end of the War was now close. On 4 November the three British divisions all attacked on a 30-mile front from the Sambre, north of Oisy to Valenciennes. 1st Division was on the extreme right; 3rd Brigade's objective was to capture Catillon and form a bridgehead east of the Canal, and 1st Gloucesters was given this task. The Battalion had moved into the front line north-east of Mazinghein on 30 October, and on 1 November A Company was attacked and suffered 12 casualties, 7 of whom died.[2] For the assault on Catillon 1st Gloucesters had under command two tanks, Royal Engineers, a section of the Machine Gun Corps and two Stokes mortars, an illustration of how the Army had developed both in equipment and organization since 1914. The Battalion attacked at 5.45 am on 4 November, under a creeping barrage. There was dense fog and, despite the barrage, the leading companies encountered several machine gun posts but pushed on, captured the bridge and established the bridgehead, suffering 32 casualties, 4 of whom died. At 5.00 pm 1st Gloucesters marched back to billets. Four years and 83 days since arriving in France, the Battalion had fought its last battle of the War.

1/5th Gloucesters was shelled frequently for the first three days of November and suffered casualties. On 4 November 75th Brigade had the task of forcing a crossing over the Sambre Canal and capturing Landrecies. Zero hour was 6.15 am in thick mist. There was some confusion, but the Battalion reached the Canal and 1/8th Worcesters came through, crossed and advanced through Landrecies. 1/5th Gloucesters then crossed and formed a defensive flank to the south, capturing 350 prisoners, guns and equipment. It had suffered 65 casualties, of whom 14 died. The Battalion advanced again on the 6th and on 9 November marched to Preux-au-Bois, holding a church service the next day, as it was a Sunday. The last entry in the War Diary reads: 'News of Armistice received, very little interest – a few Véry lights let off in the evening. A.A. guns dismounted.'

On 2 November 8th Gloucesters had begun to advance from Cauroir to Eth, encountering no opposition. On 6 November the Battalion was in support for action near La Flamengrie, and from there it continued to advance until by 11 November it had reached Bettrechies. The Battalion War Diary makes no mention of the end of the war.

Notes

1. Francis George Miles VC (1896–1961) was born in Clearwell in the Forest of Dean. He left school at thirteen to work for the Princess Royal Colliery Co. In December 1914 he enlisted with his stepfather, Frederick Clack, in 9th Gloucesters. He was evacuated from Salonika with a poisoned foot and was then posted to 8th Gloucesters. While attached to the Royal Engineers he was the only survivor of 50 men buried by a mine. Once recovered, he was posted to 1/5th Gloucesters, with whom he won the VC. After the war he returned to become a 'free miner' in the Forest of Dean and in the Second War enlisted in the Pioneer Corps. He is buried at Clearwell.
2. Among those killed with 1st Gloucesters on 1 November was Lt Arthur Skemp, who survived only eight days at the Front. He had tried repeatedly to join the Army from the outbreak of the war but he had been the Winterstoke Professor of English at the University of Bristol and was turned down repeatedly because his teaching ability was deemed too valuable.

Part XI

AFTER THE WAR

Chapter 60

A New World Emerges

The fighting had ceased, but the world was in a mess and not at peace. An armistice is an agreement to stop fighting, but a state of war still exists until a peace treaty is signed. Kaiser Wilhelm II, who had gone to Spa in Belgium from Berlin on 29 October 'to be closer to his army', abdicated on 9 November, and two days later Germany signed the Armistice. The Ottoman Empire, which had existed for over 700 years, the Habsburg Empire, created in 1700, and the German Empire, which was only founded in 1871, had now all sued for peace. Meanwhile, among the Allies, the Russian Revolution, begun in 1917, still had some way to go before the Soviet Union was formed in 1922. France and Britain, including their empires, had suffered millions of casualties, as had all the other main belligerents, and were effectively broke. As if all this was not enough for statesmen, diplomats and politicians to sort out, the dying was not yet over: the world was in the grip of Spanish flu, the deadliest influenza pandemic ever known. It began in January 1918 and lasted for two years until December 1920, spreading world-wide. It is estimated that 10 to 20 per cent of those infected died and that overall between 50m and 100m people perished (3–5 per cent of the world's population).[1] This compares with the 16m combatants and civilians who, it is calculated, died in the First World War.

The Ottoman Empire was completely broken up. Much of what happened was a result of what is still referred to as the Sykes-Picot Agreement between Britain and France, overlooking the fact that it was largely masterminded by Sergei Sazonov, Tsarist Russia's Foreign Minister. It was signed on 16 March 1916, on the assumption that the Allies would win. It led to the creation of the British Mandates in Palestine from 1923 to 1948 and Iraq from 1920 to 1937, while the French ruled Mandatory Syria and Lebanon from 1923 to 1948. It also broke Britain's pledge to the Arabs, made through Lawrence of Arabia (Colonel T. E. Lawrence), to create a national Arab homeland in greater Syria; this promise had induced the Arabs to revolt against the Ottoman Empire in June 1916 and was a key factor in the Allied victory in the Middle East. In June 2014, when ISIL (Islamic State of Iraq and Levant) proclaimed a Caliphate, one of its aims was to reverse the effects of the Sykes-Picot Agreement nearly a century after it was signed.

Greece decided that this was the right moment to launch an attack against the Turks in order to achieve a reunion with historic Hellenic settlements in Turkey, an ambition of Greek nationalism for some 80 years. They invaded Turkey in June

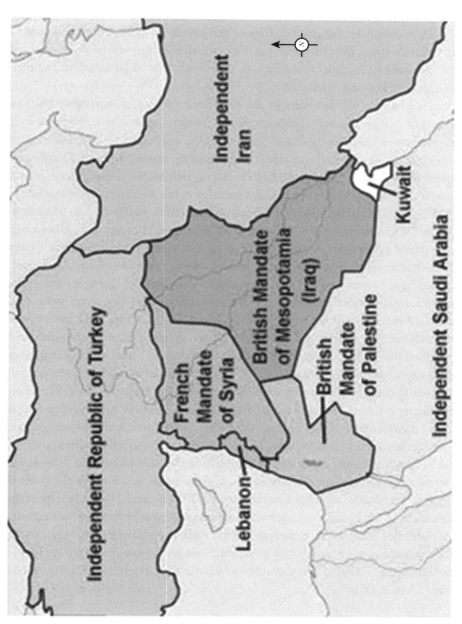

Map 35 The Mandates Created by the League of Nations after the War

1919 and were initially successful, getting close to Ankara before Kemal Atatürk rallied the Turks and overwhelmed the overstretched Greek army. The subsequent Treaty of Lausanne between beaten Greece and victorious Turkey included an agreement to exchange the minorities on each other's soil and so led to the end of the Greek presence in the coastal cities of the eastern Aegean which had existed since Homer's time. One of these was Smyrna, now Izmir, which had remained almost completely loyal to the Allies in the Great War. The hostility between Greece and Turkey still exists today.

Charles I became the last ruler of the Habsburg Empire in November 1916 on the death of his great-uncle, Emperor Franz Joseph. When the fighting in Italy began to turn against the Austrians in June 1918, he started to look for ways to preserve his empire by political rather than military means. In early October he indicated to Woodrow Wilson, the US President, that he was willing to enter into an Armistice and on 16 October issued a manifesto, but his efforts were too late to prevent his empire's dissolution: what became Yugoslavia was formed on 6 October, Poland on 7 October, Czechoslovakia on 28 October and Hungary on 1 November.

The terms of the Armistice presented to the Germans were severe. They required the evacuation of all occupied territories, including Alsace-Lorraine, which had been German since 1871; the military evacuation of the west bank of the Rhine and the surrender of all military equipment, including the internment of all German submarines and the capital ships of the High Seas Fleet; the payment of reparations for war damage; and, harshest of all, acceptance of the continuation of the Allied blockade, despite the Armistice. This was followed by the Paris Peace Conference, which led eventually to the Treaty of Versailles, signed in June 1919 and generally considered harsher than the terms of the Armistice itself. Germany lost Alsace and Lorraine, captured in 1870/71, to France. It surrendered Silesia and West Prussia to a newly independent Poland. Its proud army was reduced to a tiny gendarmerie, and its navy and air force were abolished. Germany was forced to sign this Treaty as the only way of lifting the Allied blockade. It was seen by Germans as a humiliation, and most historians agree that it made the Second World War inevitable; as John Keegan wrote, 'The Second World War was the continuation of the First, and indeed it is inexplicable except in terms of rancours and instabilities left by the earlier conflict.' That is hindsight, however. At the time there were some who felt the Treaty was not hard enough. Two days before it was signed, the German Navy decided to scuttle their High Seas Fleet interned at Scapa Flow in Orkney.

Note

1. K. D. Patterson and G. F. Pyle, 'The geography and mortality of the 1918 influenza pandemic' in *Bulletin of the History of Medicine*.

Chapter 61

The Dead and the Living

That there was so little celebration to mark the end of the War is not surprising. Those that had survived were numb, remembering all the friends and colleagues who had died or suffered life-changing wounds. There was also concern that it might not really be over, coupled with uncertainty about 'what happens now'. Today, if a factory closes and a couple of thousand employees lose their jobs, there is widespread alarm. In 1919 hundreds of thousands of men who had fought for their country were about to lose their jobs, and many would find themselves without any other employment. It wasn't only the reduction in the size of the three Services but also the closure of factories that had supported the war effort. The start of the Great Depression in Britain was still ten years away, but the seeds of it were sown as the Great War ended.

Although the Armistice came into force on 11 November 1918, the dying did not stop then. Between 12 November 1918 and 31 December 1921 272 members of the Gloucestershire Regiment and 9 of the Royal Gloucestershire Hussars died. Some of these deaths were as a result of wounds suffered earlier, some due to sickness, particularly Spanish flu, and some due to accidents whilst still serving. Most people in Britain are familiar with the Commonwealth War Graves Commission (CWGC) cemeteries that exist wherever the British fought in the First and Second World Wars. Because they are so familiar there is a risk that we overlook quite how remarkable they are. Few Russian or Turkish soldiers were ever properly buried or had their deaths recorded. The bodies of Germans and Austrians who died on the Eastern Front have unrecorded graves, if they ever had them at all. The French lost 1,700,000 men; some of these are buried in individual graves, some in collective ones. Only the British, through the CWGC, provided an individual grave for every man, even if some were unidentified; in that case, instead of recording name, age, rank, regiment and date of death, the stone simply states: 'A Soldier of the Great War – Known unto God'. Many bodies were blown to pieces or lost in the mud, but all are commemorated as individuals on a memorial. The best known are the Menin Gate in Ypres and Thiepval on the Somme, but there are many others in various parts of the world. The process of finding all the bodies of those who had died, exhuming and if possible identifying them, was a grisly business but carried out with great dedication by Labour Companies and Graves Registration Units, without whom the beautiful and moving cemeteries that exist today could not have been established. What many will not realize is that bodies are still being found

100 years later; and when they are, if they are British, another grave is added in the appropriate cemetery. Every now and again it is possible to identify a body, in which case the deceased's descendants are offered the option of a full military funeral. In addition, after the War most cities, towns and villages erected War Memorials, generally paid for by public subscription. The design of these varies, as does what is inscribed on them, but the combination of the efforts of the CWGC and local War Memorial committees mean that those who died really are properly remembered.

On 11 November 1920 the Funeral of the Unknown Warrior took place in Westminster Abbey. Company Sergeant Major William Biddle MC, DCM & Bar, MM & Bar represented the Gloucesters.

The CWGC continued to include servicemen who died up until 31 December 1921 in its records. In 1921 25 Gloucesters died, 3 in India, the remainder in the UK, of whom 17 were buried in Gloucestershire, including Bristol. There were many who died after 1921 as a result of being wounded. One, according to Robert Brunsdon,[1] was Private William Edwin Marr, wounded with 1/5th Gloucesters on 27 August 1916, who died on 27 April 1922, nearly six years later. The family lived at 23 Central Road, Gloucester and William was educated at Tredworth School, from where he won an exhibition to King's School, Gloucester. From the base hospital to which he was evacuated in 1916 he wrote to his father: 'The beggars have got me at last in the left leg, arm and back and I am now in hospital. We attacked last Sunday night and were successful, taking numerous prisoners, and were consolidating when they counter-attacked. I got the benefit of three bombs. I hope to be in England soon.' Despite the length of time intervening, he was not forgotten by the Battalion. The Battalion Padre, Revd George Helm, took the service, the bearer party consisted of volunteers from the Battalion and All Saints Church in Barton Street was packed. The comradeship that had been forged in the trenches would endure for decades.

Many of those who had died left widows who needed to be provided for. This led to the first non-contributory State pension scheme in Britain. In addition, there was a 'dependant's allowance' for children under sixteen. On the down side, women who were accused of drunkenness, neglecting their children, living out of wedlock with another man or having an illegitimate child risked being judged by the Local Pension Office to be behaving improperly, and could lose their pension. Most regiments set up regimental associations, both to organize reunions of those who had fought together and to provide financial or other support for those in need. The Soldiers, Sailors and Families Association is the oldest Service charity, having been founded in 1885. In 1918, with the formation of the Royal Air Force, its name changed to the Soldiers, Sailors, Airmen and Families Association (SSAFA), and together with the Royal British Legion, founded in 1921, it provides support to ex-servicemen. There are a host of other specialist service charities.

Gordon le Brun may not have been typical, but his story illustrates the difficulties many faced. Gordon was born in Jersey and educated in Somerset. He enlisted in the South Wales Borderers in 1910 but purchased his discharge in 1912, giving his address as 39 Colston St, Bristol. He became a male nurse in a mental asylum but in September 1914 enlisted in 7th Bedfords and achieved rapid promotion to CQMS, before applying for a commission in December 1916. He was commissioned into 8th Gloucesters and was wounded in the chest by a shell fragment in an action on 23 July 1917 for which he was awarded a good MC. In 1927, by which time he and his wife had five children below the age of eight, he pleaded guilty to stealing £26 16s 6d from Provident Clothing & Supply Co Ltd, for whom he worked. It is clear from the report of his court appearance that he was desperate, and he was bound over for twelve months and deprived of his rank of lieutenant, but did not forfeit his MC as the magistrates did not feel the offence warranted this. He later served as a Corporal in the Band of the Hampshire Regiment (TA) and was discharged in 1938. In August 1939 he applied for enrolment in the Officers Emergency Reserve but was not accepted. He died in 1978 aged eighty-seven.

One of the major challenges facing Britain once the War was over was how to demobilize the vast number that had joined up for the duration. In 1916 a scheme had been drawn up by Lord Derby, the Minister of War, under which the first men released should be those with jobs in key industries. As these had generally been the last to be called up, however, it meant that those with the longest service would be the last to be released, and this led in 1918 to protests and demonstrations. When Winston Churchill became Minister of War in January 1919 one of his first actions was to introduce a new scheme based on age, length of service and number of times a man had been wounded in battle. This was seen to be fair and defused any further protests.

Another result of the First World War was the disappearance of what is generally referred to as 'the lost generation'. It is true that many men who would undoubtedly have contributed much to the world died or were so disabled that they could not be nearly so effective. There were also many young women who would now never marry and have children. Most families have in their family trees spinsters born around the turn of the century. For all these reasons, to many in 1919 it must have seemed impossible that Europe would ever recover; and yet, despite the Second World War, it is once again prosperous and at peace, a remarkable testimony to the survival instincts of the human race.

Finally, of course, there was the need to manage the peace and reduce the numbers in uniform in all three services. Many in the Regiments of Gloucestershire still had work to do before they could go home.

Note

1. Robert Brunsdon, *The King's Men Fallen in the Great War. The King's School, Gloucester.*

Chapter 62

Mopping up and Going Home

On 11 November 1st Gloucesters was at Fresnoy-le-Grand, and 1st Division was selected to occupy the Rhine Provinces. The British Army never loses its ability to surprise, and the next day 1st Gloucesters held a 'Special Foot Washing Parade'. On 18 November the Battalion began the 208-mile march to south of Cologne. The Colours were collected from England, so that when the Battalion crossed the Belgian frontier into Germany on 18 December it marched past the Divisional Commander with Colours uncased, in driving rain. The Battalion remained near Cologne until June 1919, sending drafts home until there was only a Cadre of 3 officers, 51 Other Ranks and 24 Boys left. They landed at Dover on 9 June 1919.

2nd Gloucesters was in Orljak in Macedonia on 11 November, having been 'at peace' since 1 October. The strength of the Battalion was just 289 all ranks. Men were going sick and some were dying of malaria and pneumonia. A cable from the King to the Commander-in-Chief read:

> I warmly congratulate you and all ranks under your command upon the brilliant success achieved in concert with our Allies, resulting in the surrender of the Bulgarian Army. I fully realise the hardships and unfavourable climatic conditions which have rendered the service of the troops especially arduous and therefore still more praiseworthy.
> GEORGE R.I.

Initially, the Battalion worked quarries to provide material to improve the roads, but then began to march north, reaching Orljak on 10 November. It was then warned of a move to Batoum on the Black Sea and entrained for Salonika on 31 December. By now the Battalion had received reinforcements and its strength was 16 officers and 627 other ranks. The ship sailed through the Dardanelles before reaching Batoum on 8 January 1919. On 17 January 2nd Gloucesters entrained for Tiflis, where its role, along with the rest of the British garrison, was to resist an attack by the Georgians. On 19 February D Company, consisting of 2 officers and 112 other ranks, with transport and mules, set out from Tiflis on the 200-mile journey to Ararat, in the shadow of the biblical Mount Ararat, to garrison the area; it had immense difficulty keeping the peace between Tartars, Kurds and Armenians.

The company returned to Tiflis on 24 March. Then Second Lieutenant Barnfield set out with a servant and interpreter to investigate 'the Zode affair', although what this was is not clear. He travelled for ten days by car, sleigh, boat and on horseback, often with an Armenian escort, seeing people living in desperate conditions. By the end of May the Battalion had been reduced to cadre strength and it was relieved and sailed from Batoum back to England, together with Colonel Vicary's horse, 'The Sikh', which had accompanied him throughout the War.

1/4th Gloucesters moved from Vezzena to Val Portule in Italy on 11 November and on to Cornedo on 15 November. In January the process of demobilization began, gathering pace in February and leaving a cadre of just 7 officers and 43 other ranks to hand in the remaining stores and leave for England on 11 March 1919. The Battalion would in due course reform as a volunteer battalion in the Territorial Force based in Bristol.

1/5th Gloucesters were at Preux-au-Bois about 20 miles east of Cambrai in Northern France on 11 November. 25th Division did not advance into Germany, so the Battalion remained in France, from where they demobilized; eventually, a cadre returned home to Gloucester as another volunteer battalion in the Territorial Force.

It was well over a year before those serving in 1/6th Gloucesters got back to Bristol. The Battalion began marching on 4 November to Taranto in Italy, where it remained until 23 February 1919, when, leaving one company behind, it entrained for Brindisi to sail to Scutari in Albania and Montenegro. Then in May 1919 the Battalion went to Egypt, where it was based outside Alexandria, committed to garrison duties. The company left at Taranto never rejoined the Battalion but demobilized in September, whilst in Egypt the size of the Battalion initially increased as others disbanded; but gradually men were demobilized and by 14 December 1919 there were only 4 officers and 26 other ranks left. This final cadre and the Colours reached Bristol on 25 March 1920, having been abroad on active service for 5 years and 7 months.

2/5th Gloucesters had been at Maresches, 8 miles south of Valenciennes in Northern France on 11 November 1918. The Battalion War Diary records:

> 0855 – Wire received from XVII Corps as follows: 'Hostilities will cease at 1100 hours today Nov 11th. Troops will stand fast on line reached at that hour, which will be reported to Corps HQ. Defensive precautions will be maintained. There will be no intercourse of any description with the enemy.'

The next day, the Battalion repaired a railway line nearby. On 27 November it moved to Domqueur, 10 miles east of Abbeville, where it remained for over two months, training, filling in trenches, playing games and undertaking education in preparation for civilian life. In January demobilization began and by February there were about 10 men a day leaving, while drafts from other battalions arrived. By 5 April the Battalion was at Harfleur, 7 miles from Le Havre, and although the War Diary does not record the disbandment of 2/5th Gloucesters it ends on 31 July 1919. In his foreword to *The Story of the 2/5th Gloucestershire Regiment 1914–1918* by A.F. Barnes Major General Sir Colin Mackenzie, GOC 61st Division 1915–18 wrote:

> The 2/5th Gloucesters during the war showed they possessed in a high degree the qualities of their county; qualities which are of the essence of real England; steady, deep and true; and under the leadership of Colonels of special distinction the Battalion went surely forward, from good to better, with a quiet growing confidence in itself, which nothing checked or daunted . . . I may say, as commanding the Division, that I knew 2/5th Gloucesters very well, and their Colonels, and valued them accordingly. I always had confidence that they would carry out any task given them if humanly possible, and my confidence was rewarded in many dark days and dubious issues.

7th Gloucesters was in Kazvin (Qazvin) in Northern Persia on 30 October when the Armistice with the Ottoman Empire was signed. By 11 November the Battalion had reached Sandar, 32 miles from Bandar Anzali, where it embarked for Baku on the Caspian Sea. It immediately began to form part of the garrison, principally guarding key points, until on 24 August 1919 it entrained for Batoum, where the Battalion boarded a steamer to sail to Constantinople. Once at Constantinople, demobilization accelerated, until on 17 October the remnants of 7th Gloucester amalgamated with 8th Ox and Bucks Light Infantry.

8th Gloucesters was in France at Bettrechies, 12 miles east of Valenciennes on 11 November. The Battalion War Diary makes no mention of the Armistice, but the Battalion continued to train every day. On 25 January the Divisional Commander presented the King's Colour to the Battalion and on 21 February a draft of 10 officers and 167 men entrained to join 2/5th Gloucesters; the Battalion War Diary ends on 31 March 1919. In 1921 Lieutenant Colonel Archer-Shee erected, at his own expense, an oak memorial cross outside the village of Longueval overlooking the site of 12th Gloucesters' first attack on 29 July 1916. In 1986 it was replaced as a fitting memorial to a special battalion born in the City of Bristol.

66th Division, including 9th Gloucesters, was ordered to form part of the Army of Occupation and began a march to the Rhine on 16 November, arriving at Civey on 12 December. Initially, the work involved salvaging German war material, but there was also education and ceremonial drill. On 2 March 9th Gloucesters moved to Solingen to join the Southern Division of the Army of Occupation. In June a company plus a platoon worked on creating a racecourse at Mergeim, and Lieutenant Francombe took part in the Army Athletic Championships. He did well, and subsequently represented the British in the Inter-Allied Games involving eighteen nations in Paris. Due to reinforcements the strength of the Battalion at the end of July was 38 officers and 944 other ranks, but demobilization sped up in September and the War Diary ceased on 31 October 1919.

The 13th Gloucesters' War Diary for November 1918 consists of the single entry: 'Administering Malaria reinforcements at Haudricourt. 11th Armistice signed.' The Battalion had established this camp in September, trained reinforcements and sent them forward to their units. On 3 December the Battalion handed over the camp and moved to No 1 Despatching Camp at Le Havre. On 18 December demobilization began and it continued to process personnel leaving. On 2 May 1919 the remnants of 13th Gloucesters paraded and were presented with the King's Colour. On 4 June orders were received that the infantry cadre of 39th Division was to be disbanded. The War Diary records: '7 June – Handed in all Ordnance Stores & Horses & receipt obtained. Colour Party – strength 1 Officer 4 ORs proceeded to England via Le Havre, remaining personnel demobilized. Casualties – Offrs 3 ORs 18.' Presumably the casualties referred to were due to illness.

1/1st RGH were at Bileramun near Aleppo in Syria on 11 November. The fighting was over, and although the first demobilization party left on 13 January 1919, the closing day of the campaign for the RGH was not until 24 June 1919, and even then some men were left in Syria. On 17 November 1918 the Regiment moved to the outskirts of Aleppo and into a Turkish barracks, once the accommodation had been cleaned up. On 19 November nine of those captured at Qatia were released. Drafts continued to be demobilized, and on 31 January 1919 the strength of the Regiment was 9 officers, 126 other ranks and 168 animals. A letter dated 19 January 1919 from Sergeant Lambert RAMC, serving with 1/1st RGH, reveals an air of near-mutiny within the Regiment because of the way the Brigade Commander was treating the two English regiments in his command, the RGH and Sherwood Rangers: 'He had been in India the whole of his Army life and of course doesn't know how to treat Englishmen.'[1] On 10 February the Regiment moved to Killis in Turkey, from where it patrolled local villages until 24 June, when it was at last relieved. Four officers and 143 other ranks who were not eligible for demobilization were transferred to the Sherwood Rangers Yeomanry, and the remaining 8 officers and 19 other ranks, under the command of Colonel Turner, formed the final cadre for demobilization. They reached Gloucester Station on 15 August, where they received an official welcome. On 29 April 1922 the magnificent memorial on College Green outside Gloucester Cathedral was dedicated with the inscription: 'In memory of the Royal Gloucestershire Hussars Yeomanry who gave up their lives in the Great War, 1914–1918'. The memorial was unveiled by Lieutenant General Sir Philip Chetwode Bt, KCB, KCMG, DSO, who had commanded the Desert Column in Palestine.

In 1927 the wooden cross made by Sergeant Meulbrook and dedicated to those from the 10th Gloucesters who had died which had been erected on Christmas Eve 1916 in the remnants of High Wood was removed by Colonel Pritchard and placed in Christ Church, Cheltenham, along with the Battalion's Colours, where it remains to this day; a memorial to a gallant battalion of a gallant county.

The principal memorial to the Gloucesters is, however, at Hooge on the left of the road from Gheluvelt to Ypres. It is a splendid obelisk on which is inscribed: 'In Memory of All Ranks of The Gloucestershire Regiment who Fought and Fell in the Campaigns of 1914–1918'. On the sides all the Battle Honours won by the Regiment are listed.

Note

1. Frank Fox, *The Royal Gloucestershire Hussars Yeomanry 1898–1922.*

Gallantry

The British gallantry medals awarded to individuals during the First World War were:

Victoria Cross (VC) – Awarded for an act of outstanding courage or devotion to duty in the presence of the enemy.

Distinguished Service Order (DSO) – Awarded for conspicuous gallantry and devotion to duty by an Officer.

Distinguished Conduct Medal (DCM) – Awarded for conspicuous gallantry and devotion to duty by an Other Rank.

Military Cross (MC) – Awarded for acts of gallantry in the presence of the enemy by officers of the rank of Captain and below and by Warrant Officers.

Military Medal (MM) – Awarded for gallantry and devotion to duty when under fire in battle on land to Other Ranks.

Meritorious Service Medal (MSM) – Originally awarded for meritorious service by Non-Commissioned Officers. Between 1916 and 1919 the eligibility of the award was amended so that Non-Commissioned Officers could be awarded the MSM in the field.

Mentioned in Despatches (MiD) – Not a medal but recognition that an individual had been mentioned in a Senior Officer's despatch for a noteworthy act of gallantry or service. Only after the War, in 1919, was it agreed that the individual should receive a Certificate, and in 1920 it was decided that a bronze oak leaf would be issued for the individual to wear on the relevant campaign medal ribbon.

The only gallantry medal that could be awarded posthumously in the Great War was the Victoria Cross, which normally required a citation written by an officer who had witnessed the action and three other witnesses. The only other recognition of gallantry posthumously was for an individual to be Mentioned in Despatches; this does not mean that all those who were Mentioned in Despatches and had died had been considered for the award of a VC, but that some may have been.

There were in addition to the above a number of foreign gallantry medals that were awarded to individuals but these are not included in the following table,[1] which shows the number of gallantry medals awarded to individuals in each battalion of the Gloucesters and to 1/1st RGH. It also includes awards made to Gloucesters serving with other battalions or corps. An individual could be Mentioned in Despatches several times but names are only included once in the table (Lieutenant Colonel Beasley DSO and two Bars was Mentioned in Despatches five times).

Unit	VC (Note 1)	DSO (Note 2)	Bar to DSO (Note 3)	MC	Bar to MC	DCM (Note 4)	Bar to DCM (Note 5)	MM	Bar to MM	MSM	MiD
1st Bn		9	1	38	7	40	2	132	9	8	85
2nd Bn		4	1	8	3	6		15		10	68
1/4th Bn		4		29	2	15		64	2	11	51
2/4th Bn				9	2	2		32	2	3	6
1/5th Bn	1	1		22	2	21		84	3	8	44
2/5th Bn		1		18	3	16		73	3	2	18
1/6th Bn		2		18	2	19		56		9	43
2/6th Bn				4	2	5		26	3	3	5
7th Bn		2		11	1	13		6		12	55
8th Bn	2	4		28	1	14	2	87	5	6	23
9th Bn		2		5				15		5	27
10th Bn		1		3		11		36	2	3	20
12th Bn		1		19	4	15		55		7	31
13th Bn		1		9		2		22		3	15
14th Bn	1	4		7		5		34	1	1	13
18th Bn				1		3		9		3	4
Att other units	1	13	1	39		1	2			4	9
1/1st RGH		4		6		7		8			21

Note 1 – VCs

1/5th Gloucesters: 17324 Pte F. G. Miles

8th Gloucesters: Lt Col A. Carton de Wiart, 4th Dragoon Guards, Commanding 8th Gloucesters, Capt M. A. James;

14th Gloucesters: 2/Lt H. Parsons

Gloucesters attached to other regiments and corps: Lt Col D. Burges DSO, Commanding 7th SWB.

Note 2 – DSOs

1st Gloucesters: Capt R. E. Rising, Lt Col A. W. Pagan, Maj H. Needham CMG, Maj J. R. Wethered, Maj J. O'D. Ingram, Lt Col A. Bryant, Capt D. Duncan MC, Lt Col H. N. Vinen, Lt J. R. Guild

2nd Gloucesters: Lt Col F. C. Nisbet, Lt Col K. M. Davie, Lt Col A. C. Vicary MC

1/4th Gloucesters: Lt Col S. Davenport, Maj E. C. Slade MC, Maj E. Shellard, Capt P. G. J. Guterbock MC

1/5th Gloucesters: Capt C. R. Coote

2/5th Gloucesters: Lt Col G. F. Collett

1/6th Goucesters: Maj T. W. Nott, Lt Col P. L. Coates

7th Gloucesters: Lt Col R. Wilkinson, Maj E. Barnard

8th Gloucesters: Capt C. G. Elkington, Maj B. Thomas, Capt E. B. Pope, Lt Col W. Parkes

9th Gloucesters: Lt Col J. Fane, Maj E. F. B. Witts

10th Gloucesters: Maj J. G. Kirkwood

12th Gloucesters: Lt Col H. A. Colt

13th Gloucesters: Lt Col A. H. Boulton

14th Gloucesters: Capt F. H. Toop, Lt Col W. P. S. Foord, Maj C. Hancock, Capt B. A. Russell

Gloucesters attached to other Battalions or Corps: Capt A. Mc. Inglis (Tank Corps), Lt Col J. L. F. Tweedie (Lanc Fus), Lt C. G. Toogood (1/2GR), Lt Col H. E. Wetherall MC (2/4 Ox& Bucks), Lt A. H. Radice (SWB), Capt N. F. Somerset MC (14 Armr M Bty), Lt Col T. W. Isaac (15 York LI), Lt Col R. L. Beasley (11th Borders), Lt Col H. F. L. Hilton-Green MC (10th Devons), Lt Col D. Burges (7th SWB), Lt Col A. L. W. Newth MC (11th Cheshires), Maj V. N. Johnson (12 Inf Bde)

1/1st RGH: Lt Col R. M. Yorke, Major C. E. Turner, Lt Col A. J. Palmer, Capt Lord Apsley MC

Note 3 – Bars to DSOs

1st Gloucesters: Lt Col J. L. F. Tweedie

2nd Gloucesters: Lt Col A. C. Vicary

Gloucesters attached to other Battalions or Corps: Lt Col R. L. Beasley (11th Borders), Lt Col R. L. Beasley (17th RWF), Lt Col W. P. S. Foord (19th Northumberland Fusiliers)

Note 4 – DCMs

1st Gloucesters: Sgt T. J. Knight, Pte A. E. Crossman, Sgt T. H. Eddy, Sgt J. Wilson, Pte G. V. Law, Pte T. H. Orr, Pte J. Shipway, LCpl O. Royal, Pte W. Hotchins, Pte J. Harper, Pte E. Harris, Sgt W. Smith, Sgt T. Harding, Sgt W. Duddidge, Sgt J. C. Millard, Sgt W. H. Reece, Sgt H. E. Needs, CSM J. P. Crimmins, Sgt J. Newman MM, Pte H. Edmonds, Sgt W. F. Drake, Sgt E. Nash, Sgt G. H. Horton, Pte F. J. Wilkinson, Sgt W. Biddle MM & Bar, Pte E. A. Westbury, Pte P. E. Day, Sgt A. E. Callaghan MM, Sgt W. J. Corbett MM, Cpl W. Taylor MM, Sgt H. Coles, Sgt C. E. S. Teague, Sgt I. Mustoe, Pte A. Mitcham, LCpl A. Froud, Pte H. W. Beatley, Pte A. Yarrington, Cpl J. Bishop MM, Cpl A. Holmes, Sgt C. Hunt

2nd Gloucesters: LCpl A. E. Stevens, CSM C. Hopkins, LCpl H. Keegan, Cpl A. Cullimore, CSM J. Doolan, CSM C. Webb

1/4th Gloucesters: Cpl J. A. Selwood, Sgt L. A. Walford, Pte H. Gould, Sgt A. E. Townsend, Cpl W. Perry, Cpl W. J. Bird, CSM L. R. Barrett, Sgt H. Winterson, Cpl R. E. Crossman, Pte G. R. Bennett, Cpl G. J. Collins, Sgt A. James, Cpl G. J. Fry, Sgt A. Bees, Pte A. Smith

2/4th Gloucesters: Sgt G .E. Lait, Pte R. Forse

1/5th Gloucesters: LCpl F. W. Harvey, Cpl R. E. Knight, Sgt A. Faville, Sgt J. C. W. Jennings, LCpl M. Taylor, Pte J. D. Lane, Sgt J. Huxford, Dmr E. H. G. Farmer, Sgt P. B. Cummings, Pte P. J. Millichap MM, CSM V. G. Smith, Sgt W. Middlecote, CSM W. J. Coward, Sgt R. A. Burton, Cpl S. A. Hickman, Pte H. G. A. Pike, Pte G. D. Cobb, CSM W. Bromage, LCpl A. J. Hornegold, Cpl W. Peacey, Sgt G. W. Hobbs MM

2/5th Gloucesters: Pte L. Fletcher MM, Pte C. C. Davis, Sgt H. W. Webb, Sgt F. Davis, Sgt H. Coleman MM, Cpl V. F. W. Ind, Pte D. Carney, Pte P. Pearce, Pte J. Killeen, Sgt E. G. White, Sgt H. Wood, Cpl H. F. Terrett, Sgt A. E. Barnes, Cpl E. Cobbold MM, Pte F. T. Fry, Pte G. E. Harris

1/6th Gloucesters: Pte W. J. Redmore, LCpl H. W. Moore, Cpl H. J. Glanville, Cpl H. S. Pope, Cpl T. H. Hillier, Cpl E. J. Gingell, Pte A. H. Clark, Cpl W. R. Smith, L Cpl H. Cox, Cpl F. V. Glanville, Pte R. Kerr, Sgt E. M. Pearce, Sgt E. J. Rundle, Cpl W. J. Ashmead, LCpl J. A. Needs, Sgt E. K. Courtier, Sgt R. Day, Sgt H. Mead, Sgt F. C. Kite

2/6th Gloucesters: Pte H. Jempson, Cpl W. Connock, Cpl F. A. Elliott, LCpl B. Rands, Pte E. Jenkins

7th Gloucesters: Sgt W. H. Stokes, Cpl H. Woodward, CSM J. H. Wagner, RQMS F. J. Purnell, Pte A. Timmins, Sgt H. Sheppard, Sgt W. House, CSM S. Dommett, Cpl A. Went, CSM F. Sabatella, LCpl R. Hinton, Sgt W.J. Williams, CSM R. Carter

8th Gloucesters: Pte W. G. Bennett, Pte W. G. H. Lugg, Pte A. W. Spencer, Pte H. Pugh MM, Sgt W. H. Nash, Pte H. Hobson, CSM J. J. Trunkfield, Sgt W. J. Kennington, CSM F. W. Tye, Sgt W. N. Summers MM, Sgt W. Grayson, Sgt C. Goodway MM, Pte S. A. Farr, CSM F. A. Savage

10th Gloucesters: Pte W. Ingles, Pte H. Curtis, CSM F. Croome, Pte H. Franklin, Sgt D. Davies, Sgt R. E. Goulden MM, Cpl E. Vick, Sgt A. Shoolbread, Sgt J. C. Dowle MM, Sgt S. Phillips, RSM F. H. Taylor

12th Gloucesters: Sgt R. A. McFarlane, Cpl G. S. Perrett, Sgt N. R. Pegg, Sgt J. Lewis, Sgt W. Smith, Cpl W. A. Goodlife

13th Gloucesters: Pte T. G. Boulton MM, Sgt R. A. Tresise

14th Gloucesters: CSM W. Portlock, Pte A. Blick, LCpl F. G. Preece, Pte W. E. Edwards, Sgt F. Joyner

18th Gloucesters: LCpl F. Moulding, LCpl E. Howe, CSM A. Summerfield

Gloucesters attached to other Battalions or Corps: Sgt J.A. Hughes (Royal West Kents)

1/1st RGH: Sgt T.H. Akers, Cpl H. J. Wiseman, Sgt W. G. Castle, Tpr E. G. Forrest, Sgt Bromhead

Note 5 – Bars to DCMs

1st Gloucesters: CSM W. H. Reece DCM, CSM W. Biddle DCM, MM & Bar

7th Gloucesters: Sgt W. H. Nash DCM, MM, CSM F. A. Savage DCM

Gloucesters attached to other Battalions or Corps: Sgt S. Phillips DCM (Worcs), Sgt S. Phillips DCM & Bar (Worcs)

Note

1. Sources: Peter Littlewood, *Gallantry Awards to the Gloucestershire Regiment 1914–1918*; Battalion War Diaries; Frank Fox, *The History of the Royal Gloucestershire Hussars Yeomanry 1898–1922*.

Appendix 2

Deaths

Accrding to the Commonwealth War Graves Commission, 8,399 Gloucesters and 145 members of the RGH died during or immediately after the First World War. Over 46,000 men served in the two regiments during the War, which means that a fifth of them died. It is only when one reads the names and where each individual came from that the impact on every corner of the cities, towns and villages of Gloucestershire including Bristol becomes strikingly clear. Listing simply number, rank, name, date of death and family details, where known, of over 8,500 men would require another book. These details have, however, been collated and are available on the Soldiers of Gloucestershire Museum website (http://www.soldiersofglos.com/deaths-in-the-gloucesters-and-rgh-in-ww1/). This has the advantage that they are accessible and can be updated as additional information about individuals becomes available, particularly from their descendants. The information has principally been extracted from the outstanding Commonwealth War Graves Commission website (www.cwgc.org), which includes details of where individuals are buried or, if they have no known grave, are commemorated. Additional material has come from the remarkable book by J. Devereux and G. Sacker, *Leaving All That Was Dear – Cheltenham in The Great War 1914–1918* and the National Archives. Some who did came from outside the county, a few from much further afield. How they ended up serving in the County Regiments is not always clear, but their contribution and sacrifice is.

The following table records the number who died in the Regiments of Gloucestershire between August 1914 and 31 December 1920 as a result of the Great War.

Gloucesters	Lt Col & Maj	Capt	Lt & 2/Lt	WO (Note 1)	SNCO (Note 2)	JNCO (Note 3)	Pte	Total
1st Bn (Reg) Western Front 1914–18	4	12	38	4	63	145	805	1071
2nd Bn (Reg) Western Front 1915 Macedonia 1916–18	3	4	7	2	17	48	286	367
3rd Bn (Special Reserve) UK (Note 4)	2		7	2	6	7	53	77
1/4th Bn TF (City of Bristol) Western Front 1915–17, Italy 1918	1	1	8	3	27	44	262	346
2/4th Bn TF (City of Bristol) Western Front 1916–18		2	3		17	25	228	275
3/4th Bn TF (City of Bristol) Reserve in UK (Note 5)						2	1	3
4TH Bn TF (City of Bristol), Unit not specified by CWGC.		2	21		2	16	64	105
1/5th Bn TF. Western Front 1915–17 & 1918. Italy 1918,		1	15	1	26	70	430	543
2/5th Bn TF Western Front 1916–18		5	10	1	31	80	364	491
3/5th Bn TF Reserve in UK (Note 5)							2	2
5th Bn TF Unit not specified by CWGC		1	9		9	11	60	90

Gloucesters	Lt Col & Maj	Capt	Lt & 2/Lt	WO (Note 1)	SNCO (Note 2)	JNCO (Note 3)	Pte	Total
1/6th Bn TF. Western Front 1915–17. Italy 1918	1	5	8	1	29	75	306	425
2/6th Bn TF Western Front 1916–18		3	7	1	16	52	250	329
3/6th Bn TF Reserve in UK (Note 5)					1		3	4
6th Bn TF Unit not specified by CWGC	1	3	13		3	12	48	80
7th Bn Service. Gallipoli 1915 Mesopotamia 1915–18	3	9	16	4	35	96	572	735
8th Bn Service Western Front 1915–18	3	14	34	1	49	129	759	989
9th Bn Service, Macedonia 1916–18 Western Front 1918		1	5	2	9	18	101	136
10th Bn Service Western Front 1915–18		7	30	1	31	98	495	662
11th Bn Reserve UK 1914–15 (Note 5)			6				9	15
12th Bn (Bristol's Own) Service Western Front 1915–18	1	5	24	6	33	84	640	793
13th Bn (Forest of Dean) Service (Pioneers) Western Front 1915–18	1	2	7	2	28	40	225	305

Gloucesters	Lt Col & Maj	Capt	Lt & 2/Lt	WO (Note 1)	SNCO (Note 2)	JNCO (Note 3)	Pte	Total
14th Bn Service (west of England) (Bantams) Western Front 1915–18	1	5	5		14	36	328	389
15th Bn (Local Reserve) UK 1916–17 (Note 5)							4	4
17th Bn TF (Reserve) UK 1917–19 (Note 5)						1	13	14
18th Bn Service Western Front 1918				2	3	6	31	42
Regt Depot & Masc. (Note 3)	3	3	9	1	3	3	85	107
TOTALS Gloucesters	24	85	282	34	452	1098	6424	8399
RGH								
1/1st RGH	2	5	5	2	13	29	86	142
2/1st RGH							1	1
3/1st RGH						1	1	2
TOTAL RGH	2	5	5	2	13	30	88	145
COMBINED TOTAL	26	90	287	36	465	1128	6512	8544

Notes: (1) Regimental Sergeant Major (RSM), Regimental Quartermaster Sergeant (RQMS), Company Sergeant Major (SSM). (2) Company Quarter Master Sergeant (CQMS), Squadron Quarter Master Sergeant (SQMS), Sergeant, Lance Sergeant. (3) Corporals and Lance Corporals. (4) Casualties evacuated to the United Kingdom were often posted on to the strength of 3rd Gloucesters, (5) These are likely to be deaths caused by training accidents or due to sickness.

Bibliography

Published Books

Anglesey, Marquess of, *A History of the British Cavalry 1816–1919, Volume V: 1914–19, Egypt, Palestine and Syria*, Pen & Sword, 1994 (reprint edition).

Barnes, A. F., MC, *The Story of the 2/5th Battalion Gloucestershire Regiment 1914–1918*, The Crypt House Press, Gloucester, 1930. A collection of accounts by those who fought with the Battalion. The author/editor served in the 2/5th Gloucesters.

Beresford, Christine and Newbould, Christopher, CBE, *The Fifth Gloster Gazette 1915–1919: A Trench Magazine of the First World War*, Alan Sutton Publishing, Stroud, 1993. Reproduction of all issues of the *Gazette* with introductions by the Curator and Chairman of the Board of Management of the Soldiers of Gloucestershire Museum.

Birkin, Lawrence (ed.), *A Trooper's Diary – The Royal Gloucestershire Hussars on Service 1914–1918*, Soldiers of Gloucestershire Museum, 2014. A collection of articles published in the *Gloucester Journal* between 1914 and 1918 by an anonymous trooper serving with the RGH, but almost certainly Cpl William [Dickie] George Richards.

Bonsor, James, *I Did My Duty – First World War Experiences of H. N. Edwards as Seen through his Accounts and Recent Interviews*, publisher not known, 1998. (Although elderly when he was interviewed, Edwards' recall was excellent. He served in 1/6th Gloucesters.)

Brunsdon, Robert, *The King's Men Fallen in the Great War. The King's School, Gloucester*, printed privately, 2014. Detailed accounts of how the 35 former pupils of The King's School died during the First World War. Nine of them were Gloucesters.

Buckle, Henry, *A Tommy's Sketchbook – Writings and Drawings from the Trenches*, The History Press, Brimscombe, Gloucestershire, 2012. A delightful series of watercolours from his time with 1/5th Gloucesters in 1915, edited by David Read.

Christian, Nick, *In the Shadow of Lone Tree. The Forging of the 10th Gloucesters and the Ordeal of the First Division at the Battle of Loos, 1915*, self published, 2012. A source of many contemporary letters and a detailed account of the Battle of Loos. Most of the quotes attributed to 10th Gloucester officers and men are drawn from this book.

Clifford, Rollo, *The Royal Gloucestershire Hussars*, Alan Sutton, 1991. A photographic record of the RGH, including many images of the 1/1 RGH in the Great War.

Corrigan, Gordon, *Mud, Blood and Poppycock*, Cassell. A different view of the Great War supported by meticulous research.

Davies, Martin and Teresa, *For Club, King and County: The Story of the Gloucestershire County Cricketers and the Gloucester Rugby Club Players as Soldiers of Gloucestershire in the Great War 1914–1918*, Soldiers of Gloucestershire Museum, 2014.

Devereux J. and Sacker G., *Leaving All That Was Dear – Cheltenham and the Great War*, Promenade Publications, 1997. A remarkable profile of all those from Cheltenham who died in the Great War, principally those commemorated on the Cheltenham War Memorial but also on other memorials, most with photographs.

Fox, Frank, *The Royal Gloucestershire Hussars Yeomanry 1898–1922*, Philip Allan, 1923. A comprehensive history of the RGH in the South African War and during the Great War. Most of the quotes attributed to RGH officers and men are drawn from this book.

Grazebrook, Captain R. M., OBE, MC, *The Gloucestershire Regiment War Narratives 1914–1915*, reprinted by the Naval & Military Press Ltd. This covers the 1st Battalion in 1914 and the 2nd Battalions in 1915 at the Second Battle of Ypres.

Hamilton, General Sir Ian, GCB, DSO, *Ian Hamilton's Despatches from the Dardanelles*, George Newnes Ltd, 1917. Reprinted from the *London Gazette*.

Howell, Georgina, *Daughter of the Desert: The Remarkable Life of Gertrude Bell*, Pan Macmillan, 2006.

Hughes, Mathew, *Allenby in Palestine. The Middle East Correspondence of Field Marshal Viscount Allenby June 1917–October 1919*, Sutton Publishing, 2004.

James, N. D. G., *Plain Soldiering: History of Armed Forces on Salisbury Plain*, Hobnob Press, 1987.

Keegan, John, *The First World War*, Hutchinson, 1998. Possibly this distinguished historian's best book, a highly readable overview of the War.

Lewis, John, *Yeoman Soldiers – The Royal Gloucestershire Hussars Yeomanry 1795–1920*, Teafford Publishing, 2008. (The author's father, Fred Lewis, served with the RGH in Gallipoli, Egypt and Palestine, and the book contains numerous quotes from his letters and others.)

Liddell Hart, B. H., *History of The First World War*, first published in 1930 by Cassell & Co as *The Real War 1914–1918*, an enlarged edition published in 1934 as *A History of the World War 1914–1918*.

Littlewood, Peter R., *Gallantry Awards to the Gloucestershire Regiment 1914–1918*, Spink, 2005. A comprehensive list by battalion of all the awards to Gloucesters during the Great War. (Peter Littlewood was commissioned into the Gloucestershire Regiment and was the son of a former officer in the Regiment.)

Marks, Dean, *'Bristol's Own'. The 12ᵗʰ Battalion Gloucestershire Regiment 1914–1918*, Dolman Scott Ltd, 2011. A rare account of raising and training a Service Battalion which includes much contemporary material and goes on to describe the battles it fought. Most of the quotes attributed to officers and men of 12ᵗʰ Gloucesters are drawn from this book.

Milton, Giles, *Paradise Lost: The Destruction of Islam's City of Tolerance*, Sceptre, 2008. The story of Smyrna, now Izmir, before, during and after the First World War, and the failed Greek invasion of Turkey in 1919 and its dreadful consequences.

Nash, Thomas, *The Diary of an Unprofessional Soldier*, Picton, 1991. (Thomas Nash served in 1/4ᵗʰ Gloucesters, and his diary was edited and published by his son.)

Pagan, A. W., *Infantry*, Gale & Polden, 1951. An account of command of 1ˢᵗ Gloucesters from July 1915 until March 1918.

Patterson, K. D. and Pyle, G.F., 'The geography and mortality of the 1918 influenza pandemic', *Bulletin of the History of Medicine*, 1991.

Rostron, Peter, *Gloucestershire Hero – Brigadier Patsy Pagan's Great War Experiences*, Pen & Sword, 2015.

Sandes, Flora, *The Autobiography of a Woman Soldier. A Brief Record of Adventure with the Serbian Army 1916–1919*, H. F. & G. Witherby, 1927.

Scott Daniell, David, *Cap of Honour – The 300 Years of The Gloucestershire Regiment*, third revised edition, Sutton Publishing Ltd, 2005. The story of the Gloucestershire Regiment from 1694 to 1994.

Sheldon, Jack, *The German Army at Passchendaele*, Pen & Sword, 2007.

Tuchman, Barbara W., *The Guns of August*, Macmillan, 1962. Winner of the Pulitzer Prize for Non Fiction 1962. (Also titled *August 1914* in some later editions.)

Wilson H.W. and Hammerton J.A., *The Great War. The Standard History of The World-Wide Conflict (14 Volumes)*, The Amalgamated Press Ltd, London 1919.

Wilson, Robert Henry, his letters edited by Helen D. Millgate, *Palestine 1917*, D. J. Costello, 1987.

Wyrall, Everard, *The Gloucestershire Regiment in the War 1914–1918*, Methuen & Co Ltd, 1931. This only covers the Regular and some Territorial Battalions of the Regiment. The Service Battalions are excluded.

Documents (all held in the Archives of the Soldiers of Gloucestershire Museum unless otherwise stated. The Archives contain many more papers relating to the Great War not listed below.)

1/1 RGH War Diary. This has been researched privately, principally from public records, some in Australia. It is not available on line and and enquiries relating to it should be addressed to the Soldiers of Gloucestershire Museum.

Anstey, Capt R. H., MC: 'The Raising of the 12th Bn The Gloucestershire Regt "Bristol's Own" 1914' (typescript).

Ayres, L/Cpl William F., 12th Gloucesters, 'France & Italy Reminiscences'.

Baxter, Colonel Donald, MC, 1st Gloucesters, 'Reminiscences of August 1914'.

Bazeley, Edward, 7th Gloucesters and Machine Gun Corps, memoir.

Bradbeer, Lt Col Thomas G., 'The Battle for Air Supremacy over the Somme 1 June–30 November 1916'. A thesis presented to the Faculty of the US Army Command and General Staff College, Fort Leavenworth, 2004 (available on line).

Chadband, Ernest, 10th Gloucesters, autobiography (copy held by Nick Christian, author of *In The Shadow of the Lone Tree*).

Cripps, Captain Edgerton Tymewell, RGH, always known as 'Tim', personal diary (held in the Gloucester Record Office Reference D4920/2/2/3/4).

Edwards, Sgt A. G., 1/6th Gloucesters, diary and letters 1915–18.

Howard, Sir Algar Howard Stafford, KCB, KCVO, MC, TD. RGH, diary (Aug 1915–Oct 1918) in private hands.

Kelly, Brig-Gen P. J. V., Comd 5th Mounted Brigade in Palestine, private papers held in the Imperial War Museum, Catalogue Number 19655.

Morgan, Percy, 7th Gloucesters, memoir.

Nott brothers' letters – twelve leather-bound volumes of letters from T. W. Nott, L. C. Nott and H. P. Nott 1915–17.

Peck, Pte Francis W., 9th Gloucesters, 'First World War Diary'.

Power, George, 2nd Glosters, letters (also available with comments by Richard Power on https://georgeswarletters.word-press.com).

Procter J. C., 13th Gloucesters, letters.

Senior, Mike, 'Fromelles, 19/20 July 1916 – A Success after All?' in *Stand To: The Journal of the Western Front Association*, No 83, August/September 2008. A copy is held in The Imperial War Museum.

Shipway, W. G., MBE, MC, 'My Memories of the First World War' (typescript)

The Back Badge – The Journal of the Gloucestershire Regiment. Published twice a year until 1994 and contains articles, letters and obituaries relating to the Great War.

The Donkey Walloper – The 2016 Journal of The Royal Gloucestershire Hussars Yeomanry Association (Katia Centenary Edition), which includes Tom Strickland's account plus other material relevant to what happened at Qatia and subsequently.

Tibbles, CSM William, 1/5th Gloucesters, letters.

Turle G. H. Jnr, *A Soldier's Diary 1917. The Battle for Mesopotamia*, published privately in 1998. (This is the diary of RQMS G. H. Turle, 7th Gloucesters, published by his son, who served in 2nd Glosters 1943–7).

Wilson C. A., 'Recollections of the 28th at War 1914–1918'.

Winterbotham, Cyril and Percy, letters, transcribed by Miss Iona Radice.

Index